Rays of the Searching Sun

The Transcultural Poetics
of Yang Mu

P.I.E. Peter Lang

Bruxelles · Bern · Berlin · Frankfurt am Main · New York · Oxford · Wien

Lisa Lai-Ming WONG

Rays of the Searching Sun

The Transcultural Poetics of Yang Mu

"New Comparative Poetics"
No.23

© P.I.E. PETER LANG S.A.

Éditions scientifiques internationales
Brussels, 2009
1 avenue Maurice, B-1050 Brussels, Belgium
info@peterlang.com; www.peterlang.com

ISSN 1376-3202
ISBN 978-90-5201-545-3
D/2009/5678/37

Printed in Germany

Library of Congress Cataloging-in-Publication Data

Wong, Lisa Lai-Ming. Rays of the searching sun : the transcultural poetics
of Yang Mu / Lisa Lai-Ming Wong.
p. cm. — (New comparative poetics, ISSN 1376-3202 ; no.23)
Includes bibliographical references. ISBN 978-90-5201-545-3
1. Yang, Mu, 1940—Criticism and interpretation. I. Title.
PL2924.S47Z88 2009   895.1'152—dc22   2009025009

CIP also available from the British Library, GB.

Bibliographic information published by "Die Deutsche Bibliothek"

"Die Deutsche Bibliothek" lists this publication in the "Deutsche Nationalbibliografie"; detailed bibliographic data is available in the Internet at <http://dnb.ddb.de>.

To Poets

... for those first affections

Those shadowy recollections

Which, be they what they may,

Are yet the fountain light of all our day,

Are yet a master light of all our seeing

William Wordsworth, "Ode: Intimations of Immortality"

When the search succeeds,

Feeling, at first but a glimmer, will gradually gather into full luminosity,

Whence all objects thus lit up glow as if each the other's light reflects,

...

Eternity he sees in a twinkling,

And the whole world he views in one glance.

Lu Ji, *Wen Fu*, trans. Chen Shih-hsiang

Preface

First of all, I wish to thank Marc Maufort, the "New Comparative Poetics" series editor, for his kind and speedy response to my project on Chinese-Western comparative poetics, and for his valuable advice in editing the manuscript for publication. Thanks also to Emilie Menz and her team for their generous assistance at different stages of the production.

I would like to acknowledge several editors and publishers for their permission to reprint all or part of the following articles in Chapters 2, 4, and 5 respectively: "Epiphany in Echoland: Cross-cultural Intertextuality in Yang Mu's Poetry and Poetics." *Canadian Review of Comparative Literature* 31.1 (March 2004): 27-38; "Writing Allegory: Diasporic Consciousness as a Mode of Intervention in Yang Mu's Poetry of the 1970s." *Journal of Modern Literature in Chinese* 5.1 (July 2001): 1-28; "Taiwan, China, and Yang Mu's Alternative to National Narratives." *CLCWeb: Comparative Literature and Culture* 8.1 (March 2006); "A Thing of Beauty is a Joy Forever: Yang Mu's 'Letters to Keats'." *The Keats-Shelley Review* (UK) 18 (September 2004): 188-205; "(Un)tying a Firm Knot of Ideas: Reading Yang Mu's *The Skeptic*." *Connotations: A Journal for Critical Debate* 12.2-3 (2002/2003): 292-306; and "The Making of a Poem: Rainer Maria Rilke, Stephen Spender, and Yang Mu." *The Comparatist* 31 (2007): 130-147.

Over the years, many friends, teachers and colleagues have offered intellectual support, emotional backing, or scholarly integrity. First and foremost, I wish to extend my thanks to Karl Kao, my thesis supervisor at the Division of Humanities of the Hong Kong University of Science and Technology, for his guidance in writing my doctoral dissertation on modern Taiwan poetry. This thesis provided the theoretical groundwork for many of my subsequent journal publications on Yang Mu. I feel thankful to the late William F. McNaughton, for his devoted teaching of poetry translation.

Special thanks are due to Douwe Fokkema whom I have met twice at ICLA congresses in Pretoria and Hong Kong, and to Kwok-kan Tam with whom I have worked at the Chinese University of Hong Kong. I here wish to acknowledge their encouragement.

Naturally, my knowledge of poetry and comparative literature was nurtured by a number of other scholars. I am especially grateful to Ching-hsien Wang and William Tay. C. H. Wang kindly "authorized" the Yang Mu column of the appended chronology. More than a decade ago, they both discerned the first stroke of paint in my then fledgling project, and I am pleased that they should also be present as this work is now given its finishing touch.

Finally, I am most indebted to my husband, Chun-hai Kwok, for his unwavering support and loving care.

In the process of bringing this slow-burn project to its conclusion, I owe my deepest gratitude to the great poets, who gave me the inspiration to challenge the limits of life and to appreciate this spiritual journey.

Lisa Lai-ming Wong
Clear Water Bay
Hong Kong
2-9-2009

Contents

Author's Note

I have consistently used the Pinyin romanization system for spelling throughout this book. Names of place, poets, scholars, and titles of publication well-known in the West have retained their customary spelling (either in the Wade-Giles system or the Hong Kong romanization system). The Pinyin romanization of these names is provided the first time they are mentioned in the text. Titles of Chinese poems, articles and books are indicated in English translation in the text but their Pinyin romanization can be found in the footnotes and in the bibliography.

Comparative Poetics in the Twenty-first Century

Rays of the Searching Sun: The Transcultural Poetics of Yang Mu puts forward a bold attempt to engage contemporary literary and cultural theories in the study of East-West comparative poetics. The present research has started as a belated response to the call of pioneers in comparative literature that "comparing poetry" from an Asian perspective is long overdue. In the mid-twentieth century, René Wellek regretted that when comparatists looked at "a map of literature on an international scale," they saw "the smaller literatures of Europe and the great wide world of the Orient invite exploration and study."[1] Conscious of the need for an Eastern perspective in the discipline, European scholars such as Etiemble proposed that all comparatists study "Chinese, Bengali, or Arabic," and Wellek reminded them to "keep a balance between expansion and concentration, nationalism and cosmopolitanism" (Wellek, 1970: 53). But so far the study of comparative literature in English-language publications has been largely restricted to the literary relations within the European continent or the cultural transfer between Europe and America.

Beyond a doubt, studies of transatlantic and transpacific literary relations are needed to complete a global picture of literary history. At the turn of the millennium, Marián Gálik observed that "[i]nterliterary poetics, as one of the objectives of comparative literary theory, is still in its embryonic stage, and will not achieve any even relatively serious results without taking into account comparative study of the literary genres, traditions, and conventions at least of Sanskrit and post Sanskrit Indian literatures, Arabian literatures, and the literatures of the Far East."[2] In a similar vein, Jan Walsh Hokenson claims that "the most appropriate methods of literary study will be increasingly... comparative, in the sense of addressing texts in the widening contexts of a global

---

[1] René Wellek. Presidential Address at the meeting of the American Comparative Literature Association. Cambridge, Mass., April 1965. See Wellek, *Discriminations: Further Concepts of Criticism* (New Haven and London: Yale University Press, 1970), 52.

[2] Marián Gálik, "Interliterariness as a Concept in Comparative Literature." *Comparative Literature and Comparative Cultural Studies*. ed. Steven Tötösy de Zepetnek. (West Lafayette, Indiana: Purdue University Press, 2003), 39.

intercultural poetics. To Euro-American, South American, Asian, and African comparatists, knowledge of at least two Western and Eastern languages will be essential, no longer merely desirable."[3] Sensitive to new possibilities in a globalizing world, Hokenson remarks that "at the hands of bi-cultural writers, we will begin to see continuities that we failed to notice in the hey-day of national literatures" (Hokenson, 2003: 62).

From her overview of representative examples of post-European comparative studies by Partha Chatterjee, Olakunle George, Carlos J. Alonso, Gregory Jusdani, and Naoki Sakai, Rey Chow derives a new notion of comparison "as a type of discursive situation, involuntarily brought into play by and inextricable from the conditions of modern world politics." Each critic's approach to comparative literature, though "firmly located within a specific cultural framework," is nonetheless "transcultural, with implications that resonate well beyond their individual locations." To Chow, a "post-European culture" in the field of comparative literature "needs to be recognized as always operating *biculturally* or *multiculturally* even when it appears predominantly preoccupied with itself" (R. Chow, 2004: 301-2). Such a shift from the discipline's Eurocentric orientation necessitates an inquiry into bicultural writers in order to broaden the scope for comparison. This is exactly why the present study of Yang Mu is an extremely pertinent project.[4]

Yang Mu's Significance

The poetry of Yang Mu, the winner of the 2007 International Prize for Literature Written in the Chinese Language, has held the critical attention of Chinese and Western literary scholars alike for half a century.[5] A creative writer in poetry and prose, a comparatist, and a translator, Yang Mu is highly commended as "bicultural." His signature is the lyric voice that has deeply impressed readers and critics since his first

---

[3] Jan Walsh Hokenson, "The Culture of the Context: Comparative Literature Past and Future." *Comparative Literature and Comparative Cultural Studies*, 73.

[4] Every reader should know that the pen names Ye Shan and Yang Mu may not represent the same persona, and should distinguish the persona represented by either pen name from the circumstances of the person known as Wang Ching-hsien or C. H. Wang. But for the sake of convenience and consistency, the pen name Yang Mu is used throughout the book to refer to both the poet and the person. Yang Mu had attracted the attention of Chinese readers and literary critics with the publication of *Shui zhi mei* [By the Waterside], his first book of poetry, under the pen name of Ye Shan.

[5] Translations of Yang Mu's poetry have appeared in literary journals in a large number of foreign languages such as English, French, German, Japanese, Korean, Dutch and Swedish.

book of poetry, *By the Waterside*, was published in 1960. Wrote Lucy J. Chen, "[O]ne of the most talented of the younger poets is a native Formosan: Ye Shan [Yang Mu's former penname], a Modernist... [H]e demonstrates a sure and sensitive command of the language and a very individual style of expression in his first book of verse" (L. J. Chen, 1964: 137). Commenting on Yang Mu's poetry in the late 1980s, Dominic Cheung (Zhang Cuo) considered his "the best wrought" of lyric voices, which "remains one of the foremost and the best in modern Chinese poetry today" (Cheung, 1987: 21). For twenty-first century readers, the poet has attained superb mastery over a variety of always intense lyric voices (W. Xu, 28 May 2006).

Written primarily in Chinese, the linguistic density of Yang Mu's poetry appeals to bilingual Western readers such as Joseph R. Allen who aligns him "with the international modernism of Baudelaire, Rilke, and Eliot" (Allen, 1993: 406). To Stephen Owen, Yang Mu is "a poet who works with the materials that he has, and those materials include a sense of poetic and cultural history that transcends the cultural division of the 'West' and China. He has become bicultural... [Yang Mu] offers the largest hope for the future of Chinese poetry" (Owen, 1993: 40). Continuing with Owen's theme, Michelle Yeh finds Yang Mu "a leading light in avant-garde poetry, [and] a dynamic force in the golden age of artistic experimentation in Taiwan. He influenced not only Taiwanese poetry since the 1960s but also mainland Chinese poetry... in the 1970s." To Yeh, the poet "has achieved canonical status in Chinese speaking communities all over the world. He holds one of the most important places in Chinese literary history" (Yeh, 1998: xxviii-xxiv). Asked to name the most significant works of Chinese literature of the twentieth century for the special millennium issue of *PMLA*, Anthony C. Yu put *No Trace of the Gardener: Poems of Yang Mu* on his list of only three items, describing it as "the first English anthology gathered from the prolific volumes of the Taiwanese poet Yang Mu" who "has helped to establish high modernism in Chinese verse" (A. Yu, 2001: 2060-61).

Critical interest in Yang Mu's works in non-Sinophone communities has mounted since the late 1980s. Known for its linguistic craftsmanship and erudition in Chinese and Western classics, his poetry in its form and content reveals the influence of multiple cultures, making its translation a backbreaking challenge. A few translators in Europe and the United States (some in collaboration with Chinese translators) have successfully rendered Yang Mu's poems in their native languages. Translations of some of his poetry have been published in the United States, Germany, France, and Japan: Joseph R. Allen's *Forbidden Games and Video Poems: The Poetry of Yang Mu and Lo Ching* (1993); Lawrence R. Smith and Michelle Yeh's *No Trace of the Gardener: Poems of Yang Mu* (1998); Susanne Hornfeck and Wang Jue's *Yang Mu, Patt beim Go:*

Gedichte chinesisch-deutsch (2002); Angel Pino and Isabelle Rabut's *Yang Mu, Quelqu'un m'interroge à propos de la vérité et de la justice* (2004); and the most recent Japanese translation, Tetsuji Ueda's *Kakkouzami no uta: Youboku shishu* (2006). They have made Yang Mu's poetry accessible to readers all over the world.

Unlike his modernist precursors in Taiwan such as Ji Xian, Luo Fu and Yu Guangzhong, Yang Mu is native of the place. The significance of Yang Mu's works for Chinese literature lies in the fact that they offer not only many of the finest pieces in modern poetry, but also a native Taiwanese voice. The political tensions of the Straits apart, Yang Mu poetry addresses issues that are of interest both locally and globally. From his liberal cosmopolitan outlook to a deep attachment to his birthplace, his poems feature a kind of self-reflexive consciousness and critical sensibility rarely found in the history of Chinese poetry. Furthermore, his innovative approach to both the space and the time in which he is historically situated offers a poetics of the south and a rich corpus of sea poetry that help fill a void in the Chinese lyric tradition.

Cross-Fertilization of Cultures

The poem that opens the edition of Yang Mu's collected works is entitled "Return" (1956). The fictionality of the adventure and return underscores a teenager's romantic yearning for an odyssey. More cosmetic than real, the fatigue and disillusionment felt by the time-ravaged sailor of the poem seem quite remote to the young poet, who has yet to experience life's harsher vicissitudes. But this early indication of mobility prophetically marks the trajectory Yang Mu was to take in his subsequent poetic ventures.

Like many young talents, Yang Mu in his early works of the 1950s and 1960s impressed his audience by an intimate lyric utterance that cries out for attention and love. Having left behind the frustrated loves of youth and abandoned his first pen name, Ye Shan, the poet steadily expanded his artistic world to include familial, social, and political themes. Between the 1970s and 1980s, during a visiting professorship at National Taiwan University, Yang Mu adopted a more direct mode of addressing public and domestic issues. The next two decades saw another phase of the poet's career when he ventured out to various new administrative and academic posts. He was one of the founders of the Hong Kong University of Science and Technology in the early 1990s. Back in Taiwan, he helped found the National Dong Hwa University at Hualian and served as dean of the College of Humanities and Social Sciences (1996-2001), and he was the founding director of the Institute of Chinese Literature and Philosophy (2002-4) of Academia Sinica in Nankang. In early 2000, the poet spent a month as a visiting professor at

Charles University in Prague. Meditative and intellectual, his mature works explore dialectics in literary theory, social reality, and world politics. He returned from time to time to writing short poems, which are relaxed and playful, and show his wit and humour.

The path of Yang Mu's poetic endeavours exemplifies the development of modern Chinese poetry since the mid-twentieth century. The most influential modernist movement in Chinese literary history began in Taiwan in mid-1950s. A contemporary of the pioneers of this movement, but much younger, Yang Mu witnessed and participated in the groundbreaking events of the "horizontal transplant" of Western poetic traditions. From his early worship of the romantics to his later modernist experiments, Yang Mu has consciously fashioned his own poetic style and theory by assimilating foreign influences. A translator himself, Yang Mu has rendered the works of Dante, Lorca, Yeats, Shakespeare, and a number of English poets – from the medieval to the Elizabethans, the Romantics, and the Victorians – into Chinese. In addition to making the best of European literature accessible to Chinese readers, he has helped foster an understanding of Western literary history from an Asian perspective.

A knowledgeable professor and practitioner of Chinese poetry, Yang Mu has played a pivotal role in the "vertical heritage" of Chinese literary tradition. Although Yang Mu is concerned with exploring new literary forms and poetic language in his experimentation with modern Chinese poetry, he has aimed to keep the thread running up through the poetry of the Tang dynasty and the Six Dynasties to the *Book of Songs*. Like many Chinese poets Yang Mu often looks up to past literary masters, but rather than seeking them only as models to emulate, he engages them in an intracultural dialogue as well. A scholar specializing in classical Chinese poetry and a comparatist by academic training, Yang Mu has sought unconventional ways to review Chinese classics. His bold application of Parry and Lord's theory to a reading of the formulaic elements in the *Book of Songs* caused a stir in Western and Chinese literary communities in the early 1970s. And his voluminous publication of poetry and literary criticism has contributed much towards shaping modern Chinese poetry and rewriting Chinese literary history.

Paradoxically, Yang Mu's poetic identity is both global and local. Acclaimed in the United States for his biculturalism as a poet, he is at the same time "the poet of Hualian" in Taiwan and other Chinese communities. His contribution to bringing across cultures the medieval heroic ideals, the romantic imagination, and the international modernist movement in poetry is highly commended. In addition to his cultural mobility, the poet himself is always physically on the move across the Pacific and the Taiwan Straits. Departure and homecoming have formed the dominant backdrop against which his poetic personae address social and political issues that have arisen in different times and places. He once called himself a "right-fielder": in baseball, the right-fielder is something of a witness to, rather than a participant in, the action taking place on the field – alert to it, but not fully immersed. And as a comparatist, Yang Mu the scholar serves as a mediator between the worlds he straddles. In order to formulate a modern poetics, he travels between the newest and the oldest, between the Chinese and the West, and among various disciplines. In the hands of the poet, philosophical propositions are rendered in image-based arguments, and metaphysical concerns in romantic scepticism. His vision of time and human existence is a mythical one albeit absent of gods. The sceptic's doubts make his poetic world much larger, much more expansive than any one religious or cultural system is capable of encompassing. In Eugene Eoyang's words: "Yang Mu is… a comparative figure in and of himself, and to describe his life and works is to contemplate the intersections of languages and cultures, and his standing as a world poet."[6]

Theoretical Orientation and Organization of the Book

The twentieth century witnessed the rapid growth of the discipline of comparative literature and the development of its major methodologies. There are two main approaches to the study of literature, textualism and historicism, and the sociopolitical turn has decidedly dominated the discussion of comparative literature, and perhaps substituted for it under the name of cultural studies over the last few decades. Post-colonial discourse on cultural interactions, such as Edward W. Said's contributions in *Orientalism* and *Culture and Imperialism*, has played an integral part in critics' scepticism and ambivalence towards the literary influence of one culture on another.

Shunning the culturally chauvinistic view that sees literary influence as spatial and temporal in terms of a condescending journey moving from the origin towards the receiving end that results in second-rate imitations by the belated practitioners of the art, a new comparative poetics takes influence as having positive meaning when it is something the poet actively seeks and chooses. Since the second half of the twentieth century, increasing access to Western literature either in the original language or via translation allows modern Chinese poets to experiment with and revise their theory and practice of poetry. Like rays of the searching sun, Yang Mu has shed bright light on areas of world litera-

---

6   Quoted from Eugene Eoyang, 2 February 2003, a written response to my proposed paper on Yang Mu's poetry for the XVIIth Congress of International Comparative Literature Association, Hong Kong.

ture that have been little known to his contemporaries. Critics are often conscious of the pitfalls of over-Westernization. Yet neither Sinocentrism nor self-orientalising saves poets writing in a post-colonial era. The fact that Tang poetry, which was itself the happy product of other influences, has nourished a new generation of American poetry and the European sonnet has become part of the modern Chinese lyric tradition in the last century proves dynamic exchanges cannot be simply explained away in terms of cultural imperialism or orientalist aberrations. When dealing with the cultural crisis in modern China, Yu Yingshi finds what Chen Yinke and Edward Said have in common is an emphasis on a balance between the national culture and the cultural legacy of all humankind (Y. Yu, 1995: 13). National particulars and cultural universals are equally important in facilitating the future development of human civilization. Yu concludes with his endorsement of Michael Walzer's argument that for an individual and for a society, the most fundamental principle is self-determination.[7] Undeniably, historical circumstances always limit one's options to some extent, but with sufficient knowledge, critical awareness and creativity, a poet can exercise his or her freedom to choose from the best, and therefore literary influences, whether intracultural or cross-cultural, will not be a cause of anxiety.

To many scholars, poetry does not easily lend itself to meaningful theoretically based reading, and few have brought cultural criticism to bear on their study of Chinese poetry. In addition to striking a balance between textualism and historicism, this book attempts to make use of contemporary critical theories and post-colonial discourse in order to shed new light on the interpretation of modern Chinese poetry. To historicize is the first step towards interpretation. Donald Wesling puts poetry into a network of social discourse and hears some novelistic dialogism in a poetic voice (Wesling, 2003: 33-60). This method of locating a voice is reminiscent of Julia Kristeva's notion of dialogism – reading the "insertion of history (society) into a text and of this text into history" (Kristeva, 1980: 63). A major objective of this book is to record such interactions between history and text, with Chapter 4 as the main arena for the discussion. In taking heed of the historicity in any historical reading of literature, this research also involves a textual and linguistic turn, as illustrated in Chapter 2. Chapters 1 and 3 explore the dialogic, performative aspects of the lyric voice and the mythical dimension that intermixes different cultural conceptions of time, with due consideration of the textual and the historical. What brings these

---

[7] In his discussion, Yu Yingshi borrows the notions of "thick" (particular) and "thin" (universal) from Michael Walzer's book *Thick and Thin: Moral Argument at Home and Abroad* (1995). He concludes with Walzer's argument for self-determination.

two approaches together is the poet's bicultural perspective and critical consciousness of world literary history, which will be fully fleshed out in the concluding Chapter 5. There will be an appended chronology to offer a time-line showing the poet's development and placing his works in the general historical context.

Since the lyric voice has long been a signature of Yang Mu's poetry, Chapter 1 "On the Dialogic Lyric Voice" will look into its characteristics and development. Employing poetry as a means of self-expression through a supposedly transparent language – one that can directly reflect reality – is typical of the personal mode for the youthful apprentice in the Chinese tradition and for a fervent disciple of the romantic poets. Centred on the pronoun "I," some poems confess moods such as loneliness, or reflect on a relationship. In other more expanded and developed works, the narrativizing "I" unfolds a personal story, and sometimes indulges in a philosophizing soliloquy. The personal voice yields to visual exuberance when the poet experiments with the modernist image-based approach. Yang Mu's frequent use of the second-person pronoun has created in his poems a vocative mode that attracts the reader's attention. Between the "you" and the "I," the manner of addressing in these seemingly private utterances is mostly dialogic. From his early unchecked emotional outpourings, he progresses gradually to other artistic uses of the lyric voice. The dramatic mode is adopted in the form of apostrophe and prosopopoeia. Personified voices of inanimate objects or the dead increase the imaginative opportunities of speaking behind the mask. Developments towards a fictive mode are seen in his use of dramatic monologue, which penetrates into the psychology of historical and legendary figures, and characters from famous canonical novels in both Chinese and Western cultures. Yang Mu's recent works have been increasingly dialogic, with multiple voices heard in intellectual debates and amorous conversations.

Following up on the idea of dialogism, Chapter 2, "On Intertextuality," focuses on the tension and interaction between the intertexts in Yang Mu's poetry. Intertextuality includes the Chinese literary practices of *yongshi* and *shilei* (allusion to and application of ancient sources) and Western concepts from Julia Kristeva and Roland Barthes. Joseph R. Allen's suggestions regarding intracultural intertextuality will be discussed in addition to the cross-cultural intertextuality frequently noted in Yang Mu's poetry. The examples will illustrate from a transcultural perspective the fact that Yang Mu has assimilated diverse literary materials in order to expand his historical consciousness and facilitate exploratory thinking. Rather than producing sounds that merely repeat themselves in an echoland, a poem's cross-cultural intertextuality is in fact the poet's unique mode of intervention in an event by strategically placing it in the light of intercontextuality between international affairs.

Yang Mu has written about the theme of time since the 1950s, and Chapter 3, "On Time-worlds," will explore the evolution of his ideas on temporality. Yang Mu situates time in space by inventing different time-worlds to accommodate his philosophical discourse. His notion of time as deeply rooted in poetic responses to the world is reminiscent of Giambattista Vico's idea in *The New Science* that the first human beings perceived the world in a poetic manner and of Martin Heidegger's theory that poetry plays a fundamental role in the building of worlds. Apart from universal tropes of metaphor and allegory from the Chinese and Western lyric traditions, the poet's lifelong project of the "Water-side Myth" will be examined with reference to classical texts such as the *Book of Songs* and *Chu Elegies*, as well as to Greek myths. Yang Mu's literary configurations of time will be placed into four different categories: homogenizing time, phenomenalizing time, placing time, and theorizing time. From Yang Mu's time-worlds, the reader will discover a new mode of representation that falls outside the conventional modes of linearity and circularity.

"Poetry proves not only that you live, but that others do too," says Yang Mu (Yang, 1978a: 216). Many of the poems discussed in Chapter 4, "On Alternatives to Historical Narrative," illustrate the poet's consistent effort to relate the issues faced by Taiwan to other national liberation movements around the world. His innovative analogies between Taiwan and Ireland of the 1970s and between Taiwan and Chechnya of 2000 are famous. Revisionist histories of Fort Zeelandia from a Dutch perspective and of Changan, China's centre of tradition, from a cultural pilgrim's point of view open up new readings of the colonial history of Taiwan and the Cultural Revolution in China. Post-colonial discourse and identity politics form the theoretical basis of this chapter. Both the local, native Taiwanese consciousness and the nationalist fights for independence across the globe are presented in his poems through dramatic personae from different parts of the world. This invention of a diasporic distance from the actual site of dispute is deployed by the poet to avoid immediate journalistic commentary. The poetic distance enables the poet to compare alternative ways of reading history so that he can view the issues at hand critically and reflexively.

Chapter 5, "On Transcultural Poetics," looks into Yang Mu's prose writings about his definition of poetry, his approach to verbal art, and his conception of modern Chinese poetry in global literary history. For almost half a century, critics have witnessed Yang Mu spinning out a transcultural poetics from the gems of world literature. Such works as "Letters to Keats" (1961-64), *The Completion of a Poem* (1989), and *The Sceptic: Notes on Poetical Discrepancies* (1993), which deal with the theory and practice of poetry writing, are highlighted in this chapter. Yang Mu presents in these books a personal collection of the literary works that he finds to be essential and most fertile for a modern poet attempting to transcend the boundaries between lyric traditions of different origins. In addition, his anthologies of classical Chinese poetry and his translations of English poetry and Shakespeare's plays make the models he has chosen accessible to Chinese readers and play a vital role in communicating his deepest concerns about poetry. The body of Yang Mu's works form the basis of a "Yang Mu paradigm" for the Chinese lyric tradition, and he is highly respected as "Yang Mu of Hualian; Yang Mu of the world."[8]

"Chronology of Events" in the appendix serves to help readers locate Yang Mu in a global context. Inevitably, the approach is selective rather than exhaustive. The four columns place the poet's biography along a time-line of historical events in Taiwan, China and other parts of the world. Some of these prompted an immediate response from him while others stayed in his mind as seeds that would germinate years later. The world events include those that have crucial relevance to the life experiences of the poet and to his works. On one hand, historical incidents such as the Vietnam War and the student movements in the United States undoubtedly left their imprint on him when he was a graduate student at the University of California, Berkeley, in the 1960s. The deaths of teachers, friends and acquaintances drove him to express his grief in memory of his love and affection for them, whereas the tragic demise of public figures moved him to write in sorrowful protests. On the other hand, his amazement over the reincarnation of the Lama inspired the poet to take him for an omniscient narrator who gives an overview of modern world history in a poem. Events important in a Chinese context are listed under "Taiwan" and "China." Political unrest in Taiwan finds subtle expression in some of Yang Mu's poems. Sometimes, in order to present his insight from a comparative point of view, the poet formats the poem with reference to events in all four parallel columns. A prominent example is "The Lost Ring – for Chechnya" published in March 2000.

The biographical time-line highlights the hallmarks of Yang Mu's career and public life. But only in Yang Mu's creative works can the reader glimpse the poet's emotional and spiritual experiences. Although Yang Mu has been generally considered a romantic poet whose art is praised for its beauty and transcendental truth, the columns in the appendix serve to historicize his works and lend the reader a refreshingly new perspective from which to appreciate the poet's unique approach to history and politics.

---

8   Quoted from the programme booklet, *The Fourth National Award for Literature and Art* (2000), 15.

In the second half of the twentieth century, the route Western literary influence on China took could roughly be mapped out as moving east through Taiwan to Hong Kong, followed by a surge northward into the mainland. Well acquainted with Western culture, Yang Mu also writes elegant scholarly essays in English. For example, in "Poetry Ablaze, and Ambiguous" (1986) he traces with lyrical intensity the inception of modern Chinese poetry in Taiwan in 1958 and its development up to 1986. His creative works, though replete with foreign references, were written exclusively in Chinese. In this aspect Yang Mu appears to be predominantly preoccupied with Chinese poetry, but he actually operates biculturally and multiculturally. No single literary culture is adequate to express his intricate feelings and serious thoughts. He synthesizes the Chinese and Western lyric traditions and infuses his art with the treasures of world literature. Research into Yang Mu's transcultural poetics is therefore a study from the vantage point of the oldest lyric tradition in the East – that is to say, a study of poetry in the broadest context of world literary history.

CHAPTER 1

On the Dialogic Lyric Voice

Let your indulgence set me free [*]

The history of modern Chinese poetry saw a preference for first-person poems and, in connection with such poems, vigorous experimentation on the lyric voice. Writers of the May Fourth generation in China warmly embraced the Western notion of personal poems as a literary expression of their yearnings for individual autonomy. To name only two among many, Xu Zhimo and Guo Moruo are labelled "Romantic poets" of self-expressive lyric. Yet despite their efforts to rejuvenate Chinese poetry by including new voices in colloquial language, most new poets of the early decades of the twentieth century did not really unsettle the established theory of expressive poetry; nor did they depart radically from the biographical-historical approach to literary criticism rooted in the Chinese lyric tradition. More often than not, the lyric voice was still taken to be the unmediated personal voice of the poet. Very few Chinese poets made a genuine conceptual break from the traditional paradigm of registering the voice, and thus the self, in poetry.

The Chinese literary tradition is a "realist" tradition, within which expressiveness is understood as a paradoxically dual act. Poetry expresses what the poet thinks and feels, and therefore it is an honest act of self-revelation; at the same time, however, this self revealed in a poem defines what the poet is, and thus it is also an act of self-fashioning. The seminal statement in the *Great Preface* (c.1 B.C.) to the *Book of Songs*, "Poetry speaks the heart's intent," has produced a formidable socio-political orientation of reading and writing poetry.[1] Through Confucian

---

[*] The quote is the last line from the Epilogue spoken by Prospero in Shakespeare's play, *The Tempest*.

[1] In his introduction to *Shijing* [the *Book of Songs*], the earliest anthology of Chinese poetry, C. H. Wang (Yang Mu) considers it "the fountainhead" of Chinese literature. "It is an anthology of 305 poem edited by Confucius (551-479 B.C.), as the traditional belief has it, on the basis of about three thousand compositions collected for the education of his disciples. The book remained a classic and required reading for the literati for more than two thousand years." Poems in the *Book of Songs* are all numbered and divided into fours sections: Folk Songs, Minor Odes of the Kingdom, Greater

scholarship as well as the subsequent development of literary criticism, this statement has evolved into a prescription for the cultured man. The acute awareness of an audience, whether understood as a collective judging consciousness or the impressionable masses, regulates the poet's expression of his self. This self is therefore a product of intentional construction that follows orthodox ethical standards. Since poets are taken as orators verbalizing their own intent, poetry becomes an open statement – an utterance not to be accidentally overheard but to be heard in public. In this sense, the Chinese lyric tradition is a "personal" one from the start, though the person in this case is constantly under vigilance exercised by the self and the other, quite the opposite of a free individual.

There have in fact been several instances when poets and critics such as Lu Ji (261-303) argued for a poetics of emotions. Instead of assuming an equivalence between intent and poetry, Lu Ji took a more sophisticated view of poetic language: "The Lyric, born of pure emotion, is gossamer fibre woven into the finest fabric."[2] Poetry, to him, is an art work whose origin lies in emotions. Nevertheless, expressive theories that sanction individual private emotions remain marginal or obscure within mainstream poetic discourse. During the influx of Western culture in the early twentieth century, powerful personal feelings were given free rein in new poetry. Experiments with English and German Romanticism enabled poets to confess their inner thoughts and sentiments. But these individual voices were soon drowned out by the collective voice of political lyricism following the outbreak of the Sino-Japanese War in 1937. Even for many modern Chinese poets, the notion of writing in order to commune solely with one's own soul remains baffling.

In contrast, monologism that seems to ignore the audience is characteristic of Western lyric and is widely accepted. Since the rise of the printing press, lyrics, which are primarily addressed to the ear, have been read as an inward-looking, monologic literary form. A lyric is supposed to record the thoughts of an introverted genius, writing in isolated self-reverie. The poem is regarded as a spoken thought or a

---

Odes of the Kingdom, and Odes of the Temple and Altar. For further discussion, see C. H. Wang's "Introduction" (Minford and Lau, 2000: 71). As for the "*Daixu*" [Great Preface], its date of composition is uncertain. Stephen Owen is reasonably sure that "it was no later than the first century A. D. Many readers accepted it as the work of Confucius's disciple Zixia and thus saw it an unbroken tradition of teaching about the *Book of Songs* that could be traced back to Confucius himself [c. 551-c. 479 B.C.]" (Minford and Lau, 2000: 626-7).

[2] Chen Shih-hsiang's translation, as quoted in Yang Mu, *Lu Ji's* Wen Fu *Jiaoshi* [*A Comparative Interpretation* of Lu Ji's *Essays on Literature*] (Taipei: Hongfan, 1985), 42.

confessed emotion to be heard only by the poet himself or by a historically specific addressee, while the reader is given the role of involuntary eavesdropper. The reader suppresses her own presence and suspends her judgement because she is not supposed to be the speaker's confidante. John Stuart Mill's description of lyric as "an utterance overheard" has become a definitive approach to the genre.[3]

However, recent scholarship on lyric in the West brings back the addressee as indispensable and suggests the presence of multiple voices in a poem. Indeed, although Bakhtin assigns poetry to monologism, his own writings about speech genres seem to argue otherwise. In Bakhtin's theory, "addressivity" is considered a constituent in an utterance and the addressee can assume different forms: "The addressee can be an immediate participant-interlocutor in an everyday dialogue, a differentiated collective of specialists in some area of cultural communication, a more or less differentiated public," and lastly "an indefinite, unconcretized other (with various kinds of monological utterances of an emotional type)."[4] This fourth type of addressee, flexibly and imaginatively described as the "indefinite, unconcretized other" in a monological utterance, can readily be found in lyric. Thus the dialogic component in poetry cannot be precluded. In addition, many modern poets and literary critics – T. S. Eliot, Ralph Wilson Rader, David H. Richter, and Samuel Maio, among them – have detected other voices in lyric besides that of the poet musing to himself.[5]

---

[3]   In his essay "What is Poetry?" (1833) John Stuart Mill writes, "Eloquence is heard, poetry is overheard. Eloquence supposes an audience; the peculiarity of poetry appears to us to lie in the poet's utter unconsciousness of a listener" (Mill, 1976: 12). Northrop Frye, harping on the same note, says, "The lyric is the genre in which the poet… turns his back on his audience" (Frye, 1957: 271). In a seminal essay on lyric, Jonathan Culler gives a detailed historical survey of lyrical theories and presented insightful observations about the changing critical approaches to reading lyric in the late twentieth century. See Jonathan Culler, "Changes in the Study of the Lyric" (Hošek and Parker, 1985: 38-54). Related works by Culler include: "Apostrophe," *The Pursuit of Signs: Semiotics, Literature, Deconstruction* (London: Routledge, 1981), 135-54; "The Modern Lyric: Generic Continuity and Critical Practice," *The Comparative Perspective in Literature: Approaches to Theory and Practice.* eds. Clayton Koelb and Susan Noakes (Ithaca and London: Cornell University Press, 1988), 284-299; and "Comparing Poetry," his Presidential Address to the Conference of American Comparative Literature Association in 2001, *Comparative Literature* (Summer 2001): vii-xviii.

[4]   M. M. Bakhtin, *Speech Genres and Other Late Essays.* Trans. Vern W. McGee. eds. Caryl Emerson and Michael Holquist (Austin: University of Texas Press, 2004, c. 1986), 95-98.

[5]   A seminal article on the voices in poetry is T. S. Eliot's "The Three Voices of Poetry," in *On Poetry and Poets* (New York: The Noonday Press, 1961), 96-112. It was first delivered in 1953 at the eleventh Annual Lecture of the National League and has invited numerous critical responses. A few that are relevant to this discussion

In the Chinese academic milieu, too, the lyric voice drew renewed critical attention in the mid-twentieth century. Well acquainted with Western literature and intellectual history and arguing against an intentionalist poetics, Chen Shih-hsiang (Chen Shixiang) and Chow Tse-tsung (Zhou Cecong) attempted to unearth a legitimate origin for a spontaneous lyric voice by re-reading the etymological roots of the word *shi* (poetry).[6] Their arguments are mainly based on the primary etymons, "ᘜ" and "ᘩ." Chen deduces that poetry is "derived from and remained closely associated with the concept of beating rhythm with the foot on the ground, as graphically represented by the archaic character 'ᘩ.' The beating of rhythm with the foot clearly indicates the primordial art of dance, in which both music and song were embryonically one" (Chen, 1969: 378). In seeking the origin of Chinese poetry, Chen emphasizes the rhythmic elements of dance and song accompanied by spontaneous emotional utterance. Thus, poetry is an entity that is born naturally, directly expressing the poet's personal thoughts and feelings, rather than made self-consciously. To distinguish his concept of poetry from the Aristotelian model, Chow takes a closer look at the dancer's foot, concentrating on the movement and the direction towards which the toes point. His conclusion is that poetry inherently entails rapid movement and orientation to a goal. Both notions, "flow" and "direction," are characteristics of time. When enacted in human terms, time becomes a personal initiative, unrelated to the awareness of auditors or spectators. From a comparative perspective, Chen's and Chow's etymological re-readings of the word "poetry" illuminate alternative interpretations of

---

of Yang Mu's lyric voice include: Robert Langbaum, *The Poetry of Experience: The Dramatic Monologue in Modern Literary Tradition* (Chicago and London: University of Chicago Press, 1985, c. 1957); Ralph Wilson Rader, "The Dramatic Monologue and Related Lyric Forms," *Critical Inquiry* 3 (1976): 131-51; David H. Richter, "Dialogism and Poetry," *Studies in the Literary Imagination* XXVIII. 1 (Spring 1990): 9-27; Peter Hühn, "Watching the Speaker Speak: Self-Observation and Self-Intransparency in Lyric Poetry" in *New Definitions of Lyric: Theory, Technology, and Culture,* ed. Mark Jeffreys (New York and London: Garland Publishing, 1998), 215-244; Charles Martin, "The Three Voices of Contemporary Poetry" in *The New Criterion* (April 2004): 34-7; and Samuel Miao, *Creating Another Self: Voice in American Poetry* (Kirksville, Mussouri: Thomas Jefferson University Press, 1995).

6   Chen Shih-hsiang's essays on the topic include "The *Shih-ching* [Shijing]: Its Generic Significance in Chinese Literary History and Poetics," *Bulletin of the Institute of History and Philology, Academia Sinica* XXXIX (1969): 371-413 and "In Search of the Beginnings of Chinese Literary Criticism," *University of California Publications in Semitic and Oriental Philology* XI (1951): 45-63. For further discussion, see Chen Shih-hsiang, *Chen Shih-hsiang wencun* [Collected Essays of Chen Shih-hsiang]. eds. Ye Shan and Lin Hengjie (Taipei: Zhiwen, 1972). Chow Tse-tsung's essay is "The Early History of the Chinese word Shih (Poetry)" in *Wen-lin: Studies in the Chinese Humanities.* ed. Chow Tse-tsung (Madison: Wisconsin University Press, 1968), 195-210.

the embryonic stage of the genre and liberate the individual utterance from any decorous intent. They thus have opened up fertile theoretical ground for developing a modern Chinese lyric.

At the same time, literary experiments with the lyric voice began to flourish in Taiwan in the 1950s. Various poetry magazines such as *Blue Star*, *Epoch*, and *Modern Literature* nurtured a generation of young poets who successfully assimilated the influence of Romanticism and modernism in their works. Among them, Yang Mu has been the most prolific and influential. Immediately after his first book of poetry came out in May 1960, Yang's lyric voice was heard as distinctive and drew great praise. Lucy J. Chen found this "native Formosan" to be the most talented of the younger poets, noting that he has a "sure and sensitive command of the language and a very individual style of expression."[7] Yang was soon recognized as the best lyric poet of the 1960s. Zhang Mo declared, "The poet has already found his own poetic voice" and "judging by creative writing alone, the world poet [W. B. Yeats] is no better in craftsmanship than Ye Shan [Yang Mu]."[8] Evaluating Yang's poetry in the late 1980s, Dominic Cheung considered his "the best wrought" lyric voice, which "remains one of the foremost and best in modern Chinese poetry today."[9]

This chapter sets out to analyze the lyric voices in Yang Mu's poetry, examining how these voices bring the Chinese and Western lyric traditions together – not simply fusing the two but using their interaction to reflect on each culture's uniqueness. The first section, on the personal mode, considers the traditional attachment of the lyric "I" to the poet in both Chinese literary practice and English Romantic convention. Here, the interpretive strategy is to take the poet as leading one life and read in each poem a concrete meaning related to that life. In these poems, the addressee usually belongs to one of the first three types identified by Bakhtin. The second section, on the vocative mode, explores the poet's ability to draw the second-person pronoun, "you," into a communicative context to inhabit an exclusive poetic world of two with the speaker. Although only one voice is heard, the dynamic relationships between "you" and "I" make many of Yang's poems implicitly dialogic, as the utterance gains meaning through the presence of an addressee of the fourth type.

---

[7] Lucy J. Chen, "Literary Formosa," ed. Mark Mancall. *Formosa Today* (New York: Praeger, 1964), 140-1.

[8] Zhang Mo, "Shuizhimei de lianyi: lun Ye Shan de shi" [The Ripples in *By the Waterside*: on Ye Shan's Poetry] in *Xiandaishi de touying* [Projection of Modern Poetry] (Taipei: Taiwan Commercial Press, 1967), 119.

[9] Dominic Cheung, *The Isle Full of Noises: Modern Chinese Poetry from Taiwan* (New York: Columbia University Press, 1987), 21.

The third section looks into the dramatic mode, as expressed in either apostrophe or prosopopoeia. This strong presence of a voice forms "a signifying disposition... which fashions a judging consciousness."[10] The voice is constitutive of an object of signification, whether an addresser or an addressee. As this object is constructed, acquiring an identity and a consciousness, it forges a perspective on its own; at the same time, the object itself is elided and loses its clear contours. In this third section, the animation of a speaking subject and its listener is analyzed as the dramatization of a communicative situation. The use of a dramatic speaker invents a "subject of enunciation," which takes shape "within the gap opened up between signifier and signified that admits both structure and interplay within."[11] Thus the dramatic mode foreshadows the fourth dimension of Yang Mu's lyric voice – the emergence of a fictive persona in a dramatic monologue. Whereas the first section focuses on the biographical identification of the poet-speaker, this section explores the dialectics between the poet and the speaker by focusing on the subject of enunciation and the subject of the enounced. Although Yang Mu is not the only modern Chinese poet who creates an imaginary voice that speaks behind a mask, his experiments with dramatic monologue are the most strategic and inspiring.

The Voice of Self-Portraiture: The Personal Mode

Yang Mu's poems have been highly regarded for decades because of their musicality and imploring, confiding tone. A significant number of his poems fall into the personal mode of expression, which is characterized by the private voice speaking in a confessional style.[12] Many of these works are viewed as the poet's record of and reflection on his personal encounters. Everyday experiences at various stages of life such as courtship, homesickness, marriage, and fatherhood find their place in his works. Although one cannot be certain that the works are purely autobiographical, there is nothing in the poems to suggest that their speaker is not the poet himself, and they correspond closely in theme and mood to events in his life. In his early works in particular, Yang Mu openly admits that the lyrical self is the author's self. "From the begin-

---

10   Julia Kristeva, "From One Identity to an Other," *Desire in Language: A Semiotic Approach to Literature and Art* (New York: Columbia University Press, 1980), 141. While I find Kristeva's ideas about the symbolic function of poetic language stimulating and her notion of the "questionable subject-in-process" relevant to this discussion, my application here is not premised on the severance of the lyric voice from "classic poeticness" and literary convention.

11   Kristeva, *Desire in Language*, 127-8.

12   To Eliot, this is the first voice in poetry, which is "the voice of the poet talking to himself." Rader categorizes this voice under "expressive lyric" and Martin calls it the "private voice."

ning till now, I have written about one hundred poems, they are purely records of my personal moods and thoughts": "If poetry does have a purpose, it is to show 'you' my feelings."[13] To distinguish his own approach from the confessional style of some May Fourth writers, Yang repeatedly stresses that poetry is the flower that grows from the soil of "contemplation and meditation." But from *By the Waterside* (1960) up to *Flower Season* (1963), the dominant voice in the poems is still his own. Though rare in his mature works, the personal voice of a husband and a father is heard in family-oriented poems such as "Hualian" (1978) and "Set Off: Sonnets for Ming-ming" (1980), a prothalamion for his bride and a piece dedicated to his new-born son, respectively. In Joseph R. Allen's opinion, "Yang's poetry tends to describe a narrative arc that shadows a biographical line."[14] He argues that

> generally his [Yang Mu's] poems are ultimately grounded in his everyday world and we are induced to read them as records of actual events. He may venture into the abstract in the course of the poem, but this is usually only to "annotate the concrete." His world is subjective and lyrical, but it is *this* world, and we strive to unravel the poem so that we can see into it. (Allen, 1993: 415)

Along this line of a biographical-historical reading, the following discussion will unravel the worlds in some of Yang Mu's poems.

As soon as his first book of poetry came out, Yang Mu's unique lyric voice was recognized. The title poem, "By the Waterside" (1958), which depicts an impatient youth sitting listlessly by the waterside, listening to the gurgles of the stream, to the annoying laughter of girls, and, most importantly, to the adolescent call for adventure and love, is the most impressive work of the period. At eighteen, the poet vividly created the voice of a lonely youth. Half complaining and half grudging, spoken to nobody and for nothing, the monologue shows a sensitive youth's restlessness, and his conflicted desires to approach and to avoid the other sex. A vague reference to some addressee for his amorous attention appears in another poem of the same year, "The One in Black" (1958):

> It comes, and it goes. Sweeping between my eyelashes
> Standing for a while at the door, remembering the sound of the waves
> O, the one in black is the cloud! Before the heavy downpour
>
> I take down the scene of rain from the window
> Take down the aged shades of parasol trees
> Take you down

---

[13]   Yang Mu, *Yang Mu shiji I: 1956-1974* [Collected Poems of Yang Mu, Volume 1: 1956-1974] (Taipei: Hongfan, 1978), 605 and 608.

[14]   Joseph R. Allen, *Forbidden Games and Video Poems: The Poetry of Yang Mu and Lo Ching* (Seattle and London: University of Washington Press, 1993), 410.

The indeterminacy of the subject engaged in actions such as sweeping, standing, and reminiscing allows them to be assigned to "it," "I," or "you." The water imagery creates ambiguity, as the identity of the one in black drifts between the gathering cloud and a human addressee. "You," like the imminent rainstorm, distracts and disturbs the speaker. Compared with the indefinite request in "By the Waterside," with its indeterminate object – "No, let nobody come" – here the active repudiation "Take you down" more clearly sketches a person and situation. There is a tension between toughness and tenderness in Yang's poems of the 1950s, showing that the speaker is rather uncertain of the appropriate response to his churning emotions. The impatience and uncertainties that are features of the adolescent mood eventually find their expression in romantic love.

Most of the early poems written by Yang Mu in his teens and twenties are songlike, with rhymes and refrains, and some of them were actually made into songs. The use of interjection and the repetition of words within the short space of a line or stanza forge an earnest, intimate tone. Yang Mu's love poems are the most popular of his early works because of their delicate presentation of subtle feelings. "Icy Little Hands" (1960), "When the Wind Blows" (1961), and "Your Feelings" (1976) are representative works depicting scenes that readers can almost feel with their sense of touch as well as see and hear. "Icy Little Hands" can serve as an example:

> Ever since then, mountains roll eastward
> Wave after wave, in the rosy tides
> Let me gently hold your icy little hands
> In the rain, let me gently hold
> The rosy, icy little hands of yours
>
> ································
> Let me gently hold your hands of rose
> I am the bonfire of the chilly night
>
> ································
> I am the bonfire then
> Let the flame flick the frost off your clothes
> Sit here by the stove
> Let me, let me gently hold your icy little hands   (lines 1-5, 9-10, 17-20)

The repeated lines function like refrain or chorus, and help create the poem's earnest, imploring tone. "When the Wind Blows" is another famous example:

When the wind blows
Bells tingle in the hallway
Little orioles swoop down; the curtains flap
You lean against the fence, turning away from the flowers, away from the
    bridge
To the colourful clouds in the hazy West

When the wind blows, I will recall
When the wind blows, I gaze at your beautiful surmise under a straw hat
The twilight lingers on your shoulder
The sandy gale gnaws the lips of a southerner like me
You live in my billowy bosom
Standing side by side, we watch
From our shoulders the dusk softly falls
Softly it falls

Yang Mu's fondness for enjambment reinforces the flow of the confession. His frequent use of dashes, ellipses, and question marks at the ends of lines and stanzas seems to suggest an excess of powerful feelings that can be neither contained nor fully verbalized. The emotion in the poem is only half-articulated, leaving much to the reader's empathetic imagination. For a short period, a youthful impulse to sentimentality was often evident in his writing. In some poems, such as "Winter Airport" (1964), interjections pile up, conveying a sense of being overpowered by emotions:

Open a packet of cigarette
Let the living have eternal life
An effect of chance
And a pure chance extremely pure

....
O maple O maple, so it sings
O wilderness O wilderness
So it sings   (lines 6-9, 31-3)[15]

The young poet's self-conscious search for a breakthrough in poetic style soon resulted in a radical change in his writing. *Legends* (1971) displays a marked departure from his early sentimental yearnings. The decreased use of punctuation and interjection shifts the reader's focus onto the words themselves. Though there is little repetition, Yang exhibits mature mastery of verbal rhythm. These poems display Yang's conscious effort to write Chinese as a learned language and the poetic utterance a cultivated talk.

At the same time, Yang does not wholly abandon the musicality of the ballad form, and the refrain remains his favourite poetic device. His

---

[15]   Yang Mu, *Collected Poems of Yang Mu, Volume 1*, 264.

strong belief that musicality contributes to the organic unity of a poem is made clear in the afterword of *Taboo Games*. Yang is a renowned scholar of the formulaic lyrical form in the *Book of Songs*, and he views repetition with variations as almost essential to giving *vers libre* a coherent form. In many of his longer poems, such incremental repetition serves a function more lyrical than narrative. For example, the refrain "At the coast where the *kuroshiro* current surges" appears seven times, at regular intervals, in "Seven Turns of the Coast" (1980). At its best, repetition also has thematic significance. For example, "An Elegy of One Hundred and Twenty Lines" (1977), Yang's famous one-stanza poem, relies on auditory and visual form to perfectly render circularity of time: "at the speed of time / as it whirls: the day before / today the day after" (lines 20-2); "the cycle of time. The day before the day before / the day before today the day after" (lines 32-3); "to live or to die / is after all an order of renewal / the day before today / today the day after" (lines 112-5).[16]

Another of Yang's notable poetic devices is the deliberate injection of unconventional linguistic features into Chinese writing. For example, after he began his undergraduate studies, he started to introduce English terms and phrases into his poems: "'C' major" in "My Midnight Song" (1960), "For I was such a fool" in "Coda" (1961), and "Penelope" and "Calendar Girl" in "To Cross the Milky Way" (1961). He has continued his direct borrowing from foreign languages in most of his writing, prose and poetry alike. Sometimes he inserts references to his birthplace or to his overseas experiences. Unlike many nativist poets, Yang Mu rarely deploys dialectal variations in Chinese writing to fashion his Taiwanese identity. Among the exceptions are "Warm Days" (1963) and "Hualian" (1978), which use Hualian dialect to build up a distinct image of his home-town. Incorporating local details also helps him to present his Hong Kong experiences since the 1990s. For instance, typhoons figure in the climax of "To an Angel" (1993), bypassing the city, and of "Typhoon Signal No. 3" (1997), sweeping across it; and a local species of butterfly, Rothschild (*Troides helena spilotia*), is featured in "Butterfly" (2005). By such means, the speaker creates a fresh voice to present his current mode of thinking, and at the same time reminds the reader of his specific locales in different periods of his life.

In several of his mature works of poetry, Yang Mu speaks directly of his identity and beliefs. A poet's voice reflects the mind, in this case a scholarly mind prone to meditation and intellectualism. Moreover, as noted above, a poet's obligation to verbalize his intent in poetry is rooted in the Chinese lyric tradition. A keen awareness of national and

---

[16] Like the function of "day" in the repetition, the Chinese character "日" repeatedly appears in the lines, constituting the visual effects.

cultural mission has been expected of intellectuals since the May Fourth Movement, and Yang Mu also expresses this type of obsession with the nation in a few poems.

At the historic moment of 1979, Yang Mu lamented the loss of identity on both the individual and the national levels owing to national and international oppression. "In Memory of Einstein" (1979) and "A Song of Sorrow – Dedicated to Lin Yixiong" (1980) show a direct, conventionally assumed unity of poetry, poet, and society. They are both written in a conversational style in which the poet-persona makes his enunciative position as a Taiwanese clear. The imaginary conversation with Einstein is an appeal to an international audience to pay attention to Taiwan's national and cultural issues of identity. The poem dedicated to Lin Yixiong is a requiem in which the poet speaks for a Taiwanese dissident whose family members were murdered in the aftermath of the Formosa Incident.[17]

As the framings for a nativist Taiwanese consciousness and for Taiwan as a national entity were both suppressed by the hegemonic presence of a greater power, first the Guomindang (the Nationalist Party) and then the People's Republic of China (PRC), Yang's personal mode of self-portraiture could represent the collective voice of his people. An assistant professor at Princeton, Yang displaced his concerns into an imaginary conversation with his "neighbour" and "colleague," Albert Einstein. Instead of showing fanatical, emotional patriotism, in "In Memory of Einstein" he discusses comparable events in Israel and China. Here a Taiwanese converses with Albert Einstein, who worked out the theory of relativity but possesses an unmistakable, un-relative identity of a Jew in exile:

> Last night, you walked toward me, friendly. In the shades of the blossoming lily magnolia, wearing an old legendary woollen sweater, you couldn't help asking me why I hadn't written a poem for you, Albert Einstein, the great physicist, the Jewish saint. "Besides," you said, "your office is just next to mine. Haven't you ever thought of me when you walk in and out?"[18]

> A great physicist, a Jewish saint, Albert Einstein. It is said that to modern men your most stunning discovery is relativity, in 1919, related to the universe. Yet I don't understand, so it is not related to me – because I am a disciple of relativity, too. I have heard your name, but I don't know you

---

[17] Lin Yixiong was a provincial senator, who was arrested during the "Formosa Incident" in December, 1979. In February 1980 his mother approached the Amnesty International Osaka office for help. The next day Lin's mother and twin daughters were murdered, apparently as an intimidating act. Yang Mu's poem was meant to be a requiem for the dead and a prayer of sympathy for Lin.

[18] Yang Mu taught at Princeton University in 1979, and his office was next to the one that Einstein had used.

In the shades of the blossoming lily magnolia, you tempted me to write a poem to commemorate you. "Besides," you couldn't leave me alone, "this year is my hundredth birthday. You study in the office. Haven't you ever heard the sound of a moving chair or my coughs next door? In my old age, I didn't think about physics. Most of the time, I thought about the Jew."

Relative to your wrinkled forehead, outside the window, it is strewn with cornelian cherry now waiting for the warmth of spring to blossom, to flare. I stroll in the corridor and seem to hear your footsteps at the other end of the courtyard. But that could be only echoes of my own footsteps. Oh, no. It's you who is strolling and thinking of Israel; I think of Taiwan

Science fascinates me. As I don't understand it, the more fascinated I am. You can't move me, Albert Einstein, I'm sorry. It's true. Israel can. After the snow, I have heard people talking about you. This little town has become famous because of you. Spring is here, they will still talk about you. Summer, autumn, winter

I'm sorry, I can't write a poem to commemorate you; nor can I join the crowd to talk about you. I did listen enthusiastically to a Jew glorifying Israel many years ago, though. As regards relativity, in 1919; in that year, astonishing events happened in our China too, such as the May Fourth Movement

Albert Einstein, have you ever heard of the May Fourth Movement? Mr Democracy and Mr Science, our blood and tears. Many people died for democracy and science in China. There is always a time when cornelian cherry scatters all over the place, illuminating me thinking of what you said, Raffiniert ist der Herr Gott, aber Boshaft ist Es Nicht

Your confidence and wisdom are engraved on the wall above the fireplace in the lecture hall. I ponder in the shades of lily magnolia and the light of cornelian cherry. I believe that truth is attainable, so are democracy and science. Relativity has no relation to me, but I am moved by Israel's aspirations. The Jewish saint, the great physicist, can you be moved by my Taiwan?

(March, 1979)

This poem is loaded with anxieties and contradictions, as are the issues of national-cultural identity for a Taiwanese. The shifts of alliances in world politics in the late 1970s that led the United States and Japan to withdraw recognition of Taiwan had a tremendous impact on identity discourse among Taiwanese. "In Memory of Einstein" exhibits tensions between physics and metaphysics, a scientist and a scientific outlook, and an individual and his nation. Einstein's theory of relativity is not related to the poet, because he does not understand it. But he *is* impressed by aspirations towards Science, elevated to a metaphysical concept and abstracted as transcendental values. Science and democracy are cornerstones of the May Fourth Movement. Yang Mu deliberately picks the year 1919 to juxtapose the theory of relativity (actually first proposed in 1905) in the West and the May Fourth Movement in China. Interestingly, although he denies any connection between relativity and himself and thus rejects both a theory of physics and Einstein, the scientist, he declares at the same time his admiration for the collective pursuit of "truth" embodied in the metaphysical concepts of science and democracy in China: "I believe that truth is attainable, so are democracy and science." Only when the individual is subsumed under a master narrative, such as Science or Nation, can his appeal be heard. Tensions can be felt in the persona's shifting frames of self-identification. The cultural frame of reference, "our China," is problematized by the more specific identity claim, "my Taiwan." In this poem, what captures the poet's attention is not a theory of physics or a famous scientist but the meaning of relativity in relation to the problems of Israel and Taiwan, countries whose national-cultural identities are themselves relative – bound to the twists and turns of world politics.

"A Song of Sorrow," the most emotional of Yang Mu's works, is a poem of three stanzas of ten, ten, and seventeen lines, respectively. It is a dirge for Lin Yixiong's mother and daughters, killed on 28 February 1980 when Lin was still in jail as a result of the Formosa Incident of December 1979. In this purge of dissidents, the Guomindang regime persecuted innocent people like these women. The "song" is also meant to comfort Lin, who was kept away from home.[19]

What are gone are not only mother and daughters
the earth of peace, the promise of years
....
What is gone is the dream, not the perseverance
What are gone, gone are the veins of times
....
The last generation is too bitter, the next cannot
be bitterer, be bitterer than this, than this generation   (lines 1-2, 11-2, 19-20)

The sense of loss and bitterness is joined with the laments for the dead as the poem protests against the reign of terror.

The third stanza is semantically complete in ten lines but it lingers on for another seven lines, as the motifs of home and return are repeated in fragmentary phrases.

Heavy rain wails over the sea outside Yilan
Sunlight dimly slants at the trembling slopes
The north wind weeps in the valley, knowledge
The rock crunches in the cold brooks, words and speech

19   Owing to the censorship in Taiwan, the poem was published in *Ba Fang* [Eight Directions] in Hong Kong in 1980. The poem made its first appearance in Taiwan in 1995 when it was placed in *Yang Mu shiji II: 1974-1985* [Collected Poems of Yang Mu, Volume 2: 1974-1985] (Taipei: Hongfan, 1995), 478-81.

> Are equally fragile. We silently pray
> May the humble stars at midnight dry our tears
> Build a solid bridge, let
> The anxious mother and the frightened daughters
> Leave the city and the dust, escort
> Them (mother and daughters) to return
> To the home of plentiful marshes and rice paddies in the plain
> Return to the home of plentiful marshes and rice paddies
> Return to the plain, to guard their timeless
> Home of plentiful marshes and rice paddies in the plain
> Return to the marshes and rice paddies
> Return to their timeless
> Home in the plain.   (lines 21-37)

If the mother and daughters cannot be in their home alive, the poet prays that they can find their way back home in death, to guard and rest in their eternal, ideal home. The pathetic chanting of "home" and "return" establishes the scene as rural Taiwan at peace – a setting in which life can continue and be complete, undisturbed.

In these two poems, the foregrounding of personal and national identity by invoking proper names is an explicit, performative act of history writing. Yang Mu commemorates the innocent victims of white terror in Taiwan and aligns the political issues of Taiwan with those of Israel. The poet's coherent, straightforward discursive voice is heard. Homeless, dejected souls, both dead and alive, are offered solace in the dirge that invents an imaginary home for the longing gaze. That he draws his Jewish neighbour across space and time to be his imaginary listener to their shared concerns demonstrates the urgent need for communication. The complexities of the Taiwanese consciousness, the ambivalent, indissoluble cultural ties with a modern China exemplified by the May Fourth Movement, the oppressive Jiang regime, and the national status of Taiwan in the international milieu sum up the predicaments of the poet's portrayal of identity in that historical period.

Such transparent treatment of history through a personal, lyrical voice is rather uncharacteristic of Yang Mu's usual practice in creative writing, however. Here, the lyric voice creates multiple perspectives from which cultural identity can be conceived. The shifts between "our China," "my Taiwan," and the imaginary "home of plenty marshes and rice paddies in the plain" reveal the difficulties experienced by Taiwanese – whether on the island, in diaspora, or in prison – in locating a home. For an expedient fashioning of a cultural identity, many Taiwanese writers, like Heng Fu, chose to sever their ties with the May Fourth Movement in favour of a link with the Japanese and the West in fashioning the history of modern Taiwan poetry. Yang Mu eventually took a radically different path.

When Yang taught in Taiwan the second time between 1983 and 1984, he was engaged in unprecedented social and political commentary, which appeared in a weekly column in the newspaper, *United Daily*. These essays were collected in *Interchanges* (1985). In the same year, he published "Someone Asks Me Questions Concerning Justice and Righteousness" (hereafter referred to as "Someone"), a long poem reflecting on issues of ethnicity in Taiwan. In a pseudo-conversation, the speaker plays the role of a sympathetic and understanding listener and lets the addressee fully express his doubts and worries. Though the speaker is accommodating, he comprehends the mainstream discourse and is not without reservations.

The poem in large part focuses on a letter, whose facticity is repeatedly emphasized as specifics about its content and form are given. In "neat, well-organized writing," the letter is "signed with / real name, and ID number / Age" (lines 2-5). It is historical writing: the life history of a youth and a youth's life in history. As the speaker reads the letter, its content is continually interrupted by his introspection, retrospection, and digressions that mix in external realities on an almost ahistorical level. The intertwining movements of closing and opening, together with the dialectical play between the particular and the general and between the factual and the fictional, are staged in Yang Mu's writing of a reading of a writing.

The letter is declared to be factual and real. It is said to be a logical exposition, written in a critical, analytical style with substantial illustrations that support impressive arguments. However, what its lucid presentation conveys is a series of doubts about justice and righteousness. The letter receives no reply, nor are its doubts quelled. The first line quoted below states the topic for discussion:

Someone asks me questions concerning justice and righteousness
These need no symbols – these
Are realities that ought to be treated as realities
The sender is a person good at analytical thinking
Having taken a year course on business management, he changed to law
Spent six months in the army, made two attempts at the recruitment examinations for judges
The rain stops
To me, his background, his agony
His accusations and protests are incomprehensible
Though I try very hard, facing a pot of bitter tea
Try very hard to comprehend. I believe it is not examinations
That provoke him, because they are not included in his illustrations
What he talks about are some sophisticated questions, precise and to the point
Neatly organized, concluded in a series of perplexing

> Doubts. The sun pours onto the grassland behind the banana trees
> Glittering on the bare branches. These cannot be
> False, in the remaining warmth
> To insist on a vast expanse of coldness   (lines 42-59)

The insistence on incomprehension frees the author from the guilt of appropriation. He does not try to speak on behalf of the letter writer, nor does he claim to be inside the head or stand in the shoes of the other. He is pondering the other's puzzles, which, despite the writer's analytical thinking and succinctly presented arguments, cannot be clarified.

The letter, as it is read throughout the poem, contains only one central literary image: the "twentieth-century pear," invoked as a sigh in an aside by the rational letter-writer.

> In the frail chest grows a small,
> Lonely heart, as he wrote earnestly:
> "Precocious and fragile like a twentieth-century pear"   (lines 19-21)

This pear, which seems to be beside the point and is often dismissed from the main line of arguments, keeps returning. When it first appears as a casual emotional outburst, the reader brushes it aside as irrelevant to the central concern with justice and righteousness. The symbol is taken lightly because it does not fit in a serious discourse on concrete realities. Stylistically, the pear is an interruption that disturbs the overall impression of a rational exposition.

> ... Alas, what is meant by a twentieth-century pear –
> They are found on the highlands of the island
> In a climate similar to that in the north China plain, a rich, fertile
> Virgin territory, in circuitous ways, a kind of nostalgia-healing
> Seeds imported, to bury, sprout and grow
> They blossom to bear this fruit, a fruit not found in books
> A pathetic shape, colour and scent
> Nutrition value unknown, besides
> Vitamin C, it does not really symbolize anything
> Besides a heart, indeterminate, belonging to him   (lines 32-41)

Yet a closer look reveals that the story of the twentieth-century pear parallels the story of the letter's sender. He is apparently a second-generation mainlander of mixed parentage, born and brought up in a community of servicemen, like the pear introduced to Taiwan from mainland China. To the letter-writer, "'Place of origin makes me carry, everywhere I go / A homesickness by birth,' he says, 'like a birthmark'"; but ironically, "'Only that place which my mother has never seen is our / homeland'" (lines 90-7). Hardly a casual detail, the pear is deeply symbolic, an inscription that cannot be passed over. Questions concerning justice and righteousness cannot be answered if one tries to ignore hybridity and its impact on identity.

The account of the experiences of the person writing the letter provides a summary of Taiwan's history in the twentieth century, as lived by its general population. The letter lays out the genealogy of a person of mixed origins. Born to a mainlander father and a Taiwanese mother, the young man has grown up in a village of army families, where the military immigrants from the mainland view their settlement in Taiwan as temporary. It is merely a refuge as they prepare for the eventual recovery of their homeland across the strait. The young man's acquisition of language reflects his mixed ancestry. As a boy, he practised calligraphy of the Tang dynasty, associated with his father, while from his mother he learnt to speak in Taiwanese Mandarin, his "mother tongue." Even a critical incident in his family's story underscores how deeply he is embedded in a larger historical and ideological context. On a hot, stuffy night, his father left them after a fierce quarrel phrased in "Heated words heavily accented in his native dialect, not really intelligible / To his only son, the heir to his lineage" (lines 69-70). The young man does not know the whereabouts of his father since that time, but he speculates that the mainlander has gone to the highlands, where the climate is close to that of north China. There, he will continue to cultivate and grow the newly imported fruit, the twentieth-century pears. This young man spent most of his time with his mother, who has taught him to sing Japanese nursery rhymes and told him children's stories of "Momo Taro and the Island of Monsters." In his childhood memories, "Half asleep, half awake / he saw her [his mother] unravel the military uniform, with scissors and threads / make it into a pair of pants and a small quilt jacket" (lines 75-7). The Taiwanese mother is portrayed as a quiet, patient, and persevering figure, who preserves her native dialect, draws on Japanese cultural productions to entertain her child, and transforms the military uniform into children's wear. Her mixing of what is available, whether local or foreign, including imports from the colonizers (the Japanese) and the outsiders (the soldiers of the Guomindang), is a formative influence on generations to come.

The heart can be viewed as a metonymy for identity, but it is an imported identity, "precocious and fragile." Identity, in post-colonial Taiwan, is like a twentieth-century pear, uprooted from its native soil and transplanted elsewhere.[20] In post-colonial discourses, questions of identity confusion or diffusion are approached through various stereo-

---

[20] Another significant example of using pear for a discourse on identity is Luo Fu's poem, "Peeling a Pear at Midnight." In his poem, the pear is nationalized as a Korean pear, in which the persona sees himself. The pear's yellow skin and white heart are symbolic of the two innocent peoples, the Korean and the Chinese, who have suffered in modern history. Contrary to Luo Fu's symbolic application, Yang Mu's use of pear is not to designate a national identity, but to problematize and destabilize such a notion.

typical tactics of racial identification such as language and skin colour.
Yang Mu problematizes these tactics, however. The mother tongue of
the son of a mainlander is the language of his literal Taiwanese mother.
Significantly, Taiwanese identity and anti-patriarchal consciousness are
deeply implanted in him. His skin, represented by a birthmark, is also
inherited from his mother, though the constructed longing for the unseen
homeland leaves some imprints in the hybrid's mind.

At the peak of the identity discourse in Taiwan, the young man is
situated in the interstice between the insider and the outsider of the
province. His experiences may be common among many Taiwanese of
his time, yet he is not considered "Taiwanese" enough. If hybridity is a
historical fact, as inscribed in the life of the young man, then it is an
issue that must be taken seriously in the discourse of Taiwanese consciousness. The key to his identity, constructed by tracing an ancestral
origin, is its repression, which is mentioned almost as a slip of the
tongue: "the twentieth-century pear." What constitute the pear, the
transplant, are histories – histories of different groups of Chinese people
in the twentieth century.

The effects of denying distinctions in identity are no less pernicious
than those of essentializing identity. Using fruit imagery much like that
in "Someone," Arif Dirlik warns that

> there is a world of difference between the description of a nectarine as a hy-
> brid, and its representation in terms of the multiple contradictions implied
> by the relationships nectarine-apple-peach. Phrased in the terminology of
> dialectics, it is a unity of opposites that is expressed in the nectarine, with all
> the dynamism implicit in such an unstable unity. Hybridity suggests merely
> a proliferation of alternatives, but in real life may also lead to the extinction
> of alternatives.[21]

And "Someone" concludes with a proleptic insight about hybridity.

> He is not a prophet, but a disciple having lost his guide
> His frail chest is blown up like bellows
> A heart melts in the heat
> Transparent, mobile, empty   (lines 126-9)

In post-colonial Taiwan, an essentialist view of identity based on a
unitary origin is unrealistic and ahistorical. Nonetheless, a melting-pot
notion of hybridity that negates alternatives must be forestalled. Identity
issues demand public attention, with an eye to social equality and justice. Domains of difference – diverse experiences of feelings of cultural
belonging, local community interests, and individual rights – need to be
recognized in an immigrant society. The twentieth-century pear is a

---

[21] Arif Dirlik, "Place-based Imagination: Globalisms and the Politics of Place." In
manuscript, 23.

thought-provoking image for identity discourse in the local, intra-racial context, much as the nectarine is in the global, inter-racial one.

The dialogic lyric voice is played out in "Someone" as discord. The sender's writing is not fully recovered in the addressee's reading. The poet makes no attempt to speak to and for "you." The "I" is reluctant to answer the call and refuses to take on the role of an addressee, the ideological other in a teleological trajectory. The act of reading is fully acknowledged as defective, in order to prevent the symbolic circuit of a letter arriving at its destination from closing: there are pauses, puzzlement, and occasional moments of inattention and incomprehension. Parenthetical asides are incongruously juxtaposed to the letter's rational exposition and introduce an ironic tone. That the reading is periodically interrupted by trivial matters in the reader's surroundings, such as rain, sun, a spider, or some mosquitoes, creates a comic distance from the seriousness of the letter's subject-matter. The speaker's self-reflexive acknowledgement of incomprehension points to his own limitations in discussing the problems that confront someone other than himself. Empathy, this poem suggests, does not necessarily justify or empower a poet to speak for anyone else. The reading throws questions on questions and casts doubts over doubts, in order to interrogate the presumption of understanding and to emphasize the dangers of appropriation. Contrasting perspectives are put in play and incommensurability surfaces now and then to disturb a smooth reading. The poet addresses the question of hybridity, the subtext of all the questions in the letter and the poem, by pointing out the impossibility of an impartial metalanguage in identity discourse.[22]

At times, Yang Mu is more relaxed in his self-portraiture. Romantic images of flora and fauna, and particularly of the weather, are frequently found in these works. They also often realistically depict the poet's workplaces in different parts of Taiwan, as do famous poems about the National Taiwan University at Taipei, the National Dong Hwa University at Hualian, and the Academia Sinica at Nankang. "The Campus Tree" (1983) and "A Scale Insect" (2003) appeared at the peak of different stages of the poet's career. A visiting professor at the National Taiwan University in 1983, Yang was well-known as both a comparatist and a scholar-poet. In "The Campus Tree," he portrayed himself as a mellow, middle-aged academic who reads both English "madrigals and Chinese song-poems [Yuan lyrics]" and who engages in a conversation with a little girl about a butterfly. The juxtaposition of youth with middle-age, innocence with experience, curiosity with compassion, is also pictorially rendered by a small colourful butterfly resting on an old

---

[22] For a discussion of the impossibility of meta-language in a symbolic circuit, see Žižek, 12.

campus tree. When the little girl, who loves to make colourful soap
bubbles, asks to keep a butterfly in her book, the professor is at first
bemused; but the request later compels him to meditate on life and
ageing.

"A colourful butterfly!" A little girl whispers
in amazement. I turn and look at her
admiringly (she must be a professor's daughter)
gaping at a half-open window by her side
"I want that colourful butterfly," she says
We move closer to the pansy at rest
The two wings fold up in a dream, "I want
To catch it, I want, then, I want
To put it gently in a book. It won't hurt," says she.

No, it won't hurt. But the butterfly will die
Leaving a colourful gown, dried and soulless
In the arms of pages, leaning against words
But not necessarily living in the sympathy and wisdom
That we have yearned for.
....
"But I'll remember you always."

She laughs heartily and says, "Would you like
To see a string of soap bubbles?"
....
I look out, both hands on the railing, supporting myself
String after string, bubbles drift before my eyes
The tree heroically sheds its high-held leaves
We all are old men now
Having lost our dried colourful gowns, we only have our awakened souls
In the arms of pages, leaning against words, and also
Living in the sympathy and wisdom that we have always yearned for
                                        (lines 20-33, 44-6, 55-61)

With sympathy and wisdom one gained from life, the poet speaks in the
tender voice of a sage. Even with the knowledge of what lies ahead for
every mortal, including the lovely little girl, the speaker wishes her the
best.

Twenty years later, when Yang Mu was the director of the Institute
of Chinese Literature and Philosophy at the Academia Sinica, he met a
group of boys at his workplace. Once again, he places himself among
school children, this time as "a senior research fellow over sixty"
(line 6). Leaving his office after work, the director sees an interesting
incident:

> Just at the moment I am distracted, sound waves ride on a thousand shards
>   of
> Flooding light, I see a crowd of school children
> Thronging out from the main door behind me
>
> I slow down, listening to the resonances
> Meandering through the swaying colours of a triangular flag. To the right
>   and left
> They run, before them is the lingering sun
> A boy suddenly stops and bends over to survey the ground
> Other boys follow suit, one by one, they squat down
> In a circle, holding their breath
>
> Great discovery ought to be done
> At the dawn of a hesitant, disaster-ridden century
> I turn and look down, joining their investigation for no purpose
> To verify the signs of science and humanities in the breeze
> When all the eyes are fully focused on a spot, they see
> On the ground, a *Diaepsis patelliformi* female   (lines 22-36)

Elevating the children's play to the seriousness and significance of academic research, the speaker stoops to join them in their speculation. The Romantic truth expressed by Wordsworth – that "The Child is father of the Man" – still holds; the director of the Institute is enlightened when he sees the children's hearts leap up when they behold an insect on the ground. Only through children's eyes, in their innocent and purposeless endeavour, can great discovery be possible in the new century. The last line may appear too technical and extravagant to satisfy the school children's curiosity, but was the discovery of the species *Diaepsis patelliformi* not initiated by some researcher's equally earnest observations?

In Yang Mu's poems, the voice of self-portraiture is not monolithic and singular. The narrative always includes a dialogic counterpart to mirror the distinctive viewpoints of the senior academic and mature intellectual born of Taiwan. In form and structure, as Yang's voice has matured, these poems have become much more pointed, well-organized, and increasingly polyphonic, ridding themselves of the slackness of the early poems, which had been locked in youthful sentimentality.

Between "You" and "I": The Vocative Mode

His love poems are persistently among the most popular of Yang Mu's works. One of the major reasons is his very creative manipulation of the subtle relations between the addresser and addressee in each poem. The expressivity and addressivity inherent in the lyric form are directly rendered when pronouns of the first and second person are used.

Of central importance in the communicative situation here is the second-person pronoun. According to Roman Jakobson's analysis, an "[o]rientation toward the addressee, the conative function, finds its purest grammatical expressive in the vocative and imperative."[23] This claim is close to T. S. Eliot's conception of the second voice in poetry – "the voice of the poet addressing an audience, whether large or small" – and in this section the imaginary addressee will also be considered.

Basically, an utterance "between you and me" serves the conventional function of encouraging a strong bond between confidants, which relies on the vocative mode of expression. Noting an "assumed nonfictional referent" in Yang Mu's poetry, Joseph R. Allen argues that "[w]hen Yang Mu's poem mentions an 'I' and a 'you,' their referents are 'real' people who inhabit the world we know" (Allen, 1993: 411). To be sure, identifiable addressees are present in some specific poems, such as "The First Snow" (1978), "Oral English Class" (1980), and "The Afternoon Playground" (1986). These unmistakable addresses to his wife, Yingying, and his son, Changming, construct the picture of a real family, and thus tend to prevent the reader's associations from ranging freely. Besides, the gentle, loving voice of a husband and a father is touching.

In fact, the engaging power of Yang Mu's lines does not depend on whether "you" points to an actual referent. Closest to the Western definition of lyric as an utterance overheard, the secret sharing of the addresser's inner emotions – especially those utterances addressed to "an indefinite, unconcretized other" – does not hinder the reader from responding to the affective appeal in the poem.

What the reader of love lyric finds most appealing is the indeterminacy of the addressee and the ambiguity in the relationship depicted. To analyze the emotional impacts of Yang Mu's use of "you" and "I," this section will examine the distance between the interlocutors as well as the fluidity and mobility of each. Their relationship can be viewed as spatial, and can take a number of forms: both "you" and "I" are separate, static entities; only one of them is static, while the other is mobile; the two stay apart but close to each other because of their mutual longing; both are mobile and moving in the same direction; and both are static and mobile at different times. Accordingly, the lyric voice varies in its vocative tone, which in Jakobson's opinion can be "either supplicatory or exhortative, depending on whether the first person is subordinated to the second or the second to the first" (Jakobson, 1960: 357). To put it in a way that avoids the rhetoric of power relations, the addresser in love

---

[23] Roman Jakobson, "Closing Statement: Linguistics and Poetics," in *Style in Language*. ed. Thomas A. Sebeok (New York: Wiley, 1960), 355.

poems may use a voice that displays emotions of longing, lament, or regret.

In some of Yang Mu's early love poems, "you" and "I" are described as fixed, separate entities despite sharing some features. A neat parallelism between them produces such lines as "You have sorrow / I have sorrow" ("The Second Rainbow," 1957; lines 10-1) and "O May! There is only one evening / like a tombstone; nicely carved there are / your name, my name / amid the intermingled fading clouds" ("Writing after Death," 1957; lines 10-3). Yang Mu later abandoned these tidy syntactic arrangements for more colloquial and song-like phrasing. In "Your Feelings" (1976), the pattern of lines is musical and formulaic. Within a frame bounded by "I believe I know your feelings" and "O your feelings are like the frost and snow," the poet expands the simile by adding another level of comparison: "there was once a volcano / Your feelings are like a volcano, I know." He rings variations on this theme, as "frost and snow" disguise a "volcano" in the first stanza, paralleled by "an icy cliff" concealing "a meadow" in the second stanza and "cloud and mist" covering "an ocean" in the last stanza. The reiteration of "your feelings" and "I know" brings the speaker and "you" close to each other, although the addressee puts on various guises of indifference.

In "After the Snow" (1975) the tenderness is rendered as fire opposing the cold with a gentle exhortation:

After the snow, there is a fire in the house I believe
But I am the extinguished
Fire of last winter. Someone is lighting me, stirring me
A heap of ashy, soft-speaking stars

I cannot help walking on
Because I hear a sigh
Like the fragrance of winter-sweet stealing its way to me
I hear someone turn over the pages ...
Let me interpret your dream
I come back from an alien land, to prove to you
The difference in temperature between day and night, if
You still feel cold, why don't you throw me
Into the fireplace, to set ablaze for tonight
A new fire   (lines 15-28)

Apparently the speaker is walking outside the house, imagining the addressee's activity indoors. The gentle proposal of self-sacrifice – burning himself to keep the lady warm for a night – reminds the reader of the "icy little hands" in an earlier love poem. Whereas then he was "the bonfire," now he is "the extinguished fire" of the past. When his love poems are read in a row, a distinct lyric voice is heard, which seems to sketch a continuous narrative of the poet's life experiences.

Instead of describing him sitting or standing beside his beloved, as do the early love poems, "After the Snow" illustrates another way to position the "you" and "I." The "you" reading at home is static, the target pursued by the mobile speaker. However, the approach to the addressee is made difficult by the speaker's unease and hesitation. The same pattern is found in poems of affections directed to an imaginary addressee, like the one in "Changan" (1993):

> Suppose you were born in Changan, I came from afar
>
> ....
>
> Those are your kingdom: tender, delicate, enigmatic
> With tremendous self-awareness and a little
> Unease, I slowly advance, trespassing the boundaries of landscape and borders
> A large flag forcing its way in the gale
> Imagining the distracted embroidering finger by a needle
> Pricked, a drop of blood dots the left wing of the newly sketched magpie
> The drapes swaying
> Shadows awaken by light
> Are playing on the dark hair   (lines 1, 9-17)

An inversion of classical boudoir poetry, the poem has structurally assimilated the quadripartite design prescribed for Tang poetry.[24] In place of a female lamenting in her boudoir, the poet lets the reader hear the male traveller's voice and discover his ambivalence and worries as well as his longing for the lady.

Conversely, in a number of poems "I" is static, waiting for the "you" to come to meet him. Michelle Yeh (Xi Mi) describes Yang Mu's attitude to women in poems of this kind as "passive-aggressive."[25] She quotes a number of passages as examples of the poet's invitation to a woman: "someday you will tread on the frost and look for /... / the window where I read poetry" ("Icy Little Hands"); "Want you to come to me in the wind," "run towards me" ("Snake: A Rondo," 1969); and "Please count on me," "Please come to me" ("Love Song," 1972). Whereas these early poems have a supplicatory tone, "The Boat" (1993) is characterized by a strong faith in a secret pact between the addresser and addressee that makes the waiting calm and peaceful. While the speaker is patiently expecting a boat to sail his way, he is absolutely confident that "you" will arrive someday, perhaps at the moment when

---

[24]   For a detailed discussion of this poem, see Wong Lai-ming (Huang Liming), "Liang-zhong jiedu 'Changan' de shiyan – chuantong de yu xiandai de" [Two Readings of "Changan": the Traditional and the Modern] in *Fu Xi Poetry Journal* 3 (June 1997): 86-94.

[25]   Xi Mi (Michelle Yeh), "Du shi biji: Yang Mu" [Poetry Reading Notes: Yang Mu], *Unitas* 192 (October 2000): 30.

he is distracted. The addressee's pursuit of the speaker is sometimes imagined in exceptionally sensual terms: "I am so content and well settled with that peace and nothingness / I would rather / under the trembling groping of your soft nimble fingers / feebly sink into the silence of future and past" ("Lyric," 1993).

The emotional intensity between "you" and "I" reaches its zenith in Yang Mu's poems about mutual longing. Famous precedents come to mind, including the Chinese poem "Spring Thoughts" by Li Bai (701-762) and the metaphysical conceit of the compass in John Donne's "A Valediction: Forbidding Mourning" (1633). Yang poignantly conveys similar affectionate yearning between lovers in some of his works. Gazing in a particular direction, across the lake, over a river or the sea, to the south or to the east, the poet draws a circle taking in the shore or the coast where "you" and "I" are separately located, unable to reach each other as in the poem "The Leichi River: No Trespassing" (1975):

> You felt cold so you said; at this shore
> So did the one gazing in your direction
> ....
> Even if I loudly call out, I could not
> Let you hear it. There is only me hearing you vaguely
> Say you feel cold   (lines 16-7, 20-2)

Another poem, "Story" (1994), seems to be a rewriting of "Spring Thoughts" using sea imagery:

> If the tides roll at the speed of memory
> So do I, of the same mind. If the tides have already
> During the day and night of our separation, have already
> Told the story from the beginning to the end
> A melody that meanders round and round, a tender
> Discourse, ups and downs, life and death
> A posture of making a trip in haste   (lines 1-7)

At the same time, Yang Mu's spatial image of the communicative circuit is reminiscent of Donne's compass. The lovers kept apart by a lake or an ocean are metaphorically placed on the opposite side of a circumference, not seeing but nonetheless facing each other, sharing the same centre since they have the same mind. The concentric circles in Yang Mu's poems are a recurrent image, and they carry his gentle calls.

Furthermore, ephemeral romantic love and the elusive loved ones in Yang Mu's poems are part of his heritage from classical Chinese poetry, which originated with the *Book of Songs*. The goddesses in the "Nine Songs" of *Chu Elegies* by Qu Yuan (c. 340-278 B.C.) and the Goddess of the Luo River portrayed by Cao Zhi (192-232) also belong to this lineage, on which he draws. It is interesting to note in his recent poems a frequent use of indicators of negation, "not" (*bu* or *wu*), presenting an equivocation: what is stated to be not happening actually does occur, but within the poetic process. The addressee is described as somebody who "does not speak" in "Islands" (1992) and "you" and "I" only "look at each other without a word" in "A New Song" (1996). Perhaps for both addresser and addressee, the unsaid – like the unheard melodies in Keats's "Ode on a Grecian Urn" (1820) – is the sweetest. "In quietude, I have tried to revise / A line or two: in quietude however / Weary-hearted, I want to speak, yet / There is no word for it; at last I surrender – beauty at its best" ("In Lieu of a Letter," 1991). Sometimes, the absence of response seems to make the speaker appear lacking in passion, as when "a heart stopped beating" in "Linked Rhapsodies without Music" (1992), "Gazing at the Lake" (1993), and "The Previous Life" (1996). The fall into silence and narrative ellipsis is sometimes directly confessed: "Suppose the plot is more or less / Like this" ("Linked Rhapsodies without Music"); "Do not go after the details" ("The Thing Most Melancholy," 1993); "Cannot tell the episodes in detail," and "Cannot narrate the story in full: / that is only a beginning" ("A New Song"); and "Faraway out there is indeed a story unfinished / episodes underdeveloped... / Even if we meet again in the next life / there is no way for rewriting" ("Title Lost," 2005).

Despite the lack of fulfilment in the poems, the capacity to feel is never in doubt. Few readers could miss the supplicatory tone in Yang's love poems of the 1990s, like the voice in "Islands":

> I am all ears, hoping to be able to hear
> From you but there is no sound at all. The sea
> Is calm and clear. "Isn't that the look of your eyes?"
>
> The tides passionately roll
> Taking their time to tap on the reef, up the beach
> They circulate like a regretful love-song, unaccompanied by music
> ....
> I too, mean to ask you with the huge silence
> "If you allow ..."   (lines 4-9, 12-3)

The desperate cry in the last two lines also draws in the reader: "What will not melt is memory precipitated in cold tears / Begging for help, I / ask you." Equally touching is the speaker's longing gaze that rides on the clouds to reach the other side of the globe in "The Thing Most Melancholy":

> The evening clouds at the reverse side of the sky, like a prophecy
> Are burning to reach where you stay. Those
> Still flicker between the real and the unreal
> Are the transparent old sorrows now mixed with joy

A similar penetrating gaze at an untouchable other is found in many of Yang's poems of the 1990s, such as "Gazing at the Lake" (1993).

The most memorable love stories are usually open-ended. Because they leave a sense of unfulfilment, they challenge the universal wish for unity or for dramatic resolution. It is fair to say that the Chinese lyric tradition is filled with never-ending pursuits of elusive ladies, whose prototype is the lady across the river, well established in the *Book of Songs*; the best-known examples include the opening poem, "Turtle-dove," as well as "The Reeds" and "The River Han Is Wide." In the last, an earnest lover voices his frustration: "The River Han is wide / I cannot swim across it / The River Han is long / A boat is of little help." The modern poet describes an identical situation, though the speaker in these ancient poems never has a chance to talk directly to the lady, who is always referred to in the third person. Yang intelligently explores the tension that results when a happy meeting between the speaker and his addressee is delayed. "We cannot hear the calls from each other / Only we feel in some dim place not too far away / Similar pulsations of the heart persist, as if / Something grows in a dream" ("Tree," 1985). Even if the "you" and "I" are both mobile, they are kept close but not too close, like the mist and ripples that form a sensuous pair waltzing on different but parallel planes in "Midnight" (1994):

... At that hour, you
Grow quiet like the dark waters
I am the mist, cold and thin, having lost my direction again
I cling close to the ripples drifting, alert and aloof
Keeping a transparent distance   (lines 10-4)

To a series titled "Great Masters' Love Poems in Manuscript," Yang Mu contributed "Mist and My Other Self."[26] As in many of his recent poems, the addresser loses himself and becomes an impersonal archetype when he reveals the pictures in his heart. The "you" addressed is also reduced to an archetype to whom "I" speaks using the imagery of nature. Yet even as the identities of both "you" and "I" are attenuated into abstraction, the paradoxical sense of togetherness in separation is subtly portrayed. By purifying his emotions, Yang succeeds in rendering them more intense. His creative deployment of distance and mobility, whether physical or spiritual, lends much emotional weight to his amorous utterances and at the same time keeps them from falling in their affective effects.

Critics of Yang Mu's first book of poetry, *By the Waterside*, already hailed his unique lyric voice, which at times is "sharp," and noted that

---

[26] Yang Mu, "Mist and My Other Self," in "Great Masters' Love Poems in Manuscript," *United Daily* 22 July 2003.

"there is a kind of ineffable tension" in the poetic situation (M. Zhang 1967: 117). Today's readers, carried along with the utterance thrown from "I" to "you," would agree. These love lyrics are both traditional and modern in their dialogic tension and emotional intensity, and they use symbols employed by many great poets around the world who have paid attention to the space between separated lovers. For example, the bird is a classic messenger of love in both Chinese and Western poetry, with the turtledove playing this role in the first poem in the *Book of Songs* and Edmund Spenser's poem *The Faerie Queene* (1590);[27] Yang Mu sees the bird as "the most efficient and effective agent in the allegory of love" and the embodiment of "the lover's aggressive desire in action."[28] The "blue bird" in the writings of Li Shangyin (c. 813-858), a poet of the late Tang, and the "white bird" or "white egret" that appears in the works of Lin Ling, a pioneering modern poet of Taiwan, both serve as go-betweens in Yang Mu's poems. A white feather falling in the space between "you" and "I" is almost synonymous with the revelation of love. In addition, the image of the swan borrowed from Yeats's "Leda and the Swan" (1924) adds a modern dimension of sexuality, violence, and intellectual verve to Yang Mu's love lyrics.

Yang Mu's poetic worlds are often filled with water. A constant backdrop is the tide ebbing and flowing as it carries a message of love. Fish are also significant; the mackerel is a figure for his love in early poems, while the salmon has become a dominant symbol since his migration to North America. Other classic images include flowers, falling petals, and waving reeds. More innovative is his use of insects of the tropics, such as cicadas, cocoon, butterflies, and dragonflies, which are recurrent images in his recent poems. These living creatures contribute new sound and colour to a lover's discourse, but the addresser's and the addressee's highly mannered body language – leaning on the railing, watching the world at a window, displaying a preoccupation with embroidery, playing a zither, and so on – continue to replicate that of the forlorn lover in classical Chinese poetry. The vocative mode in Yang's love poems revives these universal images in settings that are often modern and sometimes ahistorical.

There is a growing meditative, metaphysical dimension in Yang's poems published since the 1980s. Repeated references to the previous life and the next life, the dialogic tension between lovers, and the distant phantasmal figure are means by which the poet lays bare his concerns

---

[27]   Yang Mu found the western counterpart for the bird, *jiu*, in the first work of Chinese poetry is in fact the turtledove, an auspicious bird noted for its fidelity of love. See "Chapter 6: Symbol" in C. H. Wang, *From Ritual to Allegory: Seven Essays in Early Chinese Poetry* (Hong Kong: Chinese University Press, 1988), 155-64.

[28]   C. H. Wang, *ibid.*, 161 and 163.

with love, life, and wisdom. Yeats once noted: "A poet writes always of his personal life, in his finest work out of its tragedy, whatever it be, remorse, lost love, or mere loneliness; he never speaks directly as to someone at the breakfast table, there is always a phantasmagoria."[29] The interplay of "you" and "I" is further explored in philosophical debates between the Self and the Anti-self, Not-self, or Other-self in Yang Mu's mature works. Though still two voices, still lyric, they depart from an amorous world to engage in a metaphysical and intellectual discourse on time and existence, which will be examined in Chapter 3.

Apostrophe and Prosopopoeia: The Dramatic Mode

To thwart a historical-biographical reading of his works, at various stages of his writing career Yang Mu has put on masks in constructing his lyric voice. Yang spells out his literary and social concerns by using the dramatic mode – specifically, apostrophe and prosopopoeia, two figures of speech with a long history in Western rhetoric and literature. Apostrophe is literally a turning of speech from a human addressee to a thing or an abstraction, which often is itself personified. Generally given the form of exclamation or question, it is an effective means to heighten feelings. According to Sister Miriam Joseph, "by direct address [apostrophe] conveys the immediacy of the present."[30] Inherited from the bardic tradition, the exalted voice in apostrophe is not in the familiar tone of everyday speech. "The figure of apostrophe is critical," Jonathan Culler argues, "because its empty 'O,' devoid of semantic reference, is the figure of voice, a sign of utterance, and yet, a figure of voicing, quite resistant to attempts to treat the poem a fictive representation of personal utterance."[31] In prosopopoeia, an absent or imaginary speaker, or a personified abstraction or inanimate object, is represented as speaking. Joseph, in her study of Shakespeare's use of the trope, describes prosopopoeia as "the attribution of human qualities to dumb or inanimate creatures" (Joseph, 1947: 126). A. Dwight Culler regards prosopopoeia and monodrama as the precursors of dramatic monologue.[32]

---

[29] This is Yeats's opening sentence for "A General Introduction for My Work" written for a complete edition of Yeats's works which was never published. The quote is taken from W. B. Yeats, *Essays and Introductions* (London: Macmillan Press, 1985), 509.

[30] Sister Miriam Joseph, *Shakespeare's Use of the Arts of Language* (New York: Columbia University Press, 1947), 246-7.

[31] Jonathan Culler, "Changes in the Study of Lyric," in *Lyric Poetry Beyond New Criticism* (Ithaca: Cornell University Press, 1985), 40.

[32] A. Dwight Culler, "Monodrama and the Dramatic Monologue," *PLMA* xl (1975): 366.

The close relationship between apostrophe and prosopopoeia, as well as their importance in lyric poetry, has been widely discussed by literary critics. As Paul de Man puts it:

> [A]n address of one subject to another in a *je-tu* situation... can hardly be called descriptive. ... The apostrophe, the address[,]... frames the description it makes possible. It is indeed a prosopopoeia, a giving face to... entities... which are most certainly deprived of any literal face. ... [T]he figure of address is recurrent in lyric poetry, to the point of constituting the generic definition of, at the very least, the ode (which can, in its turn, be seen as paradigmatic for poetry in general). ... It does not describe an entity, referential or textual, but sets up a rapport between concepts said to be structured like a sense perception... which carries the full burden of dramatic resolution and of intelligibility.[33]

The animation of the speaker and the addressee by direct address through apostrophe or prosopopoeia raises the dramatic situation from the level of daily encounters, allowing ample room for literary representation of the lyric voice. Robert Langbaum distinguishes dramatic monologue, in which the speaker of the poem is separate from the poet, from dramatic lyric, in which the poet's self is identified with the addresser (Laugbaum, 1957: 79-82).

In this section, Yang Mu's creative experiments with apostrophe and prosopopoeia will be analyzed as ways to enact the dramatic mode of expression. In some of his early poems, Yang Mu employs the "empty 'O'" when speaking to the imaginary addressees, which include concepts, literary invention, historical figures, and the dead. In a few poems, such as "Strange Lands" (1962), the apostrophe is directed towards multiple addressees. Among a series of portraits of foreigners written in 1958, "To Alice" offers the most lively lyric voice. The poem uses the apostrophic call, "O Alice," and the imperative – "Take off the wig, lovely Alice / Let me look at you, a brunette of Lisbon" – to evoke occidental features and dramatic characters. The exotic European setting is constructed by the description of a Catholic community resounding with church bells and prayers. Other poems have a Christian aura because of Yang's frequent apostrophic appeals to "God"; for example, "O God!" is a colloquial interjection in "Star Is the Only Guide" (1958), and "O God, where are you?" has an explicit Christian meaning in "Ghost Fire" (1962).

The dramatization of the speaker and the addressee through apostrophe and prosopopoeia is vital to the fashioning of Yang Mu's lyric voice. Talking to an unknown addressee, the speaker in "To a Lumber-

---

[33] Paul de Man, "Hypogram and Inscription: Michael Riffatterre's Poetics of Reading," 32.

jack of the Nineteenth Century" (1962) stands at the same spot and holds the same leaf as a lumberjack did seventy years earlier. The poem is a meditation on the passage of time, triggered by an object – as is typical of such English Romantic poetry as Keats's "Ode on a Grecian Urn" or Shelley's "Ozymandias" (1818). In this poem, however, the prologue foregrounds the authenticity of the lumberjack, thus heightening the verisimilitude and immediacy of the apostrophic call. Two years later, Yang Mu's experiments with the lyric voice resulted in a series of poems whose titles begin with "To," explicitly modelled after works by the English Romantic poets.

That modern Chinese poetry was experimenting with the lyric voice was generally recognized in the early 1980s. In his summary of a 1981 comparative literature conference that focused on the influences of Western literature on Chinese New Poetry, Luo Qing highlights two main poetic techniques that took modern Chinese poets in new directions.[34] One is the use of abstract nouns and abstract thinking:

> Traditional Chinese poetry rarely personifies 'Virtue,' 'Wisdom,' 'Time,' 'Fate,' or 'Death' and makes them a figure of description or address. Influenced by English poetry, new poets have begun to write poems such as 'To Fate,' 'To Death,' and 'To Melancholy.' Traditional Chinese poets like to use concrete objects to communicate their abstract meanings or feelings. On the contrary, Western poets are used to conducting their abstract thinking through abstract nouns. (Luo, 1981: 89)

Significantly, the three titles cited by Luo Qing are all taken from Yang Mu's second book of poetry, *Flower Season* (1963). And all the abstract nouns he lists as rarely personified in Chinese literary tradition were explored in Yang Mu's poems, except virtue. For example, "To Wisdom" and "To Time" are collected in his third book, *Boat Lantern* (1966). It thus took more than a decade for Yang Mu's pioneering efforts to be appreciated.

The modernist impulse to replace the verbalization of intent and confessional practice with literary craftsmanship has strongly marked Yang Mu's creative works. The New Critics deliberately differentiate the persona from the poet, treating the poem in isolation as a dramatic utterance. In interpreting a poem, they focus on a poem's text to determine the attitude of the speaker, attending only to the lines themselves to establish the impact of the lyric voice. Following the modernist parameters, Yang Mu's poems of the 1970s use prosopopoeia, a traditional figure, to effect a break from the poet's early expressive represen-

---

[34] See Luo Qing, "Xifang wenxue yu zhongguo xinshi" [Western Literature and Chinese New Poetry]. *Chung Wai Literary Monthly* 9.12 (May 1981): 82-90.

tation of emotions. "A Grass for Nothing" (1972) conveys the ennui and inertia experienced by a blade of grass.

> Other kinds of grass are happier
> Some make fodder for horses
> Some are burnt to ashes
> and buried under the snow in the north.
> An end like this is no good
> to stare, to listen and to become
> Nothing but
> A grass for nothing

The voice in "A Drifting Firefly" (1969) is more dramatic, as a murder story is told from the perspective of an avenging soul. The speaker, who killed his wife by mistake, is long dead. His wife, a daughter of his enemy, appears in the poem in the form of a drifting firefly. Disguised as a boatman, the avenging soul peeps into a household and sees his enemy sipping tea after a feast. A sense of guilt and mystery suffuses the poem, with the suggestion of a bloody murder about to occur. The dramatic tension mounts when the speaker sweats at whetting his knife, but no action takes place. The whole poem verges on an open-ended drama.

A highly apostrophic subgenre in world literature is elegy. Throughout his writing career, Yang Mu has dedicated a number of elegies to his teachers and friends, including "In Memory of Qin Zihao" (1964), "Thinking of Huang Yong" (1976), "No Valediction – To Wen Jianliu" (1976), "The Death of a Professor of English Literature" (1977), "Elegy – For Qian Xinzu" (1996), and "Then Cross the River – Elegy for Wu Qiancheng in Trochaic Meter" (1999). In tones of regret, nostalgia, or defiance, Yang vividly portrays the dedicatees and his affectionate relationships with them. Given that elegy is a literary form of a relatively fixed structure and restricted themes, few poets would try playing with its conventions. Yang Mu does so, however, in "Elegy for General Palm, with a Biography" (1993).

Many readers find "Elegy for General Palm, with a Biography" a highly enigmatic work. Consisting of two parts, a sonnet and a biography written in archaic Chinese without any punctuation, in form the poem is obviously a hybrid of the West and the classical Chinese.[35] The sonnet in part 1 details the stature and personality of General Palm, addressed in the second person in a very respectful and intimate tone. For twenty-five years, General Palm accompanied the speaker and kept

---

[35]   When "Elegy for General Palm, with a Biography" first came out, the biography in part 2 was printed without punctuation. The poem is now collected in *Temporality Proposition*, with the caesura in the biography marked by dots.

vigil in his study. Between them, a deep sense of comradeship grew. Loyal but taciturn, the general stood by the desk like a guardian angel while the poet composed his works. The speaker regrets that both he and the general have suffered the cutting wounds of time. The elegiac voice aligns the speaker and the general as sharers in a common fate – ageing and mortality. The sigh of resignation is both empathetic and compassionate.

Part 2 of the poem provides the genealogy of General Palm. Following the convention of classical Chinese biography, it opens with naming: the General is named Palm, with the alias Music, a descendent of an august lineage dating back to the times of Yao. The biography can be summarized as follows: Little is known about the early ancestors before the seventh-generation descendent, called Cum-Coconut. Highly commended for his uprightness and unwavering loyalty, he was recruited to serve in the army. Resilient and firm, he aided in the conquest of the barbarians and was honoured with the title of general. Ancestral wisdom taught subsequent generations of Palms to avoid the central provinces where the soil and the climate are unfavourable. They migrated to other places and eventually settled in the south. At the time of Longan, the sixteenth-generation descendent, Pot Rare, escorted the Magic Glare's group across the sea to some foreign lands where he and his wife, Wood Witch, stayed; their descendents were abundant and flourished. The genealogy of the Palms shows that they branched into four clans. From Master Cum-Coconut, the legitimate descendent is Pot Rare, whose brother named Betel Palm is of comparable stature. The rest of the ancestors are not recorded. Many have scattered and migrated across the seas to faraway places. The biography ends in accordance with biographical formulae: the record of the death and a commentary. "General Palm joined me in 1969. It was in 1993 that after having been seriously ill for some time, he passed away at the age of twenty-five. I was much depressed by his demise and wrote a sonnet elegy to express my sorrow." The genealogy of the subject and verisimilitude of the historical development of the clans, presented in a euphuistic style, adhere to the classical convention.

By employing a highly serious literary form to treat a new subject-matter, Yang Mu cracks a joke about the extravagance of that form. The witty and playful names make abundantly clear that General Palm and his ancestors are plants, not humans. Anecdotal evidence confirms that Yang Mu's mourning is indeed directed at a miniature palm given to him by the late Professor Chen Shih-hsiang, his dear teacher and Ph.D. supervisor at Berkeley. Yang Mu kept the plant growing in his study for twenty-four years. After a semester-long stay in Hong Kong in the fall of 1992, he discovered on his return to Seattle that the plant was sick. Even as the elegy shows how the poet has treasured the plant as his companion and muse, it indirectly expresses his deep emotional attachment to his former professor. The fictional biography appears to verge on bathos and pathos, reminding the reader both of Han Yu's playfulness in "Biography of Mao Ying" and of Zhi Yong's loving affection for his retired brushes.[36] The apostrophe to a plant in "Elegy for General Palm, with a Biography" is in fact a metonymic tender address to Professor Chen. The humour in the presentation complements Yang Mu's extremely moving prose essay, "The Land in the North" (1981), dedicated to Chen ten years after his death. In this elegy for General Palm, Yang Mu expanded the dramatic mode of the lyric voice; he not only brings together in fond memory the self, the imaginary addressee (the palm), and by implication his professor, but he also gives new life to a classical form with humour and deep affection.

A look at Yang Mu's mature works proves that his early experiments with lyric voice have become a consistent poetic practice. The freedom to speak in a voice unconnected to the author's biography greatly increases the possibilities for dialogue and heteroglossia. The imagined voices enliven the dramatic situation and engage the reader. Not surprisingly, apostrophe and prosopopoeia played an important role in Yang's development of dramatic monologue.

Dramatic Monologue: The Fictive Mode

In the mid-twentieth century, Chen Shih-hsiang contrasted the *Book of Songs* and *Chu Elegies* with Homeric epic and Greek drama to underscore the major difference between the literary traditions of the Chinese and the West: the former is basically lyrical, the latter narrative and dramatic. This tripartite structure of generic archetypes in world literature highlights the Chinese lyric tradition. By adopting the dramatic monologue, Yang Mu introduced narrative and dramatic elements into modern Chinese lyric and attempted a transgeneric approach to poetry.

The dramatic monologue is generally viewed as a Western poetic form, and specifically identified with Robert Browning. The term was apparently first used in a review of Christina Rossetti's poems that appeared in *Westminster Review* in January 1871; the critic saw in her work the "dramatic monologue," a form of modern poetry "in which a selected speaker is made to let us into the recesses of his nature and lead us along private complexities of character and history" and which was

---

36 Han Yu earned a name as a humorist by a few essays based on pure fiction, one of which is "Mao Ying Chuan" [Biography of Mao Ying]. The Mao biography is in fact a fake biography of the Chinese brush. For further discussion, see James R. Hightower, "Han Yu as Humorist" (Hightower, 1984: 5-27). Zhi Yong, the famous monk-calligrapher whose script of "A Thousand-word Essay" has been much emulated over the centuries, is said to have a tomb for the worn-out brushes he had used.

"made his own by a single writer, Mr. Robert Browning." (Dwight Culler, 1975: 366) Usually the language, thought, and feeling in a dramatic monologue are attributed to an imaginary character, someone other than the poet's biographical self. When T. S. Eliot further examines the issues in "The Three Voices of Poetry" (1953), he makes a distinction between the second voice of the dramatic monologue, which is the voice of the poet talking to other people through a mask and the third voice, "the voice of the poet when he attempts to create a dramatic character speaking in verse... within the limits of an imaginary character addressing another imaginary character" (Eliot, 1961: 96 and 104).[37] According to Eliot,

> what happens, when an author creates a vital character, is a sort of give-and-take. The author may put into the character, besides its other attributes, some traits of his own, some strength or weakness... some eccentricity even, that he has found in himself. ... [A] character which succeeds in interesting its author may elicit from the author latent potentialities of his own being [;]... he is influenced by the characters he creates. (Eliot, 1961: 102)

In other words, one can read the speaker in a dramatic monologue not only as an imaginary other but also as the poet's self, giving voice behind the mask of the other. As David H. Richter puts it, the language in dramatic monologue "is always used for two purposes at once (the speaker's and the poet's) and thus it is always and forever betraying its nominal speaker by including at least one set of intentions in addition to its own" (Richter, 1990: 19).

Such dialogic interaction between the poet and the speaker in Yang Mu's poetry can be illuminated by another interaction: that between the subject of enunciation and the subject of the enounced. In "Shifters, Verbal Categories, and the Russian Verb" (1957), Roman Jakobson distinguishes "the speech event (*procès de l'énonciation*)," which contains the enunciation and the subject of enunciation, from "the narrated event (*procès de l'énoncé*)," which contains the enounced and the subject of the enounced."[38] If Julia Kristeva's notion of "the subject of enunciation" in poetic language is added to this distinction, one can read the Eliotian merging of the first voice with the third in the light of the relation between two subjects in poetry. Anthony Easthope explains, "[T]he subject of the enounced is therefore a smaller circle contained inside (concentric to) the subject of enunciation, a larger circle, which

---

[37]   T. S. Eliot, "The Three Voices of Poetry." *On Poetry and Poets* (New York: Noonday Press, 1961), 96-112.

[38]   Roman Jakobson, *Word and Language*, Vol. 2 of *Selected Writings*, 2nd ed. (The Hague: Mouton, 1971), 133-4.

lies outside it (ex-centric to it)."[39] Like what he calls "questionable subject-in-process," the subjectivity of "the subject of enunciation" is decentred. Easthope elaborates further:

> So for the subject of the enounced: the word is treated as meaning; signifier is lined up with the signified; the syntagmatic chain is carefully sustained in its linearity; discourse appears transparent; subjectivity centred, finding a fixed position where the ego is apparently present to itself. For the subject of enunciation, the word is treated as thing; the signified slides under the signifier; the syntagmatic chain is fissured and broken; discourse is revealed as a material process; subjectivity becomes decentred, as the fixed position of the ego is shown to be a temporary point in the process of the Other. (Easthope, 1983: 44-5)

The dialectic between the subject of enunciation and the subject of the enounced is necessary for the construction of human subjectivity. While the meaning constructed along the syntagmatic axis offers a cohesive single voice for the subject of the enounced (the speaker in a poem), the dramatic monologue prevents such fixity of position from rendering the subject of enunciation as a transcendental ego. In this way, the use of dramatic monologue foregrounds the process of artistic fashioning of the lyric voice, both the voice of the subject of the enounced (the personae) and the voice of the subject of enunciation (the poet, perhaps). There is a third possible voice, however: the voice of the subject which presides over the poem, ex-centric to it, that can exist only in the poem, in its literary allusions and poetic language.

Luo Qing highlights the masked subject-narrator in modern Chinese poetry in his essay "Western Literature and Chinese New Poetry": "When traditional Chinese poets employ the first person, they mean themselves. Affected by Western modern poetry, many poets start consciously putting on masks of different roles, allowing changes and variations for the subject-narrator and his point of view" (Luo, 1981: 90). In fact, a few examples from classical poetry, such as "Laments of a Woman from Qin" (883), disprove the assertion that dramatic monologue is absent from the Chinese poetic tradition. In addition, male poets in imperial China writing in the female voice contributed the subgenre of boudoir poetry to Chinese lyrics. And even though Luo Qing's claim holds true for most traditional Chinese poetry, the use of a mask was not something entirely new in the 1980s – as Yip Wai-lim (Ye Weilian) pointed out in 1971. In his afterword to Yang Mu's fourth book of poetry, *Legends* (1971), Yip reaffirms Yang Mu's position among the disciples of the English Romantics as a worshipper of the dual tenets of "beauty" and "truth." Ever since the appearance of Yang's first book of

---

[39]   Anthony Easthope, *Poetry as Discourse* (London and New York: Methuen, 1983), 43-4.

poetry, reviewers and critics have invariably pointed to the "fine excess of beauty" in the poet's works, which were often regarded an accurate record of his actual sensations and emotions. Yip's ground-breaking commentary directs the reader to pay attention to the fictitious aspects of the voice in dramatic monologue: "Our poet [Yang Mu] no longer dwells in the outpouring of feelings by improvisation; he has already acquired Browning's 'monologue,' Yeats's 'mask,' and the early 'persona' of Pound."[40] Yip sees the separation of the subject of enunciation from the subject of the enounced as fulfilling both a personal and an artistic need. "It is through the unique consciousness designated by the mask that Yang Mu can continue to indulge in the fine excess of beauty and at the same time put the excess under check by aesthetic criteria."[41]

The practice of speaking from behind a mask has sparked diverse responses in the Chinese literary circles. Cai Yuanhuang takes it as an alternative to the allusions that are conventional in classical Chinese literature. "To make our ancestors speak for us" or "to let our ancestors' situation reflect our own" is a traditional Chinese rhetorical device, relying on parallels to appropriate the persuasiveness and authority of significant historical figures. By finding an affinity with a famous antecedent, the writer can elevate the importance of his own dilemma. In "Confession and Mask – 'I' in Chinese Modern Poetry," Cai echoes Yip's comments made a decade earlier as he defines two "I"s in poetry: the "self," or the author's empirical self, and the "anti-self," or the author's poetic self, which serves as a surrogate or a mask that enables the poet to circumvent the limitations of the empirical self.[42] He lists Yang Mu among "confessional poets," who disguise the anti-self under a vengeful mask to execute something the "self" cannot do or cannot bear doing. Michelle Yeh takes a different approach to Yang Mu's use of dramatic monologue. In "Tradition and Modernity: Innovative Continuities" (1991), she argues that his adoption of historical personages is strategic: "Tradition is used, ironically, to expose its own deficiency; it is evoked only to be undermined."[43]

Yang Mu's dramatic monologues reveal a tension between the Romantic impulse of spontaneous confession and modernist poetics,

---

[40] Yip Wai-lin, "Houji" [Afterword] in Yang Mu, *Chuanshuo* [Legends] (Taipei: Zhiwen, 1971), 132-3.

[41] Yip, "Afterword," 136. Yip finds the poem, "Shanhong" [Floods in the Mountain], the representative example of the unique consciousness in discussion. See his comments on the poem on page 132.

[42] Cai Yuanhuang, "Gaobai yu mianju – Zhongguo xiandaishi zhong de 'wo'" [Confession and Mask – "I" in Chinese Modern Poetry], *Chung Wai Literary Monthly* 8.11 (April 1980): 106-21.

[43] Michelle Yeh, *Modern Chinese Poetry: Theory and Practice since 1917* (New Haven and London: Yale University Press, 1991), 138.

which privileges the impersonal and even dehumanized. Starting with
Legends, Yang gradually moved away from the expressive poetics of
Chinese lyric tradition and English Romanticism. Like his Western
counterparts who disown their Romantic legacy, announcing that as
poets they do not speak in their own persons, Yang began entrusting the
story to a dramatic speaker embedded in a specific setting. While some
of these speakers are Yang's own invention, many are not; they range
from literary characters to legendary figures and historical personages
already well-known in different cultures, and they include Miao Yu,
from *Dreams of the Red Chamber*; Lin Chong, from *Heroes of the
Marshes*; Wu Feng, a legendary hero in Taiwan; Jizi and Zheng Xuan,
figures from Confucian history; Tolstoy, the famous Russian novelist;
and a mystical Lama reincarnated as a Spanish boy born in Granada.

In 1969, Yang Mu wrote a series of poems that mark an abrupt break
from his early sentimental personal utterances. He imitates the voice of
a traditional Chinese intellectual, and shifts the settings of his poems to
cultural and historical sites in ancient China. Making close references to
famous anecdotes and allusions to classical literary texts, the dramatic
monologues carry the weight of factual discourse. Among them, "Jizi of
Yanling Hangs up His Sword" has received a great deal of critical
attention. The famous story of Jizi (576-485 B.C.) is taken from historical materials. A Confucian role model, Jizi once made a promise to
himself that after he finished his diplomatic mission in the north, he
would give his sword to the Lord of Xu, who admired it. But by the time
he got back, the Lord of Xu had already passed away; to honour his
vow, Jizi hung the sword on a tree by his friend's grave. In Yang's
poem, the phrase "studying the three hundred poems" appears twice
(lines 19, 30), each time followed by a specific consequence of that
study, which both "causes this Confucian scholar to postpone his return"
(line 20) and "makes this Confucian scholar into an eloquent orator"
(line 31). These lines convey a deep sense of regret and disapproval.

Like traditional commentators, Cai Yuanhuang takes Jizi as a dramatic disguise behind which the poet expresses his own dilemma.
Historical figures in Yang Mu's poems such as Jizi and Zheng Xuan,
Cai argues, serve as projections that enable the poet to examine his own
personal integrity. Jizi's promise is Yang Mu's promise, and self-
mockery and sighs of resignation are the only ways that he can voice his
self-denigration and guilt. But Cai supplies little evidence for his conjecture about the author's regrets about staying north – that is, in the United
States – for too long. In her close biographical reading of the poem,
Michelle Yeh also sees a direct correspondence between Yang Mu and
Jizi, but in her view it makes possible the poet's critique of the orthodox
exegetical tradition of Confucian studies: "As the mouthpiece of Yang
Mu, who is both poet and *Shijing* scholar, Jizi denounces the degrada-

tion of Confucianism with a specific reference to the distortion of the earliest Chinese poetry."[44] Though historical-biographical interpretation usefully focuses on the unity of art and life, it runs the risk of diverting critical attention from the poet's artistic achievement. For example, such a reading of Tolstoy's confession to Sonya in "Total Isolation – 1910" (1994) would likely search for parallels in Yang's life that he might be disguising and overlook the poet's persistent experiments with the lyric voice in other poems expressing the same theme of loneliness.[45] Besides, some of Yang's dramatic monologues seem to resist this interpretive approach. Miao Yu's disturbance during meditation in "Miao Yu Zazen" (1985) or the soldiers' voice in "King Wu's Encampment: A Suite of Songs" (1969), for instance, speak more to collective or universal issues.

In fact, dramatic monologue lies between lyric and narrative, and thus allows both the poet and his invented speaker a great deal of mobility and flexibility. In dramatic monologue a voice can assume new positions from which to speak with a distinct subjectivity, and such new ways of speaking can emancipate the author from the lyrical self. This fictive voice downplays the referentiality so significant in classical Chinese tradition, making irrelevant all questions about whether the poem points to an individual existing beyond the page. The focus of interest is on the affective impact of the voice behind the mask. Phelps assigns a special weight to its rhetorical features when he defines dramatic monologue: "with very few exceptions... dramatic monologue is not a meditation nor a soliloquy" but "a series of remarks usually confessional, addressed either orally or in an epistolary form to another person or to a group of

---

[44] Michelle Yeh gives a detailed historical account of the Jizi story and her arguments for a biographical reading of the poem are well grounded. See Michelle Yeh, *Modern Chinese Poetry: Theory and Practice since 1917* (New Haven and London: Yale University Press, 1991), 133-8.

[45] Here I refer to "By the Waterside" (1958), "To Loneliness" (1964), "Loneliness" (1976) as well as "Total Isolation – 1910" (1994). While the reader may hear the teenage poet's monologic utterance in the first poem, she will soon find the use of apostrophe in the next two. On the one hand, loneliness is animated as an addressee. It is personified and feminized in the 1964 poem as a weak, attention seeking girl sitting by the speaker's side: "Leaning on my [his] shoulder and falls asleep." Owing to her unsuspicious reliance, the speaker does not have the heart to reject her, sug-gesting some bitter-sweet feelings in the experience of loneliness. The 1976 poem is a dramatic monologue featuring an unconventional animation of loneliness. In lieu of the moon, the shadow, or even the wineglass in the conventional externalization of the drinker's loneliness in the classical Chinese poetry, the poet portrays loneliness as a beast, which is a permanent resident inhabiting inside the speaker's body. Having learnt to live with loneliness, loneliness has ironically become the speaker's life long companion. On the other hand, "Total Isolation – 1910" (1994) alludes to Tolstoy's taking flight from his home that presents a specific kind of estrangement from one's family in old age.

listeners. These other figures, though do not speak, are necessary to the understanding of the monologue."[46] This emphasis on an utterance's oratorical effects points to the dialogism inherent in dramatic monologue.

Like a scene excerpted from a play, the plot in a dramatic monologue is kept to a minimum while character is emphasized. Like the unreliable narrator in a first-person narration, the poetic persona's inward-looking utterance verges on stream of consciousness at times. Yet most of Yang Mu's dramatic speakers present a subjective point of view regarding their own situation, giving vent to the consciousness that conventionally is suppressed. While the avenging soul in "A Drifting Firefly" is a personal invention of Yang, Lin Chong and Miao Yu are leading characters in classical novels. "Lin Chong Took Flight in the Night: A Drama of Voices" (1974) is a conspicuous example of Yang's experiments with dramatic monologue. The drama begins with the voice of the wind, explaining how it raises an evening snowstorm in Cangzhou that forces Lin Chong to defer his trip to the fodder depot, which would soon be burnt down by his treacherous childhood friend, Lu Qian.

The more interesting voices in the same poem are those of the wind, snow, Mountain God, Netherworld Judge, and a Demon. It is rare to hear the Mountain God speak in a Chinese play, but in Act 2 of Yang's drama, the god blames himself for not being able to do much help to save the hero from his destiny:

> I am a Mountain God for nothing, I can only watch carefully
> The heavy blizzard crush
> The two dilapidated thatched sheds
> Mark me, Netherworld Judge on my left, Demon on my right
> Lin Chong must not die
>
> Lin Chong must not die
> Snow, fall, quickly fall
> Wind, blow with all your might
> Crush the two dilapidated thatched sheds
> I am a Mountain God for nothing, my spirits is in the Five Peaks
> ....
> What a blizzard –
> Taking off his felt hat, he sits before my altar
> And drinks some cold wine, miserable Lin Chong
> What are you thinking of? Miserable
> Lin Chong, don't you know who has come from the Eastern Capital
> And he is now setting fire everywhere to harm you
> Netherworld Judge on the left, Demon on my right
> Lin Chong must not die   (2.1.47-56, 64-71)

---

[46]   As quoted in Ina Beth Sessions, "The Dramatic Monologue," *Modern Language of America* LXII (1947): 506.

Instead of mystifying the supernatural design, Yang Mu's gods and nature are humanized, and thus they recall the Olympian gods of the Greeks. The monologic utterances of the wind, snow, and gods present the episodes in a Western dramatic mode.

Well known as a man of action rather than of thought, Lin Chong is shown in the verse play in great psychological depth. Only his side of the confrontation with Lu Qian is given, and the spilt blood revives his childhood memories. Lin's dramatic monologue shows how much he regrets his desperate choice of action to defend himself:

> It seems to be our childhood days
> The big peonies
> In your garden blooming
> The floating water-lilies in midsummer
> Blooming, filling hills, ponds, to be you cinnabar at school
> The easily flushed Lu Qian, why did you have to
> Why did you have to come to Cangzhou to be killed   (3.1.11-8)

Having achieved his revenge and killed his enemies, Lin Chong is greatly disoriented. The second scene of Act 3 consists of a single soliloquy in his voice:

> ... In the temple, three heads of the dead
> The drum of the watches in the Eastern Capital beats in vain, for it disturbs
>   not
> The glazed dream. Holding a spear
> I, Lin Chong, don't know where to go
> Then drink, and deep in the thistled woods
> Don't get arrested; just get drunk
> Why not just die on the spot   (3.2. 6-12)

Lin Chong, who once was the arms instructor of eight hundred thousand imperial guards at the capital, hears that "glazed dream" – "Someday when he becomes the man of the hour / Before him Mount Tai will bow" – still ring in his mind as a refrain in Act 3, scene 3. Yet his reversed fortunes now compel him to flee from the imperial guards and seek refuge with the bandits in Liangshan Marsh. The final act, Act 4, is narrated in the voice of the snow, marking Lin's trip in the freezing water as he heads towards the marsh. The four stanzas all end with the same refrain: "The mountain looks sad." The mountain, which has seen everything in human history, seems to foresee that by taking flight from the imperial centre to the margin of the society, Lin Chong will find only another site of troubles – this time with the bandits' leaders, the Righteous Seven.

Taken together, these heteroglossic utterances from the human, the natural, and the supernatural worlds support a multi-faceted evaluation of the themes in the classical works. In the dramatic monologue, thoughts and actions are re-staged in a mode of representation that offers greater philosophical and psychological depth. As the fictional characters are revised and more fully portrayed, some literary stereotypes are given new life. For example, Yang Mu's poems lend a tragic dimension to Lin Chong, an impulsive warrior, and to Miao Yu, a nun. And the apparent freedom of choice associated with psychological realism clashes with overdetermination, as the reader familiar with their stories knows what their fate must be. At the same time, the fictive voice introduces an interesting temporal dimension: as the character confesses troubles in the immediacy of the present, the reader who hears him or her is caught between two temporalities, the retrospective and the proleptic.

In a number of poems, Yang Mu employs dramatic monologue to convey his anti-war themes and political concerns. These poems both confront war in general and have particular relevance to specific wars that the poet experienced: "King Wu's Encampment – A Suite of Songs" (1969) may be read as a critique of the Vietnam War; "The Lost Ring – for Chechnya" (2000) undoubtedly comments on the Chechen wars of the 1990s; and "Lama Reincarnated" (1993) is an overview of the war-torn decades of the late twentieth century.

"King Wu's Encampment – A Suite of Songs" is a supplement to an epic fable, *The Weniad*, that Yang Mu identified in the *Book of Songs*. Having established the oral-formulaic composition of early Chinese poetry by drawing on the theory of Milman Parry and Albert Lord, Yang continued to offer new insights by his innovative reading.[47] He weaves together the Zhou epic by putting together five poems from the *Book of Songs* – numbers 245, 250, 237, 240, and 236 – in a sequence. The last poem, which shows the only battle scene, completes the poetic narrative in the epic. The conquest of the Shang by the Zhou is justified as tyrannicide, since King Shou had lost the favour of heaven and his people.[48] The epic poems have subject-matter typical of national narratives: they sing of the conquest led by King Wu and the magnanimity of the dynastic founders of the Zhou, Kings Wen and Wu.[49]

---

[47]   Yang Mu's doctoral research on the oral-formulaic composition of early Chinese poetry was published in 1974. See C. H. Wang, *The Bell and the Drum: Shih Ching as Formulaic Poetry in an Oral Tradition* (Berkeley, Los Angeles, London: University of California Press, 1974).

[48]   See "Chapter 4: Epic" in C. H. Wang, *From Ritual to Allegory: Seven Essays in Early Chinese Poetry* (Hong Kong: Chinese University Press, 1988), 73-114.

[49]   Joseph R. Allen read this slightly differently, "King Wu, the martial king, kills his own sovereign to establish the first real Chinese state; thus Chinese civilization is built on the legacy of regicide" (Allen, 1993: 427).

There are three songs of varied length in "King Wu's Encampment –
A Suite of Songs." The first one consists of only a single line: "At the
ides of January troops ford the river at Mengjin."[50] Delivered from an
omniscient point of view, it reads like a historical record giving the
details of an event: when, where, and who. In the other two songs,
however, a distinct voice is heard. The speaker in Yang Mu's poetry
seldom takes the position of an orator giving a public address on a
platform. But in the second song, the first-person plural suggests that the
singers are a group of soldiers led by the conqueror, King Wu. Like the
chorus in Greek plays, this collective speaker offers a somewhat detached overview of what is happening to the soldiers at the front and
their wives at home. The compassionate and sympathetic voice gradually unfolds the empire-building project of King Wu. This martial king
kills his fellow countrymen and seizes the original city-state of Zhou on
the "western land" in order to set up a new dynasty. Unlike the usual
national narratives, these descriptions of wars contain not heroism but
fear and tears, injury, and fatigue – elements of humanity. Empathizing
with fellow soldiers on the defeated side, the choral speaker mourns
over the anonymous dead in the battlefield. When the commander in a
temple celebrates the successful establishment of a new dynasty, the
voice narrating the event expresses ambivalence and regret. "Conquest"
and "dynasty" are personified: "Conquest himself knows no regret" and
"in the blood a new dynasty / stealthily rises in embarrassment" (lines 6,
16-7). In the last song, the speaker voices the soldiers' poignant realiza-
tion of the true nature of war:

> Do not feel ashamed of your persuasive drowsiness
> Shame and fatigue are waiting for you at the pier
> Waiting for you to board and to plunge into the waters
> To plunge into the waters to designate a brand-new widow on the western
>   land
> Widows
> Do not prepare robe or wine for the victors who return

The last piece of advice is for the widows: victory is no cause for celebration. Even if the troops do return, they will not return whole; even if
there is a victory, a celebration will only perpetuate human loss and
misery. The orator's bitterness echoes Wilfred Owen's accusation in
"Dulce Et Decorum Est" (1920):

> My friend, you would not tell with such high zest
> To children ardent for some desperate glory,

---

[50] The line is Joseph R. Allen's translation (Allen, 1993: 45). Allen offers a detailed
analysis of this poem in his essay "Density and Lucidity: The Poetics of Yang Mu
and Luo Qing" (Allen, 1993: 426-8).

The old Lie: Dulce et decorum est
Pro patria mori.

Whereas Owen quotes Horace to uncover the lie of patriotism in this poem of World War I, Yang Mu's dramatic monologue uses an ancient precedent to prompt contemplation of the meaning of modern warfare. The anti-war demonstrations that he witnessed on the Berkeley campus in the late 1960s at the height of the Vietnam War inevitably left imprints in the poet's writing. Writing from the perspective of those who suffer in the battlefield, the poet offers sympathy not to either nation but to the soldiers themselves.

Very early in his poetic career, Yang Mu conducted experiments with the voice of the dead. In "The Wanderer and the Thoughts of Him" (1958), he plays with the ambiguity of the phrase "the thoughts of him," which may refer both to the thoughts of the dead man about the world he has left and to the thoughts of the living about the man whom they miss. Speaking in anticipation of his liberation from the body (which will not occur until fifty years after death), the soul expects that he will have left his grave, his known location. Therefore, he thinks of the people who may miss him and advises them, "At noon and at dusk of the drizzling days, let the breeze/ sweep across every town, raise the wine flags between the white poplars, and look for me" (lines 8-9). In "Variations on Sorrow" (1976), the persona whispers,

Someday you can follow the river
To reach to my grave in the mountain. You might get lost
You must bear in mind the many butterflies that I drew
To lead you to the white poplar tree more than a feet taller
Than the one in the picture. Here I am...   (lines 40-4)

Whether the "you" addressed is singular or plural, the "I" in this poem implies an individual with a unique identity when alive. In this respect, the voice of the wandering soul of the Tibetan Lama in "Lama Reincarnated" (1987) is more indeterminate and fluid.

Like the imaginary Mountain God who watches the frustration of Lin Chong's hopes after he narrowly escapes from death and his subsequent fate in Liangshan Marsh, the Lama is given a fictive voice. He oversees his disciples' search for him, the "new" Lama born of the dead Tibetan avatar. The disciples set off from Kashmir in two directions. One group turned to the east; after travelling through Vietnam, Korea, and Japan, they crossed the Pacific Ocean to North America, and then went south to Mexico. In a former Spanish colony in South America, they heard the guitarists sing "Andalusia" and were enlightened. The other group took a westward trip through India, Afghanistan, Israel, and the Balkan states. Turning north, they moved across the Baltic Sea and searched through the Black Forest before they went south to Morocco. When they were about to leave for Congo via Gibraltar, they were led by singing accompanied by guitar music to Spain.

The all-seeing Lama provides a panoramic bird's-eye view that compresses the diachronic sequence of twentieth-century world history of social chaos, political upheavals and wars onto a synchronic plane. While in the fictional world of Lin Chong, Nature animated in the voices of wind, snow, and Mountain God is portrayed with a sense of justice, but her sympathy is unheeded by the human protagonist; the Lama in the modern world is the object of the disciples' quest. In Yang Mu's early poems, the dead soul's identity is hazy and the reason for others to look for him is unspecified. Lonely and narcissistic, the speaker whispers the clues offered by nature and the landscape that hint at a route to reach him. In contrast, the Lama's identity is constantly in the process of reincarnation and thus is always in-between, not determinate or indeterminate, fixed or fluid. The Lama that can be identified, whether Tibetan or Spanish, is not the eternal, transcendental Lama. Speaking from an imaginary consciousness that transcends human mortality, the Lama's voice is not entirely fictional; indeed, to some, it points to a higher reality. A higher spiritual being capable of transmigration from one existence to another by taking on different physical bodies across races, languages, and cultures puts in question the common sense of reality.

Whether the infant in Granada is or is not the Lama is of little importance. The consciousness attributed to the essence of the Lama regardless of its human form exceeds the knowledge and linguistic ability of a new-born baby; and in time, the identity of the Lama will be sloughed off like an article of worn-out clothing. Of note in "Lama Reincarnated" is the scope of this modern version of the pilgrims' progress. As their routes thread through different corners, they tie together different manifestations of human flaws into a common fate. In whatever language the Lama speaks, listeners will hear their own stories being told. The Lama has outgrown mortality and lives outside nationalist conflicts and identity politics. God is arguably born of the human fear of death; similarly, the search for the Lama can be seen as driven by a century of hatred, violence, and suffering. In times when wars rage, large and small, there is great need for some moral guidance or a religious figure from the East, who has not engaged in crusades or ideological witch-hunts, to offer some consolation and hope in the new century.

In using the dramatic monologue in the fictive mode, Yang Mu moves easily between cultures, literary traditions, and historical contexts. Besides adding new perspectives to old literary themes and character types, the poet also brings into dialogue disparate views about politics, wars, and other kinds of human conflicts.

* *
*

In analyzing the dialogic interaction between the addresser and addressee in Yang Mu's poems, we see a growing tendency towards abstraction in his lyric voice. In all modes of expression, Yang Mu's easy movement between roles makes it possible to separate the speaker from the poet. Having abandoned a sentimental, solipsist communication with himself, the speaker engages the reader not only emotionally but also intellectually. The dialogic address makes it easier to raise various local and global concerns. Conversing with different addressees, the speaker takes on political and social aspects of contemporary life, both national and international; in so doing, the poet succeeds in providing a voice for those on the margins.

Having outgrown youthful emotionalism and become more at ease with subjects of high seriousness, the mature poet is now more easily able to take life in stride with humour and serenity. The identity of the speaker is increasingly fluid, as different historical and fictional roles are assumed. In Yang's poems, as in most well-known lyrics, the voice not closely identified with a particular individual better stands the test of time. By using a dialogic lyric voice, the poet creatively opens up a poetic textual space in which the reader can participate. The communicative situation in which an "I" engages the "you" is appealing and draws in the reader. Even when it is not attached to a fixed identity, the unique lyric voice speaking of love, sympathy, and wisdom has a specific signature, unmistakably that of Yang Mu.

The structure of this chapter – with the first two sections on the personal and vocative modes in intensely private utterances focused on love, and the last two on the dramatic representations of fictive speakers and addressees – reflects the tension in Yang Mu's treatment of the lyric voice. The diversity illustrates the poet's constant negotiations between the demands of traditional Chinese literary practice and those of "modern" Chinese poetry, between Romantic sincerity and modernist impersonality. Yang Mu's increasingly sophisticated use of different modes of expression demands closer attention by the reader. Such attention is repaid by access to multiple voices that raise issues of intertextuality, time, and history, explored in the following chapters.

CHAPTER 2

On Intertextuality

Epiphany in Echoland

In the post-structuralist discourse that declares the author "dead," texts flow freely by themselves in the reservoir of literature. As they conjoin with or collide into one another, they (re)produce a "new" text by free play. This notion of recycling the *déjà lu* lies beneath the contemporary conception of textuality as a collage of prior texts. Erased or self-evasive, the author is no longer a major subject of literary concerns. The reader has been born to usurp his place, and the study of world literature examines the "reading" and "circulation" of the floating texts.[1] Working from the premise that a modern poet draws out a poem from an "immense dictionary," this chapter will look into how "intertextuality" is actively exploited in the hands of Yang Mu, whose dictionary includes a national literary tradition that valorises a conception of allusive practice markedly different from that offered by post-structuralists.[2]

Chinese poetry is famous for its allusiveness. Allusion is viewed both as a bid for verbal authority and as a manifestation of the poet's knowledge and erudition. The Bloomian anxiety of belatedness and repression can by no means be an affliction for Chinese poets, because the recognition of a precursor's signature in one's work is a compliment rather than a curse. A long-approved pattern of borrowing gives the neophyte permission to enter into a tradition and helps keep that tradition alive. "Factual Allusion and Textual Reference" – Chapter 38 of *The Literary Mind and the Carving of Dragons* by Liu Xie (c. 465-c. 520) – reads:

---

[1]   David Damrosch proposes to view world literature as "a mode of circulation" in *What is World Literature?* (Princeton: Princeton University Press, 2003), 4.

[2]   When Roland Barthes declared the death of the author, he considered a text "a multi-dimensional space" and "a tissue of quotations drawn from innumerable centres of culture." To Barthes, the writer has only the "power to mix writings, to counter the ones with the others, in such a way as never to rest on any one of them." He renamed the author as the "scriptor" who no longer possesses "passions, humours, feelings, impressions, but rather this immense dictionary from which he draws a writing." See "The Death of the Author," *Image-Music-Text*. Trans. Stephen Heath (London: Fontana Press, 1977), 142-8.

Profound and rich are the Classics and ancient texts,
Their language is exquisite and their ideas have far-reaching implications,
Their realm is vast as rivers and seas,
And fruitful as Mount K'un and Forest Teng;
They are for a literary carpenter to choose and take
And jade and pearls in abundance as gifts.
To be able to use the words of others as if they were one's own creation
Is to have perfect understanding of the past.[3]

The stylistic and rhetorical conventions of Chinese literary tradition necessitate frequent references to the past. Such allusions to earlier texts have clear functions: "In a factual allusion, one adduces a fact to support some generalization; and in a textual reference, one cites an ancient text to support a statement" (Liu, 1983: 393). Secondary materials from the past supply poetic talents with what they need to flourish: "The Classics and ancient historical records are deep and profound, and they are voluminous in quantity. They are the profound source of all writings, and the spiritual realm in which talent and imagination make their abode" (Liu, 1983: 397). Artistic craftsmanship is displayed in the discriminating and strategic manipulation of those materials: "An artificer makes judgments about timber, and a literary man makes choices among the classics. Good timber is transformed into definite form by the application of an axe; appropriate facts are turned into a part of a literary work through the exercise of knife and brush" (Liu, 1983: 401). Liu's views on the classics reflect the mainstream literary practice of cultured men. The poet worries not so much about antagonistic tension with his precursors as about finding a place for himself in the national literary history. Far from disowning his literary heritage, a Chinese poet seeks to submerge his own voice in the words of others.

In contemporary discourse, "intertextuality" does not refer simply to an allusion or image borrowed from a work in the same language – that is, a relationship with other texts within a particular sign system; the idea has developed to include a work's relation to texts from foreign cultures and indeed its broader participation in the discursive space of world literature.[4] An intertext can be a poem, a subgenre, or a particular tradition, so long as it comes from "another text, or a corpus of other

---

[3] Liu Xie, *The Literary Mind and the Carving of Dragons*. Trans. Vincent Yu-chung Shih (Hong Kong: Chinese University Press, 1983), 401.

[4] In Jonathan Culler's definition: Intertextuality becomes "a designation of its [a work's] participation in the discursive space of a culture: the relationship between a text and the various languages or signifying practices of a culture and its relation to those texts which articulate for it the possibilities of that culture." Here I expand Culler's notion to cover the cross-cultural dimension of intertextuality. See Jonathan Culler, *The Pursuit of Signs: Semiotics, Literature, Deconstruction* (Ithaca and New York: Cornell University Press, 1981), 103.

texts, that shares its lexicon and its structures with the one we are reading. This intertext represents a model on which the text builds its own variation."[5] Within the lines of a poem, some poets foreground their allusiveness by deliberately preserving the traces of earlier writings, resulting in what Michael Davidson calls a "palimtext": "a writing-in-process that may make use of any number of textual sources. As its name implies the palimtext retains vestiges of prior writings out of which it emerges, or more accurately, it is the still visible records of its responses to those earlier writings."[6] In a literary work, these records of responses generate a relationship that is dialogical, in the Bakhtinian sense: the "particular kind of semantic relation" of "[t]wo utterances, in juxtaposition."[7] Drawing on Bakhtin's theory of dialogism, Julia Kristeva offered what is still the most useful description of intertextuality: "Any text is constructed as a mosaic of quotations; any text is the absorption and transformation of another. The notion of *intertextuality* replaces that of *intersubjectivity*, and poetic language is read as at least *double*" (Kristeva, 1980: 66). In this light, a work's strategic appropriation of intertexts – including another text's title, poetic form, internal structure, imagery, or meaning – creates an intertextual space where dialogues between historical periods and between cultures take place.

In this chapter, intertextuality will be analyzed as a space that the author opens up and the reader travels through.[8] By strategically choosing his intertexts from myriad prior texts and placing them in dialogue with one another, the "literary carpenter" creates what might be called an "echoland," quite different from the echo chamber of postmodern textual free play and its anonymous quotations. In this intertextual space, it is the reader's responsibility to extract the significance of the interconnections. For the skilled reader, Yang Mu's use of intertextuality will lead to an epiphany close to the illumination prized by the modernists.[9] And this epiphany attributable to a specific artistic con-

---

[5] Michael Riffaterre, "Textuality: W. H. Auden's 'Musee des Beaux Arts.'" *Textual Analysis: Some Readers' Reading.* ed. Mary Ann Caws (New York: the MLA, 1986), 2.

[6] Michael Davidson, "Palimtexts: Postmodern Poetry and Material Text," *Post-modern Genres.* ed. Marjorie Perloff (Norman and London: University of Oklahoma Press, 1988), 78.

[7] Tzvetan Todorov, *Mikhail Bakhtin: The Dialogic Principle.* Trans. Wlad Godzich (Minneapolis: University of Minnesota Press, 1984), 60.

[8] Barthes talks about the reader as a site: "the reader is the very space on which all the quotations that make up a writing are inscribed" (Barthes, 1977: 148). In this discussion, the site is the space or the echoland where a multiplicity of inter-texts is collected by the author and re-inscribed by the reader.

[9] The title of this chapter, "Epiphany in Echoland," harks back to Hartman's remark on Derrida's *Glas*, "epiphony in echoland." See Geoffrey Hartman, *Saving the Text: Literature/ Derrida /Philosophy* (Baltimore and London: Johns Hopkins University

sciousness inevitably brings to mind the author – the designer of the intertextual patterns.

A poem's title itself may function as a sign and evoke a subsystem. As Michael Riffaterre observes, "[T]he title, instead of referring to another text as text, refers to it only as an example, or as a repository of lexicon and grammar characteristic of a code, of a conventional discourse." The dual title is a special case: "By referring to another text the dual title points to where the significance of its own poem is explained. The other text enlightens the reader through comparison: a structural similarity is perceived between the poem and its textual referent despite their possible differences at the descriptive and narrative levels."[10]

Any reader approaching Yang Mu's poems can easily spot the layers of reference in his use of titles. Among the various poetic experimentations with intertextuality on which Yang Mu embarked in 1961 was manipulation of titles, together with subtitles, epigraphs, and other prefatory material. From 1961 to 1964, his series of apostrophic poems with titles beginning with "To" are given quotations as subtitles. For example, "To Melancholy" – apparently a Chinese translation of the English title by Keats (1820) – is paired with a line by Ouyang Xiu (1007-72), while "To Wisdom" is thematically defined by its subtitle: "Sorrow is wisdom – Keats." The religious aura of "An Evening at the Chapel" is enhanced with a biblical quotation: "he is a shield unto them that put their trust in him" (Proverbs 30:5). Some poems offer guidelines for interpretation after their title, such as the instruction that "To Athena" should be read as "Ode No. 6, in 3 Modes" and the labelling of "To Death" as "A Variation on Ingmar Bergman's *The Seventh Seal.*"

Yang Mu's innovative uses of intertexts in the titles fall into several categories. Stock titles that can function as generic indicators, such as "The Partridge Sky" and "Difficult Is the Journey" – from the classical Chinese subgenres of *ci* and *yuefu*, respectively – are employed to evoke an immediate double reading of the tradition and its modern rendition. Another technique is to enhance a title by supplying quotations from foreign literature. For instance, a title from Yeats translated into Chinese is followed by a quotation from that poet in English: thus "Among School Children" (1975) is followed by Yeats's lines from his poem of the same title (1927):

O chestnut tree, great-rooted blossomer,
Are you the leaf, the blossom, or the bole?

Press, 1981), 33-66. "Epiphony in Echoland" is the title of Hartman's second chapter. "Echoland" also refers to Barthes's "echo chamber," see Roland Barthes, *Roland Barthes*. Trans. Richard Howard (London: Macmillan Press, 1977), 74.

[10] Michael Riffaterre, *Semiotics of Poetry* (Bloomington: Indiana University Press, 1984), 99 and 105.

O body swayed to music, O brightening glance,
How can we know the dancer from the dance?

Likewise, "Composed in a Frosty Night" (1985), obviously modelled after Coleridge's "Frost at Midnight" (1798), is coupled with a quotation from that poem: "'Tis calm, indeed, so calm, that it disturbs / And vexes meditation with its strange / And extreme silentness."

In some cases, the title itself mixes two or more cultural referents. For example, "Boli – Khabarovsk, 1994" (1994) plays on the Chinese and Russian names of the place in Asian Russia where the Ussuri River from China and the Amur River from Russia converge, and "Reading Eisenstein near the Fifth Day of the Fifth Month" (2000) combines languages to illustrate the confluence of two arts, literature and film.[11] "Strange Lands" (1962) is a poem in Chinese whose references bring to mind four cultures. The poem's title and many of its lines evoke Albert Camus's *L'Étranger* (1942), while its epigraphs are two quotations, one in German and the other in English: "Siehe! Dieser Becher will wieder leer werden, und / Zarathustra will wieder Mensch werden. – Nietzsche"; "Yet all experience is an arch wherethrough / Gleams that untraveled world whose margin fades / Forever and forever when I move – Tennyson." In several other poems, the poet adds intertexts within the title itself to suggest how the poem ought to be read. These are simple instructions, as seen in "Lullaby – Rhymed as 'For Emily Whenever I May Find Her'" (1976), "Story – Rhymed as Philip Glass, Metamorphosis 2" (1994), and "Then Cross the River – Elegy for Wu Qiancheng in Trochaic Meter" (1999). An initial intertext may also help to create in the reader the proper mental state to appreciate the poem's mood or the theme; thus "The Previous Life" (1996), a love song, is introduced by "He called me sweetheart, sent a dolphin ring, / And wrote me songs for drying my tears to sing."

Even at the very beginning of his poems, Yang Mu exhibits his renowned density in writing. His poetry and poetics are widely acclaimed as best exemplifying how the joining together of Chinese and foreign poetic traditions can create a viable "horizontal transplant," but at the same time he succeeds in strengthening Chinese poetry's "vertical heritage."[12] In the following sections, Yang Mu's poetry will be dis-

---

11 The two titles in the original read: "伯力 – Khabarovsk 1994" and "近端午讀 Eisenstein." The fifth day of the fifth month in the Chinese lunar calendar is the Poet Festival, commemorating the death of an ancient poet, Qu Yuan. See the detailed explanation of the legends related to this festival in note 24, below.

12 "Horizontal transplant" and "vertical heritage" are the key words in the literary debates over the development of modern Chinese poetry in Taiwan. The two terms are coined by Ji Xian in the statement: "We believe that new poetry is a horizontal transplant, not a vertical heritage. This is an overall approach, a basic point of depar-

cussed from these two different perspectives, the intracultural (intertexts from classical and vernacular Chinese literature – i.e., vertical) and the cross-cultural (intertexts from foreign languages and literatures – i.e., horizontal), thereby highlighting first the poet's national heritage and then his comparative approach to world literature.

Intracultural Intertextuality

In Chinese poetics, with its strong emphasis on tradition, the borrowing of intertexts from precursors is a respected practice. Cataloguing such references is an essential part of Chinese hermeneutics and literary criticism, and the study of classical Chinese literature has benefited much from the enormous accumulation over the centuries of positivistic and philological scholarship. Even as exceptionally creative a poet as Li Bai, he sometimes evoked the past in his poems. "Li Bai uses history to beautify the present," remarks Chow Tse-tsung of his allusions to historical facts and literary texts.[13] In a more critical reading, this dialectics between the past and the present appears not as an aesthetic enrichment but as a subversion of tradition. While a modern poem's seamless assimilation of intertexts can localize, familiarize, or personalize a literary tradition, a new poetic consciousness can be generated only by juxtaposing the differences between the prior texts and the present work. Citing an ancient intertext in order to defamiliarize or review the tradition is a more challenging approach. A reader who comprehends the intertexts in the new dimension of the "here and now" may see more clearly "what" was said "there and then," as well as its relevance or irrelevance to contemporary bearers of the tradition.[14]

Since originality for a Chinese poet has traditionally been premised on a perfect understanding of the past and a creative use of borrowed words in constructing his own work, Chinese poetry is often a tapestry of intertexts. Yang Mu is deeply read in classical literature, and his poetry is renowned for its linguistic density. Indeed, the reader may be baffled in many of his poems by what Joseph R. Allen calls "a slightly

---

ture, whether in theory or in practice," which is the second of the six tenets in the manifesto of the Modernist School established on 15 January 1956.

[13] Chow Tse-tsung, "Shici de dangxia mei – lun zhongguo shige de shuqing zhuliu he ziran jingjie" [The Beauty of Immediacy in *Shi* and *Ci* – On the Lyric Tradition and Vision of Nature in Chinese Poetry]. In *Gudian wenxue* 7.2 (Taiwan: Xuesheng shuju, 1985), 683-727.

[14] The "what" in a text is not an eternal truth that holds valid at all times, as Paul Ricoeur points out: "to interpret is to appropriate here and now the intention of the text." See "What is a Text? Explanation and Understanding" in *Ricoeur Reader: Reflection and Imagination*. ed. Mario J. Valdés (New York: Harvester Wheatsheaf, 1991), 43-64.

archaizing language, one touched with classical phrasing and syntax" (Allen, 1993: 408). But Allen ascribes Yang Mu's "elevated, intellectualized, and difficult" poetic diction not so much to his national heritage as to his immersion in Western "modern" literature: "The studied difficulty of Yang's language – from his sophisticated, academic vocabulary to his complex, hypotactic syntax – is one of the most 'modern' aspects of his poetry, aligning him with the international modernism of Baudelaire, Rilke and Eliot" (Allen, 1993: 406).

Yang Mu's poetic achievement does in fact lie in his blending of the Chinese and Western literary traditions. As noted in Chapter 1, Cai Yuanhuang views the modernist technique of speaking from behind a mask as an alternative to the allusive practice conventional in classical Chinese literature, by which the writer's dilemma gains significance by being likened to the situations of historical figures. In the process, however, the individual case is subsumed into a homogeneous poetic discourse. In the judgment of Allen, this "imitative, intratextual, and intertextual poetics in Chinese classical literature" often leads not to a new way forward but rather an evasion of personal confrontation by emulating the voice of others.[15] The Bloomian anxiety of influence is contradicted by the Chinese lyric tradition, where the latecomer's anxiety arises not from an Oedipal struggle with literary fathers but from a fear of being disowned by the dominant literary genealogy.

A few of Yang Mu's poems from the 1960s clearly display traditional Chinese poetics. It was common in classical poetry to add an intertext to the title to serve the purpose of a preface, preparing the reader for the poem that follows. In the Chinese lyric tradition, Lin Shuen-fu (Lin Shunfu) distinguishes two kinds of preface, differing in their function and artistic value: one is a statement of information and the other an autonomous entity (Lin, 1978: 75). He argues that the preface, at its core, is "the sensuous experience of a few intense moments of perception": it gives the poem's "background, setting, frame of reference, or context – a poetic situation. The preface is a thinking back to that poetic horizon within which the lyric expression occurs" (Lin, 1978: 75-6). Yang Mu employs intertextual prefaces whose structure is referential and reflective, as they envelop the expressive and intuitive lyric utterance in the poem itself (Lin, 1978: 80-1). Quotations that supplement the title colour the reader's mood; for example, "Parasol leaves, there is only one / but the autumnal resonances are countless" (from Zhang Yan, 1248-1320) evokes the Song dynasty for Yang Mu's poem "Dreaming of Parasols" (1962), and "Sitting for long, the wind becomes sad / At sunset, the mountains grow greener" (from Du Fu,

---

[15]   Joseph R. Allen, *In the Voice of Others: Chinese Music Bureau Poetry* (Ann Abor: University of Michigan Press, 1992), 12

712-770) sets the scene for "The Miserable Wind" (1964). By deploying
a classical image to introduce his poem, the poet enables his modern
work to enter into the traditional poetic system.

The Chinese tradition of following a poem's title with prefatory material provides an often-used opening for intertexts. Most prefaces in
classical Chinese poems are merely informational, recounting the
memorable poetic situation that inspired the composition, and Yang Mu
follows this model in some of his works. Consider the following
prefaces: "In memory of an Afghani friend, who once said to me,
'Panjshir Valley is as beautiful as the eyes of Chinese women'"
("Panjshir Valley," 1984); "A Tibetan Lama passed away in San
Francisco. Some years later, people discovered that the Lama had
already been reincarnated in Spain" ("Lama Reincarnated," 1987); and
"Seen at National Dong Hwa University on 20 July" ("Rabbits," 1997).

In some cases, the occasions that stimulated the poet's imagination
were exceptional. For example, "The Lumberjack of the Nineteenth
Century" (1962) was written because Yang Mu was deeply moved by a
lumberjack's words written on a paper folded around a leaf. The preface
reads:

> I got a rotten leaf by chance. On the yellowed wrapping paper is written: "A
> leaf from the tree which I had cut in the suburb of Iowa. Aug. 1895." Ac-
> cording to the Chinese calendar, 1895 was the twenty-first year of Guangxu
> during the reign of Emperor De of the Qing dynasty. Two significant his-
> torical events occurred in the same year. One is the Qing government's con-
> cession of Taiwan and the Penghu Islands to Japan; the other is the birth of
> the poet Xu Zhimo. Beholding an American leaf of the nineteenth century, I
> was overwhelmed by the immense spatio-temporal pressure, and thus made
> this poem.

This serendipitous encounter brought two sensitive minds close to each
other, a lumberjack and a poetic craftsman; by interweaving into a
single work of art different aspects of human endeavour – private and
public, literary and political – Yang reflects on the interconnections of
modern histories. In another poem, "Farewell to the Prairie" (1987), the
preface that describes its composition as "Spun from a Line Obtained in
a Dream" mystifies the poem's origin and turns it into a message from
one inspired or possessed. By pointing to a dream rather than reality, the
poet broadens the use of the preface beyond what is traditional to include such modern material as the surrealists' automatic writing or a
psychoanalytical reading of the unconscious.

One particularly creative experiment in intracultural borrowing is
Yang Mu's appropriation of the voice of Han Yu (768-824) for an
imagined interior monologue in "Han Yu's 'Mountain Rock' in Seven-
character Verse of Old Style, Continued" (1968). The poem is written in

two parts, each introduced by a seven-character sentence in Chinese that imitates the seven-character Tang verse. Its opening words, "I talk about Buddhist paintings with a monk," clearly allude to a conversation mentioned in "Mountain Rock": "the monk said the Buddhist paintings on the ancient walls are really good." Yang Mu borrows the setting and the dramatic character from Han Yu unchanged, but he explores the classical poet's preoccupations in a monologue. Half-hearted in his appreciation of the Buddhist art, in exile Han Yu is carried away by his internal demons. He is tormented by thoughts of different aspects of the gorgeous lifestyle of the central provinces: "dancing bees among gardenias," a woman behind the swaying bed curtains, and scholars writing, reading, or discussing such political events as the Xuanwu Gate Coup (lines 3-7). Besides the sensual pleasures and social activities, Han Yu also recalls his ambitions as a government official as well as a literary artist. His skill in devising oblique rhyme in the poetic style of the Han and Wei dynasties marks him out as a promising poet. Reflecting on his eminent precursors, he positions himself between Li Bai, the romantic poet who pursues "swordsmanship and alchemy," and Du Fu, who is more humane and socially engaged (lines 19, 25). Feeling listless and frustrated, Han Yu spends his time drinking and reading Han rhymed prose (lines 27-31). He begrudges his dislocation in the south, suffering insecurity and worries while his ambitions are thwarted, and he directly confesses his yearning to return to the imperial centre.

Yang Mu's follow-up to Han Yu's poem adheres closely to Joseph R. Allen's notion of "intratextuality" as "a sprung imitation, a circumscribed intertextuality" (Allen, 1992: 12). His work alludes to numerous intertexts, including Han Yu's own poem "To Zhang Gongshu on the Night of the Fifteenth Day of the Eighth Month"; rhymed prose about the dynastic capitals, such as Zuo Si's "On Three Imperial Centres" and Ban Gu's "On Two Capitals";[16] and literary works such as "Lu Zhou," Du Fu's poem in five-character regulated verse for his wife; and Sima Changqing, a historical figure known for his rhymed prose and his love affair with Zhuo Wenjun. The random juxtaposition of role models, of Buddhist emptiness and romantic pursuits, and of the classics about politics and aesthetics, exhibits the disturbed mind of Han Yu who finds it hard to anchor himself while being displaced in exile. Though the poem is in free verse, Yang Mu retains the Tang diction and imagery. The elaborate style befits the confession of the speaker (Han Yu) in the

---

[16] The three imperial centres in Zuo Si's satirical work refer to the three capitals, Ye, Zhengdou, and Jianye of the Three Kingdoms, Wei (220-265), Shu (221-263), and Wu (222-280) respectively. The two capitals in Ban Gu's rhymed prose refer to Changan of Eastern Han and Luoyang of Western Han.

poem's last line: "Above all, I love Sima Changqing the most."[17] An avowed continuation of an intratext, "Mountain Rock," Yang's poem is dense with references to the prior text and other intertexts revolving around Han Yu, thereby offering a dramatic portrayal and in-depth exploration of his personality.

Apart from the literary allusions, the density in Yang Mu's poetry is attributable to its unusually palimpsestic deployment of conventions in multiple layers of significance. The result is more a dialogical exchange than a dialectical tension, for in most cases Yang's point is not to establish one as supreme at the expanse of another but to maintain a dynamic balance that exposes the distinctness of each. Certain subgenres, quotations, and names associated with the title and subtexts of Yang Mu's poem call to mind a specific poetic tradition or a literary work, each producing in the reader certain conventional expectations. By anticipating his reader's response, the poet constructs a kind of complicity that is necessary to set his work in motion at a dialogical level. As he creatively manipulates both a literary tradition and the cultured reader's reaction, he makes them integral participants in the poem's meaning.

Typically dialogic is Yang Mu's use of intracultural intertexts from early Chinese poetry. At different levels, ranging from classical vocabulary and direct quotation to conventional code and poetic subgenre, the poet imitates and subverts not only a single text but an entire literary tradition by forcing his readers to view it differently. Inspired by the ballads in the *Book of Songs*, the poet deeply admires early poems in the folk mode, especially those produced before the Six Dynasties (222-589). Many of his artistic efforts are dedicated to bringing Chinese poetry back to its most natural, spontaneous tradition before prosody was canonized and institutionalized. Both the subversive and recuperative impulses can be seen at work in "New *Yuefu*," a section in Yang Mu's ninth book of poetry, *Someone* (1986). *Yuefu* is a label for ballads gathered from the society in the Han dynasty (206 B.C.-220). Because it expresses communal concerns, the genre has often been compared to the realist literary canon of the *Book of Songs*. Later, when these ballads were institutionalized as cultural products of the Music Bureau, they lost their close connection with the everyday realities of the people, and *yuefu* gradually became part of the ceremonial rites and diplomatic exchanges among court officials on imperial occasions. The New *Yuefu*, as advocated by Bai Juyi (772-846), was meant to turn the official *yuefu* genre on its head. Reviving the ballad form of the early *yuefu* poetry by

---

[17]   Sima Changqing's (also known as Sima Shuangru) rhymed prose is famous for its elaborate description and exuberant images. His style has been a model of *belles lettres* for literary men's imitation. Besides, Sima's love story with Zhuo Wenjun is well known. They led a poor but happy life after marriage.

using the vernacular, New *Yuefu* was claimed to be accessible to old peasant women – proof of its simplicity and plainness.

In the 1970s, New *Yuefu* itself was revived in Taiwan to counteract the sophisticated, obscure style of Westernized modern Chinese poetry. Advocates such as Lin Shuangbu favoured the expression of public themes about the native soil, nationalist sentiments, and social issues in poetry written for the masses.[18] Interestingly, Yang Mu's poems collected in his "New *Yuefu*" are in fact intratexts that destabilize generic distinctions. In the words of Joseph R. Allen, the best way to understand *yuefu* poetry "is to read it within the conventions of intratextuality" (Allen, 1992: 12). To fully appreciate the "newness" of Yang Mu's "New *Yuefu*," the poems must be read against the history of *yuefu*. Echoing the thematic concerns characteristic of the genre, the poet declares that these poems are composed in reaction to immediate circumstances, both local and global. But instead of presenting mundane daily experiences in a simple and direct way, Yang Mu problematizes the factual account of events by exposing the narratives' suppressed elements. "Song of Departure," "Large Ziye Song," and "Difficult Is the Journey" are poems in the section that illustrate how Yang Mu redeploys the subgenre to express his own innovative insights and metapoetic commentary.

"Song of Departure" (1984), which takes as its subtitle the last line of a *yuefu* poem of the same title by Meng Jiao (751-814) – "How I wish I had wings to fly to her across the sky" – wittily inverts the gender roles in conventional travel poems. A female traveller, away from home, is described as departing from an inn for another trip on a summer morning; she travels light, carrying only a handbag and a leather suitcase. She is portrayed as young, energetic, and inquisitive, a character who dares to stay alone in a hut in the wild and cannot wait to explore "a world blazingly bright." Without the subtitle from Meng Jiao, the poem would read like an objective account of a trivial event. The subtitle offers a traditional tinge of longing, but the speaker, probably a man, seems to stay outside the whole event, powerless to intervene. The highly mannered regret that women in classical poetry express at being unable to participate in the male world of adventures is turned around in Yang Mu's refreshingly modern version.

Yang Mu further interrogates the traditional depiction of a woman's longing for her man by examining a subgenre, "boudoir poetry," as typified by the Ziye songs."[19] Only two in the canon are titled "Large

---

[18]   Lin Shuangbu published a collection of New *Yuefu* in *Taiwan New Yuefu* (Taipei, Grassroot, 1996).

[19]   John Minford and Joseph Lau's introduction to Ziye songs is as follows: "The Six Dynasties period witnessed the rapid development of two types of *yuefu* ballad, the

Ziye Song," both by Lu Guimeng (d. 881) and both themselves appraisals of this form of ballad: "Among hundreds sorts of ballad / Ziye is the most pathetic / Spontaneous is the plain voice / Originated from nature." Yang Mu adopts a similar dialogic design by pairing the title "Large Ziye Song," a commentary on the form, with two lines from the classical ballad "Ziye Song of Four Seasons": "If you do not trust me / Look at the traces in the snow." Yang's re-reading of the genre from a metapoetic perspective persists throughout the poem. The introductory statement – "I was already / Reduced to Ziye" – explicitly foregrounds the fictive nature of the speaker and playfully explains the relationship between the title and the subtitle. From a critical height, the poet stoops to join the female authors of the Ziye folk-songs. Consciously, the poet compares the woman called Ziye (Midnight) of the Jin dynasty (265-420) with her modern incarnation. The docile lady in ancient times, now

Walks out of her aromatic chamber
(fancying) walks out from the courtyard
Treading through the main streets and the alleys, from her left shoulder
Hanging across her chest is a bag, carrying
   Her unfinished ballads.   (lines 11-5)

Free and independent, the modern Ziye is given a distinct identity: a writer of ballads. She knows her job well: "What am I looking for? I know / Waiting and waiting." In classical boudoir poetry, the lady's pathetic fate is to wait for her man in tears and sighs, but Yang Mu's woman leaves her house to meet him:

I was already
Reduced to Ziye of the Southern Dynasties (fancying)
Having undergone some changes, is now worldly
And mature. The man will be late
But will surely keep his appointment   (lines 23-7)

This sophisticated woman knows how to deal with a member of the other sex who "is not arrogant but not not arrogant." He might tenderly make up some excuses for being late; she would pretend to sulk, to be disappointed, or to be disinterested. Despite everything, she is in fact very happy to see him at their meeting place. This rewriting of the conventional Ziye song gives both the docile woman and the absent man active roles and offers a happy ending to the subgenre: "We walk on hand in hand, looking for / The horizon of dreams, and go back to the ancient times / the South Dynasties, and lie down to listen to the gurgling water."

Northern and the Southern. The Southern *yuefu* is generally languid and erotic... The forty-two Ziye songs are probably the best known of the Southern folksongs during this period. Legend has it that they were composed during the Jin dynasty (265-420) by a girl called Ziye (Midnight)" (Minford and Lau, 2000: 407).

By letting the story develop beyond a depiction of helpless waiting, the poet has actually expressed his criticism of Ziye songs and further elaborated Lu's sympathetic reading of the tradition.

"Difficult Is the Journey" (1982) is a long narrative poem that portrays a traveller's sojourn in Changan and his meditation on Chinese cultural history. The *yuefu* title is tied to the first two lines from a poem by Lu Zhaolin (634-c. 684): "Can you not see that beside Wei bridge north of Changan / Rotten logs lie across the ancient fields." Lu's poem is a *yuefu* composed at Changan during the early Tang, and its fourth line – depicting the alluring scenery of a prosperous imperial centre, which attracts "the mist as well as the smoke" – is alluded to in the last line of Yang Mu's poem. As the capital of thirteen different dynasties of ancient China, Changan witnessed the rise and fall of empires, and it has become a significant cultural signifier for the Chinese. Writing "Difficult Is the Journey" after he and a group of scholar-writers from Taiwan visited mainland China when it opened its door in the early 1980s, Yang Mu conjures up a parallel visit in the Tang dynasty. In this poem, his intracultural use of an actual event as an intertext illustrates a specific kind of allusive practice, *yung-shih* (*yong shi*). Kao Yu-kung (Gao Yougong) and Mei Tsu-lin (Mei Zulin) explain the phrase: "'allusion' is used here as the equivalent for the Chinese term... *yung-shih*, literally 'use event.' 'Event' is understood here as past event, something mentioned in a preexisting text. ... '[H]istorical allusion' is probably a more precise translation of *yung shih*."[20]

The group of modern travellers from the south and from a Chinese government distinct from the mainland's ruling Communist Party showed marked historical and political departures from its precursor, a group of poets (including Du Fu) who visited the capital back in the Tang dynasty and wrote a number of famous poems about the place and its lifestyle. Their visit was recalled in a dramatic scene of literary men commenting on the results of the imperial examination.

> They had come here in a group, in spring
> Dionysian talents in magnificent apparel, riding light on a life
> Of success, discussing the meaning of the exam poems
> They criticized the familial backgrounds of the top candidates with a cynical
> Look: there might be problems with the allusions, rhymes
> Oblique, while the calligraphy too falls far below standard
> "How can this be?"   (lines 42-8)

The legendary glory of the imperial centre thus remains the locus of the modern poet's contemplation and imagination, despite the fact that

---

[20]   Yu-kung Kao and Tsu-lin Mei, "Meaning, Metaphor, and Allusion in Tang Poetry," *Harvard Journal of Asiatic Studies* 38.2 (1978): 326.

imperial Changan could no longer be reached. By re-reading and re-writing the place and the journey, he throws into relief not only the difficulties in appreciating the effects of high politics in the public's daily life but also the cultural centre's temptations, which lured poets of modern Taiwan no less strongly than those of the Tang. "Difficult Is the Journey" is a clear example of a palimtext, as the writing-in-process also captures the historical fashioning of a city-in-process. Today's Changan is conceptualized from traces of prior writings about the place. This intertextuality highlights the records of its ideological and cultural significance. The poem in fact offers an alternative approach to histori-cal, national narratives of China via its ancestral capital, Changan, an approach that will be thoroughly examined in Chapter 4.

A subgenre of Chinese classical poetry called "Verse in Jest" is fa-mous for its playfulness and irony. Yang Mu's "Six Quatrains, Written in Jest" (1993), modelled after Du Fu's poem of the same title, falls into this category.[21] While Du Fu's "Six Quatrains" – contrary to its title – expresses a rather serious point about the decline of the Tang regulated verse, Yang Mu's version is exceptionally lively. The poem records an interesting dialogue between the "old" poet and a young interlocutor, perhaps a student. Unlike the professor in "The Campus Tree" (1983), who talks to a girl about the ravages of time with sympathy and wisdom, the speaker here is amused and constantly yields to the demands of the "you," who is apparently creative and eager to learn:

> The old trees are dropping their fruits
> Dotting punctuation marks on the metrical lines
> Those are not punctuation marks but musical notes, you say
> A quatrain is done in a blink of the eyes
>
> ....
> Let's talk about them in autumn, I propose
> Now please listen (You say, it is now already
> Autumn); a chorus of the sunny and the sunless times[22]
> Is roaring at the inland and the waterside; it rises and sinks
>
> The reeds are despondent for no reason
> Drooping their white heads without a word. Both he
> And you love to watch the natural flow of running water[23]
> But object to letting insects recite the quatrains   (lines 5-8, 13-20)

---

[21] "Xi shi" [Verse in jest] is a sub-genre in the Chinese lyric tradition.

[22] By the phrases "yao qing" and "wu qing," the poet plays with a Chinese character 晴 "qing" which means "sunny" while its homophone 情 refers to "affections." So "the sunny and the sunless times" could also connote "affectionate and affectionless mo-ments."

[23] The "natural flow" in the Chinese text has a dual meaning: the flow of running water and the organic structure of a literary work. The quadripartite structure goes from introduction, complication, reversal, finally to resolution.

The addressee is again given a voice to display her personality: she is a poetry lover who shares the speaker's view of poetry but is also an independent thinker. Whereas the prior text by Du Fu, who sternly accused young practitioners of causing the decline of poetic art, shows high seriousness in its content and form, Yang Mu's imitation is casual and light-hearted. At the same time – and uncharacteristically, for Yang Mu's quatrains – this poem is plain and colloquial. Some lines seem effortless, and the expression in a line or two appears as raw as a first draft. Without the heart to debate, the speaker is ready to make concessions. His tone is lenient and lax, and a touch of humour emerges from these six quatrains. Perhaps the poet deliberately makes his work live up to the name of the subgenre, believing that a poem "written in jest" ought to be joyful.

Suturing together both intracultural and cross-cultural intertexts in one poem, Yang Mu demonstrates the interconnection of the development of poetic art and film art in "Reading Eisenstein near the Fifth Day of the Fifth Month":

Under the phoenix tree you sit
Neat embroidery rises from random stitches
Fragments of light and shadow freeze, motionless
The sun strolls to the zenith

Think first of a flower-wearing poet, singing all his way
To the river; amidst frustrations and fury
He aims at the brightest, the most beautiful
Whirlpool and throws himself down, dead

And then, how she tenderly unveils in nakedness the wisdom
Born of ordeals in her three successive lives, a humility most complete
Ah, love, in a world of wantonness, and truth too
Are terror proved

I ponder – after some allusions, some concepts
And convictions – doesn't it follow that beauty and truth are inevitably fatal
    too
Composed one by one, with surreal editing
In the superb montage in a silent film

The metapoetic commentary is explicit in the title, which brings together a Russian name and a Chinese date. The fifth day of the fifth month in the Chinese calendar is commonly known as the Dragon Boat Festival or the Poet Festival. This particular date is tied to two famous intracultural allusions, as it is associated with Qu Yuan, a patriot-poet, and Lady

White, a legendary snake spirit.[24] In imitation of Eisenstein's film art of montage, this poem is structured neatly into four quatrains, each carrying an allusion; the poem reads like a sequence of edited shots of intertexts. They are organized by a clear division of labour between the pronouns: "You" is a female engaged in embroidery, a classical metaphor for artistic craftsmanship; "He" is Qu Yuan, the poet evoked in the title; "She" is the tragic heroine in *The Legend of the White Snake*; and "I" is the speaker, who compares his job of writing poetry to Eisenstein's film editing. "You" and "I" are separated by two intertexts: a subject's unrequited love for his emperor and a supernatural woman's self-sacrificing passion for a human. While the "you" is fully indulged in weaving her dreams of beauty and love into her embroidery, the self-conscious "I" is perfecting his art by editing his quatrains, just as a film director arranges his shots.

The montage of the intertexts as well as the unveiling of the creative process makes this poem metapoetic. It could be a love-poem, but only a self-critical one. Ancient virtues such as honesty, loyalty, and unfailing love are nowhere to be found in modern life; or if they are found, in some radical or abusive forms, they are nothing but "fatal" mistakes. From an ironic distance, this theme of fidelity and passion is presented in sequences replayed from old stories. In despair, Qu Yuan drowned himself in a river; and because of her devoted love, Lady White abandoned her cultivation of the Way and was imprisoned in the Thunder Peak Pagoda. These are "terror proved." And the poem's bringing together of two art forms, poetry and film, reviews a fruitful intercultural interaction of the past century. Chinese ideogram has provided modern Western artists with a source of inspiration. Pound derived his poetics of imagism from the pictorial aspects of Chinese characters, and Eisenstein founded his filmic aesthetic of montage on a poetics of juxtaposition in Chinese writing. By cultural back-translation, modern

---

[24]   The fifth day of the fifth month in the Chinese lunar calendar is commonly known as the Dragon Boat Festival which originated from a ritualistic practice of throwing rice dumplings into the river where the patriot-poet, Qu Yuan drowned himself. It was hoped that the dumplings would feed the fish in the river so that the poet's body would be spared. This Festival in commemoration of Qu Yuan is also called "The Poet Festival." In *The Legend of the White Snake*, the fifth day of the fifth month is the crucial turning point of the plot. It is a love story about Lady White, a snake spirit, and Xu Xian, a mortal man. During the Dragon Boat Festival every year, snake spirits would revert for a short time to their original shape and they ought to retreat to the mountains. So deeply in love with Xu Xian, the fairy maiden would not risk a misunderstanding by leaving him without good reasons. Finding it hard to refuse the wine offered by her loving husband, Lady White swallows the liquid that eventually paralyzes her. Xu Xian is horrified to find her wife a snake and drops dead on the spot. Therefore, in the snake legend, the fifth day of the fifth month is a crucial chapter to show the beauty of love and truth, ironically turns out to be terror proved.

literary criticism might read montage as the characteristic style of Chinese poetry. With humour and self-parody, the intertexts, "composed one by one, with surreal editing," make up a poem in the fashion of shots edited into a film.

Yang Mu effectively uses intracultural intertextuality to help create – in a reader who has some literary competence – the proper mental state for reading his work. Sometimes, his invocation of a prior text "naturalizes" the present one by giving it a place in the long history of Chinese poetry. But more often than not, Yang Mu revises as well as imitates the allusive practice in Chinese literature in a single poetic act, decoding and deconstructing a subgenre by re-encoding it in new forms. The initial mental state evoked by an allusion is only a diversion; soon the poet defies the readerly expectation he has raised, thereby commenting on the convention. His innovative use of intracultural intertexts goes beyond simply reactivating a tradition to evaluate it and renew it with metapoetic insights. By this active weaving of intertextual patterns, Yang Mu daringly modernizes and expands the subgenres and the allusive practice of the Chinese lyric tradition.

Cross-cultural Intertextuality

For about a century, the development of New Poetry or Modern Poetry in Chinese has often been intertwined with national-cultural discourses. For instance, New Poetry was a bone of contention between the National Essence Group and the New Culturalists in the May Fourth Period. Among more progressive intellectuals, the importation of Western thought and poetics helped forge a cultural renaissance in modern China. In the mid-twentieth century, Taiwanese heatedly debated Modern Poetry, which was later attacked by the Native Soil Literature Movement of the 1970s. Controversies over the putative "Westernization" of a national genre – whether understood as a revitalization of the Chinese tradition or as a sign of cultural imperialism – embroiled poets and critics. However, the literary products themselves provide evidence that transnational influences have been integral to the poetry revolution: most significantly, the English Romantics, the French symbolists, and the Euro-American modernists. In fact, the history of modern poetry in Taiwan has been captured in a botanical trope – that of the "horizontal transplant" – a hybrid genealogy that situates the genre's origin between two main sources. In the wake of modernist poetry reform in the mid-1950s, the commendation of hybridity by Hsia Chi-an (Xia Zhian) reflects its contribution to the development of Chinese poetry. To Hsia, a national, paradigmatic work of new poetry must be rooted in the hybridity of the vernacular – a combination of linguistic elements from "high and low, ancient and modern, Chinese and the West."[25] Literary components from the past and the present, the foreign and the Chinese, are all welcome as they fertilize the new plant's growth. Therefore, it is not surprising that recent analyses of modern Chinese poetry have frequently hinged on cultural notions such as "hybridity" and "biculturalism." This section provides such an analysis, focusing on the cross-cultural intertexts in Yang Mu's poetry. Aesthetics aside, the allusive practice demonstrates the poet's response to the national-cultural discourse of his times.

As noted above, the confluence of Chinese and foreign literary traditions in Yang Mu's poetry and poetics is widely recognized. "Bicultural" is the key-word in Stephen Owen's appraisal of Yang Mu's poetry:

> Modern Chinese poetry matured in the second half of this century. It matured by developing its own history and a broader knowledge of poetry outside China. ... Yang Mu... is perhaps the wisest and most gifted of the poets now in their middle age. In his work, informed equally by Chinese and Western poetic traditions, modern Chinese poetry comes into its own, with work of intricacy and control that still loses nothing in depth or intensity.

> I have noted points of Yang Mu's Western learning, but his work is distinctive in moving easily between the Chinese and western traditions while exoticizing neither. He is a poet who works with the materials that he has, and those materials include a sense of poetic and cultural history that transcends the cultural division of the "West" and China. He has become bicultural. ... Yang Mu offers the largest hope for the future [of Chinese poetry]... because he draws two disparate histories together.[26]

In Owen's view, Yang Mu's easy movement between cultures makes the national-cultural boundary permeable as the poet blends two traditions at the expense of neither. Some years later, Michelle Yeh elaborated this notion of biculturalism in her introduction to *No Trace of the Gardener: Poems of Yang Mu* (1998): "At the most obvious level, Yang Mu's biculturalism can be seen in his wide-ranging imagery, references, and motifs, which straddle China and the West. He draws not only on classical Chinese poetry and prose but also on Western literature and culture. ... His equal erudition in Chinese and Western classics gives

---

25   Hsia Chi-an, "Baihuawen yu xinshi" [The Vernacular and New Poetry], first published in *Wenxue Zazhi* [Literary Magazine] (September, 1957), now collected in *Xiandai zhongguo wenxue pinglun xuanji* [Critical Essays on Modern Chinese Literature]. ed. Joseph S. M. Lau (Hong Kong: Union Press, 1970), 94-5.

26   See Stephen Owen, "Traditions and Talents," *The New Republic*. 22 February 1993: 40.

him a perspective from which to reflect on the two cultures."[27] To Yeh, Yang Mu's bicultural heritage offers not only a reservoir of wide-ranging literary resources on which he can draw in his own work but also a point of departure for understanding the two traditions.

Situating the poet in the local context of Taiwan, Xu Huizhi expands on the idea of Yang Mu's biculturalism and describes his writings as "cultural hybrid":

> Yang Mu is certainly a Romanticist. ... He is already a "classic" giant in the milieu of Taiwan modern literature and he will surely be one of the few [classical] paradigms. ... It can be said that Yang Mu belongs to the genteel class of Taiwan literature, who came of age after the February 28 Incident, and is a "quality" Taiwanese. ... Yang Mu's writings inherit both the "Chinese elements" of a Han Taiwanese and the native "consciousness of geography and people." As he has stayed overseas for a long period and experienced the impact of "foreign cultures" through Western classics, his writings unite all three sources of influence [Han Chinese, native Taiwanese, and the West] and become an excellent cultural "hybrid."[28]

Besides indicating the confluence of traditions, the dynamics of the "biculturalism" and "hybridity" of Yang Mu's literary practice also point to a cross-cultural dialogue between intertexts. In many poems, the treatment of a classical theme in fact embodies self-reflexive cultural critique from a foreign perspective.

Apart from suggesting an amalgam of world classics, "biculturalism" and "hybridity" can be read as a generative process of literary and cultural interactions. The hybridizing act helps illuminate not only modern readings of a national tradition but also new approaches to contemporary cultural issues. The poems discussed below have either a conventional form or a classical theme, which serves as a starting point for investigation. In each of the three poems in "Assorted Musical Modes" (1977-78), Yang Mu re-reads distinct national-literary traditions by highlighting both reversals within each tradition and interactions between traditions. These poems show how he negotiates the question of a national identity in specific historical contexts. Such poems as "The Yellow Bird" (1991), "The Lost Ring – for Chechnya" (2000), and "Temporality Proposition" (1993) are deliberate hybrids, displaying Yang Mu's strategic assimilation of foreign texts to convey his artistic and political concerns.

---

[27] Michelle Yeh, Introduction, *No Trace of the Gardener: Poems of Yang Mu*. Trans. Lawrence R. Smith and Michelle Yeh (New Haven and London: Yale University Press, 1998), *xxiv-xxv*.

[28] Xu Huizhi. "Shaonian zhi yan – Aichou zhi xin [The Youthful Eyes – The Sorrowful Heart], *United Daily News*. 2 March 1998.

"Assorted Musical Modes"

Regardless of whether they exemplify an all-encompassing cultural hybrid, Yang Mu's poems testify to the limits of the conception of a singular, unitary cultural identity. His strategy of asserting a position by exploring the interactive relations between different cultures yields fruitful results. In this respect, the intriguing trio of works that make up "Assorted Musical Modes" (*zhugongdiao*) provides an appropriate starting point for discussing Yang Mu's heteroglossic hybridity.[29] "Assorted Musical Modes" or "A Medley of Songs" is a form of dramatic entertainment that was popular in the Song and Yuan dynasties. In Wang Guowei's definition, it is "a ramification of story-telling, set to musical tunes."[30] In her essay "Outer and Inner Forms of *Chu-kung-tiao* [*zhugongdiao*], with Reference to *Pien-wen* [Pianwen] and Vernacular Fiction," Chen Lili characterizes this genre as hybrid in form and performance.[31] Formally, *zhugongdiao* is usually a rather long composition, with the body of the work framed between a prologue and an epilogue. The main work is divided into chapters, each of which ends at a critical moment of the plot. The story involves a domestic situation, whose development is intended to "give the hero or heroine realistic human dimensions [by putting] them in common, even banal, situations and to

---

[29] Mikhail M. Bakhtin sees two kinds of hybridity, the intentional and the unintentional. Unintentional hybridity is the primary historical condition of all languages upon which intentional hybridity can take place. Hybrids are culturally productive because "they are pregnant with potential for new world views, with new 'internal forms' for perceiving the world in words." Bakhtin, *The Dialogic Imagination*. Trans, Caryl Emerson and Michael Holquist (Austin: University of Texas Press, 1981), 358-360. Bakhtin's notion of linguistic and artistic hybridity is useful for challenging simplistic cultural holism. As Pnina Werbner points out, "[t]he danger that the aesthetic poses for any closed social universe with a single, monologic, authoritative, unitary language is that of a heteroglossia 'that rages beyond the boundaries.'... Intentional heteroglossia relativise singular ideologies, cultures and languages." Pnina Werbner and Tariq Modood, eds. *Debating Cultural Hybridity: Multi-cultural Identities and the Politics of Anti-Racism* (London: Zed Books, 1997), 5. When the pernicious effects of dehistorization and decontextualization are taken heed of, the evocation of hybridity can be a valuable point of departure in confronting holistic identity politics played out in literary discourse.

[30] From Wang Guowei's "Song-Yuan xiqu kao" [A Study of the Plays from the Song and Yuan dynasties] (1957), as quoted and translated by Chen Lili, in "Outer and Inner Forms of *Chu-kung-tiao*, with reference to *Pien-wen* and Vernacular Fiction," *Harvard Journal of Asiatic Studies* 32 (1972): 124-149.

[31] "The most noticeable characteristic which separates the Medley [Assorted Musical Modes] from other genres in Chinese literature is its outer form. The works are written in alternate verse sections and prose passages. Early references to the Medley in twelfth-and thirteenth-century memoirs indicate that Medleys were written for oral performances, and internal evidence in the extant works themselves further reveals that the verse sections were sung and the prose passages narrated. Thus, the Medley is a type of chantefable (chanter: to sing; fabler: to narrate)" (L. Chen 1972: 126-7).

have them deal with common, undistinguished minor characters in a common way" (L. Chen 1972: 136). In addition, *zhugongdiao* begins with a commentary that underlines a suspenseful situation and focuses the audience's attention on a particular scene, which is followed by a sudden twist in the plot (similar to an Aristotelian "discovery"). For Chen, *zhugongdiao* is important because it suggested that Chinese literature could be thought of "as plural." As popular entertainment, *zhugongdiao* is a vernacular literature intended for oral presentation; at the same time, however, its written form appeals to the reading public. It thus has dual modes of reception. In addition, because it is by definition "assorted" it displays formal features from different literary and musical sources. This classical genre of vernacular literature is certainly an early example of hybridity in form and performance.

Yang Mu's suite poem "Assorted Musical Modes" was written when the Native Soil Literature Movement was at its zenith in Taiwan. In its three parts – "Zheng Xuan Awaken from a Dream" (1977), "Marlowe Drinks" (1977), and "Wu Feng's Sacrificial Act of Benevolence" (1978) – Yang Mu goes beyond mixing formal features from within the Chinese literary tradition to include three cultural figures prominent in different national traditions. More importantly, these cultural "heroes" are depicted as being stranded in a personal, "domestic" situation at a moment of doubt and indecision.

Zheng Xuan, Christopher Marlowe, and Wu Feng are known to people today because speech or writing by or about them helped inaugurate distinct literary and cultural traditions. Zheng Xuan earned his name by annotating Confucius, the central cultural and intellectual figure of Chinese civilization, who is celebrated for his "sayings." Christopher Marlowe represents the poetic tradition of the English Renaissance, and his most famous love-poem, "The Passionate Shepherd to His Love" (1599), is an exemplum of pastoral themes and versification. The shepherd's much-discussed proposal has spurred responses over the centuries from poets of different cultures. Wu Feng, a figure from native Taiwanese myth, is a legendary martyr who surrenders his own head in order to stop head-hunting. Because he was well respected by the aboriginal people, his death reveals to them the futility of their superstitious customs. In the poem, Zheng Xuan, Christopher Marlowe, and Wu Feng are each placed in a moment of the in-between – a dream between reality and fantasy, a hesitation between yes and no, and a transit between life and death, respectively. Each stands for his particular national tradition (Chinese, English, and Taiwanese) and represents a specific facet of a culture: the intellectual, the artistic, and the moral or religious. Their utterances in "Assorted Musical Modes" are not meant to reaffirm a master narrative of an originary national culture. Instead, each is positioned on the border between commitment and resignation.

In this trio of poems, the representativeness of these cultural figures is ironically challenged by a fragmented re-presentation, which is too slippery to grasp. To situate Zheng Xuan's intellectual predicaments in a dream undercuts the solemnity of orthodox Confucian pedagogy. What stirs the annotator-persona Zheng Xuan is Confucius's voice, the Chinese collective unconscious that has been internalized as the intellectual's moral and educational mission. But the suppressed anxiety released in the dream interrogates an intellectual's self-positioning, always already overshadowed by the master's words and their endless annotations.

> So assuming that I might rank along with Ziyu and Zixia
> In Confucius's classroom, the Sage, I'm afraid, would say
> "Xuan it is who bears out my lofty thoughts!" I'm pretty sure he would
> What about such peers as Yan Hu, Zai Yu, Ren You, then?
> How would I look in respect of their expertise?[32]   (lines 34-8)

Confucian scholarship is representative of a national tradition discursively formed over time, but the manifest content of the dream shows the Confucian scholar's doubts and uncertainties. Such anxieties actually destabilize his foundational position within the Confucian tradition. The poem invites a psychoanalytical reading. If dreams are understood as symbolic discourses, often regressive in nature, then the poem harks back to the time before both an individual and a tradition were institutionalized. Affected by the residual effects of his disturbing dream, Zheng Xuan tosses in bed just as "China tosses about in [his] scholarship." Private, unconscious wishes and fears interact with possible fissures in a formidable tradition that has been consciously constructed. In this way Yang Mu foregrounds the paradoxical yet interdependent relationship between nation and individual, or tradition and narration.

A shift in scene then takes the reader to a sensuous pastoral world of romantic love. The lush landscape of an Elizabethan pastoral setting fulfils all material and aesthetic needs. Shepherds and their lasses live at ease, well-integrated into their natural surroundings. But rather than adorning the nymph with flowery decorations, the modern Marlowe scatters her into dehumanized body parts, in witty imitation of the traditional fashioning of a beauty in Chinese literary practice. In "Marlowe Drinks," "The familiar but indifferent eyebrows" introduce "the eyes, the meteors that slowly fly near at dawn" (lines 19-20). For the modern Marlowe, "the arms, a pair of Oriental catkins" (line 32) are not to be embraced, since the addressee's existence can be felt only between two mutually reflecting mirrors. This "you" is as indeterminate as an answer held back.

---

[32] Quotes from "Zheng Xuan Awaken from a Dream" are Yang Mu's translation. The Pinyin romanization is mine.

"If these delights thy mind may move,
Then live with me, and be my love."
You need not say a word; the hesitation
Means you, me, and the other. The secret of a sound   (lines 41-4)

The idyllic world contemplated by the ancient shepherd, containing "thee and me," is now dismantled by an intrusion of the other. Except for the opening and concluding stanzas, each stanza in the poem – containing four lines quoted from Marlowe's text in Chinese translation and two lines by Yang Mu – verbally corresponds to a depiction of the love theme in two mutually reflecting mirrors. In the sixteenth century, the pastoral ideal may be deployed allegorically to criticize current affairs. To dwell content and contained in an enclosed garden can be an act of self-defence, shutting out menacing powers from the outside world. In Yang Mu's reconstruction, this tension inherent in pastoral literature since its inception is magnified. In the form of a dramatic monologue, the poem orchestrates a dialogue not only between thee and me, or between Marlowe and Yang Mu, but also between the pastoral ideal of eternity and its subtext of ephemerality. Whereas Christopher Marlowe's poem submerges daily realities into pastoral plenitude and timelessness, Yang Mu's poem brings the hidden awareness of loss and absence to the surface. This "bicultural" engagement – of the past and the present, and the English and the Chinese – juxtaposes prelapsarian yearnings with postlapsarian regret in its representation of a love theme.

What we might call a "trialectics" emerges in "Assorted Musical Modes" as Wu Feng, the most marginal and the most recent of the three cultural figures, enters the scene. The poem has already declared "The Sage never dies,"[33] and Confucius's words and the English shepherd's proposal have proven to be similarly immortal. Nonetheless, this Chinese-English "bicultural" symmetry is broken when a third figure is inserted. A Taiwanese tradition disturbs a Chinese one by presenting a narrative that refuses to be enclosed within the latter. Wu Feng's presence in this suite poem problematizes the notion of a homogeneous Chinese national culture, because he is deliberately estranged from the discursive Confucian practice and fully aware of his own foreign ethnicity as a Han Chinese among the indigenous people of Taiwan.

... I know the Confucians at last
The concern they claimed for the world is but an empty speech
Words are their pathetic refuge
I have chosen commitment to life to prove

---

[33] The quote is from line 2 of "Zheng Xuan Awaken from a Dream."

The Sage is innocent. It is the commentators who are ignorant and blind...[34]

(lines 43-7)

Wu Feng, a faithful follower of the Confucian way, has discerning self-consciousness. He dismisses the discursive mediation of Confucian scholarship, which has degenerated into mere empty speeches. In order to put a stop to the aborigines' practice of head-hunting, he prefers living the Confucian ideal – offering his own head – to simply telling them the moral. But the effects of this decisive act of self-sacrifice are uncertain, swinging between his sinicization of and his naturalization by the aborigines.

Deities of the Sky, spirits of the Earth
Life is dispensable, but I am still
Frightened so; yet after death
They will probably forget Wu Feng once and for all   (lines 61-4)

At the threshold between life and death, Wu Feng's fear of mortality and futility is more touching than Jesus's appeal to his Father on the Mount of Olives before his crucifixion, for Wu Feng clearly knows that his death is final – and perhaps futile as well. He could be devoured and consumed as one of the many offerings in the aboriginal rituals. This poignant demonstration of indeterminacy in the process of cultural translation also captures with particular aptness a specifically Taiwanese perspective.

Zheng Xuan, Christopher Marlowe, and Wu Feng have continued for centuries to constitute a significant part of their national traditions because signification works. Placed side by side, they constitute a composite cultural identity for modern Taiwan poetry. On the one hand, this trio combines the assortedness of various "monologic" traditions to create a hybrid identity. On the other hand, the three poems are in fact supplements to the cultural myths of the three "national" traditions.[35] They feature liminal moments of their respective orthodoxies. In each section, a national tradition is fabricated by stock images that apparently structure a familiar narrative central to its cultural theme. But by drawing on a rich repertoire of "off-centre" images, Yang Mu injects a mobilizing force into these framed moments of liminality. The trio's

---

[34]   The translation of this quote is an adaptation from Cissie Kwok and Yang Mu's translation. See "Wu Feng," in *Twentieth-Century Chinese Drama: An Anthology*. ed. Edward M. Gunn (Bloomington: Indiana University Press, 1983), 500.

[35]   Supplement is here used in the Derridean sense. The dangerous supplement in a discourse is the subversive element that threatens to deconstruct its conventional reading. See Jacques Derrida, "...The Dangerous Supplement..." in *Of Grammatology*. Trans. Gayatri Chakravorty Spivak (Baltimore: Johns Hopkins University Press, 1976), 141-164. See also Paul de Man, *Allegories of Reading: Figural Language in Rousseau, Nietzsche, Rilke and Proust* (New Haven: Yale University Press, 1979).

"assorted musical modes" each invokes a lyric voice that sings – but over, it soon becomes clear, an ironic distance. Insofar as Yang Mu's work exemplifies the production of a cultural hybrid, it displays not a hybridity that blends all in a melting-pot, as Xu Huizhi suggests, but what Bakhtin calls intentional hybridization: a hybridity created by different voices bursting out in heteroglossia. As the suite poem was written at the time of Native Soil Literature Movement, it signifies the poet's attempt to provide alternatives to the binary opposition in the dominant discourse between the native and the foreign, between Chinese nationalism and Westernism. By inserting a destabilizing third speaker to form a trialectics, the poet throws into relief the complexities of the identity issue in Taiwan.

"The Yellow Bird"

"The Yellow Bird" exhibits a cross-cultural blending of two distinct literary referents from the Chinese and English traditions. The poem's story alludes to a famous Chinese classical poem, "A Song of the Yellow Bird in the Field," by Cao Zhi. At the same time, the poem's overall structural design and narrative points of view are borrowed from Shelley's well-known poem "Ozymandias" (1818).

Apparently, "The Yellow Bird" is a retelling of Cao Zhi's fable about a youth who saves a yellow bird from a net. Once freed, the bird "swoops down" to thank the young man.

> Windy it is up on tall trees
> Waves roar in the sea
> When the sharp sword is not in hand
> There is no point making numerous friends
>
> There are no birds to be met
> But a sparrow hawk that plunged into a net
> Those who trap the bird are gay
> A youth feels sad, witnessing the bird's fate
>
> Wielding his sword, he cuts the net
> The yellow bird is set free to fly
> Flying, and having flown up to reach the sky
> It swoops down to show the youth its thankfulness

Annotators have related the poem to a historical incident. In 220, when Cao Pi, Cao Zhi's brother, succeeded to the throne as Emperor Wen of Wei, he plotted to eliminate all his brother's friends in order to consolidate his own power. Ding Yi was one of those friends, and he was well aware of his perilous position. He went to seek help from a military leader, Shang. By writing "A Song of the Yellow Bird in the Field," Cao Zhi tried to appeal to Shang's kindness and goodwill, hoping that Shang might do for Ding Yi what the youth did for the yellow bird. Nevertheless, Ding Yi was executed.

At the level of its plot, Yang Mu's poem is a swirl from its precursor's. The initial situation is the same – a bird waits to be rescued from a net. Yet a similarly benevolent act yields very different results:

> That was ancient times
> Someone saw an avenging yellow bird
> In a net struggling
> Up there on a tall tree, the bleak wind blew
> In the distant land of future, the waves leapt
> He jumped off of his horse, wielded his sword and cut the cords
> The yellow bird flew into a sky of emptiness, the youth
> Was shocked and shaken, in an instant, his hair all whitened
> His blood bleached pale, his attire broken
> Into pieces, his bow dropped
> His arrows scattered, the colour of the flag changed
> But still in his right hand, a sword. Yes, a sword
> Dustless, glamorous
>
> – someone from the corn and millet fields returned
> and told me a shocking event   (lines 26-40)

Once liberated, the bird in this modern incarnation plunges into an abyss of nothingness. Just as shockingly, the youth's hair immediately turns white after his decisive act. The present version abandons the monolithic narration of benevolence and justice found in its classical source. Although the poem ends as it begins, the circular structure does not resolve the doubts that have been raised, and the fable now lacks a moral.

In addition to making a parodic reference to a classical Chinese text, "The Yellow Bird" adopts the technique of double narration from Shelley's "Ozymandias," which begins with a speaker reporting, "I met a traveller from an antique land, / Who said..." Shelley's tale is about the traveller's encounter with Ozymandias (Ramses II), an Egyptian king long dead, in the form of the ruins of his immense statue. The king's majestic look, fashioned by the sculptor's hands, is in fragments, but his steadfast voice is carved in the epitaph on the pedestal: "My name is Ozymandias, King of Kings, / Look on my Works, ye Mighty, and despair!" An arrogant mortal's declaration of his own worth rings loudly. What the traveller sees, however, is empty desert and Ozymandias's boasts lingering only in plastic arts and poetry – the residues of human achievements, diminished by the centuries. The multilayered narration in the voices of Ozymandias, the traveller, and the narrator turns the king's words into pathetic, unwitting self-mockery.

Clad in Shelley's poetic form, Yang Mu's "The Yellow Bird" highlights the layers of mediation and deepens the Romantic scepticism about the meaning of events and their causes. It is a report about some-one bringing back from a knight "a story of yore / about the yellow bird." Yet the further detail that it is "an avenging yellow bird" suggests some untold story from the bird's past that offers a motive for revenge. That the poem ends by repeating its opening lines – "Someone from the corn and millet fields returned / and told me a shocking event" – implies the continuous dissemination of a tale that denies narrative closure.

Indeed, the intertexts in "The Yellow Bird" can be read as fables im-parting some universal truths. "A Song of the Yellow Bird in the Field" illustrates that a compassionate act will be rewarded with appreciation and gratitude, whereas "Ozymandias" preaches against human vanity and the desire for absolute power. Yang Mu recognizes the two "truths" available to him in these prior texts and utilizes them in the echoland. When Romantic irony comes into dialogic collision with Chinese morals in "The Yellow Bird," the outcomes vividly reflect contemporary con-cerns. Since 1989, the old structures established in the mid-twentieth century have been shaken. People have witnessed historic world-changing events such as the June Fourth Incident in the People's Repub-lic of China, the fall of the Berlin Wall in Germany, the disintegration of the USSR and of the Soviet bloc, and the consequent reshaping of Eastern Europe. The myth of invincible rule has been demystified, but the meanings of the liberating changes have yet to be defined. As a new world order is in the making, Yang Mu deploys the two different cul-tural models and lets them enter into a Bahktinian semantic relation, thereby creating a new critical stance on international affairs.

"The Lost Ring – for Chechnya"

Intertextuality is a two-way street. An allusion in a text makes the discovery of a foreign culture the occasion for rethinking one's own. "The Lost Ring – for Chechnya" took its origin from an item in an American newspaper. The creative process involved both translational and transnational transfers whose details are worth examining.

In 2000, Taiwan was ready to hold its second presidential election. Shortly before the March vote, the state council in Beijing released a controversial White Paper on the PRC's Taiwan policy.[36] Beijing pro-posed a rough "deadline" for reunification and threatened to use drastic measures, including military force, to achieve it if Taiwan refused to

---

[36] Among the three most promising candidates, two have diverged from the unification agenda. Under the shadow of the ruling Guomindang's "state-to-state" theory, Lian Zhan inevitably needs to negotiate with the separatist scheming. The pro-independence candidate of the Democratic Progressive Party, Chen Shuibian, repre-sents the separatist claims of the opposition party; while only James Song Chuyu de-clares a pro-unification stand.

enter political negotiations. Despite Beijing's war threats, the Taiwanese people saw themselves as a sovereign country electing a president. Obviously, Taiwan's twenty million people were in a state of political uncertainty.

On 2 March 2000, a fortnight before the presidential election in Taiwan and three weeks before an election in Russia, "The Lost Ring – for Chechnya" appeared in Taiwan's *China Times*, offering a most timely comment on the political situation. The poem is dedicated to Chechnya, which was newly engaged in the Second Chechen War, launched by the decision of Prime Minister Putin to regain control of the separatist province of Chechnya. The move was popular among Russians and undoubtedly helped secure him the presidency in the March election. The subject matter of the poem comes from the oral testimony of a Chechen woman named Hedi, who narrowly escaped death when she and other women were attacked by Russian soldiers looting Grozny, the capital of Chechnya. After her account was given to Human Rights Watch in a hospital in a neighbouring republic, Ingushetia, it was disseminated to Western correspondents. Hedi's story appeared in an article in the *New York Times* on 6 February 2000.[37] The news caught the attention of Yang Mu, who happened to be in New York. Inspired by the event, the poet "translated" it into a Chinese poem.

By bringing Chechnya to the attention of Taiwanese readers and Chinese communities worldwide, Yang Mu turns the full light of a global concern for ethnic independence on local anxiety. By smoothly bringing "foreign" news into the "Chinese" language and a "Chinese" literary form, the poet creates an illuminating analogy to the Taiwan question. The prologue of the poem, titled "A Letter Home," reminds readers of two famous lines from a classical Chinese war poem, "With flames of battle raging for three months / A letter home is worth a treasure" ("The Prospects of Spring," by Du Fu).[38] The letter, which summarizes the news item from the *New York Times*, is followed by a narrative poem of thirty-two stanzas.

"The Lost Ring" depicts the transformation of an innocent, peace-loving youth into a resolute soldier. The speaker in the poem is the

---

[37] See Michael R. Gordon, "Rights Group Says Russians Executed Grozny Civilians." *The New York Times* 6 February 2000.

[38] "A letter home" in Chinese can be a letter from or to home. The two lines are from Du Fu's poem, "Chun Wang" [The Prospects of Spring]. An alternative translation of "three months" is "the third month" or "March." This time reference is applicable to both the second Chechen war, which has lasted for more than three months and the Taiwan situation where the presidential campaign has been in progress under military threats from an offshore power. These political and military conflicts would elicit their effects in March when presidential elections in both Taiwan and Russia were scheduled.

brother of a Chechen victim, Hedi Ivana. But whereas Hedi was focus of the news report, Hedi Ivana is kept off-stage in Yang Mu's work; she is the guardian angel to her brother, who is at the centre of the action. Unlike the real Hedi whose ring was stolen off the finger when she was pretending to be dead, Hedi Ivana's death is implied near the end of the poem when her ring is found on the finger of a Russian soldier whom her brother accidentally kills in the dark. Contrary to conventional literature that sanctions the embrace of adult values and national narratives, there is no glorification of this youth's initiation into soldierhood. Instead, the poem conveys a deep sense of regret and helplessness. Through the youth, Yang Mu constructs civilian "visions of community and versions of historic memory" and gives "narrative form to the minority position" that the Chechens occupy.[39]

That Yang Mu chose to speak to his native country from the Chechen position in March 2000 is telling. As noted above, the fall of Grozny aided Putin in winning the Russian presidency. In a voice of resistance, the youth prays in the last line of the poem that Chechnya will rise again and calls independence "the spring prophecy of rebirth." Yang Mu encloses this Chechen message in a letter home, which he concludes with a note of affectionate advice: "Roads are slippery on rainy days. Be cautious." The poet, together with the Taiwanese people, was anxiously anticipating what Taiwan's spring election might bring.

Intertextuality is visibly recorded in this poem, yet a more significant point for discussion is what might be labelled its "intercontextuality." Using a mixture of discourses on war, the poet allows the narratives of independence to be voiced by real and fictional speakers of different cultures. From the *New York Times* to the *China Times*, "The Lost Ring – for Chechnya" reviews transnational issues of the *Times* and of our time.

"Temporality Proposition"

In addition to bridging the global and local in addressing social and political concerns, Yang Mu has employed cross-cultural intertexts to develop a new path for modern Chinese poetry. An analysis of "Temporality Proposition" can illustrate his comparative poetics in practice.

As its title suggests, this poem is a philosophical and poetic discourse on time. The discussion begins with a speaker contemplating what he was, is, and will be in the precarious world to which he is bound:

---

[39] Yang Mu's text works like the discursive doubleness deployed by hybrid agencies in Homi Bhabha's conception. See Homi Bhabha, "Culture's In-Between," in *Questions of Identity*. eds. Stuart Hall and Paul de Guy (London: SAGE, 1996), 58.

By the lamp, on my grey hair I ponder
Wasn't the snow particularly heavy last winter?
At midnights, alone I sit in the precarious world
From the bottom of my heart, I miss you

The worries are for the stars, methinks
Some will have their names removed from Capricorn in spring
But I recognize them every time I look into the mirror
On my temples they have settled for years

Perhaps, for that laurel the concerns are
It puts out flowers despite the wounds? So you ask
This has never occurred to me before autumn
When Wu Gang is tired to death, it is my turn

The literary images that the speaker invokes are all situated in an indeterminate process: some are trying to balance themselves, some are
about to retreat, and others are starting a journey, following or looking
for a route. From the signs of the zodiac to the Chinese myth of the
moon, the poet draws on inanimate nature as well as the living world of
plants, fish, and humans for ideas about time. Before a dewdrop evapo-
rates at sunrise, before clouds gather and disperse in no time, and before
mackerels dive off unnoticed in an instant, their struggling moments of
existence construct the ephemeral world.

Time is manifested in a paradox of mutability and continuity. Collec-
tively, mortals enact their existence spatially in groups, and temporally
in the action's repeatability. In the Chinese myth, up on the moon Wu
Gang's Sisyphean task of chopping down the laurel and the laurel's
repeated regeneration inscribe them in a never-ending drama. An individual may, one day, leave his job behind, but the work is never over; it
is simply taken up by the next in line. Wu Gang passes his axe to the
persona "I"; similarly, in the final stanza, "I" will keep "you" company
for a while on "your" way to Byzantium – a legendary itinerary for
every artist after Yeats. The tension between the futility of labour and
the will to transcend limitations bespeaks the timeless paradox of the
living world. In this poem, activities are caught at one moment in a
process, at the very instant before they are terminated or suspended.

Yang Mu's artistic design is to juxtapose intertexts from literary representations of time in different cultures. Of all the poems Yang Mu has
published to date, "Temporality Proposition" is the only one with annotations, which mix classical and vernacular Chinese, English, and German. Apparently, his aim is to highlight the use of cross-cultural intertextuality. The last stanza stages a dramatic encounter of the earlier texts
in an echoland.

In the aging days, tenderly I continue
Playing the zither, to see you off sailing to Byzantium
At where it is about to end and not yet, suspended – silence
Über allen Gipfeln ist Ruh

The intertextual symphony reaches its climax in these four lines, which contain a buried allusion to Li Bai's famous poem of farewell, "To Wang Lun."

Li Bai was about to leave in a boat
But suddenly he heard someone singing from the shore
Peach Blossom Lake is a thousand feet deep
But deeper does Wang Lun's affectionate farewell touch me

Wang Lun's song of farewell to the Tang poet is here replaced by the music from a zither, and the role of the persona is reversed – it is now the "I" who produces the music and sends "you" on a trip. For those who are about to part, time is but a mixing of memory with desire, the past joining with the future in the present. As represented spatially, a journey of quest and discovery is juxtaposed with one of recollection and nostalgia. Hence, Yeats's horizontal trip across an ocean to Byzantium is followed by Goethe's vertical trips to his old dwelling on the hill-top, where he carved and re-carved his famous "Wanderer's Nightsong" (1780) on the wooden wall three times. In temporal terms, the persona, as an accomplished artist, is now playing some music to keep "you," an apprentice artist, company when setting sail to Byzantium. The artist-mentor has been playing the zither for some time and will continue to do so in the near future, but there is no promise that this will go on forever. However sweet the music is, there will be a time when it comes to a halt and "you" will have to carry on the quest to Byzantium alone. The old feelings in the note of farewell embedded in the Chinese allusion are put to new use, as the poet adds a reminder that the final exit from time is inevitable. With its variety of intertexts, the last stanza covers different dimensions of time, including its Romantic sublimation in the spatial image of a peak and a temporal trope of silence. The proposition breaks off at a lofty place where one looks up to some point beyond, at a moment of silence when the music, no longer heard, becomes sweeter than ever.

In "Temporality Proposition," Yang Mu creates a cross-cultural dialogue of discursive temporalities. An individual voice that raises the issues of time draws voices of poetic wisdom from Chinese, Irish, and German literature into a philosophical discourse. The discussion is not summarized in a conclusion but is suspended in quietude over all hilltops. Yet despite its collage of intertexts, the poem is not rendered as post-modern textual free play. It relies on a self-conscious poetic form to evoke a mental state for contemplation, and the repetition of what has already been said in world cultures is structured in a way that implies universality and continuity. Not only does the poem enact the modernist conviction of transcendence through art, it also demonstrates Yang Mu's cosmopolitan outlook in poetics.

*   *
*

Owing to intercontinental travel and the electronic highway, cross-cultural communications in the twenty-first century are faster and easier than ever. Only with an adequate understanding of the intertextual encounters in the echoland can the shape of world literature be compre-hended today. In addition to referring to the intersections between one text and a multiplicity of intertexts in an immense dictionary, "intertex-tuality" also designates a text's cross-cultural participation in the discur-sive space of world culture. It thus points to a new concept of world literature, premised on the fact that "a work only has an *effective* life as world literature, whenever, and wherever, it is actively present within a literary system beyond that of its original culture" (Damrosch, 2003: 4-5). Specific literary referents from different discourses and cultures offer multiple perspectives on an event in a given corner of the world. Poets can position the local in the global or vice versa to gain greater insight into some current state of affairs. By presenting variations on a single theme, the intertexts offer the reader an enlightening range of meanings.

While Yang Mu's poetry is often described as exhibiting a density that at times leads to obscurity, one may remember Barbara Johnson's observation about Mallarmé's poetics: "Obscurity is an excess, not a deficiency, of meaning" (Johnson, 1980: 68). Yang Mu's linguistic density, built on intracultural and cross-cultural intertextuality, fosters an interpretive multiplicity that is difficult to pin down once and for all. Whether read through the botanical metaphor of grafting ("vertical heritage" and "horizontal transplant") or in a spatial metaphor ("inter-"), this poetry carefully selects its subjects from the immense world dic-tionary. By his artistic and strategic interweaving of well-known texts from disparate cultures, Yang Mu succeeds in addressing issues of regional or universal interest from a transnational perspective. The re-vision of humanity has been the concern of literature worldwide; in the new century, it can be arrived at through an epiphany that emerges from an echoland of world literature.

CHAPTER 3

On Time-worlds

Tell the running water: I exist[*]

Time can by no stretch of the imagination be considered a novel theme in literature, and running water is undoubtedly a universal trope for representing it. For the Chinese, the written inscription for time that outgrows human history is a pictorial image of ripples "永" in a seal character, suggesting that the river continues to run to eternity. This image of constant movement is built into many Chinese words for time, such as "running years" (*liunian*) and "running light/days" (*liuguang*). In Chinese as in many other languages, time is figured in spatial terms. Common temporal indicators include "pass," "come," "go," and similar verbs, as well as prepositions such as "front" (*qian*) and "back" (*hou*).[1] The human experiencer of time is positioned at the centre, where he is static, watching time pass him by as persons and things change. At the midpoint of the ever-flowing river, the human presence is transient but unique, as Heraclitus, the ancient Greek philosopher, pointed out long ago: no one can step into the same river twice. Man is a lonely traveller who makes a single journey in the infinite flow of time. The Yeatsian tripartite aphorism that describes life as "What is past or passing or to come" captures a dread that preoccupies the human mind. The universal fears of mortality and futility have precipitated an extreme loneliness when one measures one's brief presence against Time. There seems to be no way to relieve John Keats's twin anxieties: "When I have fears

---

[*] This is the last line from a sonnet by Rilke: "should earthliness forget you quite,/ murmur to the quiet earth: I'm running/tell the running water: I exist" (lines 12-14). See "Sonnets to Orpheus," part two, no.29. in *Rainer Maria Rilke*. Trans. J. B. Leishman and Stephen Spender (New York: Everyman's Library, 1996, c. 1957), 162.

[1] For the verbs, "pass," "come" and "go" work similarly in the English discourse of time, but for the preposition, Chinese works differently. Thinking of "events in the front" means remembering the past and "things at the back" refer to the future," which is the opposite of "looking ahead" or "looking back" in English. For a discussion of temporal indicators in Classical Chinese poetry, see Huang Churen, "Time as running water: from temporal indicators in classical poetry to Chinese concept of time" ["Shijian ru liushui: you gudianshige zhong de shijian yungyu tan dou zhong-guo ren de shijian guan"], *Chung Wai Literary Monthly* (April 1981): 70-88.

that I may cease to be" and "on the shore / Of the wide world I stand alone." But in such fears, he certainly was not alone. In the seventh century, too, a Chinese poet, Chen Ziang (661-702), sighed when he visited Jibei lou:

> There are no precursors in front of me
> Nor are there any followers behind –
> Thinking of the long-standing cosmos
> Alone, I sob sadly.

Much of drama and literature more generally is derived from the brevity of life and vanity of the world. There are abundant examples of early Chinese poetry hinged on temporality. Subgenres such as Ziye songs and Songs of Four Seasons are organized by the cyclical changes observed in nature, and different seasons and amounts of sunlight traditionally have gender associations. The Chinese dualism related to light – *yin* (dark, absence of sunlight, feminine) and *yang* (bright, sunny, masculine) – extends to the preoccupations of the sexes in different seasons; thus "Female indulged in thoughts in spring" and "Male feel miserable in autumn."[2] In spring, women are affected by the *yang* atmosphere and think of men; conversely, in autumn, men feel the *yin* and yearn for women.[3] A more widely adopted interpretation of the line suggests the thwarted desires of women and men at different stages in life. While young women have romantic yearnings in their youth (spring), men regret that they have not realized their career goals when they approach old age (autumn). These two seasons are combined in the Chinese term "Springs and Autumns" (*Chunqiu*), an idiomatic expression for human history.

More prominent in the symbolism of time than seasons is the river. "Four seasons are like water gone," wrote Meng Jiao. Central to this category are Changjiang (or the Yangtze River; literally, "long river") and the Yellow River, the cradle of Chinese civilization. Both rivers run east, and therefore "water gone east" is a common expression for time lost. Confucius once sighed before a river: "Time passes in this manner, no matter it is night or day." Su Shi (1037-1101) similarly expresses his regrets: "We are no more than summer flies between heaven and earth, a grain of millet on the waste of the sea! It grieves me that life is so short,

---

[2]   The line is quoted from section 10 "Muiqingfan" of a classical text *Huainanzi*. See D. C. Lau, ed. *A Concordance to the Huainanzi*, CUHK ICS The Ancient Chinese Text Concordance Series (Hong Kong: Commercial Press, 1992), 87.

[3]   This is Zheng Xuan's interpretation of the line as suggested in his annotation of a poem titled "Qi Yue" [The Seventh Month] in the *Book of Songs*. See Zheng Xuan's annotation of *Mao Shi*, section 8.

and I envy the long river that never stops."[4] Li Bai laments: "Time has left me, as the day of the day before cannot be kept / Time now disturbs me on the day of today that is trouble-fed." And Tao Yuanming's response to this cosmic sorrow is "Hiding my tears for the water already ran east / I follow time through historical changes."

As Chen Shih-hsiang observes, the Chinese conception of time lacks a supernatural or religious dimension. As a result, Chinese poets contemplate the finite time in a life span, and believe that when the water runs east into the sea, there is no return to the past or progress to a higher stage of existence. Chen uses the concepts of "finite time" and "the infinite" to explore the multiple layers of temporal discourse in "The Inlaid Psaltery," by Li Shangyin. He quotes two lines in the poem – "This feeling might *abide* until it becomes memory, / But at the time *already* one is in sorrow enmeshed"[5] – showing the poet moved by his own direct encounters with the changes in life, experiences that shaped his perspective on all changes in human history. Chen sees this as an epiphany about time, but not liberation from it. He points out that the whole poem is filled with passions, and finally concludes on a note of emotional depth (Chen, 1972: 60). The Chinese do not ascribe the infinite to a transcendental realm beyond the human world. It is almost a fact of nature, like the river against which humans measure their own insignificance. As the Chinese place human mortality in the natural cycle of life and death within infinite time, a sense of "cosmic sorrow" dominates their reflections on time.

Invested in Chinese literary tradition and sceptical about all religions, Yang Mu rarely deals with the religious dimension of time in his poetry. A more useful approach to his treatment of time is suggested by Paul Ricoeur, who (drawing on Heidegger's discussion of human time) breaks the concept into three levels: the first level is "temporality," characterized by "the finite structure of time arising from the recognition of the centrality of death, or, more exactly, of *being-towards-death*"; the second is "historicity," which "refers to our way of 'becoming' between birth and death," a "*stretching-along* of life" characterized by repetition; and the third is "the prevailing of everyday-life structures over and against those of temporality... and of historicity... called

---

4   The lines are quoted from Su Shi's first prose poem on the Red Cliff. See *Selected Poems of Su Tung-p'o*. Trans. Burton Watson (Port Townsend: Copper Canyon Press, 1994), 95.

5   Chen Shih-hsiang's translation and emphasis. See Chen Shih-hsiang, "Shijian he ludu zai zhongguoshi zhong zhi shiyi zuoyong" [The Poetic Signification of Time and Scansion in Chinese Poetry]. In *Chen Shih-hsiang wencun* [Collected Essays of Chen Shih-hsiang]. eds. Ye Shan and Lin Hengjie (Taipei: Zhiwen, 1972), 61.

within-time-ness."[6] In other words, human time is *lived* time, an idea premised on human mortality and one close to Yang's primarily philosophical concerns about human existence.

As always, pitted against the finitude of mortal time is the immensity of cosmic time. In this light, the human experience of time can be classified in two ways: into the particular and the universal, as in Aristotle's approach, or into what is *in time* and what is *out of time*, as in Murray Krieger's approach (in the context of literature):

> through the typographical *figura*, the unredeemed sequence of chronological time can be redeemed after all into the divine pattern, that eternal, spatial order which exchanges history for eschatology. With every moment existing doubly – both in the temporal order and in the timeless structure – history remains history even while it is rewritten as a divinely authored myth. Every act or person seems random, arbitrary; yet each is a necessary signifier that partakes of the single Transcendental Signified. In borrowed form, this paradoxical relation between what is in time and what is out of time is also turned into a model for poetic form.[7]

Likewise, Yang Mu's poetry treats time on two levels. When he deals with mortal time, his starting-point is a historical reinscription of time as it is privately or publicly experienced. As the poet has grown older, his attempts to repeat and to retrieve significant encounters in time have incorporated specific metaphors and narrative forms. The recent tendency of the poet is to unite mortal time and cosmic time by synthesizing the collective wisdom and imagination about the temporal from many cultures.

Yang Mu's discourses on time vary widely at different phases of his poetic career; they include a direct description of a boring summer afternoon, a surrealist experiment disguised in an apostrophe, a nostalgic evocation of ancient tradition, and a simulacrum of disparate cultural referents, expressed with the precision of classical philosophy or the indeterminacy of post-modernism. By situating time in a virtual world, Yang appears to be carrying out what Susanne K. Langer has called the poet's business: "to create the appearance of 'experiences,' the semblance of events lived and felt, and to organize them so they constitute a

---

6   Paul Ricoeur, "The Human Experience of Time and Narrative," *A Ricoeur Reader: Reflection and Imagination.* ed. Mario J. Valdés (New York: Harvester and Wheatsheaf, 1991), 101-2. Despite the fact that in his essay, Ricoeur is mainly concerned with the treatment of time in narrative forms, I find many of his observations relevant to this discussion of time-worlds in Yang Mu's poetry.

7   Murray Krieger, " 'A Waking Dream': The Symbolic Alternative to Allegory." *Critical Theory since Plato.* Rev. ed. ed. Hazard Adams (Fort Worth: Harcourt Brace Jovanovich College Publishers, 1992), 1248.

purely and completely experienced reality, a piece of *virtual life.*"[8] In each time-world, the poet creates a semblance of life, which "is abstracted from immediate, personal life, as the primary illusions of the other arts – virtual space, time, and power – are images of perceived space, vital time, felt power" (Langer, 1953: 217). Similarly, in his essay "Poetry and Possibility" Paul Ricoeur sees literature as "a creation of productive imagination which projects a world of its own" (Ricoeur, 1991: 452). This fictive world proposed by Ricoeur at once offers "the horizon of possibilities which constitute an environment for people... where we could dwell" and has a horizon "which recedes when we approach it, which has always an inexhaustible capacity," thereby suggesting "a world whose horizons are never definite" (Ricoeur, 1991: 453).

The projected experiences of human reality in Yang Mu's different time-worlds cover all three levels that Ricoeur describes – "within-time-ness," "stretching-along of life," and "being-towards-death" – moving from mundane concerns to more philosophical modes of thinking, and from the particularities of mortal time to the universal order of cosmic time. And over half a century, the poet's approaches to and definitions of time have evolved in significant ways, which fall into four major categories. First, in writings that identify time with dates and events, Yang situates his poems in "real time" or the objective "homogeneous time" in contemporary life.[9] He draws out the "within-time-ness" of subjects that range from everyday routines or special occasions in his own life to social, political affairs in Taiwan and the world. Second, in poems that offer conventional literary renditions of time as measured in the natural rhythms of days and seasons, flora and fauna, ageing and death, the poet phenomenalizes time. Doing so makes possible a poetic method of discoursing about time in a cross-cultural blend of images and symbols. The third approach features Yang's meditative and philosophical musings about time. As his focus shifts, so does the poetic function, from presenting a historical record to creating an incarnation of time. Time is spatialized and place is temporalized in a myth. The fourth strategy is the one Yang has used most consistently: he theorizes about mortal time and cosmic time by capturing the dialectical tension of a quest both unique and repeatable. The passage of time is metaphorically represented by departure and return: the speaker is constantly

---

[8]   Susanne K. Langer, *Feeling and Form* (New York: Charles Scribner's Sons, 1953), 212.

[9]   Walter Benjamin coined the term "homogenous time" to refer to time measured by clock and calendar, which is a point of reference for global communication in contemporary life. See Walter Benjamin, *Illuminations*. Trans. Harry Zohn (London: Fontana Press, 1992), 252.

leaving for Byzantium and longing to return to Elysium. This treatment of time is closely connected to the themes of memory, childhood, and homesickness, but the circularity suggests what is out of time in the "Transcendental Signified" of time.

Homogenizing Time

A small number of Yang Mu's poems are directly related to events involving his actual circumstances and acquaintances, and feature his responses to occurrences in real life. This personal experience of time is closely tied to a community and its customs, and poems of this kind articulate the rhythm of Yang's life in his social worlds. The incidents he describes can be matched to their biographical origins in his own experience of marriage, fatherhood, travel, and the like.

When Yang Mu began writing poetry, he found images of time in the natural cycle of days, nights, and, seasons, on which artificial measures such as calendars and timetables are imposed. For example, "By the Waterside" (1958) features a summer afternoon, in "The Night at a Small Station" (1958) focuses on "Saturday," and "Chinese Roses Bloom" (1957) mentions "May 1956" (line 2). "Days" (1957) is about January, "The Feeling of October" (1959) about October, and "The River Gone" (1962) about the end of spring in May. Titles are not always reliable indicators of subject-matter, however; thus, the event that concerns "An April Tune" (1959) might have taken place in any month of the year. New discoveries and excitement are recorded like diary entries. "In the diary, a thousand pages of pleasure – walks, exams, and kisses," says the speaker in "To Cross the Milky Way" (1961; lines 76-7).

Yang Mu is particularly sensitive to nature's seasonal changes. The young poet painted time with natural images such as those found in the Songs of Four Seasons genre in classical Chinese poetry; in "The Road in Autumn" (1957), he writes: "October is on the treetop / Red are the maples / Why can't their shades cover too November and December below?" To him – as works such as "The Departure of Autumn" (1956), "Outside the Fence" (1958), and "The Impression of Late September" (1961) demonstrate – the ideal time is evening of an autumn day. But it seems that following his more extensive reading of poetry in his undergraduate studies, Yang Mu gave up the habit of attaching a specific date and month, or a season, to a poem, save for a series of poems written in the mid-1980s: "Mid-autumn," "A Mid-autumn Night," "The Approach of Autumn," "Autumn Song," and "Composed in a Frosty Night." His poems are often set in autumn or spring, a choice that both echoes the Romantic preoccupation with mortality found in such works as Shelley's "Ode to the West Wind" (1820) and Coleridge's "Frost at Midnight" (1798) and reflects the Chinese gender associations with the two seasons, mentioned above.

One poem that is seminal in the poet's treatment of time is a short lyric about a youth's experience of a few summer hours. For a teenage boy, one day is too long for meditation in solitude. "By the Waterside" (1958) records the youth's boredom and anxiety during a midsummer afternoon. Time is measured by the speaker's observations of nature: running water, the position of the sun, and flowers dispersing pollen in the wind. In this poem, one hears the complaints of a lonely youth waiting for an imaginary girlfriend or anticipating a romance, prompted perhaps by "the wind, the go-between" (line 9). But the possibility of being swept into the power of quarrelsome girls dampens his spirit, and he finally deceives himself into believing that after four afternoons of "waiting" he wants nobody to come. Similar restlessness is found in "Burning Afternoons" (1958), whose last stanza expresses a youth's suppressed desire for the girls he seems to despise. These poems of the listless, torturous afternoons project a specific time-world: a small community in which boys and girls are socialized. The youth's veneer of resignation or outright withdrawal vividly captures the within-time-ness of the events during adolescence.

Imitating the practice of classical Chinese poetry, Yang Mu made some titles into descriptions that include specific dates and names of places and people. Among these are "Watching the Melting Snow with Yu Guangzhong in Michigan on 2 April" (1966), "Watching the Mist with Xiaoming on 17 December" (1988), and "Leaving Clear Water Bay on 10 December" (1993). Calendar time marks "the extensive, public, and datable character of the temporality of being-there," and dating a poem assigns to "each significant event a place in the ultimate scheme of all possible dates" (Ricoeur, 1991: 343-4). These poems commemorate the lived time privately shared between kinfolk and friends. In addition, Yang Mu has written a few occasional poems in response to well-known public events, such as the 1979 Formosa Incident in Taiwan, Beijing's June Fourth Incident of 1989, the Chechen Wars of the 1990s, and the catastrophic Taizhong earthquake in 1999. Shunning journalistic descriptions, the poet forges in these poems the kind of "metaphorical relation of present consciousness to the 'having-been'" that Ricoeur seeks: "When the expression of our debt to the dead takes on the colours of indignation, of lamentation, or compassion, the reconstruction of the past needs the help of imagination that can place it 'right before our eyes'" (Ricoeur, 1991: 353). Yang gives his poem "At Dong Shi, 81 Days after the Earthquake" a subtitle quoted from W. B. Yeats – "Move most gently if move you must / In this lonely place" – that creates a tender tone of care for his fellow countrymen who suffered in the disaster.[10] A period of more than two months is long enough for outsiders to forget what the news was about, but too short for much progress to have been made in relief work and in the physical and emotional rehabilitation of the injured. Those who have not yet recovered from the trauma of their sudden loss of home, family, and friends need more time to regain their strength, undisturbed; thus anyone who happens to go to the site of the earthquake ought to "move most gently if move [he] must."

But the most horrible and disastrous events in the late twentieth century were caused by humans, not nature, and they too demand our compassion and sympathy. In "A Song of Sorrow – Dedicated to Lin Yixiong" (1980), a requiem for the victims in the Formosa Incident, the speaker mourns for Lin's loss of his mother and daughters in the period of white terror under the Guomindang's rule in Taiwan. "You Will Come Back Alive" (1989), subtitled "Mourning for Those Who Died in the June Fourth Incident," echoes the implicit pledge made in the last stanza of "The Lost Ring – for Chechnya" (2000): "the spring prophecy of rebirth." It is the poet's belief that those who sacrifice themselves for a noble cause never die: they live in people's memory. According to Aristotle, poetry is distinguished from history by its focus on presenting the plausible – what could have taken place. Effective dramatization of historical events requires that they be believable, as if they were happening right before our eyes. In addition, in their quasi-historical character, narrative poems such as "The Lost Ring – for Chechnya" look forward as well as back, uncovering not only of what might have been hidden in the actual past but also what may happen in similar political situations in the future.

By homogenizing time, Yang Mu recaptures it as a sequence of chronological events experienced privately and publicly. From a restricted world of a single individual to the social circle comprising his peers, the poet's time-worlds expand and multiply to convey the pulse of life in the contemporary world, local and global.

Phenomenalizing Time

Because literature is concerned with giving form to life, life manifested in time is naturally of paramount significance to poets. Poets' attempts to concretize time are to a large extent circumscribed by the three aspects of temporality named by Ricoeur: "within-time-ness," "stretching-along of life," and "being-towards-death." Mortality and historicity are usually rendered on two levels, as the poet makes use both of images from the actual world and of literary conventions. Lyric

---

[10] Yang Mu, *She shi* [Intervention] (Taipei: Hongfan, 2001), 76-9.

poetry, because of its brevity and intensity, is less situational and referential in approaching the structures of everyday life.

For existentialists, one way to "recover the 'whatness' of time [is] by experiencing the 'poetry' of time not in its immediacy, but in its mediations, accumulated over time in History."[11] These mediations, sedimented over time, are presented in poetry's imagery and figures of speech. Time is phenomenalized as external realities. The existentialists may view history as the transcendental signified of time, but poetry has the power to overcome the verbal and thus temporal sequence by spatial imagination. In Joseph Frank's opinion, a poet by juxtaposition can move the temporal art of poetry towards space:

> By this juxtaposition of past and present... history becomes ahistorical. Time is no longer felt as an objective, causal progression with clearly marked-out differences between periods; now it has become a continuum in which distinctions between past and present are wiped out. ... Past and present are apprehended spatially, locked in a timeless unity that, while it may accentuate surface differences, eliminates any feeling of sequence by the very act of juxtaposition.[12]

The most striking of such surface differences are poetic images. As Northrop Frye observes, "in the lyric, where the associative process is strongest and the ready-made descriptive phrases of ordinary prose furthest away, the unexpected or violent metaphor that is called catachresis has a peculiar importance. Much more frequently than any other genre does the lyric depend for its main effect on the fresh or surprising image" (Frye, 1957: 281). In the poems discussed below – "Daffodils" (1961), "To Time" (1964), and "Temporality Proposition" (1993) – images and literary conventions are directed towards the phenomenalization of time.

To ground poetry dealing with time in the natural phenomena of days and seasons seems to be a universal poetic practice. A Taiwanese born at a rural seaside town east of the island, Yang Mu brings into his poems Hualian's landscape, together with the life of its insects, plants, and humans in an agricultural setting. As in ancient communal poems, the seasons in Yang Mu's works often organize the natural world and human activities in a neat order.[13] His predilection in his poetry for the evening and the latter part of a year has continued throughout his career. Unlike other Taiwanese poets, Yang Mu often represents winter by

---

[11] H. J. Blackman, *Six Existentialist Thinkers* (London: Routledge, 1994, c. 1961), 106

[12] Joseph Frank, *The Widening Gyre: Crisis and Mastery in Modern Literature* (Bloomington: Indiana University Press, 1963), 59.

[13] One famous example of these communal poems is "The Seventh Month" in the *Book of Songs*.

references to snow in North America, displaying an outlook shaped by his years of living far from his birthplace. Yang's literary references likewise reflect a kind of trans-Pacific travel. His easy movement between Chinese and Euro-American poetic conventions, discussed in Chapter 2, has conspicuously marked his discourse on time. Sometimes these are obvious cultural translations of intertexts (e.g., Coleridge's "Frost at Midnight" in Yang Mu's "Composed in a Frosty Night"); but more generally, he adopted the practice of phenomenalizing time by amalgamating images and poetic allusions from different cultures very early in his writing. "Daffodils" is a prominent example of this method:

> The stars of the past whisper at our back
> We, not knowing why, quarrel
> Lie down, and in a lullaby
> I carefully count them falling to the valley floor
> quietly turning into fireflies drifting
> Softly they float across our heels
> under the starlight, in the shadow of flowers
>
> Oh, this may be a barren hill, a deserted pier
> Yet we row the same boat
>
> Following the flow of time, we easily glide
> Unaware of having already sailed seven seas
> A thousand years a dream, vast waters
> I turn and look at you, on your temples
> stars have shed their white flowers
>
> Daffodils, in the books of ancient Greece, look down at themselves
> – the stars of today whisper at our back
> We sit face to face at the north window
> Vaguely going through the yellowing letters

This poem contains universal images such as "fireflies" and the colours commonly associated with time's passage – grizzled hair in the "white flowers" on the addressee's temples, the "yellowing letters," and the diminished light in the "shadow of flowers." Humans are all in the same boat, drifting down the river of time; while the phrase "seven seas" has a Western sound, "a thousand years a dream" is typical of classical Chinese poetry. Most cultures use river imagery to convey the idea of life's continuous flow without stop or reversal. Self-indulgence in looking at oneself, as implied by the allusion to the Greek myth of Narcissus (another name for the daffodil), is here self-reflection on ageing. When Narcissus checks his image in the water, he sees not beauty but mortality. After a lullaby in a dream, "we" have grown old overnight. The singularity of the moment reminds the reader of Hamlet's observation that life is no longer than the time needed to say "one." That "[t]he stars of the past whisper at our back" (line 1) appears to define the past as behind us; but when the present is in our hands, we spend our time quarrelling and counting the falling stars. Yet before long, "the stars of today whisper at our back" (line 16), as if the present has already abandoned us and the immediate future offers a quiet reverie of the past as we sit "vaguely going through the yellowing letters" (line 18). Time rapidly passes us by, regardless of what we do.

In "To Time" and "Temporality Proposition," the opening line establishes the illusion of a monologic discourse. "To Time" begins with a question about what forgetting means; "Temporality Proposition," with a speaker engaged in deep thought. The reader is immediately confronted with a virtual world, as the poem's very first words "effect the break with the reader's actual environment" (Langer, 1953: 214). Lyric brevity requires the omission of circumstantial details of the kind important in the mundane world. The speaker, as well as the reader, is thrown into a philosophical musing about time.

Poets usually talk about time in terms of events that have occurred in history. In fact, only time can tell what time is. But how can that occur, if not through a human agent who has experienced time? What can the human agent tell, if he or she does not phenomenalize the abstract into concrete things and events? In "To Time," Yang creatively confronts these questions with a counter-question: what is forgetting? Oblivion is the opposite of memory, an emptying of memory's contents. Hence, forgetting is necessarily a negation of the past, an idea caught in the image of "an echoless forest." Forgetting can be experienced only when one's efforts to remember are thwarted. Yang's concept of time is opposite to that of the chronology of historical narrative. The human agent plunges into a scene or an event in a single moment, but the instant freezes, without a before and an after. The narrative is broken; remembering is disrupted. In a surrealist turn, time is spatialized in a cluster of disconnected visual images, to show time out of joint in the act of forgetting:

Tell me, what is meant by "forget"
What is meant by "completely forget" – decaying wood covers
A dying universe and the ageing moss
Fruits have ripened, fall onto the obscure earth
When summer changes into autumn, they rot in dull dark shades
When the two seasons' contents and scarlet
In a push to free themselves
Suddenly become dust
When the fragrance of flowers is hidden in the grass, as stars fall
Stalactites droop downwards, to receive the rising stalagmites
And as the footsteps of a stranger
Going through the red painted arch, going through the drizzles

Freeze at a fountain
Are frozen into a hundred statues of nothingness
This is "forget," between you and me
Between the brows has been trodden a deep valley
As an echoless forest
Holds a primitive worry
Tell me, what is meant by "memory"
As you have been lost in the sweetness of death
What is meant by "memory" – as you blow out a lamp
And bury yourself in eternal darkness

In "To Time," the composite, complex experiences of oblivion are preserved in a quick succession of images that consume time without coalescing in a whole. The movements in the poem remain in unresolved tension: the "falling" stalactites and "rising" stalagmites never meet; "drizzles" fall and freeze when the "fountain" shoots upwards, but they do not join to produce an image of linearity or continuity like that of the running river of time.[14] Oblivion does not simply mean a total blankness of mind. It refers to a failure to recall, which leaves the person who suffers it in a trance of seeing and not seeing. The brief noun phrases, sudden contrasts of association, and abrupt jolts of motion all help to convey what forgetting is like – a hazy and impenetrable realm. The impediments to memory lie in the absence of logical links.

Human time is "lived" through experience: encounters with objects, people, and events. Near the end of the poem, the question of memory arises. Memory is private recollection, whose content is gradually built up over time. Light, the concrete reality, is shut out so that past events can be more easily visualized in the dark. Night and darkness conceal one from others or from oneself as well as from the present, thereby allowing things below the level of consciousness to emerge. Yet in the course of time, memory, too, will be shut away from consciousness, and all will go black. What always remains is the helpless but futile search – that is, forgetting. At the end of this one-stanza poem, the discourse about forgetting and memory abruptly breaks off. In retrospect, the question posed is neither open nor rhetorical. It simply reflects the genuine bewilderment of a youth whose file of memory is still rather small. The puzzle can be clarified or answered only by time, not by words.

---

14   For a discussion of tension and contrast in the poem, see Lai Ruihe, "Shi Ye Shan de 'Gei Shijian'" [Deciphering Ye Shan's "To Time"]. *Longzu shikan* [Dragons Poetry Quarterly] 9 (July 1973): 205-6.

The questions raised in "To Time" are later picked up by a middle-aged speaker in "Temporality Proposition."[15] Apparently continuing the dramatic situation presented in the earlier verse, this poem depicts the contemplation of time as taking place in the middle of the night: "By the lamp, on my grey hair I ponder / Wasn't the snow particularly heavy last winter?" "Temporality Proposition" begins with the voice of an individual meditating on the ravages of time. The proposition of the title is unravelled in quotations from poetry and in references to myth and philosophy. In its synchronic voyage through signifiers and cultures widely separated in space and time, it exhibits temporal compression. The allusions to cultures in the East and the West are rendered in a mixed mode of vernacular Chinese and classical Chinese that dates back to the Jin dynasty.

Formally, "Temporality Proposition" falls neatly into rhymed quatrains.[16] The poem begins with the human experience of time as epitomized by grey hair, which is perhaps the most common signifier in the discourse of ageing. This is a universal fate: all men are bound by time, and that knowledge of mortality and mutability forms a bond between them. The musicality of the regular rhyme scheme makes the poem strike the ear as very English, and very Wordsworthian. But whereas Wordsworth stresses the connection of an individual with his past self despite the changes he undergoes through time, Yang disrupts this continuity in the human experience of time. Within-time-ness is manifested by images taken from an indeterminate process, caught in an instant as persons and things move towards extinction. It is precisely this feeling of "not yet but about to" that epitomizes time. Time cannot be contained in a stasis or fixed as a "timeless" point – it is always wavering on the edge between the immediate future and the ultimate end. "Temporality Proposition" concludes with allusion to Goethe's "Wanderer's Night-song" (1780), whose last two lines read: "Wait; soon like these / Thou too shalt rest."[17] It is precisely this present act of waiting, of anticipating some "soon"-to-be-realized future ("shalt"), that encapsulates the philosophical and poetic discourse on time.

The "not yet" is a state of hope and patience; the arrival at the end suggests human oblivion and rest in the enveloping silence of nature. The sublimation and thus the erasure of the speaking subject into a peaceful sleep are ambivalently depicted. The waiting in the instant before falling asleep, before life retreats into death, is a moment of

---

[15] The poem's title is also the title of Yang Mu collection of poems *Shiguang mingti* [Temproality Proposition] (Taipei: Hongfan, 1996), 46-8.

[16] For the poem's English translation and for a more detailed reading, see Chapter 2.

[17] For a translation of the poem, see Johann Wolfgang von Goethe, *Goethe: Selected Verse*, trans. David Luke (London: Penguin, 1986), 50.

unfathomable mystery. This moment is temporality. Viewed in this light, "Temporality Proposition" seems to echo Heidegger's conception of time and being. Time, in Heideggerian terms, is "a time of need because it lies under a double negation, the notion of no-more of the gods that have fled and the not-yet of the god that is coming" (Blackham, 1994: 103). In the philosopher's post-theological formulation, "Being/ *Dasein* is seen to be an existence already found in the world in the condition of becoming and therefore facing an open future with the power to be, and bound up with other beings in the world" (Blackham, 1994: 95). To Heidegger, human existence is anticipatory; concerns about the power to be in the world of becoming characterize the mode of existence. To Yang Mu, the experiential condition needs to be addressed in their immediacy. A man's concern for his personal existence is expressed by contemplating what he was, is, and will be in a "precarious" world in which he is found and to which he is bound – a world of natural, mythic, and literary realities.

The individual voice that ponders time in "Temporality Proposition" invokes many voices of wisdom to participate in the poem's pseudo-discussion. In this way, Yang Mu creates a traffic of discursive temporalities in multiple cultural trajectories. Time is represented in spatial terms to emphasize temporality as a process of becoming. Yang Mu's treatment of time here recalls David Harvey's succinct description of the spatialization of time in his discussion of Karsten Harries:

> The "language of beauty" is "the language of a timeless reality." To create a beautiful object "is to line time and eternity" in such a way as to redeem us from time's tyranny. The urge to "devaluate time" reappears as the artist's will to redeem through the creation of a work "strong enough to still time."
> ... The aim of spatial constructs is "not to illuminate temporal reality so that [we] might feel more at home in it, but to be relieved of it: to abolish time within time, if only for a time." Harries here echoes those famous modernist formulations of Baudelaire, "one can only forget time by making use of it," and T. S. Eliot, "only through time, time is conquered."[18]

On the whole, the philosophical discourse in "Temporality Proposition" is formally contained in a regular temporal structure composed of quatrains and rhymes. Yet despite the sense of equilibrium and fulfilment in this poetic form, the poem's ending is tentative and incomplete. Temporality means this continuous struggle to attain balance when sailing through life before the ultimate destination is reached. The "not yet but about to" also captures the excitement and tension in the human experience of time.

---

[18]   David Harvey, *The Condition of Postmodernity: An Enquiry into the Origins of Cultural Change* (Cambridge: Blackwell, 1997, c. 1990), 206.

Within time, humans continuously seek after Being in a world of Becoming. Expressed in literary terms, the self-conscious weaving of poetic form and the repetition of what is already there in world literature are structured in two common modes of representation: linearity and circularity, or mutability and repeatability. At the same time, Yang Mu emphasizes a metanarrative of becoming. "Temporality Proposition" ends in what Frank Kermode calls an "aevum" – something neither historical nor eternal, but "a third order of duration" between the flow of time and the timeless.[19] At the "no more" of time and the "not-yet" of its negation is silence, the culmination of the temporality discourse. Keats offers a similar insight in his "Ode on a Grecian Urn" (1820):

> Keats' notion of silence is combined with his notion of time. ... Preserved and sanctified by time, it keeps its original freshness and appeal. ... The paradox of the Urn, as of all true works of art, is that it transcends time by making a single moment last for ever and so become timeless. ... In the act of creation, when all faculties are harmoniously at work together, time does not so much stand still as vanish.[20]

The longing is yet unfulfilled. The word "silence," which suggests sound by its negation, is as empty as "oblivion" in "To Time." In silence and stillness, the process is suspended in a moment of anonymity and timelessness: time vanishes, and no more spatio-temporal measurements are possible.

By retrieving the artistic experiences of time from the reservoir of literary treasures in human history, Yang Mu spells out doubts and anxieties about temporality in the form of a trip, whether taken in the narrator's consciousness or on the river of time. In "Daffodils" as in "Temporality Proposition," the poet acknowledges a Cartesian notion of self in time: "the pastness of experience and the onwardness of time" is understood with a consciousness of one's existence in the presence of both the past and the present (Salvesen, 1965: 11). Even though the tight interweaving of images in "To Time" may allay fears of oblivion, the weave threatens to unravel, as the temporality proposition can be broken down into the always-already seen signifiers underscored by a metapoetic commentary. The repetition of images and the cross-cultural allusions give shape to a form of life encompassing within-time-ness, stretching along of life, and being towards death, at once particular and universal. The imaginary voyage represents both a personal quest and a

---

[19]   The notion of "aevum" is borrowed from Kermode's discussion in "World Without End or Beginning." See Frank Kermode, *The Sense of an Ending: Studies in the Theory of Fiction* (London: Oxford University Press, 1967), 70.

[20]   See Maurice Bowra, *The Romantic Imagination* (Oxford: Oxford University Press, 1950), 143.

collective human destiny. This persistent exploration of a route in life
for poets helps build up a mythic dimension in Yang Mu's poetry.

Placing Time

Poets often convey the movement of time with spatial metaphors,
and thus many poets in effect locate time in a place. Although Yang Mu
prefers to write abstractly, the names of exact locales where he confronted new experiences sometimes find their way into his poems. For
instance, his first trips across the United States in the mid-1960s were
recorded in the titles of some poems. After Yang had settled down at the
University of Iowa's Master of Fine Arts program in Iowa City, he made
several visits to other American cities. Between 1964 and 1966, he used
place-names for such poems as "Lakeshore Drive" and "The Winter of
Clinton Avenue" (both referring to Chicago), and "West of Reno City."
In "The Right Bank of the Iowa River," the title is followed with even
more information: "The Writers' Studio is on the left bank. On the right
are the Arts Museum and University Theatre. 'Impressionists and Their
Roots' is currently exhibited in the Arts Museum." Similarly, in "The
Impression of Fairfield" he reports that "he went to Fairfield on the day
before 25 November 1964, Thanksgiving Day. He stayed in Dr. Charles
O'Hare's home for a couple of days and returned to Iowa in the afternoon of the 29th." Concretizing time by supplying a date, an event, and a
place, he explicitly records the poetic situation. The period of his graduate studies will be vividly remembered with such details as the Arts
Museum housing Impressionist paintings, and his exotic experience of
an American Thanksgiving, recalled with affectionate gratitude. This
journalistic recounting of places certainly provides information for a
biographical reading of a particular period in Yang Mu's life but contributes little to an understanding of his spatial treatment of time. This
section will focus on the ways in which Yang Mu concretizes time by
mapping his time-worlds in geographical locations and mythical sites; in
so doing, the poet creates a dialectical and dialogic relation between
time and space.

In his teens, Yang Mu was already beginning to explore what would
become a dominant symbol and theme in his poetry: the motif of travel,
interconnecting the different time-worlds in his life as he attempted to
pin down time in space. The first poem in his *Collected Poems* is "Return" (1956), a mystification of time that depicts an exhausted traveller's
homecoming: "I return from the mist" (lines 2, 9). The speaker is tired
of his adventures and is taciturn about the past. Many of Yang's early
poems about time are imaginatively retrospective, showing the teenage
poet's consciousness of ageing, mortality, and human finitude. The
young poet's description of the future by means of a fictive past experi-

ence is itself anticipatory or prefigurative.[21] Over a writing career that has lasted more than half a century, Yang Mu has unveiled his early mystification of time by presenting everyday experiences in lived time; and his mature contemplation of time compels him to work towards a myth that views life as a quest to defy temporality by labour.

Labour in Yang Mu's poems often takes the form of a journey. Instead of "returning" and staying in his home-town, the speaker is constantly on the move, taking a train ride, a boat trip, or a trans-Pacific ocean voyage. The early poems give a strong sense of their locale: Hualian, a town on the east coast of Taiwan. Having grown up at the seaside, the poet has cultivated his poetic imagination on the tides, the moon, the stars, and the Milky Way. Like the Greek poets who were fascinated by unknown seas, the teenage poet was bored by the bounds of the land and could not wait to set sail and explore. In "The Harbour Is Bored" (1957), his persona displaces his boredom onto the harbour – "But I believe we are about to lift the anchor" – and worries that "This dockyard and the dam are formidable obstacles." The young traveller determines his compass location and positions himself in the east and the south. The time-worlds are also configured by stars and rivers: consider "Will the traveller in a hurry follow the star-lit map?" ("Footprints," 1958) and "He cannot grasp such a map without S or N" ("The Wind Passes," 1958). "Pursuing the unknown on the star atlas / I take leave of this sunny coast" concludes a long poem titled "The Coast of Dan Shui" (1961).

The frequent returns and departures of the speaker make him as busy as the questing hero of mythology. Perhaps time requires an unyielding search in different time-worlds before a hero (like one seeking Heidegger's "being") discovers any ultimate meaning: "Being is new, and yet, since it must be sought after and can never be fully or finally possessed, it is far off" (Blackham, 1994: 106). The discovery is forever put off, making the adventure in Yang Mu's poetry an endless one.

Road Map – *"murmur to the quiet earth: I'm running"*

Hualian is the Elysium to which the poet frequently returns. He gives the title of his birthplace to two unusual biographical poems, each dedicated to a woman he loved, "Take You Home, Back to Hualian" (1975) and "Hualian" (1978). More often than not, the home-town is evoked as a longed-for place. Whereas "Daffodils" shows the journey as a poetic glide down the river and thus gives some hazy, dreamlike impressions

---

[21] Paul de Man, "Time and History in Wordsworth," *Romanticism and Contemporary Criticism*. eds. E. S. Burt *et al.* (Baltimore: Johns Hopkins University Press, 1993), 82.

of time, the departures from and returns to Hualian all help to concretize the local landscape and the scenery seen from both sides of a train.

That conquests are imaginary and adventure induces weariness in Yang's early poems is indicative of an anticipatory nostalgia that is both retrospective and proleptic. In his mature poems, the focus of nostalgic longing is the local landscape, immune to the ravages of time. "Looking down at – Li Wu Stream 1983" (1984) and "Looking up to – Mount Papaya 1995" (1995) can be read as companion works eulogizing the poet's birthplace, Hualian. The quotations from a Romantic poet and a historian that preface the two poems respectively are particularly striking. The poetic vision of life in "Looking down at – Li Wu Stream 1983" is underscored by Wordsworth's epiphany in "Lines Composed a Few Miles above Tintern Abbey" (1798):

> For I have learned
> To look on nature, not as in the hour
> Of thoughtless youth; but hearing oftentimes
> The still, sad music of humanity,
> Nor harsh nor grating, though of ample power
> To chasten and subdue.   (lines 88-93)

On the other hand, a sense of sublimity in "Looking up to – Mount Papaya 1995" is explicated by a historian's wisdom regarding human time: "But my pride was soon humbled, and a sober melancholy was spread over my mind by the idea that... whatsoever might be the future fate of my history, the life of the historian must be short and precarious – Edward Gibbon." The poet uses these quotations to evoke in the reader the desired mental state for grasping the poems' philosophical contemplation of time.

Facing the quiet valley and the mountain, the speaker reflects on the brevity of human life when compared to the immensity of nature. Necessarily earth-bound, the stream looks up at the musing speaker in the earlier poem, while the mountain and the man meet face to face in the later one. The reciprocity in such gazing at nature – particularly a communion between man and mountain – is characteristic of the Chinese lyric tradition. They are never tired of the other. Mount Papaya always wears a "youthful look," indifferent to the poet's presence and absence, though those movements punctuate his life. The mountain is invincible, unaffected by the wars in modern Chinese history and unshaken by the earthquakes that have rocked the region from time to time. At a moment bound to cyclical time, the poet's mind is lifted up by the mountain's sublime stillness:

> ... I hear the rippling echoes, when I rest on the memories steeped in
> Enormous peace and enormous regret, looking up to
> Eternity. The immense quietude in blue gradually grows

Till it fully fills our human world
Its look, which I've tried to imitate over the years, never
Alters. The clear bright eyes now turn my way
In due respect, I rise and salute, speechless, alone
Transient as the willow in the wind   (lines 40-8)

The contact with nature is a confrontation with temporality. Attributing self-knowledge to the influence of nature is also reminiscent of Wordsworth's contemplation at Tintern Abbey. Human frailty and insignificance are embraced in quiet recognition.

"Composed at the Crack of Dawn" (2001) depicts a train ride from Hualian to Taipei and back in two stanzas. Those who have taken the trip would recognize in the poem the landscape on the east coast of Taiwan and the numerous tunnels through the hilly side of the island. The poet spatializes the past and the present by the routes of return and departure in two twelve-line stanzas. The speaker is described as a frequent passenger commuting between home and the outside world. "A train speeds across the much travelled vale" is the refrain that marks these two-way journeys. When the traveller leaves home in the morning, his mind is filled with his "long-lost motives" revived in the present, "memories" of the past, and "prophecies" about the future, while "[o]n the left, the mountains quietly fly backwards in the foliage-green air" (line 6). Soon thereafter, in the second stanza, the speaker returns home and meditates on the sequence of lived time:

A train speeds across the much travelled vale
The wheels heavily clank, penetrating my drowsy defence
Shaking the fortified mind – afterwards the whistle follows
Bellowing before the tunnel, afterwards the darkness slides at once
Into a waking dream.   (lines 13-7)

The stanza ends with a symmetrical description of the mountains: "On the right, the mountains retreats in layers like ant-hills / Unconsciously retrieving the originary starting point / When a train speeds away from the once much travelled vale" (lines 22-4).

A second party beside the speaker is mentioned in each trip. In the first stanza, the train speeds past a "God of the Soil" housed in a public shrine. This "earthly" god sits there permanently, "calculating how myriad destinies / Are to occur in stormy rain / In the moonlight, and on windy days" (lines 9-12). The deity is not on the train; he is outside of time, watching the human drama. In the second, a sparrow perches on a bench in a vacant train compartment. By mistake, the bird had flown into the compartment when the train was gathering steam for its departure. "The sparrow hops day and night; suddenly it grows old /... / On its wings, time glitters, withers" (lines 18, 20). For every human being, life is a journey moving away from birth towards death. In the course of time, all past motives, memories, and prophecies sink into the unconscious; the departure from birth is paradoxically a return to the mysterious originary state before existence. On the road, the traveller murmurs to the stream, the mountains, and to the rail route that he has been "running" from place to place, making much of his earthly experiences to become what he now is.

The Waterside Myth – "Tell the running water: I exist"

The building blocks of what this section is calling the waterside myth began being put in place when Yang Mu started writing poetry. His birthplace, Hualian, was its direct cause. From his classroom window, the young poet watched waves rolling in fine weather, or crashing in rough seas; he saw the tides wash away the sand, sea-foam carpet the beach, and water gurgle down a stream or swirl violently about the shores – and all these audio-visual images of water find their places in his poetry. His surroundings also offered other source materials for his productive imagination. From the daily chores of fishermen in all kinds of weather, he had different fish for meals and poetry. The mackerel was often personified as his addressee: for example, "Mackerel, you are my mackerel" ("Vacation on a Mountain," 1959) and "You are my mackerel in spring" ("That Era," 1960). In some poems, salmon, a species of fish popularly believed to return to where it was born to spawn, is introduced as an agent that transverses the sea in search of its origin.

In this discussion, the term "waterside myth" obviously refers to the title poem of the young poet's first book of poetry, *By the Waterside* (1960). But the mythologization of the waterside is initiated by the poet himself in "Warm Days" (1963): "On warm days, come with me, let's go boating" – "come with me, on warm days, at the waterside is the woods, beyond the woods is the mountain / In the mountain lies a bridge waiting for travellers" (lines 7, 20-1). In this light-hearted love song written in the local dialect, the long-awaited romance does materialize, and the happy world of young love is captured in "a legend of the mountain, the waterside myth" (line 6). Fifteen years later, in a poem written after the failure of his first marriage, the poet has his old self "buried at the waterside" ("The Death of 1977," 1978; line 36). Yet Yang Mu's fascination with the sea has never left him. In "Seven Stars Coast" (1996) there returns "[t]he sound of the waves [that] has drowned / the colours of time" (lines 1-2). And this sound recalls to the speaker and the reader the distant thought of "how the pollen happened to fly across the river to the other shore / the territory of quails and fireflies, and of a boy" (lines 12-3) – the boy who spent four afternoons waiting by the waterside in 1958.

Throughout his fifty years of writing, Yang Mu has retained an elemental emphasis on water that has further nourished the waterside myth. In analyzing myth, Ricoeur draws on poetry for a comparison and finds that "Poetry and myth are not just nostalgia for some unforgotten world. They constitute a disclosure of unprecedented worlds, an opening on to other *possible* worlds which transcend the established limits of our *actual* world."[22] At the waterside lies one such possible time-world for Yang Mu. Unlike the landscape of Hualian that can be named and mapped, the sea is a fluid world. Since rivers are a cradle of human civilization and a universal metaphor for time, the young poet employs running water to symbolize a linear progression of time with no return. The gurgling water measures the time of a summer afternoon in "By the Waterside" and a legendary trip leading down-river to the seven seas in "Daffodils." At times, the speaker is on a river bank watching the flow of time at his feet; at other times, he is in a boat with other humans on his life journey.

When the physical world is expanded to embrace the ocean surrounding the island, Yang's favourite metaphor is the tides. In "The Coast of Dan Shui" (1961) a refrain appears – "when the tide flows" (lines 1, 66, 71) – that has been a signature of Yang Mu's water imagery ever since. For example, in "On a Cliff" (1963) "[A]llow yourself some nostalgic feelings, when the tide flows" expresses the youth's anticipatory nostalgia; in "Coming Back from the Beach" (1978), the speaker is lost in thought about the political situation at home and hears the sound of a bugle that "drowns the restless tides" (line 14), a signal of the social turmoil in Taiwan. In "Seven Turns of the Coast" (1980), the opening line, "At the coast where the *Kuroshiro* current surges," is repeated regularly after every seven lines (lines 9, 17, 25, 33, 41, 49). The rhythmic movement of the current, like a repeated note in a song, marks the family as an anchor for the poet's drifting life. In some more recent poems, tides are used as a vehicle for deep emotions and thoughts: consider, for example, "I lean over to watch the tides ebb and flow / and let my thoughts be stranded there" ("Leaving Clear Water Bay on 10 December," 1993; lines 1-2) and "Morning and evening tides of the blood" ("The Previous Life," 1996; line 1).

The scope of the waterside myth has grown with the poet's travels in the actual world. Though the early poems composed at the coastal town of Hualian depict only a one-sided view of the ocean from Taiwan, Yang Mu's residence in the United States supplies the speaker a transcontinental perspective. "Manuscript in a Bottle" (1974), his famous poem about home, has a dual view that demonstrates his new perspective, from across the Pacific Ocean:

---

[22] Paul Ricoeur, "Myth as the Bearer of Possible Worlds," in *A Ricoeur Reader*, 487.

This time the sun sets in the west
Through the cypress before my eyes. The tide
This shore. But I know every wave
It all began at Hualian. That time
I asked in surprise, in that remote place
Is there a shore?
Now, that shore, this shore, there is only
The drifting starlight

Now there is still only a ray of starlight
Shining on my wearisome sadness
I ask the turbulent waves
"Do you miss the beach of Hualian?"
I don't know, if a wave rages
Towards the beach on Hualian – after being backwashed
Does it have to pass ten summers before arriving here?
It must be a moment's determination to be involved
To be fixed in the second of turning over, suddenly
The same wave comes
Quietly sploshing onto this deserted shore
....
I don't know, when a wave
Surges onto a deserted shore, this time
I must decide: what's the best thing to do?
Maybe, I'd better become a wave too
Suddenly turn over, in a moment's backwash
Be involved in the quiet sea
Sploshing onto Hualian
The beach

But when I step into the sea
The light mass does not vanish, the water level rises
A strip of the beach on that shore gets wet
When I walk on, or even get submerged into
This deserted shore, seven feet to the west
I don't know, in June, Hualian, oh, Hualian
Is there a rumour of tsunami again?

The intimate connection between the shores at both ends vividly captures the speaker's homesickness. Though the suggestion that his immersion into the ocean might cause a tsunami at the Hualian coast is clearly hyperbole, the apostrophic call implies a move to erase time and distance in his yearnings for home.

In real life, the poet eventually settled down in his American home. His two places, Hualian and Seattle, actually refer to two different historical realities. In "The International Dateline Concerto" (1980), the poet writes: "We've met at the most fanatical whirlpool. Whirlpool / Is

on the other side of the International Dateline; on this side is our kingdom" (lines 148-9). In fact, the poet and his second wife initially met in
1978, shortly before the United States recognized the People's Republic
of China and withdrew official recognition from the Republic of China
in Taiwan. In Zeng Zhenzhen's opinion, "Yang Mu composed 'Returning from the Beach' [1978] to express his anguished concern for the
peace of Taiwan Strait."[23] Despite having secured a stable home for his
family in the United States, the poet feels caught between two homes; he
continues to project his longing for the opposite shore and lets the ships
carry his homesickness across the ocean.

> At the coast where the *Kuroshiro* current surges
> Behind the thick fog is the garden for giant whales
> Where ships sail past regularly
> They sail past, heading for Taiwan, our home.
> ....
> At the coast where the *Kuroshiro* current surges
> A big ocean liner is actually there, proudly lifting its anchor
> It lifts its anchor, heading for Taiwan, our home
> ("Seven Turns of the Coast," lines 25-8, 33-5)

The tie between an expatriate and his birthplace is like a hidden umbili-
cal cord that consistently tugs at him and reminds him of the way back
to his origin. In many poems, this native instinct of home-coming is
animated by fish imagery. Though the mackerel is a long-established
image of a seafarer in Yang Mu's poetry, only the salmon is used as a
symbol for the traveller on the mythical home-bound voyage.

In this poetry, a return to the past or the origin closes a circle by repeating some early metaphors. Thirty years after his return from the mist
("Return," 1956), Yang Mu wrote in "Coming Back from the Sea"
(1987): "Those actually resemble the fancies of a previous life / when I
happened to pass the surging spring tides of a foreign territory" (lines 1-
2). Having sailed in different time-worlds, the mature traveller has come
to the knowledge that much of human time is spent hoping and waiting.
This stretching-along of life is punctuated by appointments real or imagined. Rather than displaying youthful restlessness, as in "By the Waterside," the speaker in "A Definite Sea" (1992) has a sense of mission:

> But I have already known everything about past and future, life and death –
> the mind
> Consolidates its shape against the huge fabulous backdrop
> I look around and see, soft breezes and tiny waves stealth virtually
> In them must lie a certain ineffable revelation
> ....

---

[23] Zeng Zhenzhen, "Sound of Water Mountains: Sea Imagery in Yang Mu's Poetry and
Prose." In manuscript, 37-8.

Even in a water-world of the strangest kind, with or without a sound
The spirits who have got lost for long are counting down time as usual
Awaiting my promised, impassionate arrival –
Please let me help them one by one, in the post-traumatic flare
Of the twilight! I will lead them out of game:
The habitual gossips, jealousy, and complaints   (lines 3-6, 11-6)

Instead of avoiding trouble-ridden interpersonal relationships, the speaker here finds himself experienced enough not only to handle their complexities but also to help disentangle them for good.

In later poems, the mature speaker often whiles away his hours by waiting and keeping watch patiently. "Village Sonnets" (1990) begins with a gaze towards something in doubt – "what is happening on the opposite shore" – a typical gesture in Yang Mu's poetry since the late 1980s. Separated by an ocean or a lake, the two persons on opposite shores communicate by the tides, the waves or the currents, or the wind, a go-between that brings them together in real time, though marked by different hours of the day on either shore. As in some early poems, mist is used to represent ineffable emotions. Yang Mu contributed "Mist and My Other Self" to the love-poem series "Great Masters' Love Poems in Manuscript" published by *United Daily* (22 July 2003); in it, the silhouette of a lady positioned in green foliage is faintly sketched on a mirror in the spring moonlight. The gaze in the dark mist is mystifying. Yang's poems frequently employ other forms of water, including ripples, rain, and snow, and tears and blood constantly remind the reader of the internal wounds of the speaker and the addressee. "The heart is bleeding" in "Amazement" (1993) and "Wild Ginger Flower" (1997), while tears are flooding the eyes or running down the cheek of the addressee in "The Previous Life" and "Typhoon Signal No. 3" (1997).

The waterside world also has a mythic dimension, inhabited by imaginary figures in such poems as "Geometry: River Goddess" (1974) and "The Water Nymph" (1999). Famous river goddesses in classical Chinese poetry include the elusive fairies sought after in Qu Yuan's "Nine Songs" and "The Goddess of the River Luo" in Cao Zhi's works. Allegorically, the quest for the river goddesses in Qu Yuan's "The Goddess of the River Xiang" and "The Lady of the River Xiang" represents the poet's attempt to seek the favour of the Prince of Chu, who, on the bad advice of his ministers, had dismissed the poet and sent him into exile. In Cao Zhi's work, the Goddess Luo is the heroine in a tragic romance. In "Geometry: River Goddess," Yang Mu's re-creation of the figure alludes to these classical archetypes.

> She who arrives across the water
> Is a goddess. The distinct oars carry the boat along
> Almost without a sound,
> A chaste, white boat emerging
> Between the pavilion and the willows.
>
> A goddess is coming, like the chimes of
> A bell floating across the water
> Only to sink in an instant –
> Moonlight on her shoulder,
> Frost on the prow and the stern. (lines 1-10)

In her classical attire and manner, the goddess is unreachable. Fashioned from close allusions to Qu Yuan's poems, the goddesses are metaphors for personal ideals: "She is gliding, and yet she does not seem to come / Any closer, but afar lingering / There. For whom does she tarry on the islet in the middle of the water?" Yang adds, "I hear the fair lady beckoning me. / We shall fly away together / And build a home in the midst of the water" (lines 15-7, 43-5).[24] He sees this quest to gain the other as a quest to realize the self. For the poet-patriot Qu Yuan, serving the Prince and his country was the only vision of a meaningful life; but the search in the river and his death by the water seem to initiate a transcendental approach to existence. Besides, the river goddesses are figures of undisputed beauty:

> A goddess, like a startled swan on the wing,
> Gracefully rises the phoenix, her beauty surpassing
> Chrysanthemums in autumn and pine trees in spring.[25] (lines 26-8)

Like the addressee compared to a "summer's day" by Shakespeare in Sonnet 18, the river goddess transcends time and is forever young in the poems by Cao Zhi and Yang Mu.

The same qualities apply to the poet's own creation in "The Water Nymph." Like Aphrodite, the water nymph in Yang Mu's myth is also "foam-born":

> If the present is absolutely born of the past:
> The tides are almost noiseless, taking turn to
> Rise and fall. I saw a person about to
> Turn and dance, in order to enter the present

---

[24] These lines in the Chinese original by Yang Mu incorporated quotations from Qu Yuan's poems, "The Goddess of the River Xiang," and "The Lady of the River Xiang" respectively. Much of the translation of "Geometry: River Goddess" is borrowed from Yang Mu's.

[25] From Cao Zhi's poem, "The Goddess of the River Luo." See also Lawrence R. Smith and Michelle Yeh's translation in *No Trace of the Gardener: Poems of Yang Mu*, 79-80.

In the future...

....
... O the water nymph
I saw the back wash of silvery waves let layers of
Glittering lights sink into the fine sand, and softly
Sing, like our humble life
Forever retreating   (lines 7-11)

The rendition of time here echoes T. S. Eliot's temporal cycle in "Burnt Norton" (1935): "Time present and time past / Are both perhaps present in time future / And time future contained in time past." Yang Mu, however, downplays Eliotian intellectualism by inserting the illusory water nymph in a fairy-tale setting. A mythical figure, the water nymph herself embodies the past, present, and future because, as the concluding line points out, she is capable of self-renewal by becoming "the daughter of herself."

The circularity of time in water imagery appears in many other poems by Yang Mu. "An Elegy of One Hundred and Twenty Lines" (1977) presents the past, present, and future being spun together in a whirlpool "at the speed of time / as it whirls: the day before / today the day after" (lines 19-21). Some of his more recent poems such as "Pindar's Odes – 472 B.C." (2000) and "Reading Einstein on the Fifth Day of the Fifth Month," portray a figure that emerges from and vanishes into a whirlpool. People and events in the actual world are fleeting and easily washed away. The transient nature of mundane reality is further elaborated in the metaphor of a typhoon, the whirling of air currents that gather and disperse physical materials in no time.

In addition to fairies and female images, some of his recent poems contain phantasmal figures from "the previous life" that further reinforce a mythic dimension. The past returns to the present in the second sonnet of "Village Sonnets" (1990): "Here / In a shower I saw the apparel / like a copy of that in the previous life" (lines 1-2). The Chinese prefix "previous" or "front" (*qian*), used in the compounds "previous life" (*qiansheng*), "previous body" (*qianshen*), and "previous events" (*qianshi*), actually refers to the self or to incidents in the past. Though the phrase sounds metaphysical, "the previous life" in Yang Mu's poems may refer to a recollection of people and events in the actual past that will not go away, or a continuation of the lyrical self's subjectivity through time. Yang's romantic heritage is obvious as he quotes from Coleridge in the afterword of his latest collection of poems, *A Scale Insect* (2006):

Oft o'er my brain does that strange fancy roll
Which makes the present (while the flash doth last)
Seem a mere semblance of some unknown past,
Mixed with such feelings, as perplex the soul
Self-questioned in her sleep; and some have said
We lived, ere yet this robe of flesh we wore.[26]

By evoking the previous life, the poet enhances the sense of time's continuous cycles. For example, the poem "The Previous Life" portrays a female figure keeping a vow that transcends mortal time; while "Title Lost" (2005) presents a similar figure equally committed to her cause, the lyric voice admits that he misses the chance of completing a story in this life but denies the possibility of doing so in the next. It is what returns from the past that makes sense of the present, and there is a hint at a future into which the lyrical self can venture. This ever-ongoing theme of story making renders the world of the waterside myth atemporal. Set against what is out of time, such as immortal fairies or the resurrected previous life, the insistence of the speaker's witness that he saw them born of the running water is in a uniquely human way to declare "I exist."

Nonetheless, many of the worlds in the waterside myth are built upon the waterscape in the actual worlds where Yang Mu has stayed, including the river banks and the coastal towns of Hualian in east Taiwan and Dan Shui in Taipei; the beach of a Canadian island near Vancouver; West Point, in upstate New York; the reef and the islands at Clear Water Bay in Hong Kong; and the lake near his home in Seattle. To his productive imagination of time-worlds he adds his everyday experiences in his trans-Pacific and cross straits travels. Typically in his recent works, the poet's interplay of mobility and stasis on land or in the sea, in a dialectics of progression and repetition, lends itself to an abstract theorization of time.[27]

Theorizing Time

A professor at a North American university and a Romantic poet who has much faith in beauty and truth, Yang Mu inevitably feels uneasy about the contemporary deconstruction of the Romantics' tenets.

---

[26] "Sonnet: Composed on a Journey Homeward" (1797), as quoted in Yang Mu, *Jiekechong* [A Scale Insect] (Taipei: Hongfan, 2006), 153-4.

[27] The titles of Yang Mu's literary autobiography also reflect the author's special treatment of time discussed in this section. The memoirs were published in a series of prose work: *Shanfeng haiyu* [Storms over Hills and Ocean] (1987), *Fangxiang guiling* [Direction Back to Zero] (1991), and *Xiwo wangyi* [Then as I Set Off] (1997), now collected in *Qi Lai qianshu* [The Former Book of Mount Qi Lai] (Taipei: Hongfan, 2003).

Though Ricoeur affirms language's "capacity to open up new worlds," contemporary theories problematize this power of language. The lessons Yang Mu learnt from the literary debates in Taiwan in the 1970s have made him keep an arm's length from battles over discourse. Pondering concepts of knowledge, love, and beauty, the poet says in "A Brief Enlightenment" (1978):

> If we
> Observe Time in the running water
> What we observe may not be
> Time, but the mindless
> Running water   (lines 29-33)

If meditation on Time is inevitably solipsistic, how do humans differentiate between "systems and essence," phenomena and beauty? (lines 22-3). Yang Mu's answer is uncompromising:

> Rather than degenerating into mere phenomena, Beauty
> Had better stay forever
> In the abstract consciousness
> Of the universe   (lines 25-8)

Instead of further theorizing time, the poet usually lets his own literary experiments in poetry serve as a statement of purpose. "A Poem on Poetry" (1995) is an interesting exception. The poet stages in the speaker's interior monologue a debate between systems and essence:

> And then Time restores from abstraction
> Its concrete signifiers; from far and near, they fall into a form
> And disperse. Perhaps, once I deliberate a discourse
> I slip and the personality splits
>
> "Indeed, it is because on a noonday
> Of yore, you saw trees indulge in their
> Foliage, birds made no sound, not
> A shred of cloud in the air, stranded in deep thoughts
> Philosophically close to a theological realm, the cosmos
> Abruptly stopped its operation for your arbitrariness"
>
> On a graph paper, Time freezes
> Initially (but let free conceptual space
> Unfold until it opens infinity to infinity), I
> Wrestle with a moment by repeated numerical measurements
>
> "Quantity? What deserves your attention is in fact
> what you have learnt from experience
> Poetic truth: how the life of mortals
> Can be expressed in appropriate images and meter
> Surely, a fly has a life in infinity, relative it is
> Just as you try to hold eternity in an hour"

I am tired of evidential research, examples
And metaphors, rhetorical devices for expressing intent
Skills (and creeds), lest before writing
Is done, the moon has extinguished the sun

"A quest, a search, to the edges of the earth
of the marine kingdom, and the outer space, to find a place for sounds
the constantly changing signification for the sensitive mind
And for the inscape, what is in and out
In a complementary union – eternity
Is the divine artwork you have carved from Time"

Worse still, language never fully captures the meaning
Comparison and symbol at times may seem
Vivid, I regret my lack of practice
Sometimes, words are but a barrier, a sin

"Galileo stores the stars he collected
in his slim cylindrical lens, yet
he knows, the size and distance are inevitably
reduced, relative to the immense cosmic space
Your poem itself is but a discovery of specific
Details, a daring mind applying some reading strategies..."

Bold misreading is meant to subvert
the high-flown writing. The malicious wind
Failing to find its way back to the originary tapestry, once and for all
Put the web exquisitely wrought to deconstruction, and annihilation

"Poetry itself discovers more than specific details
Wise reading strategies directed by a daring mind
allow your encounters and thoughts to expand
To dramatize, to extend with time to eternity
To open infinity; at last you will be amazed that
Only poetic truth is the truth that orders Time"

The personality split allows a dialogical exchange of views between Romantic faith and post-modern deconstructive strategies. A well-reasoned debate, whose argument proceeds by turns, exhibits the dialectical argumentation of the intellect. In the quatrains, the scholarly side of the speaker initiates an academic investigation in the most popular theoretical jargon, as time is examined through various concepts from semiotics, formalism, and deconstruction. In addition, a scientific methodology is applied to quantify time by mathematical measurement and to locate it in graphic space. Research based on philological and other evidence is subject to interrogation by sceptics on language. Furthermore, Romantic expressive intentionality and modernist organic unity are both rocked by deconstructive reading. Well-read in critical theories, the scholar finds that in the contemporary scene, a discourse of time is full of fissures and uncertainties, if not entirely impossible.

Against the declarative statement in a scholar's voice, the poetic side of the speaker counter-argues in the six-line stanzas using different figures of speech. Refusing to be fixed by clock-time, "noonday" manifests itself in nature's inertia. Owing to the heat and strong sunlight, the living world comes to a stand-still in a nap. A universal poetic juxtaposition of the ephemeral and the eternal is encapsulated in succinct allusions to two representative cultural figures, William Blake and Zhuangzi (c. 369-c. 286 B.C.). To English Romantic poets and Chinese Daoist philosophers, the significance of time in one's life cannot be quantified in hours or years. Time is relative: a life of less than a day for a summer fly, or of almost a century for a human, is but a moment in the face of infinity. Yet one can grasp the bliss of eternity in an hour. Yang Mu proposes a poetic project for capturing time with signifiers of different worlds – on land, in the sea, or in outer space. He bridges the conventional gap between scientific and poetic approaches to explore the mystery of time by turning Galileo's astronomical research into a literary process. A productive imagination helps Galileo connect the stellar images and thereby reveal the true picture of the cosmos. With such a daring scientific mind, a poet can use a creative reading of specific details to discover and conceptualize the poetic truth of time.

Even though the scholarly and poetic statements are made in turn in the debate, there is no real parity between the two stances. In this philosophical negotiation, the literary approach gains the upper hand and concludes the controversy in a poet's voice: "Only poetic truth is the truth that orders Time."[28] Men live in time under the shadows of temporal constraints, but poetry lives outside of time. In a metatemporal realm, poetry not only transcends but also orders time.

Yang Mu's tendency to let poetry triumph over human time may not appear very innovative, when his work is placed among that of the European Romantic poets. Yet in an age of post-Romantic theories and post-structuralist discourse, his unyielding faith in poetry is unrivalled. The poet knows well that he is writing in a dramatically different world, a world in which time is efficiently and rationally organized to facilitate global communication. The entire globe is divided into time zones, which impose a universal standard on public time. International travels shorten the vast gaps in space, and virtual meetings between people as they are living in different hours or even different dates is a normal part

---

[28]   Yang Mu's emphasis on poetic truth can be seen in his admiration for the Keatsian notion of "Beauty and Truth," and Goethe's autobiography, *Poetry and Truth*. For further discussion, see Chapter 5.

of contemporary metropolitan life. In homogeneous time, people thousands of miles apart learn simultaneously, through the World Wide Web, about an event in one corner of the world. This simultaneity dissolves the singular, unitary concept of linear time and undercuts a sense of chronological sequence. For example, in "The International Dateline Concerto," the poet plays with the eleven-hour difference that separates Seattle and Taiwan. Being able to lift themselves off the ground, modern men can be temporarily liberated from the earth's revolution. Such liberation suggests the possibility of being able to order time by gaining distance from it. From this intellectually detached position, Yang Mu reviews different discursive approaches to temporality and challenges the conceptual models of time.

The sun, the primordial indicator of time, has recently become the locus of Yang Mu's poetic-philosophical discourse of temporality. In most cultures, the natural measures of time come from the sun, as concretized in a sundial. The sun (日) is a character that also serves as a radical in other Chinese characters, functioning like a mathematical constant –for example, in the Chinese temporal indicator of "now"(時).[29] From the sun comes "light" (*guang*), a component built into such Chinese words for time as "running light" (*liuguang*), "day and night"/"bright and dim" (*guangyin*), and "time" (*shiguang*). The cyclical alternation of light and darkness dictates how humans conceive of and visualize time. The strength of sunlight and the sun's location and movement are Yang Mu's stylized, individualized expressions of temporality, as "Rays of the Searching Sun" (1998) clearly illustrates.[30]

1
The hasty shower beat the roof and stopped, like arrows
Leaving medieval stains on the window pane
Hesitantly I look around, gripping in hand for defence
A book. When rays of the searching sun instantly
Enwrap the world, like an enormous flag laying a total ambush
Before my eyes
Wishing to prove that violence and beauty, as well as sympathy
Are now getting ready on the edge of the toiling universe
Ready to move into darkness, I see someone sitting by me

---

29 Chen Shih-hsiang explains the Chinese character "*shi*" (時) not as "time" as it is commonly understood, but as "here and now." He illustrated its use by Confucius's teaching about learning: "when the time comes timely, put what you've learnt into practice."

30 Here I use the first version of the poems "A Poem on Poetry" and "Rays of the Searching Sun" as they appeared in *Lianhe wenxue* [Unitas] (January 1996) and *United Daily*, 18 Feb. 1998 respectively. Both poems are now collected in *Intervention*, the latter one under a revised title, "Rays of the Setting Sun." See *Intervention*, 108-12, and 30-7. I personally prefer the original title because the temporality proposition it conveys is a powerful irony.

In a wicker chair at the window. A Brandenburg concerto
Is softly playing upstairs, in the air
A nostalgic aura reigns
A little lost, worried
A little. Time, because of your gaze
Freezes on the wall

2
I am certain that someone is sitting by me, at the window
In the night wind, the betel palms shoot tall. Time
Carves its furrow deep into the circulating heartbeats
Having come to realize in quietude that the floating
Sentiments are like two people in reverse hours
Losing their command of speed, letting it extend to infinity
But rays of the searching sun, having tiptoed across the meadow
Are now shining on the watchful fence
Impurities in the air are purged, light and darkness
Engaged in unending wrestles, noiseless
Lifeless. If in the mute scent of tea, love and
Mercy could be savoured, please sit by me at the window
Watching them go round the depths of heartbeat
Extend to infinity
Time stops

3
The tide is on the flow, towards us
The heart and the will, apparently sunk deep in thoughts
Are calculating before the turbulent whirlpool
The blood, hidden in the drifting shadows
Surges like faint echoes
If every individual in this universe, by minute
Changes; coffee whirling round a silver spoon
And in every change lies a message
My nerve sinks in the huge stillness
And the endless chill – as if congealed
Grows or changes no more. Meanwhile, the tide takes a stride
Up the beach. The clouds press low
Over a carnation, I look for a position
To watch the rays of the searching sun on the sea
Flickering as ever, countless
Messages, some anxieties. Time –
If only time allows

4
It is exactly this moment, still and safe, I am afraid
This is it; when the rays of the searching sun adjust their intensity
Repeatedly, shining on the faraway apple trees
And behind the blind, a teapot almost cold

Warm but secretive, between a magpie
And a bat, like embroidery of random stitches
Now spread itself before your indolent gaze
You will then notice on the leaves of summer fern
Tiny insects glitter by their fluttering wings
On both banks of the drain, in their stellar formula
They roar, competing for your attention, perhaps
I guess our shoes are soled with fine sand
Such come-and-go is good, in such a moment still and safe
What has been seen is the afternoon sea
What have gone round a lap to catch up, are time absolute
And time relative, averaged out

Unlike "A Poem on Poetry," which features the internal debate of a split ego, "Rays of the Searching Sun" presents the same voice throughout, speaking from different locations. The poem's four parts alternate between Western and Asian locales.[31] Medieval literature and European music (part 1), like "coffee" and "carnation" (part 3), imply a Western setting; in contrast, the betel palms (part 2) remind the reader of Taiwan, whereas tea, magpie, and bat evoke a Chinese setting, described as "faraway" from the "apple trees" suggestive of the poet's home in Seattle (part 4). In the first two stanzas time freezes under the gaze. The speaker is sitting at the window, with a companion perceived but not physically present. Simultaneity in the sense of togetherness annihilates the relevance of homogeneous time. Temporal differences are cancelled out; time stops and sinks into timelessness. Parts 3 and 4 depict the speaker at the coffee table or tea-table, contemplating what is going on at the beach. The cyclical ebb and flow of the tides remains a common metaphor for time in Yang Mu's poetry. The rhythmic adjustment of the sunlight adds to the orchestration of temporality.

It is interesting to note that time seems to freeze in one particular period of a day – afternoon. The four parts presenting the two settings are illuminated by an afternoon sun. What is repeated is the human action during tea-time in the afternoon, though the liquid that is drunk may be coffee or Chinese tea, depending on the locale. Afternoon in one place, say an Asian city, occurs in the middle of the night in the United States. Conversely, afternoon in the United States corresponds to early morning in south-east Asia. But unlike the early morning, afternoon is the time when the sunlight is about to grow dim, as if the searching sun were ready to leave for another place and continue its quest.

---

[31] Given that men and commodities travel across continents, the details that feature a particular locale may be found in places away from their cultural origins. The contrast deliberately made by the poet is here taken as signifying a difference of location which contextualizes the sun's search and renders it thematically relevant.

The interplay of stasis and motion builds up a creative discourse of time. As the speaker sits and time freezes, time is lived in the subjective experiences of human action and consciousness. On the other hand, manifestations of the restlessness of within-time-ness – the rain, which falls and stops; the betel palms, which shoot up tall; the music in the air; the pulsation of heart-beats – all punctuate linear time by their brief presence. They stretch along life like a running river. Despite the fact that every individual changes in every minute, the continuous movement of the tides in the sea and the sun in the sky, reinforced by images of the whirlpool, blood circulation, and "coffee swirling round a silver spoon," underscores the progress towards death. The turbulent world constantly in motion provides a dramatic contrast to the restful posture of the speaker. Absolute time, like cosmic time or the time secretly shared between two like-minded individuals, is atemporal. But to the contrary, human time told by clock and calendar is relative: it is the time that many things to be done, always attended by the anxiety that it may run out. Absolute time and relative time can combine to reach poetic truth: there is simultaneity and continuity at "the stillpoint of a see-saw."[32] In "this moment, still and safe," the shared indolent gaze sustained by the searching sun can freeze time and order it.

A primordial indicator of temporality, the sun is itself atemporal – being both in time and out of time. "Rays of the Searching Sun" offers a metacommentary on the discourse of time when it takes issue with the artificial measurement of "real time" and attempts to do away with linearity and circularity, which thus far have been the two dominant modes of representing temporality. The experiential value of eternity is measured not by a moment's duration but by its intensity. Rather than seeing an absolute moment in literary imagination such as Blake's "eternity in an hour," Yang Mu engages the modern sense of "homogeneous time" in intercontinental travels. Trips across the Pacific take on the added meaning of a temporal journey, as often a few hours must be debited from or credited to the traveller's measured "present." Advancing or retreating in time, two minds meet across the Asia/America split, and in so doing, they transcend time: their temporal consciousness lies where past and future are gathered at the absolute stillpoint of the see-sawing between present and future. This realistic contemporary experience of temporality successfully liberates the representation of human time and cosmic time from the dominant spatial patterns of linearity and circularity.

---

[32] W.B. Yeats, *Essays and Introductions* (London and Basingstoke: The Macmillan Press, 1985, c. 1961), 503.

*   *

*

By homogenizing, phenomenalizing, placing, and theorizing time, Yang Mu has created a number of time-worlds for his discourse on temporality. Unlike the adventurous youth in the early poems, the speaker in the later works seems to be more meditative. Linear progression gives way to a cyclical repetition. In a mystical union, past, present, and future are projected onto each other. The continuity within changes is accentuated, while the contingency in events is downplayed. Like the "I" in "Rays of the Searching Sun," the speaker appears motionless, sitting by the window watching different worlds and pondering over time. Despite the lack of movement in individual scenes, intercontinental travel is taking place – "off-stage," between sections. Though static, the speaker in Yang Mu's recent works actively observes in detail the phenomenal changes in nature. The image-based approach echoes his practice in early poems. As one who is aware of his own changes over the course of time, he would not complain about waiting but would confess to the sublime mountain that he has been running, and the struggles of life are written on his face. Or he admits to the running stream that even if he cannot step into the same river twice, he nevertheless exists.

Forgetting occurs as earthly time slips; time can be arrested only in relation to the world one inhabits. Time exists doubly, as Krieger says, "both in the temporal order and in the timeless structure." By redeeming time in dated records, in phenomena, in places, and in a self-authored myth, Yang Mu recaptures lived time using signifiers and patterns that render the transcendental signified in a poetic form. The poems in this chapter demonstrate the poet's development towards the abstract theorization of time. His cosmopolitan reading of shifting and overlapping time-frames updates temporal consciousness in a globalized world.

In the light of historical consciousness, some of Yang Mu's poetic time-worlds might appear atemporal, remote from the sense of history as public time lived in and by the masses. For a more socially and politically oriented reading of time, Yang Mu has adopted a dramatic new approach that will be examined in the following chapter.

CHAPTER 4

On Alternatives to Historical Narrative

History may be servitude, /
History may be freedom [*]

"The river rushes east and gone with it the waves and roars / the dynamic heroes since time immemorial."[1] In many famous classical Chinese poems, time runs like a river for both the individual and the dynastic era. The flow of events is thus figured as natural and inevitable.
Today, we are reminded of the "cunning passages, contrived corridors"
in historical narratives where the supposedly natural stream of events is
in fact subject to political writing and rewriting.

History, in the form of a unitary national narrative, is charged with
the political agenda of legitimizing the ruling party. Despite the rise of
post-colonial discourse, history-writing's use of a single voice has rarely
been questioned. On the contrary, people liberated from the colonizer
have now obtained the right to speak and their desire for decolonization
has facilitated the same singular, essentialist approach to the past.
Writing projects of "recovery" rely almost exclusively on the testimo-
nies from the minority position. During the early period of national
independence, it is common to see histories proliferate in order to rescue
the suppressed past. Since this table-turning strategy employed by
literatures of resistance is still trapped within an oppositional imagination, history writing continues to perpetuate its servitude to those in
power.

Much of Taiwan's past has been decided by external powers, and
whenever its sovereignty changed hands, its national narratives under-
went dramatic rewriting. Under the rule of the Dutch in the early seventeenth century until 1662, Taiwan was then a Japanese colony from
1895 until the end of World War II. At the Potsdam conference of 1945,
Japan surrendered control of the island to the Republic of China, repre-

---

[*]   The lines are quoted from T. S. Eliot's poem "Little Gidding."

[1]   The opening lines of Su Shi's poem, *"Nian nu jiao: Chibi huaigu"* [Meditations on
History on the Red Cliff].

sented by the Nationalist Party (the Guomindang). Although the Chinese Communist Party established the People's Republic of China on the mainland in 1949, Taiwan remained the Republic of China under the Guomindang until Chen Shuibian, the leader of the Democratic Progressive Party, was elected President in 2000. For more than four hundred years, the people of Taiwan have suffered from a troubled national identity and an unsettled international status.

There are at least three main master narratives in Taiwan's quest for a national-cultural identity. The first is told from the perspective of the Han settlers who dreamed of recovering the mainland from an illegitimate ruler. This narrative was enacted twice: by the Ming subjects against the Manchu in the seventeenth century; and by the Guomindang against the Chinese Communist Party since the mid-twentieth century. The historical situation was complicated by the increase of cultural influence from the West, resulting in the second essentialist narrative, which pitted Chinese-ness against Westernism in the literary milieus of the 1960s. This oppositional imagination developed further ramifications in subsequent decades. Between the Modern Poetry Debate in the early 1970s and the decline of the "Native Soil Literature Movement" in the early 1980s, there emerged a nativist Taiwanese consciousness, which is distinct from the Chinese cultural nationalism of the past.[2] Subsequently, the third narrative, which developed in the 1990s, laid out a separatist agenda. With the President of the Democratic Progressive Party as the figurehead, the turn of the millennium marked the post-Guomindang era in Taiwan.

While many writers and poets were politically engaged in the discursive formation of one or more of these national narratives, Yang Mu has kept himself apart from this reality. This chapter will scrutinize several of his long poems by placing them in the context of critical moments in the history of Taiwan. Instead of responding directly to these historical events in his work, Yang Mu has confronted them via an indirect path. There are two innovative trajectories that Yang takes: one is to re-stage

---

[2]   The Modern Poetry Debate and the Native Soil Literature Movement are prominent examples of some Taiwanese writers' reactions to the prevailing modernism in Taiwan's literary scene. These movements are in step with the 1970's general call for a nativist literature, resulting from the patriotic sentiments of anti-westernism and resistance to imperialist exploitation. The Modern Poetry Debate began in 1972 and lasted for about two years. The debate involved academic scholars and modernist poets. Modernist poetic experiments were denounced for their obscurity, European style syntax and lack of social and political engagement. The Native Soil Literature Movement, which promoted a nativist, socially responsible literature in a realist style, reached its zenith in 1977-78. Many key figures of the nativist group later decided to realize their political agenda directly by making public protests. The nativist movement dramatically subsided in the face of government intervention in 1979.

the events from a temporal distance; the other is to couch them as allegorical moments in a foreign land. By adopting and emplotting the historical facts and figures in his lyric testimony, Yang Mu assimilates the local historical turmoil into a larger backdrop of monumental world events. Given the paradoxical possibilities of inhibition and liberation, the poet neither forces histories to perform a national service for Taiwan nor uses them to promote a political agenda in his works.

History Plays and Histories Play

In the context of Taiwanese literature's depiction of history, Yang Mu's poetry has succinctly demonstrated the cultural practice of intervention, similar to what Homi Bhabha proposes:

> [It is] a space of intervention in the here and now... To engage with such invention and intervention... requires a sense of the new... an insurgent act of cultural translation. Such art does not merely recall the past as social cause or aesthetic precedent; it renews the past, refiguring it as a contingent 'in-between' space, that innovates and interrupts the performance of the present. The 'past-present' becomes part of the necessity, not the nostalgia, of living. (Bhabha, 1994: 7)

In Yang Mu's works, the Chinese tradition of historiographical writing in poetry is adopted not only as an aesthetic precedent but also as a means of inversive intervention. The poet writes "history plays" in which different "histories play." His approach to the contemporary political conditions is both an echo of and a dissent from the mainstream narrative of Taiwan in which he is historically situated.

The poems selected for this section can be located in "post" situations such as post-Dutch Occupation in Taiwan and post-Cultural Revolution in the PRC. "Fort Zeelandia" (1975) discusses the end of the Dutch occupation around 1662, while the "The Story of Five Concubines" (1983-4, 1990) relates to the fall of the Eastern Ning Kingdom into the hands of the Qing in 1683. Both hinge on crucial events in the change of ruling regimes in the seventeenth century. "Difficult Is the Journey" (1982) gives an account of a traveller's traumatic encounter with the Chinese cultural imaginary, represented by the ancient city of Changan. The traveller's experience is understood in terms of the long separation between Taiwan, and mainland China. Here, the unitary-voiced narrative of History contests with the histories that it tries hard to suppress but fails to erase. The poems are history plays in which disparate histories come into play. At the same time, Yang Mu's unconventional approach to writing about the past and the national-cultural critique that such an approach entails will be investigated.

Strictly speaking, among the poems analysed here, only "The Story of Five Concubines" can be generically categorized as a "history play."[3] Other examples such as "Fort Zeelandia" and "Difficult Is the Journey" are poems that display dramatic qualities, such as conflicts of values and roles, as well as the expressive power of masked dramatic monologue. The elision of the poet's subject position offers a variety of enunciative perspectives from which the dramatic personae can intervene in the widely accepted version of History. Instead of orchestrating a stable, continuous account of History, individual personae speak through fissures in national narratives and challenge their invented coherence, questioning what Jonathan Arac calls, an explication of the silence.

National narratives held a positive understanding of the course of... history, and their writers believed it was a responsibility of culturally ambitious and important narrative not only to show but also make explicit this understanding. Literary narrative denied any such responsibility, challenged any such understanding, and developed techniques to supersede such explicitness... [S]tudies has most often struggled to reincorporate literary narrative into a

---

[3]   Apart from "The Story of Five Concubines," Yang Mu wrote only one other history play, *Wu Feng* (1979). Since *Wu Feng* is a verse drama that Yang Mu published separately from his books of poetry, it demands a full-length discussion that falls outside the scope of this chapter. However, a brief recapitulation of this history play will serve as a starting point for discussing how different histories emerge in Yang Mu's narratives. *Wu Feng* is based on the story of a martyr in a native Taiwanese legend. Wu Feng is a Han settler to the island who sacrifices his own head in an attempt to stamp out the local head-hunting customs of the aborigines. His death reveals to the natives the brutality and futility of their bloody rituals, which they have finally given up. In Yang Mu's treatment, the friendship between Wu Feng and the aborigines is placed at the poem's forefront. However, their cultural differences surface in face of a crisis. By putting two disparate perspectives in confrontation with one another, Yang Mu re-mobilizes the mythical function of an earlier narrative as a method of transforming its ideological make-up. Unlike the common Han-oriented stereotypes of superstitious savages, in Yang Mu's portrayal, the aborigines are good-natured and conscientious. The clash is one of conviction, not of values and personality. Both Wu Feng and the aborigines try, to the best of their abilities, to serve the people they love. The conflict, therefore, rises to the height of antagonism found in Greek tragedies. Wu Feng's self-conscious doubt presented in soliloquies highlights the ambivalent position he holds as an outsider to the tribe.
    By this re-vision of the aborigines, Yang Mu places the dialogue between two competing narratives, the Han and the aboriginal, on equal footing. Yang Mu is rewriting both the text of the Wu Feng legend and the aboriginal version of Taiwanese history. Refusing a simple rejection of one or another, Yang Mu departs from the Han hegemonic practice of monopolizing benevolence for the self and racializing brutality in the other. Different from monolithic national narrative of the Han and the aborigines' decolonizing cultural revival, Yang Mu's articulation of their encounters redeems the aborigines as well as Wu Feng. For an English translation of the play, see Cissie Kwok and Yang Mu, "Wu Feng," in *Twentieth Century Chinese Drama: An Anthology*. ed. Edward M. Gunn (Bloomington: Indianna University Press, 1983), 475-513.

renewed national allegory, undertaking to explicate what was programmatically, even polemically, left silent. (Arac, 1997: 148)

In "Fort Zeelandia" and "The Story of Five Concubines," voices of both the central colonizers and the marginalized colonized, are amplified to engage national narratives in dialogue. From "Difficult Is the Journey," a traveller's dramatic monologue animates the shadows of a suppressed history that lie beneath the communist agenda written on the billboards.

In colonial narratives, the emphasis on the colonizers' power and victory is normally justified by the inferiority of their subjects. Said's post-colonial reading of "Leda and the Swan" operates on the assumption of a lack, or absence, in the colonized.[4] If Yeats's "Leda and the Swan" suggests that Leda is only able to gain the strength to resist her attacker through the acquisition of his knowledge and power, then the poet is implying that her empowerment is false. Seizing the power and knowledge of the colonizer cannot guarantee national liberation, as Fanon warns us.[5] The power and knowledge that the national bourgeoisie appropriated from their ex-masters only serves to perpetuate colonial rule in new forms even after national independence.

Reading "Fort Zeelandia" against poems of decolonization, one can see that Yang Mu's adoption of the gendered metaphor of colonization as sexual intercourse is in fact an inversion of the discourse's patriarchal hegemony. Fort Zeelandia was a sandy peninsula off the southern coast of Taiwan, the first region on the island to be colonized in 1624. The Dutch spent over ten years building a fortress there and making it the site of their governor's residence. After a nine-month siege by Zheng Chenggong, the Dutch surrendered the Fortress to Ming China in 1662. Fort Zeelandia is a significant historical site, which marks the beginning of Taiwan's colonial experiences. In Yang Mu's approach to the writing of colonialism, Fort Zeelandia is situated at the historical moment when Dutch rule was about to end. This was the last moment of the European occupation of Taiwan and the Dutch soldier's confession at this moment is an insertion of an alien voice into the monolithic "Chinese" version of national re-unification. Yang Mu's gendered representations such as

---

[4]   Edward Said, "Yeats and Decolonization," in Terry Eagleton, Fredric Jameson and Edward W. Said, *Nationalism, Colonialism and Literature* (Minneapolis: University of Minnesota Press, 1990), 90.

[5]   Frantz Fanon traces three phases in the evolution of a national culture during decolonization. "In the first phase, the native intellectual gives proof that he has assimilated the culture of the occupying power... In the second phase, the native is disturbed; he decides to remember what he is... [In] the third phase, which is called the fighting phase, the native... turns himself into an awakener of the people; hence comes a fighting literature, a revolutionary literature and a national literature" (Fanon, 1963: 222-3).

describing the landscape as a female body or portraying national resistance as buttons on woman's clothes, are stereotypical, yet they illustrate that the agent for change is not necessarily male. Unlike "Leda and
the Swan" in which the colonized cannot save herself except by adopting the other into the self, the colonized in "Fort Zeelandia" represented
by a dominated local female fights back with her exotic otherness. This
resistance frustrates the male vanity of conquest. The violence of change
is mutual, as both the colonizer and the colonized are altered by their
experience. Fort Zeelandia is the site of colonial violence and foreign
administration, where contact and pacification between two peoples
takes place.

> The huge canons have rusted, gun-fires
> Vanished into the fragmented pages of history   (lines 29-30)

The canons have rusted to indicate that military or sexual violence
becomes impossible or irrelevant over the course of time. In the end, the
Dutch soldier has grown accustomed to a quiet counting of the twelve
buttons and a slow unbuttoning of the new clothes, suggesting that a
different relationship has developed between the colonizer and the
colonized. The female, though mute in the poem, wears down the inva-
sive approach by her perseverance and her adherence to local customs.
The history of the Dutch surrender inscribed solely as a military defeat
by a "Chinese" national army is revised. Inserted into the national
narrative are both the nativist resistance to colonial rule and the colonizer's naturalization on the tropical island. "Fort Zeelandia" ends in a
chanting of "Ilha Formosa," another name for Taiwan, coined by the
exotic gaze of the European explorers and now reclaimed by the native
islanders.

> ... Ilha
> Formosa, from afar, I have come to colonize
> But I have come to surrender. Ilha
> Formosa. Ilha
> Formosa   (lines 49-53)

"Fort Zeelandia" and "Ilha Formosa" create an exoticized and eroticized
identity for the island. These names are imprints of colonial experiences
constantly revived and almost endeared to people, especially in the
nativist discourse. The prosopopoeia to "Ilha Formosa" is an evocation
of a Taiwanese-ness, characterized by colonial experiences and thus
distinguished from a monolithic "Chinese-ness." In Yang Mu's "Fort
Zeelandia," the interpellation is invoked not to affirm one's self against
the other, but to problematize the Dutch colonial project and the Chinese
national recovery in the light of their surrender. This "monologic"
utterance can be taken in a Bakhtinian term as the site where "an intense
interaction and struggle between one's own word and another's word is

being waged." [6] The Dutch soldier's confession opposes the Dutch narrative of conquest and at the same time casts doubts on the Han celebration of national recovery ascribed solely to Zheng Chenggong's military success. The Dutch soldiers in diaspora and the local people on the island are agents living at the juncture of authoritative national narratives between two *nations'* historical battle in 1661. In Yang Mu's poem they spell out disparate narratives from their marginal positions.

Following the chronology of events, "The Story of Five Concubines" is a sequel to "Fort Zeelandia." To put an end to the Dutch Occupation of Taiwan, which had started in 1624, a fierce battle was fought at Fort Zeelandia in 1661, resulting in the defeat of the Dutch and the victory of the Ming troops led by Zheng Chenggong. In October, 1661, Zheng, who was granted a dynastic surname, Zhu, set up the regime of "Eastern Capital" on the island. It was the "Eastern" capital in relation to the capital on the mainland, now fallen into the hands of the alien Manchu to become part of the Qing dynasty. "Eastern Capital," suggests that the Ming Empire in the east took Taiwan as a temporary refuge while planning the Ming's eventual return to the mainland. The ultimate ambition of Zheng was to expel the Qing and restore the Ming. When Zheng Chenggong died in 1664, his son, Zheng Jing, succeeded him by dubious means. Zheng Jing renamed the Eastern Capital "Eastern Ning" in order to establish a Ning kingdom independent of the Ming. Under his rule, the power and prospects of the Ning regime declined. Despite a few conquests along the coast east of the mainland, conspiracies and corruption reigned on the island. Across the strait, the Qing Empire prospered and became a great power.

"The Story of Five Concubines" consists of three fragments from an incomplete verse drama. The play captures the liminal moment when the Eastern Ning kingdom of the Zheng family was about to fall in 1681. In contrast to the "official" History of high politics, which is usually written by male inscribers from the ruling regime, "The Story of Five Concubines" impresses its readers with its diversity of experiences from multiple perspectives, including the female one. Similar to "Fort Zee-landia" the history writing in this poem is intermixed with individual people's experience of history as they lived it. Unlike "Fort Zeelandia," however, each of the three fragments presents a distinct framing of the historical event within a specific role: Madam Xiu, one of the five concubines of Prince Jing, Shen Guangwen, a poet-cum-historian, and

---

[6]   When Mikhail M. Bakhtin delineates his notion that utterance is a "complex and dynamic organism," he says, "[w]ithin the arena of almost every utterance an intense interaction and struggle between one's own and another's word is being waged, a process in which they oppose or dialogically interanimate each other" (Bakhtin, 1981: 354).

Zhu Shugui, Prince Jing of Ning Kingdom. The soliloquy in each fragment challenges the version of history propagated by the Han patriarchy.

"Fragment I: She Foresees the Catastrophe" (1983) opens with a
question addressed to the concubine, Madam Xiu, "What date is it
today?" While formulating an appropriate response, Madam Xiu reveals
her insight into the historical circumstances she finds herself in. She is
shrewd and self-conscious, fully aware of what her role will be in
history, because of her gender.

> Oh summer, a magnificent theatre
> Happy and bright. All living creatures
> Fit well in their pre-given positions
> And grow. Let us too, before a meticulously designed
> Setting, concentrate on playing our designated roles
> To please and beg, to envy and love madly
> In blood and tears, to perform a play well.   (lines 21-7)

A real-life play will be staged and the female actors will have to perform
in it. The concubines and the princesses have to commit suicide with the
emperor at the fall of the dynasty. This was the fate of the females in
Chinese patriarchal culture, as it is the destiny of the concubines in a
displaced Ning kingdom offshore in Taiwan. The ritualistic sacrifice is a
significatory act of female loyalty. The female body and life are com-
modified as the properties of an emperor. If the territory cannot be
protected and the palace cannot be removed and brought with them, the
escape of the royal family through death is both total and final. The
prohibition against the concubines falling into the usurper's possession
illustrates the patriarchal fetishization and hegemony over the female
body.

The traditional gendered code of conduct assigned to the concubines
is clear. However, the concubines do not accept their fate without
question. It is brought to the fore and identified through Madam Xiu's
awareness of, and interest in, the dramatic plot. Thus, this Han tradition
of patriarchal hegemony over the female is deconstructed. Madam Xiu's
recognition of what is demanded of her in order to complete the sacrificial practice makes the scene ironic. The juxtaposition of the seasonal
activities of living creatures in nature with the female's fated role in
such a historical moment is allegorical. The ants' and bees' "pre-given
positions" in nature are compared to the "meticulously designed setting"
in which the concubines are required to "perform" their "designated
roles." What happens in the natural cycle highlights what is unnaturally
demanded of the female in the "man"-made historical cycle. With this
awareness, Madam Xiu's compliance is not a result of loyalty or sub-
mission, but an indication of her professional ethics as an "actress." If
she commits suicide at the end of the play as the plot demands, her

suicide will signify nothing more than the performance of an act she has chosen to do, which destablizes the conventional narrative of female allegiance to the nation and patriarchal culture.

An official narrative of events connected by their long-term and immediate causes is common in history writing. "Fragment II: Shi Lang Sets off from Mount Tong" (1983) presents such an account of Taiwan history in the seventeenth century. Shen Guangwen, the persona in this fragment, was a subject of the Ming dynasty under the threat of persecution when Zheng Jing rose to power. His writing career prospered after the Qing Empire took over Taiwan and he is considered the founder of Taiwanese history and literature.[7] In the poem, Shen Guangwen plays the role of poet-historian. Through a flashback, Shen gives a historical account of the Han takeover of Taiwan in 1661 and at the same time recounts the battle waged by Shi Lang in 1681.

In Shen Guangwen's narrative, Shi Lang was once the sworn brother of Zheng Chenggong. In 1651, following a conflict caused by jealousy and a power struggle, Zheng killed Shi Lang's father and brother. Several years later, Zheng departed for Taiwan and settled on the island. Shi Lang spent thirty years plotting revenge for the death of his family members. His chance finally came in 1681 when the Qing emperor, Kangxi entrusted him with the task of recovering Taiwan. Shen Guangwen's soliloquy is delivered as Shi Lang sets off from Mount Tong for Taiwan, just as a tempest was eminent. This is the same moment when the catastrophe is about to befall the concubines and the Ning ruler in Fragments I and III respectively. Shen's version of history chronicles the events affecting the masculine members of the story, and women have no part to play in his narrative.

The persona in the third fragment is Zhu Shugui, Prince Jing of Ning Kingdom. The soliloquy in "Fragment III: Prince Jing of Ning Kingdom Sighs in His Life of Refuge" (1990) shows the prince's despair immediately after the fall of his realm. Zhu is the ninth generation descendant of the founder of the Ming dynasty, and he seeks refuge in Taiwan at a

---

[7]   Shen Guangwen (1612-1687) is the founder of Taiwanese poetry. Shen was born in Zhe Jiang and was a subject of the Ming dynasty who was stranded in Taiwan owing to a typhoon. Since Shen wrote poems to satirize the military government of Zheng Jing, he would have been persecuted in the East Ning kingdom. It was only in 1685 when the Qing Empire took over the island that Shen and Ji Qiguang and fourteen other writers set up Dongyin shishe [The East Poetry Recitation Society], the first poetry society in Taiwan. This society sowed the seeds of traditional Chinese poetry on the island. Ji wrote, "There had been no people in Taiwan until the arrival of Sian [Shen Guangwen]; there had been no writing until the arrival of Sian." See Chen Qianwu, "Taiwan shi de wailai yingxiang" [The Foreign Influences on Taiwan Poetry], *Li* 146 (August 1988): 4; and Liao Xuelan, *Taiwan Shishi* [History of Taiwan Poetry] (Taipei: Wuling Publishing Company, 1989), 18-20.

time of political turmoil. Now a fugitive from the Qing army, his sighs show his humble wish to dismantle the wall that imprisons him, so that he can find a way to flee.

> ... Oh sigh if you may
> If sighing, or weeping, or wailing
> Can burst open your bottled up chest
> Let those shames and furies gathered over time
> Leak, from the back of your mind, or pour
> We shall all sigh loudly   (lines 12-7)

Zhu Shugui is contemplating a heroic exit. This last act of a play can be taken as a dramatic climax to honour the Zhus, paying the last tribute to the Ming, who has now reached its final fall. The prince's pathetic urge to allow his kingdom and his very identity to disintegrate is a plea for liberation from the national narrative, which has circumscribed his existence.

> ... Oh sigh if you may
> Weep, wail. Let the furies of the universe
> Blow up, to shock the cosmos
> Make the tempest shake my way out
> Of the broken walls at the southeast; Make mountains and rivers tremble
> Whip the cracked earth, for the sake of the ancestors
> Create a genuine doom for the last time   (lines 22-8)

Zhu's wish to run away is an irony that explodes the ancestral narrative. In contrast to the sacrifice demanded of the female in Fragment I, the national myth is inverted by the myth-bearer, the Ming descendant. What the prince wants is a wham, not a whimper, for staging a dynastic annihilation. But for the individual himself, the human desire to escape from death is more important after all.

The three fragments that make up "The Story of Five Concubines" offer three different perspectives on a single historical event. The conventional national narrative separates into various strands of family history, individual predicaments and explorations of the burdens of being female in a patriarchal world. The characters in the verse drama do not compete to be authentically represented; instead each occupies a separate scene, enjoying an equal right to speech. The concubines whom history objectifies, marginalizes, and obliterates are placed at the centre of the stage, spotlighted by the poem's title. The historical significance of their story is thus restored. The poet-historian's organized narrative in the second fragment is written in linear fashion with a strong sense of causality, following the common practice for a documentary record. Zhu's fantasy for a boisterous and flamboyant last act has a deconstructive effect on the orthodox national narrative but is tainted by the speaker's pathetic wish for survival.

The dramatic figures are situated on a temporal "national" border at a dynastic turn. The concubines, the poet-historian and the fugitive prince are not placed together in service of "free play." Rather, their separate presences in three different fragments offer multiple narratives that underscore the constructed nature of historical realities. Just as there are different ways of imagining time, there are different histories. Like the designated roles in a play, no speaker is more or less fictional than the other. The concubines are inside a gendered historical imagination, which is over-determined and under-discussed. A historian's imagination utilizes proper names and dates – signifiers that claim to be credible documentation of the signified – and achieves objectivity and reliability. The historian's failure to document everything is made conspicuous when the female voice in the preceding fragment is immediately erased by his official account. In History, women's proper names do not count. Only the surname of the Zhus carries historical significance for the royal family of the Ming. Ancestral inheritance and continuity is the basis of the Han patriarchal hegemony. The prince's ambivalence towards this burden of familial-national tradition and duty exposes the fissures in the grand narrative. While the first two fragments were written in 1983, this third fragment was added in 1990, and the verse-drama was first published in 1997. The poem traces the gradual dissolution of the Han legitimacy in Taiwan after the 1987 abolishment of martial law. Incomplete though it is, "The Story of Five Concubines" stages different histories that play against one another with moving dramatic tension.

Yang Mu is at his most powerful when he deploys a mixture of poetic forms and referents to render the very moment of national-cultural crisis itself. The poet often fractures a text by intercutting it with other writing. He lets the speaker's train of thought and observations bring disparate texts together and draw the verse forward. This precarious and temporary suturing of different referents at the intersection of positionalities is itself a performative act. Conceptualizing the subject as a product of multiple locations, Lyotard says:

> A *self* does not amount to much, but no self is an island; each exists in a fabric of relations that is now more complex and mobile than ever before. Young or old, man or woman, rich or poor, a person is always located at "nodal points" of specific communication circuits, however tiny these may be. Or better: one is always located at a post through which various kinds of messages pass. No one, not even the least privileged among us, is ever entirely powerless over the messages that traverse and position him at the post of sender, addressee, or referent. (Lyotard, 1984: 15)

In Yang Mu's poetry, the nodal point of communication circuits is usually animated by a dramatic persona who is situated at a historical juncture. This persona's dramatic monologue spins out a narrative of history, which is displayed as constructed, or sometimes, deconstructive. A prominent example of such a dramatic persona is the traveller in "Difficult Is the Journey."

"Difficult Is the Journey" is a poem taken from the section labelled "New *Yuefu*" in Yang Mu's ninth book of poetry, *Someone*. "New *Yuefu*" was first advocated by Bai Juyi (772-846) and is a poetry that strives to be accessible to the common people, through simplicity and plain language. Interestingly, Yang Mu's poems collected in this "New *Yuefu*" section are in fact texts that destabilize generic distinctions. Observing the thematic characteristic of New *Yuefu*, the poet admits that these poems are composed in reaction to present-day local and global events. Instead of presenting the mundane daily experiences in a simple and direct way, however, Yang Mu problematizes the factual account by exposing the events' suppressed narratives. Among the poems in the "New *Yueh-fu*" section, "Difficult Is the Journey" is a notable example of how two contrasting historical readings of a place come into play.

"Difficult Is the Journey" is a long narrative poem delineating a traveller's sojourn in Changan, and his meditation on Chinese cultural history.[8] The title is followed by the first two lines from a *yuefu* poem of the same title by Lu Zhaolin (634-c. 684): "Can you not see that beside the Wei bridge north of Changan / Rotten logs lie across the ancient fields." The last line of Yang Mu's poem alludes to the fourth line of Lu's work, which depicts the alluring scenery of a prosperous Changan enticing "the mist as well as the smoke." Since Changan was the capital for thirteen different ancient Chinese dynasties, it has witnessed the rise and fall of empires and become an important cultural signifier for the Chinese.

The accumulation of cultural and historical significance can invest a location with meaning, causing a conceptual shift to occur. An attachment to such a site can help to form an identity, as Caren Kaplan observes:

> When a "place on a map" can be seen to be a "place in history" as well, the terms of critical practice have made a significant shift... The notion of a politics of location argues that identities are formed through an attachment to a specific site – national, cultural, gender, racial, ethnic, class, sexual, and so on... Location can be seen to be a place in relation to history, used... to unpack the notion of shared or common experience. (Kaplan, 1996: 25)

---

[8]   Intertextual references of this poem are plentiful. Besides Lu Zhaolin's poem of the same *yuefu* title, Yang Mu mentions two other poems, which have significant impact on the motive and mode of writing in his work. They are Du Fu's "Beizheng" [A Journey to the North] and Li Shangyin's "Xing ci xijiao" [A Journey to the Western Suburb]. See Yang Mu, "Afterword" in *Someone*, 176.

In Chinese culture, the imperial centre is an embodiment of rich literary and cultural treasures; the yearning for Changan has been a persistent theme in classical and modern Chinese poetry. "Difficult Is the Journey" begins with a prelude, composed of stanzas one to four, in which the persona records his journey to Changan and into History.

> A donkey-drawn cart clumsily rolls down the street
> I stand before a loess alley, gazing at History
> Before my eyes, a crowd of shadows wriggles on the red wall
> Dry, peeled off; it seems that among them is me:
> Wrapped up layers over layers behind the billboards, a thin one that
> Hardly bears the spring chill. People push towards me
> Slanting body temperature gradually touches my blood and bones
> I turn to distinguish left and right, and find that they are but overlapping
>   shadows
> On the wall, the shapes are false. I then understand
> How alien and alone, insignificant and insubstantial, I am
> And cannot help shivering in the twilight that has survived since ancient
>   times   (lines 1-11)

As a traveller strolling in Changan, the persona sees History as distorted and broken shadows projected onto the red wall. The wall determines who is inside and who is outside, and establishes who is at the centre and who is on the periphery. It is a screen on which History can be read and written. The colour of the wall upon which History is inscribed simultaneously conjures up juxtaposing images of Changan's palace walls in imperial China, the wall under the Gate of Heavenly Peace (Tiananmen Square) from the People's Republic of China as well as the Red Wall of communist Russia. Historically and ideologically Changan is a hybrid of all these places. The wall's shadows are fragmented beyond recognition, wrapped up in billboards and big character posters. Apart from the traveller, no local inhabitants care whether the shadows are false or not.

> ... but I know
> Their interests lie in chestnuts, cigarettes
> Flour, vegetables, salt, and lard
> And in snow, pasture, and floods outside the city wall
> I gaze at the magnificent Goose Tower. Their
> Interests lie not in the tower, nor in me   (lines 32-7)

At a historical moment when people are busy earning their livelihood, the cultural and religious symbolism of the Big Goose Tower falls into oblivion.[9] In contrast to the persona who makes an intellectual pilgrim-

---

9   In Changan, there are Big Goose Tower and Small Goose Tower. Big Goose Tower
     is located at Cian Temple [Temple of Benevolence]. Big Goose Tower is where the
     famous Buddhist monk, Xuan Zhuang, kept the Buddhist scriptures. In addition, the

age to Changan, the city's local inhabitants lead their lives outside its influence. They are cultural exiles unaware of the importance of reviving their precious cultural tradition.

The traveller's outsider's gaze perceives a fissure in History. He resists the temptation of oblivion, which conceals and represses memories of past glory, by repeating his elegiac laments for the loss of a cultural China. These laments are punctuated by the refrain, "Can you not see." This refrain introduces three nostalgic outbursts in stanzas 5 to 6, stanzas 7 to 10 and the last five lines of stanza 10 respectively. The first appeal addresses the loss of art and poetry. One of Changan's famous sites is the Forest of Calligraphy Steles. Calligraphy is a literal inscription of art, poetry and history. These works of calligraphy and carving contain important information, including the canonical texts; records of visits to the Forest; people's historical preoccupations and pastimes; as well as poems, proseworks and the epitaphs of different dynasties. These writings not only display the evolution of literary skills and calligraphic styles, but also exhibit the everyday life and current events of different historical periods.

> Can you not see the miserable wind at the tower of Cian Temple
> There hide the ghosts and gods, and there poetic spirits sob
>
> (lines 38-9)

The rich cultural life enjoyed by the ancestors is now nowhere to be found. Nonetheless, the persona continues his journey, eventually coming across a man who sells fiction. To the traveller, searching as he is for cultural China, this fiction-seller's face is both familiar and unfamiliar.

> That face is a face that I cannot recall, not
> Old nor young, without joy and without
> Sorrow. That is an extremely familiar face –
> I have seen it in books; a face I have imagined and fashioned
> A boatman, a ricksawman, a herdsman
> Fleeing for refuge in ancient times, making connections and ties in modern days
> He is literate; he has seen *The Strange Phenomena Witnessed in the Last Twenty Years*[10]

---

goose is significant because in a Buddhist myth, the Buddha performs a miracle by coming down to the human world disguised as a goose and gives his life to bestow his favours on mankind.

[10] This is an intertextual reference to a novel, *Ershi nian mudu zhi guaixianxiang* [The Strange Phenomena Witnessed in the Last Twenty Years], written by Wu Yanren and published in 1910. This novel is regarded as one of the four major novels of late Qing. The poem is probably a record of the trip to the PRC Yang Mu and other writers took by invitation in 1981 when the country started to open up. It can thus be read as Yang Mu's confrontation with and meditation on the history of post-1949 China. At that time, most Chinese in the mainland still lived under fear of political purge and

> He has seen workers, peasants, soldiers;[11] he looks up
> Astonished – he has seen me too   (lines 54-62)

Unlike Tiresias who has seen all and has suffered all in T. S. Eliot's *Wasteland*, this face is indifferent and unaffected by all that it has witnessed. The encounter between the persona and the fiction-selling figure dramatizes how an individual conceives History and how History perceives an individual in return. This face "has seen" people and events in history as if it "has seen" a novel. By cataloguing what the face "has seen," the poet stresses this "seeing," which sweeps over both immediate realities and fictional writings in an all-levelling glance. The textuality and fictionality of History is foregrounded and illustrates its weakness. Revived by a traveller from Taiwan, who has seen Changan in books, in calligraphy, and in poetry, the imaginary cultural Changan rises from repressed narratives and astonishes the indifferent History.

At the moment when the traveller is about to be appropriated into the anonymous masses of the past by the fiction-seller's sweeping glance, he recognizes the familiar/unfamiliar face of History/Fiction. In a self-alienating examination, he sees how he appears in the eyes of History.

> My temples grey as an alien's, and I
> Am actually an alien who has travelled thousands of miles to this place
> Standing independently in the cool shades of the tower, gazing at
> History: its dust, its mud, and its blood
> I heard the sonorous clamours of swords and spears, the cries for a
>   break-through
> The devouring flaming tongues, the falling roofs
> Thunders, lightnings, rainstorms and gales
> The refugees' song of exile   (lines 63-70)

After the Cultural Revolution, Changan has become an anacoluthon that ruptures the narrative of the cultural imaginary. The poetic distancing of the persona as alien from the locals questions the cultural grid on which Chinese intellectuals of the past have situated themselves. The locals are preoccupied with the demands of daily subsistence and political practice. Changan is now a cultural signifier that is purged of its usual signified. The persona is an alien who feels culturally dislocated but paradoxically he has become a culturally dislocating supplement to the stable, homogeneous historical narrative fabricated by the present regime.

---

in material destitution. Since this poem was written in 1982, this line may refer to what had happened in the PRC from 1962 to 1982, including the Cultural Revolution (1966-1976), which directly impacted the cultural environment of China represented by Changan.

[11] These three categories of the population, workers, peasants and soldiers, make up the "proletariat" in the PRC.

In the PRC of the 1980s few people would have the traveller's mind-set and expect to see the cultural Changan. The historical circumstances did not allow such nostalgic imagination. Thus the "I" is an unexpected and unwelcome supplement that astonishes the figure of History who has seen all. The sweeping glance of History, which is used for collect-ing and absorbing stray details and residues into a homogeneous narra-tive, finds it hard to assimilate this alien's anticipating gaze. The persis-tent gaze functions like a dangerous supplement, as an inherent, internal "otherness" which impedes from within the "smooth-running" history writing of the ideological apparatus.

The second emotional outburst introduced by "Can you not see" de-scribes the traveller's forlorn leave-taking:

> Can you not see the dark clouds sweep by the west side of Baishui
> The official path is haunted by weeping willows...   (lines 71-3)

The persona's position in this cultural matrix is ambivalent. He is not exactly an exile, reiterating laments for a lost paradise. Following classical Chinese poetry's traditional portrayal of travellers, the persona ponders the cultural centre from a window in the night.

> ... Starlight of March
> Glitters, and floats across the silent north
> Oh China! A guard patrols under the iron gate
> Keeps watch and stands in the shadows of swaying willows   (lines 94-7)

The traveller's quest for the essential, cultural China is doomed. China is watched over by the iron gate and the guard, who stands on an ancient land. The guard does not realise that the site has for a long time been renowned as a place of deep feelings and history. He stands amidst the swaying willows, unaffected by the city's literary and cultural refer-ences to sentimentality.

> Attentively, I look and listen, wishing to find
> Some sound, to grasp the pulse of the old city
> Sallow and dark, yet an undying face
> Wishing to sketch the dawn upon the night   (lines 105-8)

To his disappointment, the traveller finds only ruins in the land which "was once as fertile as home." Changan, which was a metonymy of cultural China, now means only ruins in the north for the traveller. He occupies an ambivalent position between being an exile and a tourist. The poem is a record of the traveller's inquiry and a report of the effects of the journey on him. He is not a shopper-spender tourist who goes to Changan for sightseeing and souvenirs. Having known the place from literary and cultural representations, he journeys there for a re-cognition of these representations locally. The traveller is a cultural exile who learns that Changan, the marked space of a national culture, is now nowhere to be found.

His lament reaches its height through incremental repetition of lyrical chanting. In the last five lines, the persona cries:

> Yet can you not see
> Can you not see that beside Wei bridge north of Changan
> Where travellers walked into daybreak, in those days of yore
> Where thousands of steed sped by, today only the cold
> Mist mixes with deserted smoke. Can you not see   (lines 124-8)

The pathetic, insistent appeals to take heed of the lost treasures of the national tradition exemplified by the passion, exuberance and beauty of Tang culture, seem to be futile. The rhetorical question used in classical poetry, "Can you not see," is an apostrophe marking a striking scene. Here, the question is asked three times, as resolute attempts to draw the inhabitants' attention to the cultural deprivation in their lives, but at the same time, the repetition betrays the speaker's despair. The accelerated refrains of "Can you not see" mount in a crescendo, only to fall into an affirmation of blindness – "you cannot see."

If Changan is the centre upon which a system of cultural coordinates can be set, this centre no longer holds. Roaming in the ancient cultural capital, the shadow of the traveller and those of the local people merge to compose a picture on the red wall. Yet, the traveller's and the locals' preoccupations never meet. The mobility of the traveller results in the discovery of his banishment from the cultural imaginary. The transposition of the lyric voice into Tang poetry parallels the transformation of the unitary personal voice into the cultural one. The sense of loss is intensified by the disturbances caused by an absence, not so much an absence of the memorable past as the absence of the memories of the past. Fragmented but continuing connections between the lost Changan, which acts as a point of departure for the cultural imaginary, and the present Changan the traveller finds as a site of everyday realities, can still be made. The persona's encounters during his sojourn are staged as critical commentary on the cultural ruptures caused by a historical upheaval.

The journey is difficult indeed because the traveller locates himself on a specific itinerary. This wish to return to the pre-communist, national-cultural China is a problematization of diasporic imagination. An attachment to a special cultural and literary site that used to serve as the basis for diasporants' identity formation is proved irrelevant, if not unfeasible. The traveller's discoveries urge a rethinking of the place-based consciousness of the cultural home. The anxiety and despair experienced by the traveller uncover the tension between the disparate national narratives suggested by the Changan symbol.

Compared with the common cultural practice of re-narrating the past by re-establishing a place, "Difficult Is the Journey" is a meta-criticism of this construction of a cultural identity in the present. The politics of location in identity discourse argue for a place-based conception of self, but one has to note that the chosen site is always open to historical revisions, as Caren Kaplan reminds us,

> that site must be seen to be partial and not a standard or norm... the stakes in the politics of location lie in the effort to address a perceived gap between poststructuralist relativism and rigidly essentialist articulations of identity. (Kaplan, 1996: 25)

Through the encounter of the persona's questing gaze with History's all-seeing glance, Yang Mu addresses this gap between perceptions and juxtaposes disparate history writings in the poem.

In addition, "Difficult Is the Journey" displays the performative power of deploying the past to demystify the present. The incessant references to "seeing" and "not seeing" indicate the relationship between blindness and insights in a way John Berger suggests,

> The past is never there waiting to be discovered, to be recognized for exactly what it is. History always constitutes the relation between a present and its past. Consequently, fear of the present leads to mystification of the past. The past is... a well of conclusions from which we draw in order to act. (Berger, 1972: 11)

In the poem, the traveller is an outsider, attaining an existence free from the historical frame of the present. By a *drawing* from different materials of the past, he *draws* in his mental picture a different Changan of the present. His preconceived idea of Changan as a cultural Mecca makes him see the lack, or absence, in the place he has come to. The ancient Changan is detached from its physical location and it becomes a cultural imaginary that travels with the persona. It is no longer a place, nor an origin, but a set of cultural signifiers drawn from the past. While History continues to fashion a singular, unitary narrative through fiction, the open-endedness of the poem questions the nature of history writing itself. The poem's chanting is a double-bind of record and erasure, in-between "can you not see" and "you cannot see."

If as Berger says, fear of the present leads to mystification of the past, perhaps, hope for the future lies in the demystification of both the past and the present. In this section, the three poems of Yang Mu are read as history plays in which the field of national discourse becomes a field of contention, peopled by different subjects voicing their individual consciousness. Voices of the native Taiwanese, the female and the diasporant, articulate contested stories of a historical event or a historical site. The "lived" experiences of the participants rupture the orthodox narratives, whether it is the Dutch imperialist conquest, the Ming glory built upon the national recovery of Taiwan and upon the subject's royal allegiance, or the place-based cultural imaginary of Changan. Yang Mu's attempts at demystification are in fact a political critique. They are history plays in which disparate histories play against each other, allowing a myriad of alternatives for addressing the national-cultural narratives of Taiwan and of China from some peripheral positions.

Writing Allegory:
Diasporic Consciousness as a Mode of Intervention

Literature has always been allegorical. Fredric Jameson's homogenization of the third world into a unitary experience of colonial oppression results in what he terms a "national allegory," which overemphasizes a nationalist response in literature. However, Madhava Prasad considers the national framing of third-world literature to be justifiable under specific historical circumstances. Allegories facilitate such framing and serve to highlight the emergence of a nation.[12] From Prasad's point of view, allegorical correspondences help to fabricate a readable narrative to clearly delineate the contours of a nation. Owing to "allegory's capacity for including (self) critical layers of discourse," there is always a subversive potential latent in the self-alienating nature of allegory (Prasad, 1992: 80). Common to recently liberated nations is a struggle to dismantle colonialism in order to provide for a new order. Narrative is often seen as an effective apparatus to prevent the obliteration of a national culture.[13] Nevertheless, one should take heed of equally essentialist post-colonial tendencies in depictions of colonial rule and pre-colonial order. Allegorical writings are sites for negotiating alternatives to such bi-polar discourse.

The Greek roots of the word *allegory* are *allos*, "other," and *agoreuein*, "to speak." Thus, allegory allows the "other" "to speak" or lets one "speak" from the position of the "other." Allegory is never an ontological enunciation of a self-identifying act. A parallel structure of events or ideas is implied in an allegorical narrative. Allegorical reference is intermittent and it often contains an embedded ironic tone.

Similar to allegory, diasporic consciousness operates in its distance from, as well as its link to, a structured correspondence. Diaspora is

---

[12] In Madhava Prasad's words, "The greater visibility of the national frame of reference in Third World literature may be a function primarily of the historical conditions under which these nations came into being." See Madhava Prasad, "On the Question of a (Third World) Literature." *Social Text* 10.2-3 (1992): 78.

[13] Narrative here does not refer to a genre-bound concept. Instead it is taken as a novelistic tendency that can frequently be detected in the discursive formation of national and cultural identity.

defined and interpreted in terms of the myth of origin. As William
Safran has written of "diaspora":

> *the Diaspora* had a very specific meaning: the exile of the Jews from their
> historic homeland and their dispersion throughout many lands, signifying as
> well the oppression and moral degradation implied by that dispersion
>
> ... I suggest that... the concept of diaspora be applied to expatriate minority
> communities whose members share several of the following characteristics:
> 1) they, or their ancestors, have been dispersed from a specific original
> "centre" to two or more "peripheral," or foreign, regions; 2) they retain a
> collective memory, vision, or myth about their original homeland – its
> physical location, history, and achievements; 3) they believe that they are
> not – and perhaps cannot be – fully accepted by their host society and there-
> fore feel partly alienated and insulated from it; 4) they regard their ancestral
> homeland as their true, ideal home and as the place to which they or their
> descendants would (or should) eventually return – when conditions are ap-
> propriate; 5) they believe that they should, collectively, be committed to the
> maintenance or restoration of their original homeland and to its safety and
> prosperity; and 6) they continue to relate, personally or vicariously, to that
> homeland in one way or another, and their ethnocommunal consciousness
> and solidarity are importantly defined by the existence of such a relation-
> ship. (Safran, 1991: 83)

These conceptual characteristics of diaspora suggest that diasporic
consciousness is a kind of spatial imagination and it allows the allegorical use of role-playing in a self-alienating act. Compared with allegory
as an alibi defined by its absence from the site of its referent, diasporic
consciousness is an alibi that denies its absence. The use of allegory in
the diasporic consciousness is always already distanced from identity
because of its ambivalent position between revelation and concealment.
In Paul de Man's conception,

> Whereas the symbol postulates the possibility of an identity or identifica-
> tion, allegory designates primarily a distance in relation to its own origin,
> and, renouncing the nostalgia and desire to coincide, it establishes its lan-
> guage in the void of this temporal difference. (De Man, 1983: 207)

Diasporic consciousness, manifested in the significatory act of writing
allegory, is a means of representing the post-colonial condition because
such a consciousness is constituted by a double awareness oscillating
between the society of residence and the society of origin. Like allegory,
diasporic consciousness prevents a full correspondence in a symbolic
mode by a discovery of temporal and spatial differences. Diasporants
supplements the national narrative and defers its closure because of both
their distance from the homeland and their commitment to return. The
existence of diasporants prevents their homeland from creating a coherent national narrative, because a key group is not present.

The language of identity is always important in identity politics. This discursive formation is based on the deployment of metonymic images from a referential system such as place of birth, race, ethnicity, class, gender, language and religion. The nation-building impulse calls for the narrative associations of these images to create a coherent identity. Diasporic consciousness is a deconstruction of such referential systems of identity. In their place diasporic consciousness substitutes a new referential system based on "the pathos of a temporal predicament in which man's self-definition [in this context, a man's identity] is forever deferred" (De Man, 1979: 199). It is the myth of homeland that defines diasporic consciousness and at the same time determines its allegorical fictionality.

Diasporic consciousness is one of the prevailing moods underlying modern Chinese literature. "The obsession with China" is not only a dominant theme in contemporary novels, but also provides a major subject for other genres of Chinese literature in the twentieth century.[14] Many Chinese writers, living and working in diaspora, bemoan the loss of home and yearn to return to a cultural origin located in ancient China. Jameson developed the notion of the "national allegory" based on an analysis of the novel, which is the predominant literary form of the West. Nonetheless, many of the elements in his argument and in the subsequent debates related to it, can be applied to an investigation of modern Chinese poetry. The dilemma facing the lyrical self in many contemporary Chinese poems can be interpreted as the collective cultural experiences of both national resistance and nation-building. The national, realist demands on modern poets at different historical moments, as shown in the identity construction schemes in numerous literary debates, reflect the political dimension in the writing and reading of poetry. A parallel between the individual and the national destiny

---

[14] The phrase "obsession with China" was coined by C. T. Hsia in 1961 and it has become a set phrase among critics of modern Chinese literature. In C. T. Hsia's opinion, "[w]hat distinguishes this 'modern' phase of Chinese literature [the pre-1949 Chinese literature of the early twentieth century] alike from the traditional and Communist phases is rather its burden of moral contemplation: its obsessive concern with China as a nation afflicted with a spiritual disease and therefore unable to strengthen itself or change its set ways of inhumanity. All the major writers of the period – novelists, playwrights, poets, essayists – are enkindled with this patriotic passion" (C. T. Hsia, 1999: 533-4). Hsia sees this obsession with China persist in post-1949 Chinese literature. Among younger Taiwan writers the obsession "takes the form of nostalgia, implying at once a regret over the loss of the mainland to communism and a poignant appreciation of the greatness of their mother country" (C. T. Hsia, 1999: 563-4). See Appendix 1: "Obsession with China: The Moral Burden of Modern Chinese Literature" and Appendix 3: "Obsession with China (II): Three Taiwan Writers" (1975) in C. T. Hsia, *A History of Modern Chinese Fiction*. 3rd edition. (Bloomington and Indianapolis: Indiana University Press, 1999, c. 1961), 533-54 and 563-86.

is expected so that the national character of the creative works can be safeguarded.

Significant literary debates about the national character of modern Chinese poetry took place in the 1970s in Taiwan. In the early 1970s, nationalism increased owing to successive historical events, such as the Diaoyutai Incident in 1970, Taiwan's withdrawal from the United Nations in 1971, Richard Nixon's visit to Beijing as well as the termination of official relations between Taiwan and Japan in 1972. These diplomatic and political setbacks had a traumatic impact on the Taiwanese population. Operating at this time, the Modern Poetry Debate (1972-74) was deeply influenced by zealous nationalism and anti-Westernism. The fervour of the subsequent Native Soil Literature Movement for promoting a realist and nationalist literature in opposition to avant-garde experimental writing was a disguised protest against imperialistic influences from the West in aspects other than the literary.

Being one of the few prolific native Taiwanese poets, Yang Mu has been a focus of critical attention since the 1960s. His early poems, under his first penname Ye Shan, have been highly praised for their lyrical quality. However, when anti-imperialism was in vogue in the 1970s, he became a target of criticism from many nationalist critics who regarded his works as alien and antagonistic to Taiwanese readers. Yang Mu's involvement in the debates about identity politics is interesting. There is no doubt that he is a diasporant as he first went to the United States to study and has been teaching there since the mid-1960s. Unlike many diasporants, his residence in a foreign nation is more a choice than a necessity. His place of birth in Hualian positions him on the periphery in Taiwan. What is more, as a Taiwanese poet, he is geographically distanced from the specific cultural milieu of mainland China. As a contemporary poet, he is temporally distanced from Changan, the imperial centre in classical Chinese poetry, and from Beijing, the political-cultural centre of Modern China. In the geo-political mapping, he is physically removed from the political and administrative centres of Beijing in the PRC and Taipei in the ROC. Such temporal-spatial distance from these centres of traditions proves an advantage to Yang Mu, who manipulates this diasporic condition to explore controversial identity issues from a transcultural, cosmopolitan perspective.

Writing Allegorically from the Outside

When referring to people and events in life, one is always an outsider. To any referent, poetry is outside; so is language itself. Yang Mu is always self-conscious of this truth in his writing. To admit this "outsidedness" is a humane, liberal and realist attitude to life. Indeed, Ye Shan [Yang Mu] fashions himself an outsider in "The Right-fielder of

Romanticism," the preface to the Hongfan edition of *First Essays of Ye Shan* (1977), which is often regarded as the poet's self-defining Romantic manifesto. In this essay he writes about how one can be an *out*sider *in* a baseball game. The important thing is that this kind of "outsidedness" is allowed by the rules of the game. The poet frames the preface between an opening paragraph depicting a youth's sweet loneliness in playing the role of right-fielder, and a concluding paragraph on Yeats, whom he also describes as a right-fielder. Book-ended between the two right-fielders is a numbered discussion of the different meanings of Romanticism. The romantics' accommodation of discrepancies and their courage to think and act outside of the prescribed norms is exemplified by Yeats who is often called "the last romanticist." To Yang Mu, the term should be read as "the romanticist to the last." In the last paragraph, the gist of romanticism is presented as "Yeats's problems":

> By an overview of Yeats's life, I find that he was all along a lonely person. Among his Irish friends, he was a discriminated right-fielder, a lonely outsider, chewing a blade of grass picked from the earth – that should be shamrock leaf – looking at his friends inside the game discussing about slaughters, about creating "a terrible beauty" with flesh and blood. I believe that Yeats surely loved Ireland no less than MacBride and others did, but he had chosen a completely different path. I can imagine if Yeats were there in the crowd watching his teacher anatomize a pigeon, at the moment the blood spilled, he would certainly turn away and force his way out, to stay at a loss in the corner.
>
> I am still pondering over Yeats's problems. (Yang, 1977b: 11)

Yang Mu focuses on Yeats as an outsider from his revolutionary, nationalist Irish contemporaries. Written in Seattle on St. Patrick's Day, in 1977, the poem is Yang Mu's statement of his own national-cultural position in a complex allegorical grid reference. At a moment when Yang Mu was criticized for being an outsider to "Chinese-ness" by the realist critics, this preface is a timely response.

Echoing his confessed outsidedness, Yang Mu uncovers the ideological aberration in other people's avowed claims of "insidedness." Contrary to what the title of his prose work *The Spirit of Berkeley* may suggest, Yang Mu has no intention of appropriating any claims of social activism. As a writer despite one's great sympathy, one can only observe and report from the outside. Stripping off the pretence of being inside is a more authentic and realistic way of showing concern for different social groups.

> It is said that we should presume that we know how the rural labourers feel. For example, when we see lights of the fishing boats, it is said that we must not praise these lights as poetic but ought to think about the hardships suffered by fishermen... If we always observe life in great sympathy – a pre-

sumably great sympathy – we would only become entirely an outsider. Yet I wonder, we cannot but remain no more than an outsider.[15]

To the poet, admitting one's outsidedness does not damage one's ability to participate in society. Instead, an allegorical distance from the subject allows an array of searchlights to probe the matter.

Yang Mu's writings often stood out as an anacoluthon at different critical moments of political controversy in Taiwan. Yang Mu did not construct a cultural identity based on the national imaginary of Chinese-ness, nor did he create a sensation of belonging to the time and place of the immediate present. In the poems, he shows his concerns via refraction by drawing the reader's attention to some people and places other than those of China or Taiwan. He talks about Ireland, about an Indian in the United States, about Spain, and about Chechnya and Russia. The Irish-Spanish-Chechen themes, as well as the concerns for diasporants, are incongruous with the Taiwanese nationalist or nativist discourses of the last few decades. This conscious distance from the discursive mainstream is representative of Yang Mu's using allegory as a mode of intervention.

"My nostalgia is 'Irish'"

Yang Mu's contributions to *Dragons Poetry Quarterly* are conspicuous examples of this allegorical approach to identity discourse. Among the five poems published in the magazine, three were written on "foreign" subject-matter (two about Ireland and one about an Indian in the United States). The other two are apparently "Chinese" poems (one on Du Fu and the other on a Chinese hermit) that are in tune with the manifesto of the *Dragons*, a "national" literary magazine, which aims to play the "Dragon music" and perform the "Dragon dance."[16] The presence of three "foreign" poems in such a periodical is worthy of critical attention.

Despite all of the false impressions of exoticism it may convey, the Irish theme is present in a number of Yang Mu's poems written in 1971-

---

[15]   The essay in discussion is "Shangu jizai" [Observations in a Valley] written in June 1976, collected in *Bokelai jingshen* [The Spirit of Berkeley] (Taipei: Hongfan, 1977), 39. Yang Mu's notion of "outsidedness" is intended to be a dialogue with the writers of the Native Soil literature. In January 1978, Yu Tiancong wrote an essay, "Yuhuo yu shuangchong renge" [The Lights of the Fishing Boats and the Double Character] as a response to Yang Mu's essay and in a moralistic way dismissed Yang's notion of "outsidedness." See Yu Tiancong, *Minzu yu xiangtu* [Nation and Native Soil] (Taipei: Yuanjing, 1981), 70-1.

[16]   The *Longzu shikan* [Dragons Poetry Quarterly] uses the dragon as a cultural emblem for Chinese-ness and has stated in their Manifesto that their mission is to "play our own gongs, beat our own drums" and "perform our own dance of the dragon."

72. Three poems of the Irish series are "Sailing to Ireland" (1971), "We Want to Go Sailing Too" and "Ireland" (1972).[17] In the Taiwanese cultural climate of anti-Westernism, Yang Mu's depiction of Yeats's problems was considered a "foreign" issue to readers and critics. The Irish themes in Yang Mu's poems were then taken as proof of the "outsider" mentality of a "western" trained poet. The first two poems, which focus on sailing, evidently in imitation of Yeats's "Sailing to Byzantium," are selected for this discussion.

Sailing to Ireland

> A terrible beauty is born
> – Yeats

On Saint Patrick's Day
I hang a shamrock leaf on your door
And yet the sound of the executioner's gunshots
Keeps reaching here. Here
Where, after a shower, the breeze
Flies over the withered expectation of
The apple trees – my nostalgia is Irish

As nostalgic as an Irish winter evening
When God passes by the graveyard of the revolutionaries
And wonder what he can properly do to John MacBride
Who violently bled, and died
Daffodils have not bloomed yet
The call to arms is still clear; moreover
There are many others jailed in the city

So they will not even wait till Easter
To knock down my shamrock with their bayonets
And trample it. Now that spring is here
And the clouds play easily over the sea
The salmon multiply rapidly in the mountain creeks
The new play of May is being rehearsed and staged
And people have finally forgotten what happens

On Saint Patrick's Day[18]

---

[17] "Sailing to Ireland" was written on the 20 March 1971 and published in *Modern Literature*. "We Want to Go Sailing Too" and "Ireland" were both written in 1972 but published two years later in the *Dragons Poetry Quarterly* in January and December of 1974 respectively.

[18] This is Yang Mu's translation. See Chi Pang-yuan [Qi Bangyuan] *et al.*, eds. *An Anthology of Contemporary Chinese Literature – Taiwan: 1949-1974*. Vol. I: Poems and Essays (Taipei: National Institute for Compilation and Translation, 1975), 292.

That in the early 1970s Yang Mu focussed his thoughts and writing on Yeats, who kept himself apart from the revolutionary Irish nationalists of his day, is an allegorical admission of his own Taiwanese national-cultural position. That "Sailing to Ireland" is subtitled by the quotation, "A terrible beauty is born," foregrounds the inter-textuality of this poem with Yeats's "Sailing to Byzantium" and "Easter 1916." Almost sixty years after Ireland's Easter Uprising, the speaker reflects on Irish memories of white terror, which included casualties, deaths and imprisonment. The Irish "winter" is enacted by the ruling regime, personified as an executioner or an anonymous "they," who violently suppress those who try to fight their bayonets with shamrocks. In the poem, spring re-animates nature and people, while burying unpleasant memories. Violence and bloodshed during the revolution might have been forgotten in Ireland where independence was partially achieved in 1948. A similar History was about to be re-staged in Taiwan when political unrest and white terror erupted in the late 1970s.

In Taiwan's prevailing anti-Western nationalistic discourse, Yang Mu's concerns for the Irish struggle for a national cause seem irrelevant. Opposing the simplistic designations of self and other as "Chinese" and "Western," the poet's positioning of himself at the exotic margin is particularly provocative. "Sailing to Ireland" was easily dismissed as another product of Western influence. While critics bemoaned the poem's imported sentiments of frustration and emptiness, few read a separatist agenda behind the translated event. If Byzantium represents Yeats's utopia for art and craftsmanship, Ireland, as characterized by Yeats's literary texts and life, becomes a model for a Taiwanese poet who is engaged in a comparable artistic pursuit and facing similar political dilemmas. What this Ireland-Taiwan analogy shows is how History affects the content of a poet's works and how the poet has negotiated History's demands.

The second poem on the Irish theme, "We Want to Go Sailing Too," further investigates the issues of the Irish independence movement, which also bears a close resemblance to the political situation in Taiwan. The dominant anti-imperialist sentiments exhibited in the Modern Poetry Debate uphold a Chinese national identity as the unique, ultimate locus for positioning a poet's identity. In the poem, the tension between an unyielding commitment to the cause and ambivalence about how that commitment should be enacted dramatizes the cultural and political dilemmas of intellectuals in that historical moment.

Such a palm, so thin, so delicate
An obscure constellation I don't think I can read it
(Whether you go east or west
It is the same misery that awaits you
To find yourself finally lost)
Footmarks are playing on the wall   (Yang Mu's translation 1975: 285-6)

In the poem the wish to set sail is persistently brought to the fore by the seafarer's audacity described to be dark green. Green is the colour for Ireland and greenish blue is the colour of the sea, symbolizing migration. Initially the collective lyrical self "we" wishes to set off for a voyage, with a "parabolic audacity turning straight" while in the last refrain, this desire for audacity becomes delicate and incomprehensible. What consistently sustains the desire to set sail is the wish to take a risk, regardless of the possible parabolic swirl in the itinerary. The inhibiting hesitation is ascribed to the uncertainty of direction. Both the East and the West are traps where only the misery of being lost awaits "you," the seafarer. Inscriptions cannot be deciphered. Palmistry offers no reliable indications, nor can one read the star atlas for a clue. Footmarks, which are considered traces of the ancestral and cultural origin in Native Soil Poetry, are now misplaced on the wall, on the border between the inside and the outside. The dilemma of being caught between the East and the West epitomizes the poetry debates of the 1970s: one can hardly decide which course to take, despite having the audacity to commit to a cause. In this poem Yang Mu unlocks the East-West dichotomy and disputes the simplistic designation of individuals as either nationalists or compradors. To him, many of the most thoughtful and socially concerned intellectuals are involved in sophisticated meditations on their positions in the in-between.[19]

References to the anxieties inherent in the Irish struggle for independence constitute Yang Mu's alternative outlook on the national narrative in the Taiwanese Modern Poetry Debate. Many critics take the intertextuality as merely a manifestation of the poet's aesthetic inclination towards western romanticism. Nonetheless, a close study of the inter-contextuality illuminates a parallel between Yeats's anxiety over the "terrible beauty" born of the Irish national struggle against the British and Yang Mu's scepticism of the nationalist obsession with the

---

[19] This perplexing East-West dilemma has appeared in a number of Yang Mu's works from the 1970s. For example, in his prosework, "Guihang zhier" [Flying Home II] written in October, 1975, Yang Mu writes, "To return to the east from the west, the plane goes west instead. This is certainly baffling... Deep in thoughts, I wonder why returning to the east, the plane goes west instead... Summer vacation is about to end. Having been home to visit their relatives, overseas students are on their way flying to the west, even though their planes go east instead." See Yang Mu, *The Spirit of Berkeley*, 11.

"Chinese" heritage in Taiwan. The ideological make-up of the Modern Poetry Debate displays a Chinese cultural nationalism that the poet finds problematic. At such critical moment of identity crisis, Yang Mu's slight hesitation on the issue does not mean he is turning away from reality. On the contrary, the cautious attitude registers his deep concerns about the complexities of the political situation. This hesitation echoes Yeats's ambivalence as Edward Said sees it when he contextualizes the poet in his post-colonial cultural mapping.

> For Yeats the overlappings he knew existed between his Irish nationalism and the English cultural heritage that both dominated and empowered him as a writer were bound to cause an overheated tension, and it is the pressure of this urgently political and secular tension that one may speculate caused him to try to resolve it on a "higher," that is, non-political level. (Said, 1990: 80)

Like Yeats, Yang Mu is well aware of his position as in-between his Taiwanese nationalism and his Chinese cultural heritage. His reference to Yeats does not simply invoke the difficulties in en-siting one's cultural identity but points to a more complex problem: the construction of cultural identity itself in the post-colonial context.

> [D]espite Yeats's obvious and... settled presence in Ireland, in British culture and literature, and in European modernism, he does present another fascinating aspect: that of the undisputedly great national poet who articulates the experiences, the aspirations, and the vision of a people suffering under the dominion of an offshore power. (Said, 1990: 69)

In this very early stage of debating cultural identity in Taiwan in the 1970s, Yang Mu interrogates the binary enclosures of identity in the name of the East against the West, or a national "Chinese-ness" versus the imperialist Westernism. The insertion of the Irish question into the identity discourse creates an allegorical correspondence for re-thinking "Chinese-ness" from the peripheral Taiwanese perspective.

There is a great deal in common between Yeats's cultural tension with the British tradition and Yang Mu's relationship with the Chinese. Given his acute awareness of a cultural heritage transplanted from a neighbouring island with a different history, Yeats's need for a national signature underlines his decolonization project. This post-colonial predicament can be resolved by retrospective decolonization: an imaginary recovery of the land, a redevelopment of the native language and a myth-making "by which the land was seen... in a state that antedated its alienation by imperialism" (Said, 1990: 78). Said regards Yeats "as an Irish poet with more than strictly local Irish meaning and applications," and "as someone whose poetry warned of nationalist excesses" (Said, 1990: 87-9). When Yang Mu claims that his nostalgia is "Irish," this is not meant to be read in a strictly literal or nationalist sense, because in the poems Yang Mu depicts not only heroic deeds performed for a nationalist cause but also the terror born of "nationalist excesses." Yeats codified his Celtic concerns and cultivated a distinct Irish national-literary consciousness through the medium of the English language. To Yang Mu, the Taiwanese colonial experiences of being ruled by other races, such as the Dutch in the seventeenth century and the Japanese in the late nineteenth and early twentieth century, should not empower the monologic, coercive tyranny of Chinese nationalism. He addresses the Taiwan question from the local Taiwanese perspective through a translation of Yeats's concerns. Being one of the few young native poets who had earned a voice in the literary milieu, Yang Mu's alternative cultural outlook on Taiwan's complex identity issues was both daring and innovative. His preoccupation with Ireland not only puts forward a direct dialogic response to the dominant nationalist "Chinese" identity discourse in Taiwan, but more importantly, it allegorically proposes a hidden separatist agenda. In this light, Yang Mu's Irish theme in the 1970s is a forerunner of the Taiwanese nativist project for independence in the 1990s.

"His Brahman smile, I believe / Has evolved from misery"

Jameson's notion of "national allegory" and Safran's concept of "diaspora" are both premised on the idea of a home-bound consciousness. Writing based upon this notion normally represents the collective memory or vision of the homeland. However, in Yang Mu's treatment, as seen in his poems on Irish themes, the home is situated at a distance from the Chinese setting. The diasporic consciousness is generated in a story of a displaced persona's homesickness in a host society. "An Indian" published in the *Dragons Poetry Quarterly* 13 (1975) is an example of this diaspora theme.

In "An Indian," Yang Mu's protagonist sits on a terrace carpeted by fallen leaves in late autumn while reading an aerogramme from home. The image of the Indian becomes increasingly clear as his three appearances are rendered in filmic terms as a long shot, a medium shot and finally a close-up:

> An Indian, sitting on the stairs
> Read a letter, an aerogramme
> That was in late autumn last year
> Floating on his face were
> The Brahman smile
> And misery too
>
> Hunger turns into new songs
>
> He is still sitting
> On the stairs of late autumn last year
> A thin and dark Indian

Is reading a letter, an aerogramme
Yellow leaves gather on his
Introduction to Economics

Turns into new songs

He sits on the stairs carpeted with fallen leaves
An Indian, barely twenty
His look, comes from the bank of the River Ganges
He is reading a letter; the words on the aerogramme
Have evolved from the Sanskrit, I believe
His Brahman smile, I believe
Has evolved from misery

The Indian is a diasporant studying economics in a foreign country. His national identity is given in the title and stated as the subject of the opening line. His cultural identity is first painted by his facial expression, which is a smile with a tinge of sadness, reminding one of a Brahman.[20] His racial identity emerges when his skin colour is mentioned in his second appearance. Lastly the close-up focuses on his physical appearance or "look," which bears the imprints of his origin. An additional identifier comes from the letter written in a distinct script evolved from the Sanskrit. The two short refrains separating his three appearances point to the social and economic problems of his home. The national-cultural identity of "an Indian" is thus completed in the portrayal through his birthplace, race, religion and language. By narrative associations of "hunger," "misery," and the youth's studying *Introduction to Economics* abroad, a brief national history is written.

The diasporic consciousness of this Indian student is marked by his thoughts of home. Images of the ancestral homeland and the present post-colonial nation are superimposed on each other to form the myth of India. Hunger and poverty surface as an epilogue to his letter reading and they are transformed into the refrains of new songs. These songs suggest the Indian's preoccupation with what he hopes to eventually contribute to his nation through his study of the *Introduction to Economics*. The transcendent Brahman smile invokes the Hindu attitude to life, inherited from the national culture that originated by the River Ganges, the cradle of Indian civilization. The prominent theme of this poem is a diasporant's obsessions with his nation. India travels through space via airmail, and through time, from the ancient civilization on the Ganges to the modern academy of the West, as an integral part of the Indian's college life in a foreign country. Because of the diasporic distance, there

---

[20]   In Hinduism, a Brahman is a member of the highest Hindu caste. The word is a cognate of Brahma, the essential divine reality of the universe. Brahma is the eternal spirit from which all being originates and to which all returns.

is room for new songs, for new hopes and expressions, which the Indian student can hope for, as indicated by his smile.

There is neither "Dragon music" nor a "Dragon dance" in this poem. What one can find is the depiction of the unique Indian culture, the Hindu attitude to life and most importantly, his attitude to the new songs. These new songs are not yet formulated nor incorporated into a national myth, but they are committed to the restoration of the prosperity of Home, which epitomizes the ethno-communal consciousness of an oriental student in the West. The encounter with this Indian, mediated through the gaze and the language of a Chinese man, evokes the possibilities of new songs. During the process of articulating these songs tensions between the national Indian objectives and the denationalizing power of global capitalism arise. Impending problems of cultural identity and economic imperialism will need to be negotiated. If this story of an Indian student is a national allegory of post-colonial India, the presence of this Indian theme in the *Dragons Poetry Quarterly* is an allegory of Chinese diaspora displaced in an Indian cultural site. The Indian's anxieties echo those of the Taiwanese in the 1970s.

Taboo Games:
Intervention of "an incomprehensible great romance"

The title of Yang Mu's seventh book of poetry, *Taboo Games*, introduces the Spanish theme that the poet worked on in 1976, at the 40th anniversary of the Spanish Civil War. Besides the title poem, two others were written in the same period: "Spain 1936" and "Ballads: On the 40th Anniversary of Lorca's Death." "Taboo Games" is a Chinese translation of the title of a piece of classical Spanish music for guitar, *Romance Anonimo*, also widely known as "*Juegos prohibidos*" in Spanish and "*Jeux interdits*" in French.[21] The poem is set in Granada, the hometown of Federico Garcia Lorca (1898-1936), during the Spanish Civil War. The persona wants to teach a kind and curious girl the history of a tormented country through the poem's Spanish setting, music and poetry. These signifiers of Spanish-ness are invoked to recount the suppressed history of the struggle against tyranny and to raise the girl's historical consciousness. On a literary level, the signifiers are deployed to allegorize the poet's concerns with another historic place and time.

---

[21] The title of Yang Mu's poem "Jinji de youxi" is translated as "Forbidden Games" by Joseph R. Allen in *Forbidden Games and Video Poems* (1993) and adopted by Lawrence R. Smith and Michelle Yeh in *No Trace of the Gardener* (1998). I render the title as "Taboo Games" to capture the poem's close intertextual relationship with the central theme of taboos found in Lorca's *Romancera gitano* or *Gypsy Ballads*, which Yang Mu translated into Chinese in 1966.

As a prelude to the Spanish theme, "Taboo Games 1" starts with leaves swaying in the afternoon breeze, accompanied by guitar music. The thoughts of Granada, when understood in terms of the taboo themes in Lorca's poem, *Gypsy Ballads*, form invocations of desire and repression. A similar theme is expressed around issues of sexuality in poem No. 5 of Lorca's work, "The Gypsy Nun":

> The Church growls in the distance
> like a bear on its back.
> How well she sews! What needlework!
> But dearly would she embroider
> the flowers of her fantasy
> on the straw-coloured cloth.
>
> ....
>
> Through the eyes of the nun
> two horsemen come galloping.
> A last inaudible sign
> loosens her tight chemise,
> and, seeing clouds and hills
> in the desolate distance,
> her heart of sugar
> and verbena breaks.
> Oh, what an exalted plain
> with twenty suns above!
> And what upstanding rivers
> does her mind's eye see!
> But she keeps to her flowers,
> while above her, in the breeze
> the light plays chess
> on the window's jalousie   (Trans. Havard, 1990: 59)

In Yang Mu's "Taboo Games," the Spanish guitar music is a prelude introducing a picture of the nun. "Taboo Games 1" opens as follows:

> Afternoon
> Outside the screened window, leaves are softly swaying
> swaying a sentiment, an incomprehensible great romance
> (The G chord is difficult to master, she says. Her hair slides to the left.)
> She looks down at her ring finger
>   with difficulty pressing down the wind of Granada
> A nun at the window says her rosary; by chance she looks up
> faraway a wanderer's horse slowly passes by
> The horse is really slow.
> She has already finished counting the twelve beads
> The wanderer disappears on the horizon. As Lorca says...   (lines 1-9)

The tension the nun feels between spiritual and carnal love tests the limits of taboo. Yang Mu psychologically represents how the nun represses her erotic desires through the chanting of the rosary. His depiction echoes Lorca's treatment of the gypsy nun's sublimation and erotic catharsis, which Lorca has her display through the act of embroidery.[22] The poems do not confront these taboos, instead displacing them in acts of substitution. Yang Mu's poem is a taboo game: both admitting the proscribed action and concealing it. The repression and sublimation through allegorization precipitates a political catharsis. Yang Mu's mourning for Lorca is a regret of the kind of life that must be led during the white terror either in the Spain of 1936 or in Taiwan in the late 1970s.

Yang Mu's reference to the guitar's G chord conjures up scenes of Granada, the Gypsy's romance, Lorca's poetry and his murder.[23] In *Gypsy Ballads*, the turmoil and torture imposed by interdiction is crystallized into "bitterness," a recurrent motif in many of the eighteen poems. Similarly, the flavour of Spanish music is heavily dosed with notes of bitterness in Yang Mu's work. "Taboo Games 1" sets the subdued but bitter tune of the entire poem.

> Chinaberries pass perpendicularly through the stave – moment
> after moment, dot after dot, lower and lower, bitterer and bitterer
> one dot lower than another, one dot
> bitterer than another – the sounds
>
> Finally fall onto the ground. She looks up
> and sees me melancholically listening to the inaudible leaves
> softly softly swaying outside the screened window – afternoon

The melody of *Romance Anonimo* is mixed with staccato gunshots. The fall of Lorca is superimposed upon the image of the fall of pots of violets, the fall of Chinaberries from the trees, and the fall of the musical notes from the stave, all dropping into a cluster of low, bitter sounds.

Many motifs in "Taboo Games 3" correspond to poem No. 4 of *Gypsy Ballads*, "Somnambular Ballad." In that poem, Lorca paints his gypsy portraits in green. As the green emerald hues radiate from the girl's green flesh and hair while she awaits someone on a green veranda, the colour characterizes her overwhelming youth and the bitterness of unripe fruit. Her powerful attraction is paradoxically indicative of bitter love (Havard, 1990: 53). In "Taboo Games 3," Granada is a colour and a language, connoting both Spanish joy and pain. The green coloration in Yang Mu's poem is employed to paint the wind and the horse, suggesting a picture of hope and freedom on a Spanish meadow:

---

[22] For a detailed discussion of this idea of sublimation, see Robert G. Havard's "Introduction" to *Gypsy Ballads*, 16-7.

[23] Lorca was murdered in 1936, most probably for his dissident views against the tyrannical Spanish Government under Francisco Franco (1892-1975).

Try to remember
the great care, in Granada
Try to remember your language and pain
green wind and green horse, yours
language and happiness –   (lines 1-5)

However, the pursuit of desires in the face of taboos always causes anxiety and injury. In "Somnambular Ballad," the stairs, which the girl's father and the young horseman climb to reach her on the green veranda where moonlight showers and water resounds, seem to be endless:

Now the two friends climb
towards the high veranda.
Leaving a trail of blood.
Leaving a trail of tears.   (Trans. Havard, 1990: 55)

The bleeding horseman is trying to fulfil his last wish: to meet the bitter girl. The father is in mourning in their house, lamenting the loss of self and home: "But I am no longer myself / nor is my house my house." The premature death of the girl annuls the effort they spent to reach her, despite the blood and the tears.

In "Taboo Games 3," Yang Mu suppresses the tragic plot of the source text in which the girl died by introducing a kind and curious girl to the scene. This girl is learning to play the Spanish guitar and speaks the polysyllabic language. The persona wishes to deliver this girl into the hands of St. Michael so that she can be taught about Granada, about history and about great compassion. However, the poem's sense of futility remains and is presented in the death of a youth under the fig trees. The youth wears a clean cap and leaves his home on Sunday, probably on his way to a church. He knows Lorca's poems well but his premature death, caused by political persecution, deprives him of the chance to serve his community as a peasant or a soldier. In "Taboo Games 2" the line, "In tears, in blood" acts like a Greek tragedy's choral commentary. It is borrowed from Lorca as a mourning refrain for Spanish history and Lorca's fate. Violence and bloodshed, together with insecurity and melancholy hover throughout "Taboo Games."

"Taboo Games 4" ends on a concluding note, as if a conclusion can be obtained from the Spanish lesson. The persona comes to realize that when music and love are gone, life can still continue to fulfil itself.

When music is lost (say, now)
the story is still there, the hero alive
....
even if he is killed on an alien land   (line 13-4, 33)

The alien land can be the homeland, which is now alienated by a "Spanish" white terror. The owner of the residence sighs, "But I am no longer myself / nor is my house my house," because the guitar is replaced by guns, the donkeys are taken over by the cavalry and the music of the great romance is finally drowned in the staccato shooting. The white terror perpetuated by the state apparatus in Spain is similar to what occurred in Taiwan. "Taboo Games" are played at the threshold between the invocation of the taboo and the temptation to overstep it. The poem celebrates Lorca by protesting against the Spanish fascist regime in particular and against all totalitarian rule in general. The persona mulls over these issues at the border of the city of Granada, as well as on the peripheries of all marginalized places. His poignant political contemplations offer insight into local Taiwanese issues from a global perspective.

In another poem on the Spanish theme, "Spain – 1936," Yang Mu adopts a less dramatic and more meditative approach to the same issues. This poem appeals to the world to take responsibility for the deaths of Spanish poets and philosophers in 1936:

> In the memories of olive trees, wishing to grasp
> the philosophy of Miguel De Unamuno[24]
> That must be 1936, before we
> were born, in a place faraway
> Miguel De Unamuno died; he died
> in the existence of existentialism. That is 1936
> In the memories of fig trees, a poet
> died too; he did not exist in our existentialism
> Federico Garcia Lorca
>
> How does a nation make sense of
> the death of poets and philosophers?
> In 1936. How does a people
> mourn for those hovering in the air
> those souls that won't go away? I ask
> "Can you answer me?" I search in your eyes
> only to find a frustrating, cynical look
> I wish to stay away, so once again I dash into
> the mist

In the age of existentialism the murders of poets and philosophers ironically demonstrate a denial of their existence, which is defined by their commitment to the chosen political beliefs. When people have the courage to think and act against totalitarian rule, death is not final since their spirit cannot be explained away by the regime. The poem confronts the usual irresponsible, cynical attitudes of intellectuals who excel at explaining away guilt with rationality. In retrospect, this poem foreshadowed the imminent Guomindang crackdown of Taiwanese nativists

---

[24] Miguel De Unamuno, a Spanish philosopher (1864-1936).

in the late 1970s. When men die for a cause in times of political persecution, they leave a question that demands an answer. Continually
returning to the question will punctuate and puncture subsequent history
writing. Narratives of a nation and her people cannot be easily closed
but have to confront and make sense of the deaths in "Spain – 1936," in
"Formosa – 1979" and in similar events throughout human history.

A Spring Prophecy of Rebirth

The turn from the anti-Westernism of the 1970s to the anti-Chinese-
ness of the 1990s reflects not only the changes in world politics but also
the complex national consciousness of the Taiwanese. In the last decade
of the twentieth century, Yang Mu located another site for his poetic
explorations. The poet's thoughts on Russian history are shown in such
works as "*Boli* – Khabarovsk 1994, " "Loneliness 1910," and
"St. Petersburg," which are set during the Russian Revolution.[25] These
poems were written in the mid-1990s at a time when Yang Mu taught in
Hong Kong.

After the signing of the Sino-British Joint Declaration in 1984, the
people of Hong Kong waited for more than a decade for the day their
home was handed over to the People's Republic of China. As a result,
Hong Kong endured a period of anxiety and uncertainty. The re-
unification of Hong Kong with the PRC paradoxically suggests the
"liberation" of Hong Kong from both communist and colonial connotations. The local people regarded the re-unification with ambivalence.
Yang Mu's Russian poems reflect his concerns about these political
events. The 1997 re-unification forced many Hong Kong people to flee
their birthplace and seek a home elsewhere. His Russian poems demonstrate Yang Mu's commitment to democracy and they also examine
issues of flight and desertion in extreme situations. "*Boli* – Khabarovsk
1994" is about a Russian soldier running away from the red guards. The
refuge he finds on a hill at Khabarovsk is symbolic. Khabarovsk is the
converging point of the Ussuri River (*Wusulijiang*) and the Amur River
(*Heilongjiang*) running from China and Russia respectively.[26] Rivers are
common motifs in classical Chinese poetry, signifying time, memory
and history, but usually only segments of a river were employed for
these purposes. Yang Mu's innovative decision to represent the merging
of two rivers from different nations extends the motif of the transcultural
connection between the USSR and the PRC. Caught between two

---

[25]   The three poems were written in 1994. They are now collected in Yang Mu's
eleventh book of poetry, *Temporality Proposition*, 80-90.

[26]   Khabarovsk (*Boli*), the second largest city in the Russian Far East, is about thirty
kilometres from the Chinese border. *Heilongjiang* (Black Dragon River) is the Chinese name for the Amur River, which marks the border between China and Russia.

communist regimes, the Russian soldier is stranded on the shore. He continues to have high hopes for the future because a young girl waits for him on a mountain peak. She is characterized as a source of light: a blonde in a golden dress with the sun behind her. At the heights of Khabarovsk, Yang Mu offers a bird's eye view comparison of the two communist narratives, at the same time as he expands the traditional Chinese literary trope that equates rivers with history.

"St. Petersburg" is a poem on the theme of desertion with strong political undertones. The setting is Russia before the October Revolution. "That is the night before the second revolution" – the speaker meditates at a moment of political change:

> That era, is an era about to end, our city is about
> To fall. The disappointed soldiers follow different
> Flags and drums, and wage in my heart
> A small battle   (lines 1-4)

In the beginning, the speaker's immobility is a matter of personal choice. Having said goodbye to his friends in the first stanza, he says to himself, "I stay behind alone" (line 7). As his sense of alienation grows and his fears of misunderstanding surge, the speaker's confidence sags. The lament about the unexpected departure of "you" in "You left me here alone" (line 28) indicates that the speaker's stay in the place has degenerated from an enactment of his own will to a helpless abandonment by others. The speaker's dilemma captures the mood of Hong Kong in face of its imminent liberation. Besides showing the poet's empathetic response to the anxiety of Hong Kong, the poem articulates the trialectics among the three geo-political entities bordering the Taiwan straits – the PRC, Hong Kong and Taiwan. Because the implementation of "One Country, Two Systems" in Hong Kong is considered a model for the future unification of Taiwan with the PRC, a sceptical Taiwanese perspective is embedded in Yang Mu's Russian analogy of the Hong Kong handover.[27]

Similarly, the analogy between Chechnya and Taiwan in Yang Mu's poem "The Lost Ring – for Chechnya" (2000) is not far-fetched. Since

---

[27] "One Country, Two Systems" is a concept originally proposed by Deng Xiaopeng, the leader of the People's Republic of China, during the early 1980s. It is a guiding principle for the reunification of China. The idea is that there will be only one China, but that areas such as Hong Kong, Macau and Taiwan can retain their own capitalist economic and political systems, their own distinct laws, freedoms and way of life, while the mainland adopts the socialist system. With the implementation of "One Country, Two Systems" after the British and Portugese governments returned Hong Kong and Macau to China in 1997 and 1999 respectively, the two cities have become Special Administrative Regions of China. These regions will exist under the system until 50 years after the handover.

the late 1980s Taiwan has been democratizing, which has gradually paved the way for the nation's self-assertion as an independent political entity. This newly formed notion of sovereignty and national dignity was exemplified by the presidential elections in 1996 and 2000, both of which were held under the PRC's threats of war. Coincidentally, both elections also occurred at the same time as the two Chechen wars of independence from Russia. Ironically, the analogy between the two nations' political situations was not first made by poets, but by the leaders of the two dominant powers, the PRC and Russia. In 1996 the PRC and Russia formed a coalition and signed a Sino-Russian Strategic Partnership against American hegemony. When Jiang Zhimin and Boris N. Yeltsin met in Beijing on the 9 and 10 December 1999, Yeltsin pointed out the similarities between the problems of Chechnya and Taiwan. On 10 December, the Sino-Russian Joint Declaration was released, reinforcing a mutual support on the issues of Taiwan and Chechnya. Yeltsin sided with Jiang on Beijing's re-unification stance, refusing to recognize the "state-to-state" theory, and objecting to the inclusion of Taiwan in the American-led Territorial Missile Defence. In return, Jiang supported the Russian incursion into Chechnya. The parallels between Chechnya and Taiwan were thus politically recognized.

Taiwan was ready to launch its second presidential election in 2000. On 21 February 2000 the state council in Beijing released a controversial White Paper on the PRC's Taiwan policy. The 110,000-word document, issued during the presidential campaign period in Taiwan, was widely believed to be Beijing's plan to influence the March 18 presidential election. Taiwanese people were electing a president for the new millennium and the result would certainly influence the nation's political future. The White Paper put pressure on candidates and voters, and railed against the separatist rhetoric rampant in the 1990s. Beijing proposed a rough "deadline" for re-unification and threatened to use drastic measures, including military force, if Taiwan refused to enter political negotiations. Despite Beijing's war threats, the Taiwanese people defied any attempt to usurp their electoral rights, instead they reiterated their sovereign independence, national dignity and respect for people's choice. The general will was to maintain the status quo, while avoiding any drastic move to jeopardize the island's security.

Both Chechnya and Taiwan are in a minority position under constant threat over their desire for national independence. The second Chechen war is rather different from the first in which the Russian troops suffered. In the second war, Putin successfully seized all of Chechnya, which raised his popularity and secured him the Russian presidency in the March election. In February, the Russian invasion of Grozny, the capital of Chechnya, reached its final stage. The federal forces occupied most areas of Grozny while the Chechens sought to blast an escape route through the Russian blockade of the besieged city. The refugees who survived the exodus testified to the human rights' abuses committed by the Russian troops. "The Lost Ring – for Chechnya" begins with a letter, recapitulating a news item from the *New York Times* and it is followed by a long narrative poem. From Chechnya to Taiwan, Yang's work transmits a war victim's story and connects Taiwan and Chechnya in a political analogy.[28]

In the spring of 2000, the Taiwanese people were getting ready to cast their votes for a new political future. That Yang Mu chose to speak to his native country from the Chechen position in March is telling. Compared with the global attention paid to the first Chechen war, the international press had been relatively quiet during the second war. The fall of Grozny bolstered Putin's electoral prospects in the spring. Nonetheless, Yang Mu is optimistic about Chechnya's hopes for independence. In the last line of the poem the Chechen youth looks forward to "Independence, the spring prophecy of rebirth." Yang Mu envelops the Chechen history in a letter home that ends in a piece of loving advice, "Roads are slippery on rainy days. Be cautious." The poet, together with the Taiwanese people, stands in a critical historic moment, anxiously anticipating what the spring election will bring to Taiwan.

Translation as Allegory

By incorporating Indian, Irish, Spanish and Chechen stories into his poems, Yang Mu uses translation as an allegorical means of examining modern Taiwan history. In contemporary cultural discourse, translation studies are considered the key to comparative studies in literature and culture. The word "translation" is heavily loaded with connotations of mediation, appropriation, and power play. A translator is no innocent agent engaged in a process of decoding and recoding a message. Like anyone who writes, he or she inevitably participates in a performative act of cultural construction or deconstruction. Unlike someone who only writes, however, the translator encounters two cultures, each of which confronts the other at the same time. As translation always involves a series of decisions, most importantly, selection and dissemination, the cultural strategy employed by the translator cannot be overlooked.

History tells us how political upheavals have instigated intellectual and literary transformations, which were often facilitated by the importation of foreign ideas. Susan Bassnett sees translation as playing "a

---

[28] For a detailed analysis of Yang's adaptation of Heidi's story from the *New York Times* in his poem, see the discussion in Chapter 2.

fundamental role in cultural change."[29] Specific cultural experiences at a historical juncture are often reflected in literary forms. Translation of cultural experiences is now facilitated by the speed that both humans and information can travel, creating transnational correlations that engender insights into local and global concerns.

While colonial subjection of indigenous cultures should be heeded, the subversive potential of translation is viewed as an art of resistance in James C. Scott's notion of "hidden transcript."[30] By bringing home unorthodox ideas, which constitute a source of resistance, a translator can inscribe a political agenda against the dominant culture without being held accountable for this dissident voice. The engagement of the mainstream ideology in the interplay between the orthodox and the heretic is a game that translators can safely play because the translator can claim he or she is simply translating another's ideas. This provides an emergency exit or alibi for the translator.

By resuscitating the circulation of a text or an event as "a sign whose signifié was a culture as such," Yang Mu's works show how translation participates in debating transnational affairs.[31] His texts are like the hybrid agencies of Homi Bhabha's conception. Their discursive double-ness allows a deployment of "the partial culture from which they emerge to construct visions of community, and versions of historic memory, but give narrative form to the minority positions they occupy; the outside of the inside: the part in the whole" (Bhabha, 1996: 58). In this respect, translation along with allegory and diasporic consciousness are Yang Mu's specific modes of intervention.

For decades, Yang Mu has pondered over Yeats's problems. Having spent more than ten years translating Yeats's poems into Chinese, the poet published *Selected Poems of W. B. Yeats* in February, 1997. The seventy-six poems in this selection offer an overview of Yeats's poetry. Apart from the elegant literary translation and the erudite scholarship in the annotations, what is most striking in this anthology is the "Introduc-

---

[29] "Writing does not happen in a vacuum, it happens in a context and the process of translating texts from one cultural system into another is not a neutral, innocent transparent activity. Translation is instead a highly charged, transgressive activity, and the politics of translation and translating deserve much greater attention than has been paid in the past. Translation has played a fundamental role in cultural change." Susan Bassnett, "From Comparative Literature to Translation Studies," in *Comparative Literature: A Critical Introduction* (Oxford: Blackwell, 1993), 160-1.

[30] See James C. Scott, *Domination and the Art of Resistance: Hidden Transcripts* (New Haven: Yale University Press, 1990).

[31] For the notion of circulation of sign in "translation as culture" or "culture-modelling translation," see Vladimir Macura, "Culture as Translation," in *Translation, History and Culture.* eds. Susan Bassnett and Andre Lefevere (London: Cassell, 1995), 64-70.

tion." Instead of giving a critical analysis of Yeats's exquisite poetic craftsmanship in this lengthy essay, Yang Mu focuses on the gradual creation of the Irish nation from its fluid nomadic tribal state to its declaration of Independence upon the formation of the Irish Republic in 1948. Discussions of Yeats's personal life, political endeavours and literary works make up only about half of this introductory essay. Yang Mu deliberately embeds the poet and his poetry in an Irish national narrative. The emphasis on Irish history indicates a close connection between texts and contexts, poet and history. The "Introduction" shows that radical activism is not the only path to political intervention and nation building. Yang Mu highlights how Yeats contributed to national liberation by reinforcing a distinct Irish culture. Yeats's re-inscription of the Celtic myths as well as local topographies such as the Danaan beach and Irish countryside, brings about a revival of Celtic culture that is central to the cultivation of a national consciousness. Moreover, Yang Mu establishes a connection between Ireland and Taiwan in the "Introduction" by his reference to Johnathan Swift's "A Modest Proposal." Swift's satirical "proposal" advocated, through allegory, the slaughter of Irish children by the colonizers for the convenience of colonial administration. No matter how macabre the policy sounds, Swift urged its implementation after the model practised in Formosa [Taiwan]. In Swift's portrayal, Ireland's suffering under colonial suppression is compared to that of a colony in the Far East. Given attitudes to Asia at that time in history, Swift's comparison was meant to be a grotesque analogy, however, it is a vivid cultural correlative.

Furthermore, it is interesting to note that in the 1990s Yeats and his works attracted much literary and critical attention in Taiwan. Twenty-eight years after Yang Mu published his poem, "Sailing to Ireland," Wu Qiancheng published a collection of essays on Yeats under the same title in 1999. As a result of the lifting of martial law in 1987 and the subsequent democratization on the island, the political significance of the analogy between Ireland and Taiwan has become apparent. The Irish literary revival and rebellion against Britain in the 1910s and 1920s seems to serve as a precedent to the Taiwanese cultural rebellion against "Chinese-ness." Yang Mu's preface to Wu's book is entitled "Poetry, Love and Politics." In it he makes his translational-transnational concerns explicit.[32]

---

[32] In Emily Apter's conceptualization of translation zones, the zone is one of "critical engagement that connects the 'l' and the 'n' of transLation and transNation." She uses the term "translational transnationalism" to "emphasize translation among small nations or minority language communities." See Emily Apter, *The Translation Zone: A New Comparative Literature* (Princeton: Princeton University Press, 2006), 5. Here Yang Mu's translational-transnational concerns involve contemporary international politics in a much broader sense.

Political movement itself is not the goal. What a movement aims to bring about is the persistent faith and compassion in a civil society – this is the goal of our engagement and participation. Poetry is the means to maintain our spontaneous human feelings, in our literary world, as in Yeats's literary world. Let's look at his from this place, at this time, when the twentieth century moves into the twenty-first, from Taiwan. (Wu, 1999: 21-2)

By urging his readers to align Yeats's experiences with their own, Yang Mu opens up new vistas to identity issues from a binocular "global-local" perspective. The complexities Yang Mu discerns in the Taiwanese negotiations of a national-cultural identity are revealed in his answer to the question about why he translated Yeats's poetry: "Yeats is Irish; he writes Irish poetry in English. I am a Taiwanese; I write Taiwan poetry in Chinese. The Chinese culture is certainly the ultimate reference, but I hope to help Taiwan poetry to find a form, a tradition" (Yang, 1996: 37).

Besides working towards the formation of a Taiwan poetic tradition, Yang Mu's translation also attends to the interests of the indigenous minorities. In 1999, he published his Chinese translation of *The Tempest*. Shakespeare's identification with Prospero is shared by the accomplished poet. His sympathetic reading of Caliban, who is native to the island, is of course an implied political statement against imperialism and the exploitation of indigenous people. The translation of *The Tempest*, whose emphasis is on forgiveness rather than revenge, seems to foreshadow his reconciliatory tendencies evident in later poems such as "A Draw in Chess" (2001).

* *
*

Writing about the Irish, Spanish, and Chechen themes, as well as the Indian and Chinese diasporas, Yang Mu interrogates the nationalistic, essentializing rubrics of the identity discourse in Taiwan by linking a people and a home to world history. Dwelling in another place, speaking from a borrowed position, the poet addresses the issues by re-contextualizing the immediate present in the past or in a foreign place. In the poems discussed, the nostalgia is "Irish," the post-colonial diasporic consciousness is "Indian," the political protests are "Spanish" and "Chechen." Yang Mu's writing is allegorical. Travelling across cultures and meditating on the peripheries within a culture, his poetry illuminates a composite cultural identity that is at once local and global, difficult if not impossible to nationalize. Contrary to the binarism exhibited in the anti-westernism of the Modern Poetry Debate in the early 1970s and the Native Soil Literature Movement in subsequent years, Yang Mu's cautious location of the site for identification actually foreshadowed the politics of nativist discourse of internal otherness within "Chinese-ness," which has played out in the last two decades. The nostalgia that Yang Mu has fashioned in an allegorical displacement is not nostalgia for the epic heroism of an originary culture. It is the yearning for a site – "another" context where the pressing issues of the present can be situated and raised in a trove of awakened possibilities, which are otherwise already closed.

Different from fable in which "one reads the moral back into the narrative" in order to contain a reader's experiences in a closed text, allegory enables one to read the narrative in an inflexible form with self-reflexivity (S. Stewart, 1991: 79). Distance lends perspective and makes room for comparison. Writing allegorically, just like living in diaspora, allows the flight into exile to be followed by a re-conception of home from a distance, with an identically detached artistic posture. Yang Mu's poetic approach to Taiwan identity politics entails an allegorical reading of the inside from the outside. This diasporic distance offers a global perspective from outside to reflect on the "local" national discourse. By re-staging the suppressed histories of the Dutch Occupation, the fall of the Ming dynasty, together with various foreign "national" precedents, his poems advance the re-reading of a historical event from a new critical point of view.

While some translators use translation to disguise the message of resistance and to erase their own presence, Yang Mu's translation of text or event into a transcultural discourse is endorsed with a distinct signature. Instead of taking this translational act as an escape, Yang Mu deploys it as a transnational illumination. The evocation of Ireland foreshadows the national excesses of "Chinese nationalism" in Taiwan of the 1970s, and bringing Chechnya to world attention in the new millennium reinforces the conviction of national autonomy and independence, with full awareness of the high price it will probably cost. Yang Mu's transcript of resistance is not hidden, but is mediated so that the inter-cultural references to the Irish and Chechen themes help to decipher the cultural and political issues at hand. His creative use of "inter-contextuality" allows a multi-layered structure of narratives to be doubly or triply voiced.

Cultural translation demands the recognition of the historical specificities of an event in the source culture. Yet it also proves that many of such specificities are in fact "translatable" experiences that may foster insights for people caught in a similar predicament in the culture of another place at another time. Other than imperialist moves of domination and appropriation, translation can engender "contesting and contested stories" from minority positions. Specific local concerns are often marginalized by dominant powers in world politics, but through translation and its interplay with creative writing in a different culture, what is local can reach out to interact with global efforts of protest and resistance. Dramatizing a historical moment or writing allegory from the outside, Yang Mu does not bypass the local political contingencies, but engages them more intensely in global historical contexts.

CHAPTER 5

On Transcultural Poetics

Choosing Forms of Worship from Poetic Tales[*]

"Why is Chinese poetry so short?" An English professor asked.
"Before I answer your question, I'd like to know why European poetry is so long." Said Yang Mu.[1]

Yang Mu's anecdote above succinctly illustrates the heart of East-West comparative literature: the subject for intellectual inquiry and the difficulty of finding a truly bias-free methodology. Answering a question with a question, the exchange, which took place in the 1970s, foreshadowed the critical exchanges in the decades to come. A question arising from this issue was raised by Rey Chow: "what are the power relationships between the 'subject' and 'object' of the culturally overdetermined 'eye'?" (R. Chow, 1991: 3) Comparative study of any kind requires the ability to turn the tables and the readiness to take a binocular view of the literature in question.

As discussed in earlier chapters, the traditional historical-biographical approach adopted by Chinese literary criticism can be read, not as an example of intentional fallacy as invented by the New Critics; but instead this approach's emphasis on "historicity" can be seen as foreshadowing the post-structuralist reading. The Chinese reverence for their literary predecessors and their ready acknowledgment of borrowing from them may be accused of hampering their quest for originality, but one may also argue that the ancients demonstrated an early recogni-

---

[*] The line is quoted from William Blake, "Plate 11" of *The Marriage of Heaven and Hell*.

[1] I first heard this story in 1993 in one of Yang Mu's lectures on Comparative Literature at the Hong Kong University of Science and Technology. The dialogue took place at a conference on East-West comparative literature at Harvard University in the early 1970s. Yang Mu gave a detailed account of the event in an interview with Michelle Yeh in 2002. See Arthur Sze and Michelle Yeh, "Frontier Perspectives: Three Interviews on Contemporary Poetry in Taiwan" in *Mercury Rising: Contemporary Poetry from Taiwan*. eds. Frank Stewart, Arthur Sze and Michelle Yeh (Hawaii: Manoa, 2003), 30-1.

tion of belatedness and a post-modern awareness that a writer's work is but a repository for the literary echoes of his predecessors. Living at a particular moment in history, every author writes amid these echoes. The sole way to escape their influence is to select the voice(s) that most closely match one's own. Only knowledge can expand a poet's range of options for the predecessors he chooses to echo. Yang Mu's anecdote underscores the impediments that have existed in the development of East-West comparative poetics since the mid-twentieth century. His disinterest in the literary debate between Native Soil Literature and Modernist Poetics in Taiwan in the 1970s is ascribed to a simple attitude: *"There's no point in continuing this debate because we have read very different books. Our reading lists are different"* (Stewart *et al.*, 2003: 29, emphasis in the original). The same reasoning can apply to the questions about the length of a specific kind of national poetry. Whether one finds a particular kind of poetry "short" or "long" actually depends on one's cultural assumptions about the norm.

The English professor's question reflects an Orientalist view of Chinese poetic form, which is mainly derived from classical poetry. Global literary history in the last century saw not only a unilateral trend of cultural influence from the West dictated by the route of colonial conquest, but also an increasingly dynamic interactive exchange between continents. Notions of literariness introduced by the Russian Formalists and Czech Structuralists have become a disciplinary paradigm for comparative literature since Wellek's criticism of the French school in the 1950s.[2] From a comparative perspective, literariness in world literature is in fact inter-literariness and the idea of the inter-literary process has become a major subject for scrutiny.[3] One of the pioneering Chinese comparatist, Chen Shih-hsiang, saw such inter-literary relations in generic terms:

> the dominant position of the Songs [*Book of Songs*] in Chinese literary valuation as well as creation, in contradistinction to that of the ancient

---

[2]   For example, Roman Jakobson, "The object of literary scholarship is not literature but literariness, i.e. which makes a given work a literary one." Roman Jakobson, *Noveishaia russkaia poezia* (Recent Russian Theory) (1921), as quoted and translated by Marián Gálik (Gálik, 2003: 34). René Wellek, "Literary scholarship will not make any progress methodologically, unless it determines to study literature as subject distinct from other activities and procedures of man. Hence we must face the problem of 'literariness,' the central issue of aesthetics, the nature of art and literature." See "Crises of Comparative Literature" in *Concepts of Literature*, 293.

[3]   In *Theory of Interliterary Process* (1989), Dionýz Ďurišin writes: "Interliterariness is the basic and essential quality of literature in an international and inter-ethnic context and ontological determination. This determination and its framework comprise all possible relations and affinities, individual literatures, supra-ethnic, and supra-national entities of various kinds, and the highest embodiment of interliterariness, world literature" (Ďurišin, 1989: 21).

Greek epic and drama, is an ever thought-provoking phenomenon. ... To speak of the Songs as lyric is to find for our discussion of a common language in modern criticism, as well as to distinguish them as a prototype characterizing the first accomplishment of Chinese literary creation and fathering a native tradition as truly as the ancient Greek drama and epic fathered the European. (S. H. Chen, 1969: 373-4)

To offer a conceptual framework for effective comparison, Chen set up the trinity of literary archetypes by bringing together the dominant ancient literary traditions of the world. Justly placed in juxtaposition with its western counterparts, Chinese lyric tradition stands out as the most significant subject for research in comparative poetics. At the 2001 Congress of the American Comparative Literature Association, Jonathan Culler's keynote speech called for a long overdue comparison of poetry. This chapter attempts to answer his call by analyzing Yang Mu's response to the challenge of transcultural poetics.

Steeped in Chinese and western cultures and well-versed in both Chinese and English, Yang Mu demonstrates his intercultural mobility in his poetics and poetry. His comparative perspective offers alternative readings to some dominant discourses of language and literature. Certainly one can easily tack the label of a Romanticist on Yang Mu, seeing that his earliest poetic mentor is John Keats, and his latest is W. B. Yeats. However, a close examination of his poetics proves Yang Mu's resistance to the indulgence of narcissistic musings. His brand of lyricism has an inherent urge for communicative dialogic exchange and his poems address an audience. In "Private Poetry, Public Deception," Jerome McGann exposes the hypocrisy of the rhetoric of sincerity in the romantic ideology:

> If a contradiction exposes itself at the core of Romantic self-integrity, we confront an illusion in the romantic idea(l) of spontaneity and artlessness. Romantic sincerity only presents itself as unpremeditated verse; in fact it involves a rhetoric, and contractual bonds with its audiences, which are just as determinate and artful as the verse of Donne, or Rochester, or Pope. The rhetoric of sincerity in romanticism is a rhetoric of displacement; the audience is not addressed directly, it is set apart, like the reflective poet, in a position where the discourse of the poem has to be overheard. Among the important consequence of this basic maneuver is the illusion of freedom which it fosters – as if the reader were not being placed under the power of the writer's rhetoric, as if the writer were relatively indifferent to the reader's presence and intent only on communing with his own soul.[4]

As a result of the Romantic illusion, the poetic space of the poem is exclusive to the poet, sanctioned and sacred, not to be intruded upon.

---

[4] Charles Bernstein, ed. *The Politics of Poetic Form: Poetry and Public Policy* (New York: Roof, 1990), 123.

The reader can only watch and overhear from a distance. The rhetoric of sincerity requires a conception of language as a transparent medium through which a poet can construct a reality, internal or external, that the reader can reach. The consistent feature in Romantic discourse is the referential effect.

It is fair to say that Yang Mu's concerns in his first two books of poetry are primarily Romantic. His emphasis on the expression of his own moods, emotions, and thoughts is constitutive of a transcendental ego – the poet as the point of origin for poetry. Taking the poet as a personality and poetry as life experience mixes art and life. However, a marked shift from these early commitments is found in his third book of poetry. Since its publication, there has been a conspicuous tension between Yang Mu's romantic outpouring and his modernist restraint. The strong lyric impulse pulls the poet towards Wordsworthian sincerity, while the pursuit of artistic refinement points to Eliotian impersonality. Anthony Easthope elucidates the struggle between romantic and modernist poetics by listing how "'Tradition and the Individual Talent' is effectively a point-by-point refutation of Wordsworth's 'Preface'" (Easthope, 1983: 135-6). This seminal essay by Eliot plays a central role in Yang Mu's *The Completion of a Poem*, where he explicates the relationship between a burgeoning poet and his cultural heritage. From "Letters to Keats," to other works on comparative poetics such as *The Completion of a Poem* and *The Sceptic: Notes on Poetical Discrepancies*, Yang Mu translated and assimilated the best examples from Western lyrics and critically scrutinized his own personal temperament and cultural heritage at the same time. Being selective and reflective in the cultural transfer of the western poetic tenets, Yang Mu has helped shape a new configuration of modern Chinese poetics and disseminated it in theory and practice.

A study of the influence and dissemination of a particular European literary movement such as Romanticism in the East inevitably involves an investigation into the process of translation and transfer, which is easily mistaken as a mere repetition. Lydia Liu warns comparatists of parochial conceptual aberrations towards translational and transcultural practice such as the bias that "[t]he knowledge obtained in this way cannot but be tautological," and draws critical attention to writers' inventiveness and contribution in translingual practice (L. Liu, 1995: 9). René Wellek proposed that "[c]learly there are periods of the dominance of a system of ideas and poetic practices; and clearly they have their anticipations and their survivals."[5] As the world is becoming globalized,

---

[5]   For Wellek's remark, see "The Concept of 'Romanticism' in Literary History – II. The Unity of European Romanticism," *Comparative Literature* 1.1 (Winter 1949): 172.

a cross-cultural approach is key. On this issue, Jan Walsh Hokenson's comment is most discerning:

> Writ global. As we begin to realize, here on our brink, how adopted languages, adopted cultures, adopted genres change radically under the pressures of modern migrations and at the hands of bi-cultural writers, we will begin to see continuities that we failed to notice in the hey-day of national literatures. In the creeping erasure of national, canonical, disciplinary, and other borders, we must re-vision the literary past of the last millennium in order to locate sites of cultural transfer in medieval, renaissance, augustan, romantic, modernist intertextuality, and thereby develop the analytical, comparative tools to accommodate literary history in the new millennium. (Hokenson, 2003: 62)

To reflect on the global view of the research field, Rainer Schönhaar proposes a "transcultural approach" to comparative literature in the twenty-first century. Finding that existing categories like "imitation," and "transformation" are too narrow to define what has been happening, he suggests applying Wellek's notion of "confrontation" in a "transcultural sense and manner" to study literatures of entirely different origins (Schönhaar, 2004: 248-9).

The following sections will explore new sites for national heritage and cross-cultural transfer in Yang Mu's poetics. A comparatist himself, Yang's major concern is the future development of Chinese poetry. Well aware of the Chinese traditional conception of poetry as a means to "verbalize intent" and the tendency towards historical-biographical reading in literary criticism, Yang seeks innovations through Western literary trends like romanticism and modernism. Bringing together visions of poetry from poets of various cultures such as Keats, Goethe, Yeats, Rilke, and Eliot, Yang attempts his own definition of poetry in his mature works.

As for the "Chinese" dimension in poetry writing, Yang Mu's approach is unique. The sense of affinity he feels for the cultural China of the ancient past and his demonstrated interest in early poetry such as the *Book of Songs*, classical works before the Six Dynasties, and Tang poetry resulted in well-known publications like *The Bell and the Drum, From Ritual to Allegory: Seven Essays in Early Chinese Poetry*, and *Anthology of Tang Poetry*. Sympathetic attention to the long neglected south in Chinese literary history is a dominant feature of Yang's poetics. The elegies of the south by Qu Yuan, and works about the south in Tang poetry are highlighted in his commentary. As a poet, Yang Mu is considered "the Hualian poet," honouring his commitment to his birthplace. From the small coastal town, Yang has earned fame across Asia with his "modern" poetry, which was recognized in 2007 when he was awarded "The International Prize for Literature Written in the Chinese Language." He has modernized versification not only by experimenting with new forms and *vers libre*, but also by making old forms such as the sonnet and *yuefu* new. The urbanity and mobility exhibited in his poetry illustrates his modern cosmopolitan outlook on the world. The contemporary trend of global travel expands to include the cross-cultural assimilation of language, poetic form and reading material. Hand in hand with globalization is the need to be anchored to the local. Viewing historical events through their inter-contextuality is a prevalent feature of Yang Mu's recent poems, and clearly shows his formulation of a global perspective for modern Chinese poetics. In translation, his poetry and poetics has contributed significantly to transcultural poetics in the making.

Letters to Keats

Yang Mu's professed affinity for the Romantic poets led critics to describe him as "a disciple of English Romanticism." Zhang Mo, the editor of *Contemporary Chinese Poetry: Ten Major Poets* says:

> Yang Mu is a disciple of "unsurpassable beauty." His poetry is obsessed with the overflow of "beauty" – wild surmise and stirs in nature, and it often recalls our nostalgic reverie of the simple, peaceful way of life in ancient times. He is a cloud that rises over the hills, or a chime of bells from an old temple, which does not detain your feet, but demands your heart to feel, your eyes to listen. (M. Zhang, 1977: 415)

From Yip Wai-lim's point of view, Yang Mu consistently upholds the Keatsian conviction of "a fine excess" of beauty and "is always a disciple of the overpowering beauty."[6]

There is little doubt that the influence of Keats is paramount in Yang Mu's early writings. In his teens, Yang Mu began his poetic quest with the Chinese notion of the affective-expressive function of literature and he valued poetry as the language of emotions.[7] Unknowingly echoing the Romantic rhetoric of sincerity, the youth understood language to be a transparent vehicle for rendering one's personal feelings and state of mind. In his first book of poetry, *By the Waterside* (1960), Yang Mu deliberately set himself apart from the Romantic generation of May Fourth by declaring that poetry is no longer sentimental confessions. His emphasis on "meditation and contemplation" suggests the vatic posture

---

6   In a letter, Keats wrote, "I think poetry should surprise by a fine excess... that if poetry comes not as naturally as the leaves to a tree it had better not come at all." See Letter to John Taylor, 27 February, 1818. See also Yip Wai-lim, "Afterword," in *Legends* (Yang, 1971: 119).

7   For Ye Shan's [Yang Mu] views of poetry, see Yang Mu, *Collected Poems of Yang Mu, Volume 1* (Yang, 1978b: 605-8).

of a Romantic poet's musings, whose words are meant to be overheard. Unlike some Romantic pioneers of modern Chinese poetry, Yang Mu prized "emotions recollected in tranquillity" over "an overflow of powerful feelings." He denied "inspiration" but was convinced of poetry's expressive function and yearned for effective communication.

From *By the Waterside* to *Flower Season* (1963), his method of conveying his message progressed from addressing a specific referent to confiding in an indefinite group of solitary people who are fond of beauty, eternity and unreality. Yet the lyrical self remained closely connected to the author's self. "From the beginning till now, I have written about one hundred poems, they are purely records of my personal moods and thoughts" (Yang, 1978b: 608). To the young poet, "[i]f poetry does have a purpose, it is to show 'you' my [his] feelings" (Yang, 1978b: 605). While he wrote and read poetry for his own gratification, publishing also brought much satisfaction. "I publish these poems because I enjoy the pleasure of reading others' poems," he said (Yang, 1978b: 608). This conception of the pleasures of a poetic life reflected his essential kinship with the thoughts of the Romantics, which was later systematized with his progress in literary education. Yang Mu's interest in Keats grew during his undergraduate studies in the Department of Foreign Languages at the Christian Tunghai University (1959-63). After his "rapport de fait" with Keats the young poet was able to theorize his many thoughts on poetry into a coherent belief in Romanticism. Poetry was elevated to a kind of natural law – "the law of the heart" in pursuit of beauty and truth (Yang, 1978b: 608). To him, the divine impact of poetry served to cultivate human sentiments and spiritual strength, just as a religion does. Kantian influence seemed to creep in when Yang Mu proclaimed the subject-matter most deserving of his praise to be a purposeless, purely divine beauty and selfless love. Yang Mu declared in the Preface of *Flower Season* that he worshipped John Keats above all other poets.

Acknowledgement of Keats's influence was also made in his prose work entitled "Letters to Keats." Yang Mu wrote fifteen letters to Keats between 1963-5 while serving in the army at Quemoy and later pursuing graduate study in Iowa.[8] Quemoy was the first time the poet spent a

---

[8]   Yang Mu graduated from the Christian Tunghai University in June 1963. He then served in the army at Quemoy from October 1963 to July of the following year. In September 1964, he went to the US to do a Masters degree at the University of Iowa. The fifteen letters, in the order arranged by the author, are: 1. "Lühu de fengbao" [Storms over the Green Lake] (1963), 2. "Ziran de jidong" [Stirs of Nature] (1964) 3. "Shanzhong shu" [Writing in the Mountain] (1964), 4. "Jie" [Misfortune] (1964), 5. "Zuihou de shoulie" [The Last Hunt] (1964), 6. "Lianhua luo" [Flowers of Chinaberry Fall] (1964), 7. "Xiatian de qinsheng" [Summer Music from the Piano] (1964), 8. "Hanyu" [Chilly Rain] (1963), 9. "Xiang xuwu chenmei" [To Nothingness Do

considerable period away from home or campus and from his family and friends. In solitude, the young poet began a written conversation with the poet whom he most revered. These fifteen letters make up a journal of spiritual quest, which resembles the Greek philosophical discourse. As Michel Foucault says, the struggle of the soul in the pursuit of self-knowledge is basically dialectical. A pseudo-dialogue is necessary in order to conduct a self-analysis.[9] Like a student engaged in the great Socratic discussions, the young poet engaged Keats in a conversation about the meaning and purpose of life. Their topics cover a large but fairly coherent body of thought related to themes such as nature, beauty, love, solitude and simplicity. The letters laid the foundation for the poet's later development of a poetics for modern Chinese poetry, which is Romantic in spirit and modernist in form. *First Essays of Ye Shan* (1966), his prose work that contains "Letters to Keats," has gone through several reprints and in particular the preface to the 1977 edition exhibits the poet's persistent inclination to English Romanticism. Allusions to Keats's work frequently appear in his other prose writings, such as "Science and the Nightingale" (1977) (Yang, 1982: 17-26). Keatsian aesthetics is also found in his books on poetics such as *The Completion of a Poem* (1989) and *The Sceptic: Notes on Poetical Discrepancies* (1993).[10]

It is widely known that "Letters to Keats" not only helped formulate the poet's own development of a theory for writing, but also introduced the Romantics' aesthetic and philosophical notions, such as imagination,

---

Sink] (1964), 10. "CAVEMEN" (1963), 11. "Hongye" [A Red Leaf] (1964), 12. "Di shier xin" [The Twelfth Letter] (1964), 13. "Jiaotangwai de fengjing" [The Scenery outside the Church] (1964), 14. "Lubian" [By the Fire Stove] (1963), and 15. "Zuobie" [Farewell] (1965) (Yang, 1977b: 65-143). *Ye Shan sanwenji* [First Essays of Ye Shan] was published by Wenxing in 1966 and reprinted by Hongfan in 1977. In the last three decades, it went through 17 reprints and a new edition came out in 1994. References to these letters will be indicated by their numbers in the following discussion.

9   Foucault points out the significance of dialogue and letter-writing in the process of self-formation in Greek culture. "In Plato's writings, dialogue gave way to the literary pseudo-dialogue. But by the Hellenistic age, writing prevailed, and real dialectic passed to correspondence. Taking care of oneself became linked to a constant writing activity. The self is something to write about, a theme or object (subject) of writing activity." See Michel Foucault, "Technologies of the Self," in Luther H. Martin *et al.*, eds. *Technologies of the Self* (Amherst: University Press of Massachusetts, 1988), 27.

10   Yang Mu, *Yishou shi de wancheng* [The Completion of a Poem] (Taipei: Hongfan, 1989) and *Yi Shen* [The Sceptic: Notes on Poetical Discrepancies] (Taipei: Hongfan, 1993). The opening paragraph of the preface in *The Sceptic: Notes on Poetical Discrepancies* consists of a single sentence: "This is a book that explores beauty and truth" (1). In another paragraph, the author writes, "All that I care about is but beauty and truth" (2). The poet takes a highly philosophical and intellectual approach to "beauty and truth" in this 304 page book.

beauty and truth, to Chinese readers. As apostrophic correspondences, "Letters to Keats" explicitly illustrates Yang Mu's retreat into an imaginary circle of fellow poets in nineteenth century England. In Culler's opinion, "[a]postrophe resists narrative because its now is not a moment in a temporal sequence but a *now* of discourse, of writing. This temporality of writing... seems to be that toward which the lyric strives" (Culler, 1981: 152). Lyrical in nature, Yang Mu's letters display a sense of "detemporalized immediacy," which is indeed "an immediacy of fiction" (Culler, 1981: 152). A sense of "now-ness" in the imaginary dialogue is fostered by numerous quotations from Keats's correspondence and poems, together with Yang Mu's questions and responses. In this series of exchanges, the author not only fleshed out his romantic approach to poetry, but also eventually discovered what a Chinese poet in the twentieth century ought to do in order to find a genuine voice for himself.

With an affectionate greeting to Keats in the first letter, the youthful Yang Mu entered into an imaginary relationship with his mentor.

> Never would it have occurred to you that after more than one hundred years, tonight, a wet night, when I recall a particular village amid rubble and ruins, I think of you. Did you know the Song dynasty? The beauty of Song is the surprise of the classics... I think of you, you who lived one hundred and fifty years from now. I think of the Middle Ages in your poetry; I think of those ruined fortresses and deserted courtyards in your vision too, as if withered petals drifting down at your side, sending fragrance like nonchalance, residual twilight fading in the dusk. (L1: 67)

Parallels are established between the beauty of ancient Chinese architecture and Keats's poetic vision of Medieval Europe and ancient Greece. Although the poet found that he was in spiritual union with Keats, the two were in reality temporally, geographically and culturally distanced.

> I know we are really far apart in time and in space. This separation is not only caused by barbwire and moat (as you can imagine). This is god's design. (L1: 67)

In this letter Yang Mu evokes an ancient village called "Mountain Queen," which was built during the Song Dynasty. As if creating a film montage, the author abruptly cuts from the Chinese historical site to a scene from Keats's 1818 world. "I saw you... I saw you sitting at your place in Hampstead, with the *Færie Queene* on your lap, and watching your beloved lady walk past the courtyard" (L1: 68). The direct reference to the love story between Keats and Fanny Brawne is phrased in an understanding tone between intimate friends. The seemingly random association between "Mountain Queen" 山后 and the *Færie Queene* 仙后 rests on the ideographical resemblances of the Chinese characters. Yet one will not miss the relevance of the parallel: it was the *Færie*

Queene that first awakened Keats's genius; likewise, it was Keats's poetry in addition to the beauty of ancient Chinese art and architecture that stimulated the artistic side of Yang Mu's nature.[11]

In this initial stage of the correspondences, the young poet's devotion to the Romantic path is evident. He declares to Keats, "I dedicate everything to you" (L1: 72) and "[y]our poetry is like a stain that soaks the whole world; your soul is like a lantern that lights up people's hearts, sentimental and unsentimental alike... you live forever in all places" (L1: 73). This sensitive disciple of Keats has a natural sympathy for the Romantic worship of nature and simplicity, love and beauty. "Many a time, I sat at the riverbank from noon to sunset, only for watching how the clouds gather and disperse in the running water. If only that innocent curiosity could really live on. How I wish I could own such a pure soul forever!" (L3: 81) The exquisite enjoyment of the present, no matter how fleeting, is the Romantic response to the transience of beauty. In another letter, Yang Mu translated directly from Keats's lines, "A thing of beauty is a joy forever / Its loveliness increases; it will never / Pass into nothingness" (L8: 102).[12] His devotion to beauty is a reflection of Keatsian doctrine: "with a great poet the sense of beauty overcomes every other consideration, or rather obliterates all consideration."[13] In letters such as "Flowers of Chinaberry Fall," "Summer Music from the Piano," "A Red Leaf," and "By the Fire Stove," nature and people were rendered with a Rousseauian sensitivity and sincerity. The cross-cutting of conversational fragments and the maidens' countenances with lines from Keats's poems movingly depicts Yang Mu's affectionate relationships with the other sex. His amorous feelings are captured in natural imagery: the seasonal change of flora and fauna, the weather, different hours of the day, the landscape and seascape. Descriptions of fragrance, music, light, colours, and the warmth of fire appeal to the reader's senses. Yang Mu's successful deepening of inner feelings through a sensibility and imagination inspired by nature vividly illustrates his application of Romantic aesthetics.

From letter 2 onwards, the author uses the first person pronoun "we" to refer to John Keats and himself. "You" is supposed to be Keats, the imaginary addressee in the letter, but sometimes it can be the reader or

---

[11]   On an occasion in 1812 or 1813, Charles Cowden Clarke read to Keats the *Epithalamium* of Spenser and lent him a volume of the *Færie Queene*. Keats was enchanted by Spenser's fairyland. E. de Sélincourt says, "[i]t is significant that Keats's earliest known composition is the Imitation of Spenser, written probably in 1813, and Spenser never lost hold upon his imagination." See "Introduction," in *The Poems of John Keats*, ed. E. de Sélincourt (London: Methuen and Co., 1905), xxii.

[12]   See John Keats, *Endymion*. Book 1, lines 1-3.

[13]   See Letter to George and Thomas Keats, 21 December, 1817.

anyone else. Very often, the use of "we" and "you" gives the impression that the author is sharing a view with Keats while at the same time imparting some Romantic notions to Chinese readers. One example is when Yang Mu discusses the love of nature. "Yes, 'nature' is your best friend. She is always loyal to you and looks after you. If only you are willing to be close to her, if only you are sincere to her, she is your friend and will always be with you" (L2: 76). Sometimes, the author assumes the role of Keats's spokesman in a defence of poetry.

> When I was in the third year, I was fascinated by your poetry. I read your collected works, translated your long poem and I gave "lectures" on your poems to female classmates. I explained why things of beauty are "a joy forever" and why you wrote "La Belle Dame sans Merci" and why "four kisses" tells us what true love is. I was so clever. I made up reasons for you. "The use of number in this poem is to create 'surprise.' The only thing that is worth your attention is whether it *appeals to you. Don't you think Kisses Four interesting, impressive and appealing?*" (L9: 107) [14]

"La Belle Dame sans Merci" is a masterpiece that celebrates the medieval revival with its magic charm. In his letters 4 and 5 as well as in some later poems, Yang Mu attempts to produce similar works of mystery with intense lyrical feeling and dramatic tension.

Many other letters are replete with reminders and verbal echoes of Keats. Sometimes, Yang Mu writes as if replying to Keats's letter. "In your letter, you wrote, 'How happy is such a "voyage of conception," what delicious diligent Indolence!'[15] I see... In order to feel your 'diligent indolence,' I ought to understand you, to enter into your thoughts and to reach you, not through your books but through your soul" (L3: 80). At other times, he refers to Keats's letter indirectly. "I've got to see my friend, to smoke with him and talk about the poet's *'negative capability,'* and to cultivate in myself the indolence and scepticism, or an ambitionless ambition, or a purposeless purpose?" (L8: 102-3) [16] Like

---

[14] Words in English (emphasis mine) are directly quoted from the original text.

[15] This sentence is translated into Chinese with an adaptation by Yang Mu. It is quoted from Keats's letter to J. H. Reynolds dated 19 February, 1818. The idea of diligent indolence is explained in the beginning of the letter, "I have an idea that a Man might pass a very pleasant life in this manner – let him on any certain day read a certain Page of Poesy or distilled Prose and let him wander with it, and muse upon it, and reflect from it, and bring home to it, and prophesy upon it, and dream upon it – until it becomes stale – but when will it do so? Never – when Man has arrived at a certain ripeness in intellect any one grand and spiritual passage serves as a starting post towards all 'the two-and thirty Palaces.' How happy is such a 'voyage of conception,' what delicious diligent Indolence!" Robert Gittings, ed. *Letters of John Keats* (London: Oxford University Press, 1970), 65.

[16] The term *"negative capability"* (italics mine) is quoted in English in the original text. See Letter to George and Thomas Keats, 21 December, 1817.

Keats, Yang Mu needed a literary peer to help spell out the many new concepts that dawned on him. In fact, he, together with some other undergraduate students, formed a "Cavemen" society to regularly discuss issues of humanity (L10). The impact of the ideas he obtained from these undergraduate meetings is conspicuous. Letter 9, "To Nothingness Do Sink," is composed of a stanza by stanza reflection and response to Keats's poem, "When I have fears." Each stanza quoted from the English original is followed by one or more paragraphs of discussion in Chinese. The burgeoning poet's fears that he "may cease to be" and his anxiety about "Love and Fame" are exposed. At times, Yang Mu found himself getting too old to read the poet. "Keats belongs to the youth who is very very young" (L9: 109).

There are continual signs that the poet often turned to Keats for help and guidance. Having both a sensuous nature and sound critical insight, Yang Mu was particularly annoyed with his own inadequacy. "When the world challenges you, you evade it and turn to another world. The poet owns many worlds" (L8: 102). To the young poet, Keats was a counsellor who kept him from despondency. But sometimes Yang Mu confided in his friend about feeling exhausted by his poetic expedition.

> "My soul cannot adapt to the mundane realities. What I dream of and wander in is the scenery of the Middle Ages. I follow a long poem to the classical world. It has been a long trip and I am very tired."...
> "It is because you follow a romantic poet of the nineteenth century to the Middle Ages and ancient Greece that you are now tired," answered his friend.
> "The Romantics are innocent." (L8: 103)

Here, the author's reason for exhaustion is not supposed to be a complaint. It is only natural that in the course of time, the young poet has widened his literary horizons. Yang Mu realized that indulgence in Keats's world might not lead him any farther down the road of a poetic career. "Oh, Poet, haven't you asked yourself to change? Say from sweet lyrics to a prelude of something great? What you saw are the joy and sorrow of the gods on the Greek peninsula; what I saw are the gratitude and resentments of the tribes on high mountains. We return to the peerless, darkest spot – the Heart of Darkness" (L12: 126). Looking back, Yang Mu was amazed by his own imagination of the world. "At sixteen, I wrote 'Return' [one of his earliest poems]... I often wonder: When did I write my first poem? How? What kind of powers drove me and compelled me to do it?" (L12: 123) At the age of twenty-four, he wrote, "I am lost among books, among the great poems, the fairy's loose sleeves, the stars of Victoria – they blind my way. How should I 're-turn'?" (L12: 126) Faced with diverse stimulations, the young poet compared Keats's ideas with Camus's existentialist notion of "absurdity" in life or Conrad's perception of humanity in *Heart of Darkness* (L9: 107). As a maturing poet, Yang Mu felt that he was situated in a world much more complex and unstable than Keats's, so he needed to understand it with the ideas of the great writers and philosophers of the twentieth century. "Beauty" as a system of belief appeared to be inadequate. "What are we looking for after all? All is summoned by beauty; it is a religion. I believe firmly in eternal beauty – immortal beauty, but does it co-exist with melancholy?" (L12: 123) Restless about the status quo, the young poet yearned to return in order to set off again, but in a new direction. The urge for change exhibits not only the poet's creative impulse to make something new, but also an astute awareness of his own limitations at that moment.[17]

Faced with the realities of political volatility and the rise of anti-westernism in Taiwan, Yang Mu had to confront the specificities of his own culture, language and society. In "The Scenery outside the Church," there emerges an acute consciousness of "I" as an independent author in a time and space different from nineteenth century England. "Poet, what would you say?... What we want is the sandy gale in the vast desert stretching from the north to the south, not the whispers at the altar. What we demand is something 'Chinese,' something 'poetic.' We need to go back to the East" (L13: 132). [18] The scenery outside the church implies the social realities in one's surroundings. His question on how the Creator would interpret the tragedies on earth is not only directed towards the Christian God, or gods in general, but also towards the Poet-Creators who produced great tragedies such as *Oedipus the King*, *Hamlet* or *The San Lü Officer* for the stage.[19] "The whole world was thrown into a crisis, which the Creator failed to handle, in the nineteenth century and the twentieth century, in the West and the East... About these scenes outside the church, how would the Creator explain them?" (L13: 133) The young man brooded over the role of a poet amid a crisis of human civilization. For the time being, he believed that he needed to venture outside the religion of "beauty" to find the answer.

Immediate concerns for a Chinese poet in the twentieth century were centred on how to make poetry "modern" as well as "Chinese." Importa-

---

[17] Yip Wai-lim's comments on Yang Mu's early works also point to the need for a change in poetic style, "Indulgence in the fine excess of beauty – the classic's surprises, the stirs of nature, together with clouds, knights, dreams of exotic gardens – inevitably leads to indulgence in sound effects as well. This is the case in *Flower Season*, and in *Boat Lantern* too." See Yip's "Afterword" on Yang Mu's fourth book of poetry in *Legends*, 122.

[18] The anxiety about the crisis of modern civilization echoes the concerns and images in Eliot's poem "The Hollow Man."

[19] San Lü is the title of a senior official in feudal China. The famous Chinese patriot-poet Qu Yuan was once a San Lü officer of the Chu state.

tions from foreign sources and experimentations with western techniques caused much controversy. Debates over "westernized" Chinese
poetry in the community inevitably disturbed Yang Mu, who declared
himself a disciple of an English poet. Such worries are displayed in one
of his imaginary discussions with Keats about a Chinese predecessor. "If
you want to understand the meaning of 'sublimity,' read Fang Si's
works. This is true, Poet. Could you imagine the appeal of Roman spires
in Chinese poetry? And the appeal of giant pillars, squares, fountains
and cathedrals, too. In the beginning, people said: 'Fang Si is an obscure
poet; he is Europeanized' "(L14: 136). Yang Mu's appreciation of Fang
Si's experimental introduction of German scenery to Chinese poetry is
an affirmation of the path he himself was taking.

After years of literary education in his undergraduate and graduate
studies, the last letter, "Farewell," displays Yang Mu's determination to
search for a unique poetics for Chinese poetry. "The first time I sang for
you and painted for you was a summer day; reeds were tall and green"
(L15: 142). "Two years of lingering in Iowa City are about to end. It is
now summer time too, shaded by a city of trees" (L15: 143). Summer
returns every year, but Yang Mu is no longer the same. He was now a
well-educated poet, pondering national and cultural concerns. In the last
few letters, emotional empathy gives way to theoretical analysis. Like
any adolescent, there were times when Yang Mu had to wrestle with his
predecessors on the issue of influence and identity. Yet the poet's
farewell to Keats is the result of not so much an Oedipal struggle as a
cultural dilemma.

In Praxis: Classical and Contemporary, Chinese and the West (1960-80)

Taking leave of the Keatsian world, Yang Mu continued along a
forking path: he wished to re-visit the Chinese literary tradition, and to
explore Western poetics. In his poetry from the early 1960s there is
conspicuous oscillation between the English Romantics and Chinese
classical poetry. In January 1962, Yang Mu wrote two poems, "To
Melancholy" and "To Wisdom," after John Keats's ode, "On Melancholy." 1964 saw the publication of five more of his apostrophic poems,
"To Fate," "To Loneliness," "To Time," "To Athena" and "To Death."
While "To Fate" and "To Time" are both philosophical meditations on
life, they differ in approach: the former is religious whereas the latter is
a surrealist experiment with images. "To Death" records a narrative
about a knight's life with reference to Ingmar Bergman's movie, *The
Seventh Seal*. "To Athena" is an ode to the Greek goddess and draws
upon Greek myths and Athenian architecture. Imprints of western art,
literature, and culture are visible in the content and form of these works.

In the climate of anti-westernism, Yang Mu, unlike some poets who plunged into fierce debates, answered accusations of deculturation through his own creative works. Aware of the importance of cultural roots, his apostrophic poems in the 1960s include a call to return, which is addressed to his contemporaries, "Summoning the Spirits of the Dead: To Chinese Poets of the Twentieth Century" (1962). He makes an explicit reference to the source text by Qu Yuan in the poem's title, and refers to the poem's target audience in the subtitle.

The need for such negotiations lies in the tremendous lag of more than two thousand years between the time of Chu and the twentieth century.[20] The poem's language of exhortation and choice springs from two paradoxical inversions of history: the present is oblivious of the past but the past foreshadows the present's oblivion. What the poem's flutist from the ancient past says is more than a prophecy; it is a proposed remedy to what has already happened in the present. It is ironic that the flutist, who is long dead, beckons the dead souls of the poets living in the twentieth century. The poem's irony connects the living dead in the modernist wasteland to the sleeping dead in the iron house of modern China.

Braving the frost, the ancient flutist sets his prosopopoeia to the rhythm of the bell and the drum, calling to those who have lost the sense of season.[21]

In frost-covered clothes, a solitary goose flies coldly past
A flutist stands at the old pier – come back to the East
In dream, there beats a drum; while awake, there rings a bell
O those who have lost their sense of season   (lines 1-4)

While a migrant bird like a goose knows the season and the direction of the route home, the wandering modern poets, like the dead buried under the snow, are lost forever. The flutist beckons the dead to rise from their graves. Time passes as the Qingming festival of spring is over and the summer rain in Changan stops, alluding to the golden age of poetry exemplified in *Chu Elegies* and Tang poetry. After the Tang dynasty, poets have fallen into an eternal sleep in which Chinese cultural symbols flit across their dreams: "You dream of dragons, dream of phoenixes, you dream of unicorn" (line 18).

---

[20] The mourning ritual "Jiaohun" [Summoning the Spirits of the Dead] was first used as a poem's title by Qu Yuan (340-278 B.C.) who lived in the Chu State during the Warring States Period (403-221 B.C.).

[21] "The bell and the drum" is an allusion to the *Book of Songs*, which is a collection of the earliest Chinese poems composed in the Zhou dynasty (1066-256 B.C.).

The six lines of the last stanza allude to a Tang poem "Climbing a Hill" by Du Fu, in which the third and fourth lines read: "Boundless leaves fall in the woods, the endless Yangtze River runs roaringly here."

Boundless leaves fall in the woods, so does frost
Come back to the East, O those whose sense of season lost
Theatres for song and dance have locked away the Wuyue aesthetics of two
    millennia
When the drizzles drown your route home, you wanderers
O your pale flutist
Quiet are the mountain and the sea; the Yangtze River runs East as always
                                                                (lines 19-24)

The flutist exhausts all of his energy inviting poets of the twentieth century to look up to the *Book of Songs*, *Chu Elegies* and Tang poetry for their literary models. After the decline of the Tang into the chaotic period of the Five Dynasties and Ten States (907-60) to which the Wuyue State belongs, the aesthetics of poetry from the time of the Zhou Dynasty lies dormant and locked away.

The poem undoes the conceit of having been written in the past, because a flutist in the Warring States Period could never have known so much about Chinese literary history. The public call to the Chinese poets of the twentieth century can be read as a self-address, which is in fact a self-admonition. The all-knowing flutist speaks from a timeless vantage point and his earnest concerns about the development of poetry overcome the gap of more than two thousand years in the temporal continuum. The flutist's counsel meanders like musical notes through time towards both the future and the past. These notes finally resonate in the poem, "Towards Time Immemorial" (1978), which Yang Mu published sixteen years later:

There has never been such a musical note
So bright, yet quiet
Perhaps you originally belonged to the music of the time immemorial
Having flown elegantly in a quarrelsome era[22]
Once fed up with the noises of the numbered notations, decided to leave
To hide in the forgotten *yuefu* —[23]
Pure and bright, you are the jade of Mount Kun[24]

---

[22] The quarrelsome era here may refer to the Warring States Period. The representative poet of this period is Qu Yuan.

[23] *Yuefu* is the Music Bureau established by Emperor Wu of the Han Dynasty. It collected regional ballads and set them to tunes. Later it became an institution producing court music for religious rituals or the royal family's social functions. *Yuefu* is also a subgenre of poetry accompanied by different kinds of musical instruments. As used in this line, *yuefu* refers to the poetic subgenre.

[24] The Jade of Mount Kun is a precious stone that has legendary powers of fire resistance. Its colours and lustre stay even after being burnt in coalfire for three days.

It was only when Li Ping played the *konghou* of China[25]
The phoenix screamed in amazement, then slowly you woke up
Lingering, in doubt[26]
Waiting

And that was already the earth-shaking, heaven-shattering ninth century
Autumn rain splatters and scatters on the last leaf of the great dynasty[27]
You wake up like a musical note, softly chanting
Shyly reviewing the music of the time immemorial
The singing glistens on the rain-washed leaves
Fluttering glimmers of the heart: history
Is a page of new tune reborn

Waiting, shards of light in the modern era
Gather, I hear an unchained, unrestrained song
Entering my *yuefu*, a vow defying decay[28]
To set the tune of my concluding poem
Towards time immemorial

"You," is a personification of music or poetry, and is portrayed by the Lady in the antiphonal song between Goddess Xiang and Lady Xiang in the "Nine Songs." The personified poetic music, "you," is a bright and quiet peace-lover with a free spirit. She refuses to be measured by numbered musical notations or to be institutionalized by the Music Bureau to serve the court. She leads a hermetic, dormant life in the forgotten *yuefu*, the original balladry, until someone recovers the spontaneous power of music and poetry.

The ever-lastingness of "you" is like the Orphic voice in western poetics. In one of the fabrications of the Orpheus myth, Rilke's *Sonnets to Orpheus*, the speaker acknowledges the eternal presence of poetic music: "your sound lingered on in lions and rocks / and in the trees and birds. You sing there still. / O you lost god! You never-ending trace!" (Sonnet I. 26, lines 10-12; Rilke, 2004: 57) Orpheus, the lost god of western poetry, like the ancient Chinese musical note, is forever pursued

---

[25] *Konghou* is a stringed instrument of ancient China.

[26] "Lingering, in doubt" alludes to the first line, "You linger in doubt" of "The Goddess of the River Xiang" and "The Lady of the River Xiang" from Qu Yuan's "Nine Songs" in *Chu Elegies*.

[27] Lines 7, 8, 9, 12, and 13 are adaptations of Li He's (791-817) poem "Li Ping plays the *konghou* prelude," in which lines 4, 5, and 10 read: "Li Ping plays the *konghou* of China / The jade of Mount Kun breaks and the phoenix screams," and "Earth-shaking and heaven-shattering, autumn rain splatters." The explosive effects upon nature are hyperbolic illustrations of the forceful impact of the music in *yuefu* poetry.

[28] In the original, the author alludes to some expressions of a specific *yuefu* title, "Shangye qu," which presents an unfailing devotion until the end of the world. The translation in English renders the theme instead of the quotation.

by poets. In Chinese literary history, Li He (791-817) reminded poets of the impact of a lyrical *yuefu*, "*Konghou* prelude," in his own work. Only then was this poetic music resurrected from its eternal sleep. The musical note travels across time and space and at last enters into the present concluding the poem and setting its tune. In Yang Mu's poem, musicality is not so much a choice made by the author as a gift endowed to him by the fairy of poetry.

Yang Mu traces the whereabouts and activities of poetic music from time immemorial. The story of "you" is the literary development of lyric in Chinese poetic tradition. In the west, lyric reminds one of the lyre and of poetry at the same time. Music and poetry are inseparable and its expressive effects can only live if freed from official institutionalization and social programming. Yang Mu's fondness for *Chu Elegies* and *yuefu* demonstrates the liberal inclinations in his poetics.

The nostalgia for a glorious lyric tradition is presented by a lyrical, mythical invitation to return. This is an earnest call to modern Chinese poets to "come back" to the golden age of Chinese poetry and speak in their "native" language. "Summoning the Spirits of the Dead" performs a double act of valorisation and devaluation. On one hand, the flutist's song, rich in quotations, valorises the classical poetry of the ancient past. On the other hand, the present poetic form in vernacular Chinese radically departs from the traditional prosody it means to honour. "Towards Time Immemorial" attempts to memorialize and to revive the ancient song at once. Its apostrophic tone is comparable to western poets' prayer to the Muses for inspiration.

From a self-expressive utterance to apostrophe and prosopopoeia, the auditory effects of tone and rhythm are thoroughly explored in Yang Mu's early poems. In some works such as "To Time," his apostrophic entreaties to the abstract concept, Time, dovetail with exuberant visual images. From the late 1960s onwards, the modernist experimentation of form began to flourish in Yang's works. Among them "Rain Is" (1968) is considered a manifesto poem, as its subtitle "Ars Poetica" makes clear:

> Humidity on the neck
> Spreads; up from the waist rises
> Hair of forest
> Weather –
> The mossy wilderness
> A bird flies past
> A fan's
> Fibre, feathery shadows
> Drown in the boundless terror
> Your sleeve
> For the grave of early spring

Falls off, implying
A certain birth
At first it is a fresh splash-ink
Soon
It turns into a furious
Knight charging at me

"Rain Is" illustrates the modernist poetics in praxis. The speaker's efforts to define "rain" show the reader an exercise of the imagist dictum of "No ideas but in things." The feel of rain is "objectified" in concrete images. The humid weather is musty and wet, rising and spreading in the air and the landscape as it does through the human body. The breeze is felt in the flapping wings and the feathery images dive into an engulfing boundlessness. The drizzles paint a watery scene of early spring in the manner of Chinese splash-ink painting yet the heavy downpour that follows is cast by a furious, miserable knight who threatens a head-on attack against the persona.

This poem demonstrates Yang Mu's awareness of the epistemological source of imagism, one of the most prominent revolutions in Anglo-American poetry during high modernism. Imagism is the result of a cross-cultural interaction between China and the West through the translation and theorization of Ezra Pound. To many, imagism is a happy misreading of the significance of ideogram in Chinese poetics. Artistically and wittily Yang Mu further utilizes the distinctive features of Chinese ideogram. He draws the "featheriness" and the "swooping" of the bird (鳥) visually by using repeatedly characters and radicals of a similar shape or related meaning such as "羽" for feather, "系" for silk, "韭" for grassy plants, and "隹" for birds. In addition, a strategic allocation of the words in successive lines (for example, lines 6 to 9 read vertically from right to left in Chinese) completes the pictorial representation of a bird swooping down into the boundless void. Non-Chinese readers could also recognize the graphic design in the picture.

一鳥飛過
扇的
纖維，羽影
沒入可怖的浩瀚

The visual effects of the characters are the crux of Chinese ideogram and resist translation. One may hesitate if one needs to decide whether this modernist poem is a product of westernization or a sinicization of western modernist views. This is a particularly interesting point in comparative poetics. While ideogram is an entrenched component of the Chinese language, it was rarely employed in the creation of images in classical poetry. It might play some part in riddles and limericks but it was not seriously used as a theoretical basis for Chinese poetics. Pound's misreading and dissemination of ideogram's significance encouraged many modern Chinese poets' to utilize ideogrammatic features to produce something comparable to the concrete poems of western poetry.

In Yang Mu's experiment, imagery is often put to unconventional use. Images do more than evoke emotions, they are frequently employed to present concepts and sometimes to help develop philosophical and intellectual propositions. What's more, the poetic form of lyric encompasses the poet's discourse on academic disciplines outside literature. Examples include the poems "Metaphysics," "Physics," "Chemistry," "Philology," "Theology," and "Geometry," which were all written in 1972. More light-hearted and playful in tone, each discipline is poetically sketched by a natural flow of one or more dominant images. For example, "Chemistry" is set during morning tea: "If a song sinks into / the tea newly brewed, jasmine rises / a turbid blue / Solution is alkaline." The last line sounds like a technical statement concluding a scientific report on a laboratory test. The incongruity of setting and theme infuses the poems with a sense a humour. Yang's effort to humanize and poeticize scientific subjects is later apparent in his prose writing, "Science and the Nightingale" (1977), which may be a response to I. A. Richard's "Science and Poetry." Between 1975 and 1986, Yang Mu published five substantial volumes of poetry: *Manuscripts in a Bottle* (1975), *Song of the Big Dipper* (1978), *Taboo Games* (1980), *Seven*

Turns of the Coast (1980), and *Someone* (1986), each displaying a conscious struggle to create a marked change of style.

The Completion of a Poem (1989)

To many critics, Yang Mu's first and only book of poetics is *The Completion of a Poem*. Having invested years of scholarship in both Chinese and western lyric traditions, the poet demonstrates his unique ability to navigate the transcultural confrontations of poetic materials and literary theories in this work. In his early forties, Yang Mu had already published eight books of poetry and numerous collections of very popular creative essays. He became Taiwan's most revered literary figure, whom fledging poets often approached for advice. *The Completion of a Poem* was written between August 1983 and August 1984 at a time when Yang served as a professor of comparative literature at the National Taiwan University and for a term as an adjunct professor of Chinese literature at the National Tsing Hua University. The book's subtitle "Letters to Young Poets" echoes his "Letters to Keats," but this time the roles are reversed. In this work the letters are replies from Yang Mu the mentor to both real and fictional budding poets.[29]

The Completion of a Poem, as its title suggests, is about the ongoing process of poetry writing. Supporting the letters are Yang Mu's views on the poetics of modern Chinese poetry. The embryonic and maturing stages of these views can be traced in the prefaces and afterwords of his books of poetry and other prose writings, which he has written over a span of more than thirty years. Though Yang Mu's poetic vision was well-known by the late 1980s, it does not mean that his poetics was unaffected by the literary debates in the development of modern Chinese poetry in Taiwan and China. At times he was a target of attacks. Li Zushen took this book as an apologia for poetry and likewise, Liao Xianhao considered it a defence. The correspondences between Yang Mu and the young poets can be read as a continuation of this dialogue between contemporary literary critics and poets.

The epistolary form and close textual analysis of individual poems in some letters reveal the entrenched references to at least two important works in modern Chinese literature – Zhu Guangqian's *Twelve Letters to the Youth* and Qin Zihao's pioneering work about modern poetics, *Anatomy of Poetry*. In its overall design, *The Completion of a Poem*'s tone and purpose bears affinity to Zhu's and Rilke's letters. The typically Chinese attitude that self-cultivation is a prerequisite for a literary man is present throughout but Yang Mu emphasizes the artistic and

---

[29] Some topics for discussion in various chapters of this book were in fact initiated by letters Yang Mu received from young poets in Taiwan.

intellectual aspects in the creation of poetry. The Chinese notion that "writing is identical with the writer," holds the writer responsible for his moral and political messages. Yang Mu advises the young poets to create a universal man who possesses the artistic temperament to respond sensitively to beauty and the sublime. He claims that the gifted talent can be further nurtured by nature and by adventures. A burgeoning poet should realize his aspirations by expanding imagination and experience through extensive reading and travelling, and by cultivating a free spirit. In Yang Mu's poetics, the western notion, "style is the man," is accepted as true.[30] His special emphasis on the modernist tenet of "impersonality" must not be overlooked. These Eliotian insights are cited in the letters that discuss how "historical consciousness" and "social involvement" can negotiate traditional Chinese ethical demands on writers. Rather than speaking as a personalized, historicized subject from his specific position, Yang Mu reiterates the ways a poet can participate in history and society through his art.

The book is organized into eighteen letters plus one postscript.[31] Yang Mu begins the last letter "Poetry and Truth" with an anecdote from Goethe. Yang quotes extensively from the Preface of *Aus meinem Leben: Dictung und Wahrheit* to explain how and why at the age of sixty-five, Goethe started his autobiography:

> For though in our youth we zealously go our own way, impatiently rejecting the claims of others to our attention for fear of being diverted, these are most beneficial to us in our later years when a generous expression of interest may quicken us and stir us to new activity. (Oxenford, 1974: 2b)

Having responded favourably to the request to write his autobiography, Goethe immediately began to put all of his works in the twelve volumes in chronological order. He tried to demonstrate his poetry's relation to

---

30   Some Chinese critics naturalize this western notion as "style is personal integrity," which is a misreading that brings it close to the traditional Chinese belief that "writing is identical with the writer." See Chen Fengming's interview with Yang Mu in 1977.

31   The eighteen letters are entitled as follows: 1 *"Baofu"* [Greatness of Aim] (March 1984), 2 *"Daziran"* [Nature] (November 1984), 3 *"Jiyi"* [Memory] (December 1984), 4 *"Shengcun huanjing"* [Living Environment] (January 1985), 5 *"Zhuangyou"* [Adventure] (June 1985), 6 *"Lishi yishi"* [Historical Consciousness] (August 1985), 7 *"Gudian"* [Classics] (January 1986), 8 *"Xiandai wenxue"* [Modern Literature] (April 1986), 9 *"Waiguo wenxue"* [Foreign Literature] (July 1986), 10 *"Shehui canyu"* [Social Involvement] (November 1986), 11 *"Xianshi"* [Leisure] (February 1987), 12 *"Xingshi yu neirong"* [Form and Content] (January 1988), 13 *"Yinyuexing"* [Musicality] (February 1988), 14 *"Lun xiugai"* [On Revision] (April 1988), 15 *"Fabiao"* [Publication] (April 1988), 16 *"Pengyou"* [Friends] (May 1988), 17 *"Shengming"* [Reputation] (May 1988), and 18 *"Shi yu zhenshi"* [Poetry and Truth] (May 1988). References to these letters will be indicated by their numbers in the following discussion.

the extrapoetic aspects, which include the circumstances of his life and the poetic influences on him. "But the task soon grew more burdensome, as detailed notes and explanations were needed to fill gaps in what had already been published" (Oxenford, 1974: 2b). So Goethe decided to perform the task in a different manner:

> In my attempt to respond to the reasonable demands that had been made of me and in my striving to present, in the order in which they occurred, the inner promptings, the outward influences, and the stages I passed through both in theory and in practice, I was driven from my circumscribed private life to the world outside. ...
>
> In this manner, from such observations and probings, from memories and reflections, the present narrative was born, and it is from this view of its origins that it can best be enjoyed and used and most reasonably be judged. Whatever else might be said, especially with respect to the half-poetic, half-historical treatment employed, can well be left to the text that follows. (Oxenford, 1974: 2c-2d)

To Karl J. Weintraub, the modest title of *Aus meinem Leben* indicates Goethe's attempt "to give his young life under one dominant aspect: the formation of the personality of the poet" (Oxenford, 1974: xxiii). Weintraub believes that the grand objective of the autobiography is to render "the account of the formation of a man who also was a poet – the history of an education" (Oxenford, 1974: xxix). In his Postscript, Yang Mu explains that the eighteen letters in *The Completion of a Poem* arise from circumstances similar to the genesis of Goethe's *Dictung und Wahrheit*, but Yang Mu's manner of responding is entirely different from Goethe's.

Although the Goethean notion of "world literature" proposed a journey to the Orient, few scholars have actually followed this promoting. Yang Mu's *The Completion of a Poem: Letters to Young Poets* is an Eastern attempt to connect poetic creeds of different cultural origins. As shown in its title, the book is a combination of Stephen Spender's *The Making of a Poem* and Rainer Maria Rilke's *Kaufen Sie jetzt diesen Artikel* (Letters to a Young Poet).[32] In fact, Yang Mu's work corresponds to these earlier texts in form and content. While Spender highly commended Rilke's *Duino Elegies* for introducing "new 'frequencies' into the pulsing fields of the universe," Yang finds in them "all the

---

[32] The two texts are: Stephen Spender, *The Making of a Poem* (New York: Norton, 1962, first published 1955) and Rainer Maria Rilke, *Letters to a Young Poet*. Trans. M. D. Herter Norton. Revised edition 1954 (New York and London: Norton, paperback edition, 1993). Spender's essay, "The Making of a Poem," was first published in 1946. It was collected in the book of the same title, 45-62. It should be noted that Spender published an article entitled, "Letter to a Young Writer" in 1954, a year before *The Making of a Poem* came out. See Stephen Spender, "Letter to a Young Writer." *Encounter* 3 (March 1954): 4-5.

beauty of the western culture" (Yang, 1993: 9). [33] With vested interest in Stephen Spender's career as a poet, Yang gave a brief biographical sketch of the poet in his article "Spender, the English Poet" (1976) to introduce Chinese readers to Spender's political beliefs and literary style. [34] According to Yang Mu, Spender inherited the great tradition of English poetry and, unlike his contemporaries who mourned the fragmentation of modern civilization, he affirmed the love and humanity he found in the modern world. Just as Spender showed his keen appreciation of Rilke's works by translating them into English with J. B. Leishman, Yang translated a number of Spender's poems from the 1940s to the 1960s into Chinese in order to delineate his achievement. What is common between Yang's and Rilke's letters is that each answers queries from specific correspondents and addresses the general concerns of the author's times. *Letters to a Young Poet* is a collection of ten letters from Rainer Maria Rilke to Franz Xaver Kappus between 17 February 1903 and 26 December 1908. These ten letters are Rilke's sympathetic responses to a would-be poet regarding his doubts about poetry and life. Rilke's letters sound authentic and personal. Similarly, Yang Mu's eighteen letters are dated with month and year, running from March 1984 to May 1988, with a Postscript written in October 1988. While the letters might be addressed to some specific young poets, rarely does Yang Mu mention the names of his correspondents in the letters. Only on the second last page of the Postscript are some of their names such as Zeng Shumei (L3) and Lin Yaode (L4) given. [35]

Between the opening letter and the postscript is an organized account of his critical reflections after more than thirty years devoted to reading, writing and teaching poetry. From the outset, Yang's project is pedagogical, whereas Rilke and Spender are more individually or politically engaged. *The Completion of a Poem* is not simply an ABC of poetry writing but a book for advanced students who have a fair grasp of the Chinese literary tradition and are prepared to widen their scope of knowledge to encompass western poetry. With the textual concern of the creation of a poem as a lead, Yang teases out what makes a poet and also investigates the nature of modern Chinese poetry. However, it is only by a comparative reading of *The Completion of a Poem* against the two western texts that have influenced it, that Yang's unique contribu-

---

[33] See Stephen Spender, "The Imagination as Verb," *The Imagination in the Modern World* (Washington D. C.: Library of Congress, 1962), 9.

[34] Yang Mu's essay on Spender includes some translations of his poems into Chinese. See Yang Mu, "*Yingguo shiren Shibande*" [Spender, the English Poet]. *Epoch* 43 (March 1976): 4-8.

[35] Yang Mu mentions that some of the lines quoted in Letters 3 and 4 are from Zeng and Lin respectively (Yang, 1989: 221).

tion to the art of poetry can be fully appreciated, both locally in Taiwan and internationally in comparative poetics.

To Rilke, Spender, and Yang Mu, poetry is an art only accessible to a minority of writers. To the question: "What makes a good poet?" Rilke answers by citing a poet's intrinsic existential urge to create. "To a true poet, writing is a necessity on which he builds his life" (L1). Almost like an echo, Spender says, "Poets speak of the necessity of writing poetry rather than of a liking for doing it. It is spiritual compulsion, a straining of the mind to attain heights surrounded by abysses" (Spender, 1955: 47). The role of a poet is a vocation. The same holds true to Yang Mu. He states in his first letter that poetry demands a life-long devotion and that the poets need to uphold principles of freedom and democracy. With an independent soul fortified by knowledge and illuminated by imagination, a poet is able to see through the mundane realities of the world and to embrace it, in spite of the adversities, with love and empathy. Speaking to young Chinese poets, Yang identifies the creation of a poem with the making of a poet: "Your work is the essence of your conscience and integrity, evident of the meaning of life you have committed to" (Yang, 1989: 7). Of note here is Yang's reference to the Chinese demands for a "cultured" man. Personal conduct and moral principles as well as artistic achievement are pre-requisites for a poet worthy of reverence. In his teens Yang was impressed by the works of Li Shangyin of the late Tang dynasty. Despite the obscurity of Li's poetry, he was enticed by its beauty, melancholic mood, structural perfection in rhyme and parallelism, and intellectual agility with images and diction, all of which represent the highest manifestation of the prosody of regulated verse. When he wrote *The Completion of a Poem* at a more mature age, he held Qu Yuan up as a true poet worthy of praise and emulation. Yang admired Qu's artistic achievement, but he was also impressed by the poet's faith in life and devotion to his country.

Because Yang Mu learned from Keats both that a poet "owns many worlds" (8th letter to Keats), and how to create those worlds amid mundane realities, he agrees with his foreign predecessors that all poets find inspiration and consolation in Nature and in a store of memories. In the west, Wordsworth revealed his belief in the importance of childhood in his famous line, "The Child is father of the Man," while Rilke finds "a child's incomprehension" a blessing (L6). Most poets are blessed with an ability to retain the pristine significance of their earliest experiences. Despite the fact that innocence and simplicity is a treasure usually lost to adults, poets can re-create childhood days in their original freshness through their writing. Therefore, memory is particularly important to poets. In Spender's opinion, "[i]nspiration is the beginning of a poem and it is also its final goal" (Spender 1955: 52). He sees the interconnection of inspiration, memory and imagination: inspiration is "the faintest flash of insight into the nature of reality" while "memory is the faculty of poetry, because the imagination itself is an exercise of memory" (Spender 1955: 55 and 57). To offer an alternative to the Chinese biographical-historical approach to writing about the past, in Letter 3 Yang introduces the western notion of memory and poetry as expressed in the Greek myths on the hills of Eleuther.[36] By bringing in the Greek myths and Plato's scepticism about poetry, Yang helps to broaden his readers' conception of the imaginative potentialities of language.

Compared with his two predecessors, Yang Mu incorporates a wide range of references from world literatures. Instead of the troubled conflicts about his national-cultural identity that were exhibited in "Letters to Keats," Yang is now easily able to expose his new mindset, which allows the worlds of East and West, of past and present, to meet. From Letters 6 to 9 namely, "Historical Consciousness," "Classics," "Modern Literature," and "Foreign Literature," he deals squarely with the obstacles to literary reforms in the Chinese context. Given that Chinese literature is famous for its long-established lyric tradition, innovations of modern poetry are always points of contention. Yang takes a progressive stride forward by quoting T. S. Eliot's essay, "Tradition and the Individual Talent," in the original as well as in translation: "Yet if the only form of tradition, of handing down, consisted in following the ways of the immediate generation before us in a blind or timid adherence to its successes, 'tradition' should positively be discouraged" (L6). Historical consciousness to Yang Mu is not merely an awareness of one's national past, but the knowledge of what has happened in the wider world. The poet's critical attitude towards established views of the literary past is liberating. Well-versed in Chinese poetics, Yang discusses Zen and Poetry, and comments on the two major intellectual, philosophical trends that have shaped the Chinese lyric tradition. Poets that have modelled themselves after Du Fu's axiom "rather die than stop at some mediocre lines" tend to labour at prosody and diction. In contrast, other poets distrust language because of the Zen Buddhists' teachings: "never build on words." These poets believe that poetry is the "communication of the minds, not built on words." Yang finds that these competing theories may cause confusion and neither helps young poets today. "Poetry is not Zen, nor is Zen poetry," says Yang. Chinese students are usually caught between these two established doctrines and entangled by their traditional tenets. This may be due to their misunder-

---

[36] Yang Mu's main emphasis is on Mnemosyne, the Goddess of Memory born of Uranus and Gaia and the nine daughters, the Muses, she begot with Zeus. He further explains that the Muses, the goddesses of poetry to whom poets pray, are descendents of gods, memory and the cosmos, and are taken to be the origin of poetry in the west.

standing of "tradition" as the accumulation and emulation of classical canons. In that mindset scholarship means a passive reception of indoctrination and practice therefore requires imitation. As a result, young Chinese poets take it as a compliment when their works are recognized as bearing the signature of a famous predecessor. Since the "anxiety of influence" derived from the Greek culture seems exclusively western, it is difficult for Chinese people to accept that challenging the canon can be a positive thing. Familiar with the cultural differences between China and the west, Yang Mu is tactful when confronting the formidable reverence for the national heritage. Historical consciousness in his comparative approach compels a modern poet to be aware not only of the relation between himself and his time, but also of the interdependence between his own national literature and other literary traditions in the world. Such awareness is vital before the poet even puts pen to paper.

From the perspective of world literature, Rilke's *Letters to a Young Poet* appears rather regional in its cultural scope, dwelling mainly within Europe. By contrast, Stephen Spender's collection of essays *The Making of a Poem* was written in the 1950s when transatlantic exchanges on different aspects of life were much more common. At a time when translations of contemporary American literature were over-running the Continent like an invasion, European writers were going through a crisis induced by an increasingly commercialized culture, which Spender named the "American malady... the commercialization of spiritual goods on an enormous scale" (Spender, 1955: 191-2). Between 1947 and 1949, Spender spent the greater part of each year in the United States, where he frequently stayed with Auden and Isherwood. These trips highlighted his worries about the condition and the development of British poetry. In "The Immigration in Reverse," Spender observes that English writers who had emigrated to America and returned had learned two things:

> Firstly, that immigration in reverse is extremely difficult if not impossible because America more than any other country is a womb into which you have to be reborn. Secondly, that a fiction based on the breakdown of class barriers is something we need over here: but there is little comfort in this lesson, because it is not writers but the society in which you live that has to break down class barriers. (Spender, 1955: 205)

The trend of "immigration in reverse" is undesirable because it suggests that London is no longer the centre of literary and cultural tradition for American pilgrims. Worse still, young British writers seemed to suffer the loss of their pre-American selves. To Spender that threat is "the start of a kind of internationalism which for Europeans means Americanization but for Americans means taking America with you" (Spender, 1955: 195). Spender's negotiations with the Americanization of British poets are explicit in "Goethe and the English Mind" (1949). To rescue British poetry from decline, he reiterates the significance of Shakespeare and Goethe, the fountainheads of British and German literatures, by comparing their famous creations, *Hamlet* and *Faust*. In Spender's view there is much for British writers to learn from Goethe:

> Goethe's own poetry, supremely German as it is, reaches out beyond the German into the world, toward a world literature. We are now living in that period when the writers of no nation enjoy that kind of cultural self-sufficiency which so beneficially produced a French, an Italian, and an English literature each with peculiarities of attitude which they instinctively protected from one another. ... We are in each language prey to influences coming from the outside. It is enormously important that we should be influenced by what is strong. ... There is none to whom we can look more trustingly as the father of a world literature than Goethe. (Spender, 1955: 134)

Spender senses the inevitability of influence and change, but the anxiety caused by American "cultural imperialism" drives him to turn to other national literatures in Europe. To enlist the German pioneer of world literature in the discourse is a subtle call to return to the centre of European tradition in the course of internationalization.

Spender's struggles with the competing demands of national heritage and foreign cultural influence are nothing new to modern Chinese poets. Chinese writers' ambivalence toward foreign literature is a century old. To approach texts in translation, Yang Mu promotes an attitude that is open, sincere, and enthusiastic even as he acknowledges that foreign literature is bound to suffer a loss in translation, and readers who do not read the original will receive an incomplete understanding of the text. Yang's main argument in "Foreign Literature" (L9) can be summarized by the example he cited from Keats. Keats had limited knowledge about European literature, but nonetheless found enlightening resonances in a chance discovery of a foreign-language text. In October 1816 Keats read Chapman's translation of Homer. His joy at this discovery drove him to write the sonnet, "On First Looking into Chapman's Homer," the work that established his fame. This serendipitous moment ascribed to translation initiated the five most productive years of Keats's poetic career before he died at the age of twenty-six. The same joy can be discovered by modern Chinese poets when they encounter foreign literature.

As what Damrosch says of translation: "*All* works cease to be the exclusive products of their original culture once they are translated; all become works that only 'began' in their original language" (Damrosch, 2003: 22). Like Spender, Yang Mu welcomes "fruitful misunderstanding." He is less worried about misreading works than he is anxious to be exposed to new ideas and forms. For example, to Yang Mu the Bible is a good source of amazing images for young poets. The poet's advice is that if a poet encounters a wild image or idea in a foreign poem, he should be possessed by it; the strangeness can help augment a poet's consciousness. When a foreign text is reborn into a literary system beyond its own, it begins its participation in the making of world poetry.

Yang Mu is no rootless nomad wandering among different cultures; his deep reverence for his national tradition exhibits cosmopolitanism of a comparative kind.[37] In a culture heavy with historical lessons from the past and idealistic visions of the future, there must be something for poets to revolt against and something for them to cling to. Yang Mu holds a positive attitude towards his society as well as towards the activities pursued by poets in the ancient times, the recent past, and the present. He has a strong sense of continuity that helps bridge the gaps in Chinese literary history. With a clear mission to disseminate the art of poetry and a strong faith in what he perceives to be significant for the burgeoning poets, Yang Mu's eighteen letters illustrate not only the making of a poem, but also the making of modern literature: "Based on these changing factors in our society and the unyielding aspiration to define art and literature in our age... we, as readers and writers [of poetry], through reading and creating, are in fact making our modern literature" (L8).

Poetry writing is more than self-expression or self-contained entertainment; poets may like to share their works with others in diverging ways. Yang Mu illustrates these methods from different traditions. For example, the Chinese monk-poet, Han Shan (Cold Mountain) inscribed his poems on trees and stone. Some people followed him and made a record of his works. Tao Yuanming's famous poems on drinking were collected because he asked his friend to make a fair copy of his improvisation and circulate them among his peers. Keats published a book of poems in 1817 that captured critical attention and established his fame in London. However when *Endymion* came out in 1818, it was poorly received and conservative critics hurled harsh criticism on his poems and mocked his low birth. What Yang points out by Keats's example is that despite the negative responses to his works, Keats made the most out of adverse conditions through his creative spirit, producing numerous great poems in the years before he died in 1821.

Famous stories about the friendship between western poets like Coleridge and Wordsworth, Pound and Eliot are cited in Letter 16. To Yang Mu, friendship between poets is more than an affinity owing to artistic temperament; it is also built on personal integrity and loyalty to

---

[37] See Bruce Robbins, "Comparative Cosmopolitanism." *Social Text* 31/32 (1992): 169-186.

their states. For illustration, he probes thoroughly into the background of an artwork, "In Praise of Friendship," co-painted by Xiang Xingmo and Zhang Qi of the Qing dynasty. Among Xiang's friends, four were already dead by the time the painting was completed. The two survivors were Lu Derzhi and Xiang, the painter. The painting is set in the early Qing, shortly after the fall of Ming. It was a time of political volatility during which people lost many of their friends. A poem in the painting inscribes the occasion held amid the pine trees in the mountain:

> Five old men steeped in art and literature
> Old acquaintances meet to talk about their works
> Mutual encouragement and aspiration for immortal fame
> Their spirit of painting and poetry has stayed for ever

The artwork, in images and in words, captures the significance of friendship between artists. There is a need to meet with one's friends and it is gratifying to compete, debate and share with one's fellow poets. Xiang, the painter outside the frame places his friends in an everlasting jovial gathering full of care and hope for the future. That they are kindred spirits is imagistically indicated by their head-dress. Drawn in the Qing dynasty, the five artists are still wearing the hat and scarf in the Han style after the specific fashions of the Jin, Tang and Song dynasties. This perception of the imagined community of poets imbued with cultural and political historical consciousness supplements the Eliotian notion introduced in Letter 6. By analyzing "In Praise of Friendship," Yang Mu juxtaposes his concerns for the particular in history and the universal in art.

"Reputation" (L17) solves young poets' puzzles about how to locate themselves in literary history. Yang Mu first places the contemporary Chinese poets in a temporal site more than 2400 years after the *Book of Songs*, and then evokes a pair of great cultural figures in China, Confucius (552-469 B.C.) and Li Bai (701-762). Li Bai lived 1200 years after Confucius but before contemporary poets. Despite their magnificent achievements in philosophy and poetry, Confucius regretted how sages decay like withering trees, and Li Bai died miserably by the side of the Yangtze River. Both Confucius and Li Bai, of course, had no idea about their immortal fame. With full confidence in the formidable Chinese lyric tradition, Yang Mu never doubts that great poets will be immortalized, yet in the late twentieth century, he anticipates that a modern poet can secure a place in a much broader area than within mere national borders.

Knowledgeable of both Chinese and Western cultures, Yang Mu is able to see the benefits of transcultural interactions. When Damrosch discusses the scope of a world poet's vision, he perceives world literature as it is described in Vinay Dharwadker's phrase: "a montage of overlapping maps in motion" (Damrosch, 2003: 24). Both *The Making of a Poem* and *The Completion of a Poem: Letters to Young Poets* show a reshaping of the cultural map that Spender and Yang Mu experimented with. As Spender places Shakespeare and Goethe, who are two centuries apart, together in his picture of the literary origins of Western literature, Yang goes further and imaginatively draws a trans-temporal and trans-spatial affinity between a pair of great poets, Tao Yuanming and Shakespeare (L17). Tao (365-427), a famous Chinese poet of the Southern Dynasties, had a beautiful poem misread and discarded by eminent editors such as Xiao Tong and Zhong Rong. These critics-cum-editors missed Tao's innovative analogy:

> How I wish I were her shadow in daytime
> Wherever she goes, I am always by her side
> How I wish I were the belt among her clothes
> Guarding her slim waist, I to her as close
> If I were a bamboo, how I wish I were her fan
> Stirring soft breezes in her tender hand   (As quoted in Yang, 1989: 201)

Tao and Shakespeare lived 1200 years apart, but Yang Mu wittily juxtaposes Tao's sincere yearning for his lady with the wish Romeo makes while standing below Juliet's balcony:

> See how she leans her cheek upon her hand!
> O that I were a glove upon that hand,
> That I might touch her cheek!   (Yang, 1989: 202)

The coincidence can almost be read as an example of literary borrowing from the Chinese. Cross-cutting these very distinct verse forms in a montage, Yang Mu reads this transcultural overlapping as a sign that the gift of imagination is universal to poetic geniuses. The finely wrought images impress readers of different cultural and linguistic backgrounds and stand the test of time.

A reshaping of the cultural maps does not imply a total abolition of differences. Nevertheless, a poet's ability to locate his cultural roots in the global picture bespeaks his unique stance. One thing that makes Yang Mu a most prominent "bicultural" poet is the seemingly paradoxical attributes of cosmopolitan outlook and native Taiwan consciousness in his works. Drawing on T. S. Eliot's ideas of historical consciousness in "Tradition and the Individual Talent," Yang Mu delineates a manifesto for his nativist discourse (L6). From a historical perspective, Taiwan's complex association with mainland China is analogous to the literary relationships between nations in the West. The tradition that Eliot identifies with covers a thousand years of Anglo-Saxon culture as well as three thousand years of European literature going all the way back to Homer. To Yang Mu, the Chinese lyric tradition includes a century of modern Chinese poetry as well as the classical works dated from the *Book of Songs*. Just as Western poets find their origins in Greece, it is natural that Chinese poets acknowledge theirs in ancient China. More importantly, what constitutes a distinct identity for young poets is local consciousness. Like the centrality of Anglo-Saxon culture to poets writing in English, the joy and sorrow of the four hundred years of Taiwan history is fundamental to young Taiwanese poets writing in Chinese.[38]

Proficient in both English and Chinese, Yang Mu has published all his creative works in Chinese and seems predominantly preoccupied with the Chinese tradition itself. Immune to Stephen Owen's and Spender's anxieties about deculturation, Yang is by no means Sino-chauvinistic. A comparatist in academic practice and in his outlook, Yang's approach to literatures of different cultures reveals the possibility of a fruitful exchange in their artistic and historical concerns. Allaying fears about cultural impoverishment, Yang takes a liberal, bicultural path that helps young Chinese poets better connect their worlds and conceive the meaning of world poetry.

When Said quotes Goethe's grand vision for founding the field of comparative literature, he admits that "the underlying and perhaps unrealizable rationale was this vast synthesis of the world's literary production transcending borders and languages but not in any way effacing individuality and historical concreteness" (Said, 2003: xvi). Despite Spender's ambivalent admiration for American culture and his regret for the inferiority complex that gnaws at some British writers of his time, Britain still holds as a centre of tradition for American literature and more importantly, for the rising Commonwealth literature. What Spender did not foresee when he wrote *The Making of a Poem* is that in the postcolonial world, the education of many successful contemporary writers of literatures in English was anchored by vigorous training in British literature of the past centuries.

In *The Completion of a Poem: Letters to Young Poets*, Yang Mu helps map young Taiwanese poets situated at the crossroads of the traditional and the modern, the Chinese and the Western. Native to Taiwan, Yang's shrewd consciousness of the local specificities of his homeland in relation to Chinese culture and Western literature is unsurpassed by other poets writing in Chinese. The eighteen letters addressed to young poets constitute a great literary education that will help boost the proliferation of poetry writing in Taiwan and in other Chinese communities. The comparative approach and cosmopolitan outlook

---

[38]   For a detailed discussion of the history of modern Taiwanese poetry, see Yang Mu, "The Origins of Modern Poetry in Taiwan," *Origins of Literature* (Taipei: Hongfan, 1984), 1-10 and "The Origins of Taiwanese Poetry Revisited," *United Daily*. 27 November 2004.

exhibited in the letters is indeed a solid contribution to modern Chinese poetics in the making.

The literary influence of Rilke on Spender, and of Rilke and Spender on Yang Mu, connects Europe and Asia in the map of the literary development of world poetry. Critically conscious of the challenges to the development of modern poetry in an age of transculturation, both Spender and Yang look to Goethe and Shakespeare for support or stimulation. In "Goethe and the English Mind," Spender says, "Sometimes I imagine to myself the language of the world conversing." In his mind, the world expands to reach the other continent across the Atlantic, but the medium of communication remains European. What is clearly shown in Yang Mu's *The Completion of a Poem: Letters to Young Poets* is the astonishing fact that the worlds across the Atlantic as well as the Pacific are really conversing – in Chinese.

The Sceptic: Notes on Poetical Discrepancies (1993)

Yang Mu reiterates the relation between "Poetry and Truth" in the last letter of *The Completion of a Poem*. The Keatsian conviction, "A thing of beauty is a joy forever," remains central to his concept of poetic truth. To Yang Mu, a poet is a maker of beauty and beauty is truth. When a poet scrutinizes his world honestly, he can unlock the mysteries of love and death with his own key. What may be ugly or beautiful in mundane reality will be transformed in the poetic world. Yang concludes his letters with Prospero's epilogue from *The Tempest*. Having performed his magic, the magician bows his thanks to the audience before the curtain falls. Prospero, Shakespeare and Yang Mu have done their job and like most great artists, they are confident in the worth of their art. They, like all poets who are true to themselves and their art, are happy.

Yang Mu's discourse on poetic truth includes an inbuilt theatricality and artifice, which are the major concerns of his next book of poetics *The Sceptic: Notes on Poetical Discrepancies*.[39] When *The Sceptic* came out in 1993, it won immediate acclaim and was voted one of the "Books of the Year" by *China Times* and awarded "The Best Book Award" by *The Reader*. What first captured readers' attention is the book's bilingual title, 疑神 [Yi Shen] *The Sceptic: Notes on Poetical Discrepancies*. Although the title in Chinese, *Yi Shen* [Doubting God], carries an explicit referent, "*shen*" (God), as the subject for scrutiny, the Chinese character *shen* has numerous meanings such as "spirit," "higher being," "deity," "divinity," "supernatural," "magical" or even "uncanny," which

---

[39] The book in discussion here is *Yi Shen*, hereafter referred to as *The Sceptic*. See *Yi Shen* (*The Sceptic: Notes on Poetical Discrepancies*) (Taipei: Hongfan, 1993), 304 pages.

undermine its clarity. In contrast, the title in English *The Sceptic: Notes on Poetical Discrepancies* suggests no specific subject for doubt. The thrust of the book is about the sceptical attitude, which is personified as "the sceptic" who accepts nothing at face value. Such a cynical attitude to life leads a person to observe various idiosyncrasies in the articulation of faith and belief. The restless "doubting" referred to in the title is reinforced by a quote in the prologue from Qu Yuan's *Chu Elegies*: "In a baffled mind doubts proliferate / I wish to be at peace but fail." The sceptic's continuous exploration of the unknown is paralleled to the Romantic quest in Section 11: "To me, the most touching ism in literary history is Romanticism... From my point of view, to prove that god exists or does not exist is most difficult; pantheism is not an impossible solution, but to remain sceptical about god, one would be liberal, care-free, just, gentle, and kind" (Yang, 1993: 168).

The belief in liberty motivates Yang Mu to closely examine the apparent tension between a sacred book and a poetic book. While John Butler Yeats finds "the sacred book of arts is in fact a profane book that expresses the contrary of the 'religious'," Yang Mu argues that the two are basically the same (as quoted in Adams, 1991: 289). As J. B. Yeats observes:

> There are two kinds of belief: the poetical and the religious. That of the poet comes when the man within has found some method or manner of thinking or arrangement of fact (such as is only possible in dreams) by which to express and embody an absolute freedom, such that his whole inner and outer self can expand in full satisfaction.

> In religious belief there is absent the consciousness of liberty. Religion is the denial of liberty. An enforced peace is set among the warring feelings by the help of something external, as for instance the fear of hell, some feelings are chained up and thrust into dungeons that some other feeling may hold sway; and all ethical systems yet invented are a similar denial of liberty, that is why the true poet is neither moral or religious. (Adams, 1991: 299)

To resolve this difference, Yang Mu reads a religious book as a poetical one in *The Sceptic*. Deity/God is a metaphysical signifier common to most cultures. According to Geertz, deity is "a cluster of sacred symbols, woven into some sort of ordered whole, which makes up a religious system. For those who are committed to it, such a religious system seems to mediate genuine knowledge, knowledge of the essential conditions in terms of which life must, of necessity, be lived" (Geertz, 1973: 129). Espousing a similar view, Yang Mu analyzes the transcendental concept, "god," "dao," or any logos, as a centre which "is born of false conclusions drawn from far-fetched analogies; He [it] dies of textual research and deconstruction" (Yang, 1993: 70). The discrepancies found in the sceptic's random notes can be discussed on two levels: the ideological and the poetical. As identified by Geertz, over-selectivity and distortion are methods of sustaining an ideology. Religion, like any ideology, is subject to a pernicious selectivity in which only some aspects of actual life are emphasized. In addition, those aspects that are recognized are distorted to support the ideologues. On the ideological level, what *The Sceptic* illustrates is that in most religious texts over-selectivity and distortion formulate a closed system of signification within which "god" is installed.[40] On the poetical level, discrepancies suggest differences in artistic representation employed by the individual religious systems. In this light, the sceptic's focus falls on the aesthetic considerations of each deifying process and its outcomes.

Deity, the core signifier of any religious text, is subject to its author's representation. This central signifier helps the author of a sacred text to focus and direct his art in the service of a divine truth. The deifying procedure is a creative process close to poetic writing. The potential poeticity of this universal significatory exercise has aroused the interests of many major poets. In the first section of *The Sceptic* Yang Mu begins his deconstructive reading of religion by defining it in a figurative way: "Religion is merely a firm knot of ideas" (Yang, 1993: 2). When Yang Mu renders his own Chinese transliteration of the word "ideology," he cleverly turns it into a four-character word "yidilaojie" [a firm knot of ideas]. It follows that in order to untie the "firm knot of ideas," one must untangle the process of signification. "Everybody knows the images," but the sceptical speaker claims in Section 5, "only I know the ways to display and preserve these images... Everybody pays attention to im-ages; I do not. I pay attention to the *ways* images are displayed and preserved" (Yang, 1993: 64, emphasis mine). Images are indispensable since "god" must be inscrutable. Therefore "god" needs to be hidden in shrines and mystified by images in order to show how important or omnipotent he is.

What is poetical in religious language rests in its capacity to open the reader's eyes to new aspects of reality and a new way of living.[41] In several sections of *The Sceptic*, the creative potentialities of the images of "god" are examined closely. There are many different types of god in different cultures. Gods can be male or female. In the West, there are the Christian god, and the Greek gods and goddesses on Mount Olympus. In Asia, in the coastal areas of China and in Taiwan, there are a number of

---

40   For a discussion of the ideological level of discrepancies in *The Sceptic*, see Lisa Lai-ming Wong, "(Un)tying a Firm Knot of Ideas: Reading Yang Mu's *The Sceptic*," *Connotations: A Journal for Critical Debate* 12.2-3 (2002/2003): 292-306.

41   For a discussion of religious language as poetic language, see "Poetry and Possibil-ity" in *A Ricoeur Reader: Reflection and Imagination*. ed. Mario J. Valdés (New York: Harvester Wheatsheaf, 1991), 448-62.

sea goddesses worshipped by fishermen and sailors. In some oriental cultures such as Japan, Kami (god) can reside in objects. People who are serious about drinking tea may admire "Tea gods" and study the "Tea bible" (Yang, 1993: 296). Common to most cultures, images of god are primarily man-made in the form of verbal, written or plastic arts. It is believed that the Christian god created mankind according to his own image. This world view endows humanity with a certain degree of divinity above other creatures and instils the hope that it would be possible to resemble god in appearance and virtue. Race-conscious people, however, often question the validity of such claims because it is obvious that the image of the Christian god, as embodied by Jesus Christ, is traditionally based upon a Caucasian male. The sceptic observes an interesting cultural difference: "The sculptures of arhats, are all individually given a unique appearance whereas all angels look more or less the same" (Yang, 1993: 295). Plastic arts certainly give the most direct impression of a "god." The sceptic is familiar with images of Athena, Apollo and King David through paintings and sculptures. Once a photograph of a bronze sculpture of Athena stunned him: "She is so beautiful that one dare not look at her in the face" (Yang, 1993: 118). The image is a reproduction far removed from its "origin." Yet the "godliness" of Athena lies in her beauty. Comments like these are not aimed at questioning the true face of the referent, be it arhats, angels or Athena, but at arousing readers' interest in the diverse methods of religious representation.

From his ironic distance the author sees through the different strategies of signification but at the same time makes use of them. When a question of location "Where are gods and demons?" is posed, different religions and philosophies produce different answers. To the sceptic, Christianity is a cultural construct composed of architecture, music, poetry and visual arts. The composition of soaring vaults, melodious prayers and variegated colours in a cathedral provides an ideal setting for reading Rilke's *Duino Elegies*. In this work Yang Mu finds "all the beauty of Western culture" (Yang, 1993: 9). Disciples create exquisitely designed cathedrals or temples to house their god or gods. These images represent sanctuary in times of wars and are particularly represented in the holocaust movies. Some religious systems do away with buildings and house their gods under trees. In Buddhist scriptures, different Buddhas are found sitting under different trees (Yang, 1993: 249-58). The most revered Buddha, Sakyamuni, becomes enlightened during his meditation under a Bodhi tree. Confucius, the great Chinese philosopher, often enshrined as god, is said to have taught under apricot trees (Yang, 1993: 261-2).

To locate the Devil, a priest will often say, "The Devil is in your heart." When people wondered where Dao was, Zhuangzi's (c. 369-c. 286 B.C.) reply was "everywhere":

> Then he elaborates it with examples and situates Dao in ants, in weeds, in earthware. Finally, he actually comes up with "in urine and excrement." It is really getting worse and worse.
>
> *
>
> Deep in the mountain, there is a vast mansion, a Spanish monastery with a red-tiled roof. Greeting one's eyes are pineapples all over the mountain. A breeze blows. (Yang, 1993: 20)

To Yang Mu, it is not the specific whereabouts or the validity of such locations that matter. It is the meaning attached to the place that is important. His witty juxtapositions tease the "confusion of linguistic with natural reality, of reference with phenomenalism" (De Man, 1986: 11). After citing the contingent location of Dao "in urine and excrement," the author immediately provides an image of a red-tiled Spanish monastery surrounded by the sweet breeze smelling of pineapple. A game of jostling signifiers is played here, in which disparate sets of images collide into one another. Humour and irony mark the style of these passages in *The Sceptic*, especially when they are read in a self-reflexive approach.

Like a cultural critic, the sceptic examines the discursive logic in the theory and practice of a religion by engaging a wide range of texts, drawing upon examples from numerous systems of belief. The mysterious reincarnation of a Tibetan Lama, who died in March 1984 into the body of a Catholic Spanish boy, born 12 February 1985 in Granada, was a wonder to the world (Yang, 1993: 33). The sceptic is amazed by such belief in transcendence beyond temporal-spatial bounds. In his book Yang Mu also explores Greek myths of Apollo and Athena that extrapolate "truths" beyond human experience. When it comes to the accumulation of discourses, Christianity excels in the volume of its publications and the many multi-media representations of faith. Besides the Bible, there are enormous numbers of Christian texts on many different subjects. Publications discussed in *The Sceptic* include narratives such as Chaucer's *The Canterbury Tales*, John Bunyan's *Pilgrim's Progress* and Milton's Christian epic, *Paradise Lost*, and poetry such as the works of John Donne, religious verses by Hopkins, and the sacramental sonnets of the poet-monk, Edward Taylor. Since the medieval era Christian narratives in literature have been set in monasteries and churches, and have featured pilgrims, knights, monks and clergymen whose actions have discursively established the religious system. Apart from this organized dissemination of the Christian doctrine through written texts, there are theatrical performances and cinematic versions of the crucifixion and salvation stories. The sceptic thus looks at a modern mode of indoctrination featured in the theatrical rendition of the 1960s musical, "Jesus Christ, Superstar," which was later made into a film. To him, the director plays god in an adaptation, the biblical plot can be re-staged and re-cast in any setting, for example the Ming dynasty in China (Yang, 1993: 13). In spite of the cultural differences in the form of signification, the formulaic presentation serves to perpetuate the Christian logic.

From a literary point of view, there are striking similarities in the depiction of death in religious texts and other forms of writing. The most famous contemplation of death, Hamlet's soliloquy of "To be or not to be," is used as a prelude to the topic in Section 10. Shakespeare's description of death as "The undiscovered country from whose bourn/ No traveller returns, puzzles the will," is just one of various attempts to explain and explore the region beyond life. In one category Yang Mu places the serenity of philosophers confronted with death. The ancient "biographies" about the sages reveal that Confucius knew his time had come and had actually prepared for it. Similarly, Socrates also knew about his imminent execution and accepted it: "If gods find this well, let it be." In another category, an ironic comparison is made between the ways Jesus Christ and Ah Q behaved when death was at hand. By comparing Christ, "a melancholic man" in the Bible with Ah Q, the despised clown in a famous vernacular Chinese fictional work "The True Story of Ah Q," Yang Mu analyses them not as the son of "god" or a creation of a writer, but as different poetical embodiments of the human reaction to death (Yang, 1993: 147-50).

Tactics of overselectivity and distortion are found in other kinds of discourse. Assuming the role of a literary critic in Section 15, the sceptic does a close reading of Karl Marx's 1856 love letter to his wife, Jenny, written while he was in exile in London. With the practical skills of American formalism, the sceptic anatomizes the stylistic features of the text. To him, Marx's simile of comparing his yearning for love during a period of separation to the plants' need for sunlight and rain is too conceited, although the sceptic concedes that the logic works well. However, Marx's allusions to Ludwing Andreas von Feuerbach, a German philosopher, Jocab Moleschott, a Dutch physiologist, and Pythagoras, an ancient Greek philosopher and mathematician, are rather strange in a love-letter. As a materialist, Marx would probably refute the notion of rebirth, as formulated in the Brahman belief of reincarnation in Hinduism and Jesus Christ's resurrection in Christianity. Out of love, however, Marx ends his letter with a poetic line, "Buried in her arms, and be reborn in her kisses" (Yang, 1993: 220). Marx strikes a reconciliatory note, forsaking his usual dialectical thinking and materialistic outlook for the sake of love. Such a romantic line nonetheless stands out as a rupture to Marxist logic. In this section of *The Sceptic*, Marx's well-argued love-letter is compared against a lover's speech in Gustave Flaubert's novel, *Madame Bovary*. Rodolphe says to Madame Bovary in their first meeting after a six-week separation, "Oh, I think of you constantly. It drives me to despair... Forgive me! I'll leave you... Goodbye! I'll go away, far away, and you'll hear no more of me."[42] This approach-and-retreat conflict for forbidden lovers is often a cause for dramatization in literature. Emma and Rodolphe's manneristic indulgence in theatricality constitutes a sharp contrast to Marx's letter. There is no analogy by logical deduction, but an intense emotional outburst. Marx's conceit and Rodolphe's verbiage are divergent signifying practices that exhibit poetical discrepancies in the discourse of love, "real" and "fictional." The discrepancies distinguish a scientific socialist from an artist. The discussion also reveals contradictions within a person's language. Even Marx, the god who fathered Marxism, has to admit the irrelevance of his science and resort to transcendental imagery to convey the emotional aspects of human life. A major source of pleasure in reading *The Sceptic* is the author's examination of language in a discourse and his argument about how language follows, and at times, breaks away from the system that circumscribes it.

Signification is most powerful at the critical moment when one's religious faith is put to test. Yang Mu examines several instances of religious struggle where he perceives a loss of subjectivity and a distortion of human nature. He exposes the coercive twisting of natural human responses into stereotypical piety found in the horror-soaked scenes of faithful Christians fighting lions in the Coliseum and in the bloody image of Jesus's crucifixion. The sceptic notes that the repulsiveness and eeriness of these images are actually suppressed by faith and naturalized through ritual. Violence and blood act as a kind of shock therapy to wandering souls. Sacrificial acts revive disciples' feelings of guilt and repress their human responses. What is more, the suppression of romantic love and passion in the name of god is no less unnatural. To illustrate his point, the sceptic reads Alexandar Pope's poem, "Eloise to Abelard" (Yang, 1993: 36-44). Pope voices Eloise's complaint, "Nature stands check'd; Religion disapproves" (line 259) and portrays her prayer of religious anguish rising to an ecstasy of sexual orgasm. To the sceptic, Pope's poetic treatment allows the merging of the two conflicting figures, the Christian god with the forbidden lover, Aberlard, into a referent of her intense yearning.

Unlike poetic language, which opens one's imagination, religious language is embedded with an element of commitment. The dramatiza-

---

[42] Yang Mu translated the speech into Chinese in Section 15, *The Sceptic*, 223 and the English version quoted here is taken from Gustave Flaubert, *Madame Bovary*, trans. Alan Russell (Middlesex: Penguin, 1950), 168.

tion of decision-making is indispensable in religious discourse. Common to many systems of belief, conversion usually occurs in a momentary relinquishment of the self, requiring the unconscious subjugation to the unknown. In many cultural traditions, images of nature play a crucial role in signifying such experiences. The last few pages of *The Sceptic* describe how the sceptic, on waking up from a nap, is confronted by a reservoir of "religious" signifiers. The nap, a temporary loss of mastery over one's own intellect and senses, is mysterious, like death. Yet in an uncompromising manner, the sceptic defies the signs, which include a cross, a chapel and scattering spots of light from the stained glass windows, immediately before him. These are the stock images in the Christian language of divine revelation. He refuses to allow his experiences to weave into a religious conversion. With a decisive statement, "I have to go now," the notes on poetic discrepancies end. The sceptic finally chooses to free himself from the scene of "godly" revelation and break away from their totalizing signification.

Driven by imagination and the mysteries of life, man need to invent a sign to contain the metaphysical and arrived at a name, "god." In *The Sceptic*, a variety of signs from different cultures illustrate poetical discrepancies, which become particularly conspicuous in translation. The Greek word "logos" is translated into the English word, "Word," capitalized to give it a mystic and divine flavour. In Chinese, "logos" is rendered by the character "Dao." In the Chinese translation of "The Gospel according to John," the opening sentence reads: "In the beginning was Dao, Dao was with God, and Dao was God" (Yang, 1993: 114). This line from the Bible echoes Laozi's third century B.C. explanation of the mysterious origin of the world: "I do not know its name and call it Dao" (Yang, 1993: 115). The elasticity and inexactness of the term Dao plays a crucial role in this cultural transfer, linking ancient Chinese philosophy with Christianity. However, readers are reminded of the Chinese concept of immanence as epitomized in the ever-present but unprovable Dao: "The Dao that can be verbalized is not the universal Dao" (Yang, 1993: 116). In Chinese culture, to build a system on the irreproducible Dao is self-defeating. In spite of the constructedness of signs and traces, Section 16 explains how poetical representations of the abstract and ineffable have been institutionalized into systems of belief or disciplines: Dao into Daoism, god into theology and various religions, and words into poetry, poetics and different schools of poetics. To Yang Mu, these systems are all dubious. "When there is poetry, there will be poetics. When there is poetics, there will be xy-ist poetics, yx-ist poetics, and many other isms. When there is poetics, poetry is partially lost. When there is xy-ist and yx-ist poetics, poetry is completely lost." No matter how many kinds of poetics there might be, the poet allows them to exist as long as they do not interfere with poetry. "What an author ought to do is: do the job well, then shut up" (Yang, 1993: 238-46).

Above all, the sceptic is free from "epistemological tyranny." In the beginning, "[n]ames and jargons are primarily fluid... When signs are systematized, defined and restrained into a closed system, they are turned into terminology... Selected words are polished, revised, and canonized" (Yang, 1993: 281). It is then easy to dictate the disciple's mind by insisting on an invented set of signifying practices in order to monopolize the linguistic signs and their meaning (Yang, 1993: 280). To rebel against this tyrannical control over the use of language, Yang Mu takes an ironic approach in his critique, revealing how over-selectivity and distortion formulate a set of signifiers into a religious discourse. He is amused by the circulation of world cultures that occasionally serves to produce a system by co-incidence. The introduction of Buddhism to China is a relevant example. The religion arrived in China because of a dream and a dream interpreter. During the late Han dynasty, Emperor Ming dreamt of a golden man flying to him from the sky. He called an assembly of subjects to interpret the dream for him. One suggested that there was a Deity in the West whose name was Buddha and that perhaps the dream related to Him. The emperor agreed and sent his subjects to India to gather information about Buddhism. They returned with two Buddhist monks in 65 B.C. Thus this historical cultural encounter evolving into the development of a popular religion in China was the result of mere chance: people took different layers of representation, such as the emperor's dream, seriously. The dream interpreter's assumption that the Deity in the West was Buddha; and the two Indian monks' decision to focus on the translation of the Buddhist sutras, rather than to indoctrinate people into the Buddhist Way, ended up being tremendously important. An enormously significant event in history, such as the dissemination of Buddhism in China, reveals its bathetic origins when placed under critical scrutiny. The accumulated details such as dream and wild conjecture collide in a chance encounter and however far-fetched they apparently are, they help to fabricate a coherent discourse over the course of time. All religions appear to the sceptic as examples of random methods of selecting and preserving images that are eventually tied into the firm knot of ideology.

As the dialogic relation between the book's English and Chinese titles implies, *The Sceptic* does not offer any definitive answers to the *doubts about god* raised in the Chinese title, instead it exposes *poetical discrepancies* discovered by *the sceptic*. In the words of the sceptic: "All these ways of showing and keeping the images of Him has once been a heavy blow to my mind. Deity has never grabbed me, yet those things attached to Him have grabbed my mind after that heavy but gentle blow" (Yang, 1993: 64). In *The Sceptic*, the discrepancies are more poetical than religious in nature because they point to the creative and deceptive powers of language in different discourses about "god." These discrepancies reveal the plurality, incompleteness and ideological ruptures that have been repressed by religion. The discursive construction of a religious text, like any other linguistic text, operates by tying drifting signifiers into the firm knot of "god." By showing that signifiers are empty and free-floating and the ways of suturing them are unlimited, Yang Mu reveals the infinitude of the discursivity of "god" in his deconstructive reading.

In comparison to the systematic layout of *The Completion of a Poem*, *The Sceptic: Notes on Poetical Discrepancies* is a heteroglossic assembly of fragments composed of statements, doubts, quotations and translations. Unlike in *The Completion of a Poem*, where the use of English is often put in parenthesis or accompanied by a Chinese translation, English words and jargon are assimilated into the Chinese sentences in *The Sceptic*. Some fragments are put in a question and answer form between two speakers: "I" and "the other." The book is not meant to be pedagogical; it only displays the process of critical inquiry into various topics such as: the spirit of Romanticism, the making of god (poeticity) in the ultimate service of beauty and truth, and the theorization of poetry by isms and poetics. The book ends with the sentence, "I have to go now," an echo and a solution to the prologue of the book: "In a baffled mind doubts proliferate / I wish to be at peace but fail." Deifying was once an impetus for the development of human civilization. Many types of art (temporal and spatial) are traces of the imaginative exchange between the concrete and the abstract, the profane and the divine. In the sceptic's eyes, poetical discrepancies in representation are all equal. So he regards *The Bible* and the *Anthology of Tang Poetry* as the same as any other books on a shelf, perhaps placing *The Sceptic* between the two volumes.

Choosing or Being Chosen

The Sceptic's debate between religions and poetics is conducted in a Romantic spirit, heavily infused with a self-deconstructing irony. The degree of historical validity or scientific truth of the existence of the deity under discussion is not the author's concern. What is relevant is the different ways he discovers to articulate faith and belief. The discrepancies reside not so much in the variety of deities as in the variety of poetical descriptions of the god or gods. This brings the reader back to William Blake. When Blake talks about how ancient poets animated their surroundings by naming them and thus over the course of time established various systems of thoughts and beliefs, he reminds the reader that the subsequent construction of religious systems is a result of forgetting that men have been "[c]hoosing forms of worship from poetic tales" about "[a]ll deities [that] reside in the human breast."

> The ancient Poets animated all sensible objects with Gods or Geniuses, calling them by the names and adorning them with the properties of woods, rivers, mountains, lakes, cities, nations, and whatever their enlarged & numerous sense could perceive,
>
> And particularly they studied the genius of each city & country, placing it under its mental deity;
>
> Till a system was formed, which some took advantage of, & enslav'd the vulgar by attempting to realize or abstract the mental deities from their objects: thus began Priesthood;
>
> Choosing forms of worship from poetic tales.
>
> And at length they pronounc'd that the Gods had order'd such things.
>
> Then men forgot that All deities reside in the human breast.
>
> William Blake, "Plate 11," *The Marriage of Heaven and Hell* (Keynes, 1966: 153)

According to Harold Bloom, the problem of "choosing" is at the centre of contemporary discourse about literary tradition and canonicity. All of these debates can be summarized by a simplistic but dialectical question: "Do we choose a tradition or does it choose us, and why is it necessary that a choosing take place, or a being chosen?"[43] What constitutes a choice may not be easily identified. In literary terms, the range of options available to a poet depends largely on his education, knowledge, exposure, competence, attitude and temperament. On one hand, when a poet has a full grasp of all the options before him, he is free to choose. On the other hand, because a poet is situated in a historical moment, he is limited by his spatial-temporal location and at his best he is restricted to accomplishing certain goals in the development of the tradition(s).

Given such limitations, one's option is summarized by Pindar's words: "to exhaust the limits of the possible." Certain aspects of the possible are determined at birth. Born in 1940 in east Taiwan, Yang Mu's formal schooling occurred under the Nationalist Party's system of education. His childhood memories of Japanese colonial rule and the aboriginal life in his neighbourhood have constituted an exceptional aspect in his writing of the subaltern positions. Growing up in a peaceful town facing the Pacific Ocean, his seafaring dreams enabled him to align to the Greek imagination and provided him with the oceanic imagery that supplemented the dominant river imagery of classical Chinese poetry. Taiwan's political unrest in the 1970s and his American experiences opened up a different perspective to local issues from a

---

43   See Harold Bloom's "The Dialectics of Poetic Tradition" (Adams, 1992: 1186).

diasporic distance. The macro and pluralist approach he took towards historical incidents on the island offers a third path to reflect on the binary opposition in the mainstream discourses, be they the anti-Westernism in the 1960s, the Native Soil Movement in the 1970s, or the separatist agenda in the 1990s.

In his early years Yang Mu was given a solid education in classical and modern Chinese literature, and his undergraduate and graduate studies in the 1960s equipped him with knowledge of western literature and theories. Despite his belief that differences in literary views may be attributed to differences in which texts one is educated in, Yang Mu has never given his readers a required reading list. His works themselves invoke a wide range of literary references that an aspiring poet or comparatist would be hard pressed to cover in a life time. He has both assimilated and innovated a wide variety of anecdotes, literary works and theories to spell out his own poetic vision. He has been influenced by the West's ancient heritage including the Greek myths, Medieval romance, Chaucer, Milton, Spenser and Elizabethan poetry. He has also adapted and interrogated more contemporary Western literary influence including the English Romantics and the modernists. He particularly admires W. B. Yeats, the literary figure who bridges romanticism and modernism. Yang Mu has been less influenced by female poets, although Emily Dickinson seems to hold some sway over his writing. German authors like Rilke and Goethe have also been important to him. As for the national lyric tradition, besides early Chinese poetry like the *Book of Songs*, *Chu Elegies*, and ballads of *Yuefu*, Yang Mu admires works by poets before the Six Dynasties such as Tao Yuanming. For Tang and Song poets, works by Li Bai, Du Fu, Han Yu, and Su Shi are frequently cited. An expert scholar of the *Book of Songs*, Yang Mu makes frequent references to Zheng Xuan and Jizi. A native Taiwanese poet, he pays tribute to Wu Feng, the legendary Taiwanese figure in a verse play. An extensive and inquisitive reader himself, Yang discovers interesting tales even from Karl Marx, an author assumed to be most unpoetic. An aggregate of these poetic tales finds its heteroglossic expression in the prefaces and afterwords of his thirteen books of poetry, and in *The Completion of a Poem* and *The Sceptic*. The creation of Yang Mu's poetics discussed in earlier sections of this chapter presents the historical circumstances as well as the poet's personal inclinations and scholarship, which have shaped his choice.

One significant choice Yang Mu has made in his theory and practice of poetry is to introduce drama into Chinese poetry. Drama was not part of the mainstream Chinese literary tradition until the Yuan dynasty (1250-1368) and dramatization in poetry was rare. Xin Qiji's (1140-1207) two poems about his agonizing attempts to abstain from drinks are two exceptional cases. He placed this struggle in two dialogues. The first was between the speaker and the wine glass and the second was the speaker's interior monologue, again addressed to the silent wine glass.[44] There are also some famous examples of "verse in jest" including Han Yu's (768-824) "Biography of Mao Ying" and Ouyang Xiu's (1007-72) "Exposition on Flies." However, this kind of colloquial, humorous dramatization is viewed as bathos, a rhetorical device employed occasionally by the literati, but it does not occupy a place in mainstream literary studies. Plucking these dramatic writings from the margins of the orthodox tradition, Yang Mu reinterprets Xin's drinking poems in his modernist "Loneliness" (1976). He revives the style of a mock-biography in "Elegy for General Palm, with a Biography" (1992). Yang Mu's innovative reading of the *Book of Songs* returns dramatic elements to the poems in his critical essays. For example, his appreciation for poem No. 156 "I Went to the Eastern Hills" explores the possibilities of dramatizing the thought of a homecoming soldier. Yang Mu varies his interpretive strategies in two book chapters, "Theme" in *The Bell and the Drum* and "Heroism" in *From Ritual to Allegory*.[45] In the first reading, the sight of an oriole causes the soldier to imagine his wife's remarriage, reflecting his fear of betrayal. In the second, the oriole in flight represents the returning soldier's happy recollection of his own wedding as he comes home after three years in the battlefield. When the two interpretations are read together, the poet's investigation of the complexities in human psychology is demonstrated. Yang Mu also illustrates the drama inherent in verse through his interpretation of poem No. 31 "Drum Beating," which also describes a soldier thinking about his wife. Determining which dramatic persona is speaking becomes vital to the understanding of the poem. The core of the poem lies in a love vow: "For good or ill, in death as in life; / this is the oath I swear with you. / I take your hand / As token that I will grow old along with you" (Waley, 1987: 113). The poem's mood and meaning change depending on whether the vow was spoken in the voice of the soldier or that of his

---

[44] Xin Qiji wrote these two poems in sequence. In the first poem, the wine glass agrees to leave when the speaker dismisses it, promising to return when it is next summoned. This dialogue betrays the poet's lack of resolve in abstaining from drink. The sense of humour and self-mockery is seldom found in classical poetry.

[45] The two interpretations are found in C. H. Wang, *The Bell and the Drum*: Shih Ching *as Formulaic Poetry in an Oral Tradition* (Berkeley, Los Angeles, London: University of California Press, 1974), 115-7; and C. H. Wang, *From Ritual to Allegory: Seven Essays in Early Chinese Poetry* (Hong Kong: Chinese University Press, 1988), 63-5. The first reading interprets the oriole as one of individual elements in the theme of wedding. In this reading, Yang Mu finds the poem a wistful song of worries and sorrow, while the speaker worries that his wife may have married another man. The second interpretation reads the poem as a joyful song of homecoming and a happy recollection of the wedding day. Both interpretations are convincingly presented for the sake of argument in the respective chapters.

wife. Interpreted as in the voice of the homesick soldier, the vow is his confession of combat fatigue and nostalgia. If it is the soldier remembering something his wife has said, the vow demonstrates his feeling of regret and indebtedness to her.[46] Rather than coming up with a unitary reading through the endorsement of one view and the suppression of another, Yang Mu proposes both, leaving the drama open to the audience's interpretation.

Yang Mu's sensitivity to the dramatic voice has penetrated his poetry writing, literary criticism, and translation. Many of his poems are closely related to other art forms such as painting, film, and music. Some of his early lyrics were recorded as songs because of their melodic lyric voice. The theatricality of Yang Mu's poetry lends itself to stage performance. His suite poem, "Snake: Three Etudes" (1988), was performed as a dance play in 2000. Yang Mu's poems are literary experiments, exploring the limits of disciplinary boundaries and generic conventions. He admitted that his translation of *The Tempest* gave him a chance to speak in different languages, be they the cultured verse form or the vulgar voice of the play's lowly characters. His latest publication, *English Poetry in Chinese Translation* (2007), covers selected works from *Beowulf* to the poetry of Dylan Thomas. This anthology shows a still wider range of poetic voices, such as the tender words of Christopher Marlow, the refreshingly relaxed tone of Andrew Marvell, and the fascinating bizarre rhythm of Dylan Thomas.

Writing in the twentieth century, it is only natural that "belatedness" is the universal symptom for creative writers. With a lyric tradition over three millennia old in Chinese culture and a Western counterpart that is not that much younger, it is extremely difficult, if not impossible for a poet to invent a brand new approach to his art. To most Chinese writers, literature is a means to express one's thoughts and feelings. The traditional tenet that "poetry verbalizes intent" continues, to a considerable degree, to underline the content and style of modern poetry. Yang Mu's study of foreign literature, and in particular English Romanticism, further reinforced the spontaneous expression of powerful feelings characterizing his Ye Shan period. During his graduate study, however, his turn to modernism marked his conscious control of his expression. Emotions were reined in and the lyrical voice was dramatized behind different masks. After taking leave of the English Romantic world by concluding his "Letters to Keats," *The Completion of a Poem* shows us

---

[46] The dramatic voice in "Drum Beating" was the theme for a seminar course on Comparative Literature offered by C. H. Wang at the Hong Kong University of Science and Technology in 1994. According to Arthur Waley, both "Drum Beating" and "I Went to the Eastern Hills" are about a soldier who comes home only to find that his wife has presumed him dead and married again (Waley, 1987: 112-3, and 116-7).

the theory and practice of a mature poet-mentor. Rich in experience but still inquisitive in spirit, *The Sceptic: Notes on Poetical Discrepancies* collects the random observations of a liberal-minded sceptic and this deconstructive reading of all kinds of system displays post-modern elements.

Instead of the post-modern self-annihilating act of drowning one's voice in the sea of literary echoes, Yang Mu finds a way to forge his own signature. Paradoxically deconstructive and constructive in practice, the poet takes issue with the well-established literary systems and codes. He wishes to rupture the discourse and reveal the fissure, and then to fill in those gaps. His deconstructive reading of texts and traditions is a reaction to having been chosen and confined by history and tradition. The poems Yang Mu wrote in his fifties are more socially engaged on the one hand, and philosophical and theoretical on the other. The title of his twelfth book of poetry, *Intervention* (2001), best summarizes his strategies. In the Afterword, the poet claims that he is in fact doing a knight's job: "A flag and a sword equip the knight for his charge; poetry is my act of intervention" (Yang, 2001: 138). Through the transcultural confrontations of texts and contexts, Yang intervenes in social and political affairs, as well as in the post-modern discourse of language and writing.

The poetic structure of Yang Mu's works fully supports Yang Zhao's observation of the poet's art: "Yang Mu places the newest with the oldest in a dialogical and dialectical situation."[47] By re-reading the old with the new, the poet critically reflects on classical traditions in China and the west. For example, "Changan" (1993) is a meta-poetic commentary of the fashioning of the voice "I" and the poet keeps a postmodern distance from his creation by a proposition "If I... and you..." In this poem he turns the love lyric into a dramatization of lyrical writing itself. The conspicuous "constructedness" of the formulaic love lyric, written in imitation of the organizational design of Tang poetry, paradoxically revives attention in the classical form at the moment of deconstructing it.[48] To demonstrate the dialogical and dialectical tension between the new and the old, "A Poem on Poetry" (1996) is an apt example.[49] The dialogue in the poem is an intellectual debate between imagination and reason. References to various critical theories constitute the arguments between the lyrical self and its counterpart. The discussion reveals that the laws of thought in poetry are those of non-discursive logic and in

---

[47]   Yang Zhao's comment in a seminar held at Eslite Bookstore, Taipei on 1 January 2000. *China Times* 18 January 2000.

[48]   For a full discussion, see Lai-ming Wong's article "Two Readings of 'Changan': the Traditional and the Modern."

[49]   A detailed analysis of the poem can be found in Chapter 3.

Susan Langer's formulation: *"they never apply to scientific or pseudo-scientific (practical) reasoning"* (Langer, 1953: 234, emphasis in the original). It is the laws of imagination that govern the process of poetic creation. The two voices speaking in alternate stanzas are engaged in an intellectual activity. It is a dialogical exchange of views on contemporary poetics between the Romanticist and the postmodernist. The poem opens at the moment when the speaker encounters an intellectual block and gets lost amid contemporary theories. Yang Mu respects science, but he is dubious about the post-structuralist theories of literature. As he suggests in his famous essay, "Science and the Nightingale," imagination is essential for both science and poetry. It is conceivable that while Galileo captures the constellations in infinite space through his telescope, a poet crystallizes eternity in the fine details of artistic creation (lines 35-40). "A Poem on Poetry" re-affirms the oldest Orphic imagination as a resistance to the postmodern deconstructive discourse. The poet's preference brings the reader back to ancient Greek culture. The Aristotelian spider-web (lines 43-44) summarizes the organic unity of an artwork: "A thing whose presence or absence makes no difference to the whole is not part of that whole" (Aleshire, 2001: 29). The Romantic self reasons and debates with the speaker and guides him back to faith in poetic truth. The romantic voice has the last word and concludes the discussion: "Only poetic truth is the truth that orders Time."

Erudition in ancient literary cultures does not make Yang Mu an unthinking classicist. He shrewdly detects their failings. "Pindar's Odes – 472 B.C." is a commentary on Pindar, the last lyric singer in ancient Greece. Famous for his odes celebrating horsemanship and running, which were the popular games of the time, Pindar was particularly good at portraying a male competitor's strength and skills. In Yang Mu's poem, the horseman is superb because of his divine heritage. His father is a god wandering in the south, while his mother is a sea nymph. The poet highlights the themes of beauty, magnificence and victory just as Pindar did. Unlike Pindar, however, Yang raises a question about the whereabouts of the horseman's mother. This question critiques the Greek poet for concentrating only upon the glorification of the horseman. Yang Mu notes how the theo-centric and patriarchal tradition in Ancient Greece led to the negligence of the athletes' mothers. Yang Mu's poem both criticizes and supplements the tradition of Pindar's odes.

Yang Mu has done a great deal to critique Chinese literary traditions. Canonization is a matter of choosing, but these choices carry enormous weight in literary history and generic tradition. By anthologizing Chinese poetry, Yang Mu can exercise his own choices. When he published *Anthology of Modern Chinese Poetry* with William Tay, he paid tribute to his predecessors. When he did the selection and editing for *Anthology of Tang Poetry*, he had an ambitious purpose in mind: To complete the picture, and fill in the gaps in conventional lists by paying heed to the "marginal." Opposing the moralistic criteria of traditional Confucian editors, Yang Mu includes "hedonistic" drinking poems, in particular those by Li Bai. This gives a more complete picture of the literary subjects. In his selection of Tang poems, he paid special attention to the description of the south. The south was traditionally a place of exile for frustrated poets in imperial China, and had therefore been depicted with negative images and poems about the region were seldom found in the canon. To counteract the biased northern representation of the south as a squalid, barbaric place, poems depicting the flora of the south such as "coconut trees" are deliberately included. Yang Mu restores the "Poetics of the South" to a proper position in the Chinese lyric tradition.

To Complete the Fable

In the Afterword of his tenth book of poetry, *A Complete Fable* (1991), Yang Mu links his poetic approach both to the concrete and the abstract:

> My poetry attempts to abstractize both the abstract and the concrete in the mundane world by linguistic means: my concept comes from artistic truth. I care about grammar and take heed of rhyme and sound effects. It is not my wish that a poem I write only talks about one event or a single idea. We have tried to build an acceptable abstract structure, a generative locus of infinitude. In this structure, there are unrestricted messages, resonating among themselves into infinity. This is called "abstract transcendence." This is where the power of poetry lies. (Yang, 1991: 155)

As delineated in earlier chapters, Yang Mu's literary approach avoids making poetry a journalistic record of mundane realities. When Yang concretizes the abstract, he gives material form to phenomenal concerns. As Paul de Man observes,

> The very concept of certainty, which is the basis of all concepts, comes into being only in relation to sensory experience be it, as in Hegel, as unmedi-tated assurance or, as in Descartes, as reflected delusion. If there is to be consciousness (or experience, mind, subject, discourse or face), it has to be susceptible of phenomenalization. But since the phenomenalization of ex-perience cannot be established a priori, it can only occur by a process of signification. (De Man, 1981: 33)

What Yang Mu does is to make the abstract concrete through descrip-tions of sensory experiences like aural and visual details. The passage of time is one example. Poets captures the phenomenology of time through descriptions of sensory experiences like running water, withering leaves, greying hair or a song coming to its end. When Yang Mu says that he concretizes the abstract in his poetry, what he does is phenomenalizing the abstract. Yang Mu creates an experience of the abstract, which he calls the "abstract transcendence," through the process of signification.

Nonetheless signification does not happen without the reader. To Riffaterre, the poetic significance of a poem is the moment of actualization that occurs in the process of reading between the text and the reader. The lyric voice in Yang Mu's works is famous for its imploring tone when talking to "you," the imaginary addressee. Although he does mask his poetic voice through historical or fictional figures, generally the speaker and the addressee are kept obscure. One possible identity for this ideal addressee "you" is the unknown reader. Among his later works are a few poems in which the poet talks to the invisible reader, who is usually a mute companion: "By the lamp, the one who has tea with me without a word is as quiet-coloured as chrysanthemum" ("Song of Time Lost," 1989, lines 35). At times, the speaker affirms his belief in himself: "I should have known / All these without asking; or else how come on earth / There is someone who understands everything about the rhyme and rhythm in my writing" (lines 38-40).

In *A Complete Fable* he offers various definitions of his own poetry but he concludes with the phrase "by means of language" every time. To him, "words count before everything else."[50] In this sense, poetry is a big illustrated book drawn in language. In "In Lieu of a Letter" (1991), "beauty at its best" refers to an aesthetic experience in both writing and reading. The speaker feels the temptation to "speak," to put forth a representation of "beauty at its best" by verbalizing it but this urge is finally abandoned in wordlessness. He concludes that "Beauty at its best you are" because "you" in a state of purposiveness without a purpose, sets free the will to live through the adventures that will be captured in a poem. Combing through the thickets of words to find the gem of poetry, the poet's heroic quest will not be fulfilled until he delivers the treasure into the hands of the lady. The complete fable of poetry writing and reading is like a medieval romance. Under the spell of verbal art, the unknown reader will be carried away by his or her adventures in the poetic worlds and will travel through thick and thin like a page attending to the poet-knight (lines 36-45). However, locating such a discerning reader is challenging. When Yang Mu does find one, he elevates her to heavenly status, as in "To an Angel" (1993). The poet then asks for her attention and understanding in desperate humility. A good poem is like a well-wrought spider web, produced by the brave mind of a poet but it must wait to be reproduced in the same brave mind of a reader. Simi-

---

[50] Yang Mu's emphasis on language is too conspicuous to overlook. The quote is from his prosework, "She Says My Quest Is an Escape," in *Direction Back to Zero* (1991), 121-46.

larly, the poet needs to be chosen by the reader to complete the poetic fable.

* *
*

Judging from his deep concerns for language, one may say that Yang Mu is rather conservative. While some modern Chinese poets are attracted to experiments in the western models of Abstract Poetry or Concrete Poetry which play with the aural and visual aspects of language, Yang Mu departs from the avant-garde in his serious considerations of sound and sense, form and content. He never attempts eye-catching breakthroughs that shock the reader but this does not diminish his poetry's subtle potential to subvert. The lyricism in his tone and language is so widely read and well studied that since 1993 it has earned him world renown as a bicultural poet. It has also won him the "International Prize for Literature Written in the Chinese Language" (2007).

Yang Mu has constantly tried out new poetic forms or reviewed traditional ones. Almost half a century ago, in the Afterword of *By the Waterside*, the poet made a promise in his first book of poetry: "I will always seek and make experiments, never will I be pinned down to a single style" (Yang, 1978b: 606). While some avant-garde Taiwanese poets have tried hard to produce ego-less poems through collage, Yang Mu's poems have a distinct voice. His poetry and poetics have actively looked into the fissures in established systems and breathed new life into existing discourse. Like rays of the searching sun, he illuminates Chinese and foreign poetics both by evaluating these works and assimilating them. His "Letters to Keats" was an attempt to emulate and rebel against his poetic predecessor. Troubled by the conflicts between a national-cultural identity and a foreign master, he said farewells to John Keats in his last letter. But the problem of identity still preoccupied him until he resolved it in *The Completion of a Poem*. Nonetheless, some of the doubts about poetry and religion, which he first expressed in one of his letters to Keats, "The Scenery outside the Church," were taken up again thirty years later and further explored in *The Sceptic*. The book's ending is almost a re-visitation of the letter from thirty years ago. Having pointed out the methodology of examining the doubts about god, he is happy to leave the questions outside the church, writing "I have to go now."

One of the favourite metaphors of Yang Mu's later poetry is to compare the flow of life events to the appearance of a whirlpool in a stream. The current swirls round an empty centre for a while, and depending on the water level, the whirlpool appears and disappears at different times. In "Reading Eisenstein near the Fifth Day of the Fifth Month" (2000) and "Pindar's Odes" (2000), the early image of the whirlpool in "An

Elegy of One Hundred and Twenty Lines" (1976) reappears in a more sophisticated form. More than a reference to time running speedily in its circularity, the whirlpool in the two recent poems captures the vision of beauty at its best which is always elusive and quick to vanish. As Seamus Heaney sees in Robert Frost's belief "that individual venture and vision arose as a creative defence against emptiness, and that it was therefore always possible that a relapse into emptiness would be the ultimate destiny of consciousness."[51] Yang Mu has little doubt about such views of creativity and to him poetry is "something born of nothing." He is free from the dialectics of "something versus nothing." Recurrent metaphors that move easily between different forms include the tide, vapour, embroidery, and a round trip. The endless labour in activities such as the tide rolling in and out, vapour condensing and evaporating, nimble fingers stitching and unstitching, and a traveller frequently coming and leaving, all underscore the deconstructive approach in his meta-poetic commentary and *ars poetica*.

Perhaps, the best way to talk about Yang Mu's poetics of abstract transcendence is to read "Pick it up" (1994). The poet here illustrates that a poem is but a man-made artifice by detailing the creative process of making:

> So I guess what passes before dawn
> Across the vale in our dream – the countenance that soon
> Disappears – is you. Listless, alone
> I recall upon the shimmering waters
> At the foot of a hill on the other shore
> A strand of blue mist floats
> A strand of blue mist floats like a ribbon falling
> You stoop to pick it up

What sweeps across the poet's mind is something indeterminate and impermanent. In the darkness of his dream the poet has no firm hold of the flickering thing, he can only try to guess or recall what is about to pass and disappear. It is this uncertain moment of vague recognition before full cognition in broad daylight that must be rescued. To fix the formless, he gives it the form of a strand of blue mist drifting from a hill on another shore. Aesthetic distance is kept by the image which is far away and unreachable in space and time. Time is running out, because soon the sun will rise and the mist will evaporate. Ephemeral as a spark of inspiration, the mist floats like a ribbon falling. By compression and transformation the invisible is turned into something visual, and the intangible into the tangible. In many of the short poems Yang Mu has lately published, he focuses on only one small event and unfolds its

---

[51]   See Seamus Heaney, "Above the Brim," in *Homage to Robert Frost*, 63.

details to create a purely poetic reality.[52] The poet's musings are presented in the tone of a nonchalant observer. The thoughts are half illuminated by shimmers of inspiration and are then picked up and pinned down on the page. What "Pick it up" describes is the abstract-transcendental art of poetry writing through a concretization of the abstract.[53]

A relaxed poetic style also underlines Yang Mu's recent works. "Temporality Proposition" (1993) shows that the poet is at ease with disparaging literary traditions. His choice of translating *The Tempest* (1999) into Chinese shows a preference for a play about self-recognition and reconciliation. The German translation of his poems *Patt beim Go* is titled after his poem, "A Draw in Chess" (1999), which transcends binary oppositions and ends in the Buddhist enlightenment epitomized by the Heart Sutra. With sympathy and wisdom, the mature poet learns to live in peace.

* *
*

The anecdote that opens the chapter illustrates that only one's knowledge of a broad selection of poetry and one's awareness of the transcultural confrontations can help one truly understand the question about whether a poem from a specific culture is long or short. A cross-cultural reading list will allow the poet to move between cultures and therefore offer him an array of options. Yang Mu has the freedom to choose how he employs the lyric voice, and he is able to select a local or global perspective from which to view issues of his times. Illuminated by the rays of the searching sun, the poet is able to create different time-worlds to experience and portray life, and to offer alternative voices to national narrative.

Perhaps, the ultimate knowledge from Yang Mu's poetry and poetics is that the rays that light up poetry in different corners of the worlds come not from the sun; they come from soul-searching insights within all great poets. It is after all the earth's own revolution that brings different facets of our globe to light, just as a liberal turning of the mind motivates a transcultural reading and writing of literature.

---

[52] In fact, from *Temporality Proposition* (1997) onwards, Yang Mu published many short poems, each of seven to eight lines in less than eighty words.

[53] Yang Mu's article on the topic is "Abstract and Alienation: Where Time Would Surely Forget Us," *United Daily*. 28-31 December 2004.

Chronology of Events

World	China	Taiwan	Yang Mu
		Colonial history of Taiwan 1590-1945	
		1590 Portuguese reach the island and name it Formosa (beautiful).	
		1641 Dutch take control of the island.	
		1661 Zheng Chenggong's troops conquer the island and expel Dutch in 1662.	
		1683 Manchus take the island which becomes part of Qing China.	
		1895 Treaty of Shimonoseki concludes Sino-Japanese War; Taiwan is ceded to Japan. Taiwanese are assimilated by Japan in terms of naming, language and culture.	
	1911 Fall of the Qing; establishment of the Republic of China.		
1914 World War I begins	1919 May Fourth Movement		
1918 World War I ends.			
1936 July. Spanish Civil War begins.	1936 Over 120 Communist and leftist writers, styling themselves the Chinese Writers' Association, proclaim the slogan "Literature for National Defense."		
Federico Garcia Lorca assassinated.			

World	China	Taiwan	Yang Mu
	1937 Sino-Japanese War begins		
1939 World War II breaks out.			
			1940 Sept. 6. Born Wang Ching-hsien (Wang Jingxian) in Hualian, Taiwan.
1941-45 The European Holocaust. Pacific War breaks out.			
1942 Albert Camus, *The Outsider* published.	1942 Mao Zedong's "Talks at the Yanan Forum on Art and Literature" sets out the role of the arts in China's revolutionary struggle.		
1945 May Germany surrenders unconditionally.		1945 Defeat of Japan in World War II; Guomindang takes control of Taiwan.	
Aug. The US army drop atomic bombs on Hiroshima and Nagasaki; Japan surrenders unconditionally. Pacific War and World War II end.		October 25. "Restoration" of Taiwan.	
	1946 Civil war breaks out between Nationalists (Guomindang) and Communists.	1946 The Committee on Popularization of the National Language is formed.	1946-52 Attends Ming-yi Elementary School, Hualian; first cohort of students after the restoration of Taiwan.
1947 India and Pakistan become independent nations.		1947 February 28th Incident.	

World	China	Taiwan	Yang Mu
	1949 Communists under Mao Zedong's leadership defeat Guomindang in civil war; the Chinese Communist Party takes over mainland China.	1949 Guomindang government retreats to Taiwan; millions of people flee from mainland China to Taiwan.	
		May 19. Martial Law is imposed.	
	October 1, Mao proclaims People's Republic of China (PRC).	May 24. Legislative Council passes the Betrayers Punishment Act.	
		1950s-1960s "White Terror" Era.	
		1950 Chiang Kai-shek resumes presidency.	
1950-53 US heads UN forces in Korean War.		Guomindang government establishes the Chinese Literature and Art Awards Committee and the Chinese Literature and Art Association, which promote anti-communist and anti-leftist ideas.	
		US aid begins.	
		Ban on the publication of Japanese-language news.	

World	China	Taiwan	Yang Mu
	1951 China and the Vatican break off diplomatic relations.	1951 *New Poetry Weekly*, the first poetry journal in postwar Taiwan, published.	1951 Reads popular fiction.
			1952-58 Attends Hualian Middle-High School.
	1952 "Three Anti Drive" ends; "Five Anti Drive" begins.	1952 The use of Japanese and Taiwanese as languages of instruction is forbidden.	1952 Reads *Xi you ji* [Journey to the West] and *Shui hu chuan* [Heroes of the Marshes].
	Eileen Chang flees to Hong Kong.		
	1953 First Five Year Plan begins.	1953 Modern Poetry Society is formed; *Modern Poetry Quarterly* founded.	
	1954 Du Pengcheng publishes *Guarding Yanan*, which is banned in 1958 as General Peng Dehuai is purged. Du is later accused of conspiring against Mao Zedong in the Cultural Revolution.	1954 March. Blue Star Poetry Society is formed. June. *Blue Star Weekly* founded. October. Epoch Poetry Society is formed; *Epoch Poetry Quarterly* published.	
1954 The International Comparative Literature Association (ICLA) is founded at Oxford University. Officers elected include Fernand Baldensperger, TS Eliot, Jean-Marie Carré and Carlo Pellegrini.			

World	China	Taiwan	Yang Mu
	1955 Period of "New Democracy" ends and collectivization begins.	1955 President Chiang calls for writers devoted to "Combat literature and art."	1955 Starts writing poetry and publishing under a number of pen names, including Ye Shan, in local and Taipei newspapers and journals.
			Begins editing, with Chen Jinbiao, a poetry weekly, *The Seagull* (named by Hu Chuqing, his teacher of Chinese from Hunan, China), and a literary supplement in *East Taiwan Daily*.
1956 Suez Crisis.	1956 Mao Zedong proclaims the slogan "Let a Hundred Flowers Bloom, Let a Hundred Schools of Thought Contend."	1956 Modernist Poetry Society is founded by Ji Xian.	
		Literary Magazine is started by T. A. Hsia.	
	1957 Anti-rightist Campaign begins.	1957 *New Poetry Today* and *Literary Star* are founded.	

World	China	Taiwan	Yang Mu
1958 Nobel Prize in Literature: Boris Pasternak. The worldwide success of *Doctor Zhivago* causes Pasternak to be severely criticized in the USSR, and he declines the Nobel Prize in Literature in 1958, fearing that if he leaves the USSR he will not be allowed to return.	1958 First Five Year Plan fails. Great Leap Forward intended to speed up industrialization fails. The national movement of "New Ballad" starts.	1958 Hu Shi becomes the director of Academia Sinica. May 4. Invited by Chinese Literature and Art Association, Hu Shi gives a talk proposing the introduction of a liberal literature and the revival of the revolutionary spirit of May Fourth Literature.	1958 Studies in Taipei, where he becomes acquainted with such poets as Qin Zihao, Huang Yong, Ji Xian, Luo Fu, Ya Xian, Zhou Mengdie, Yu Guangzhong, Chu Ge and Xiong Hong.
1959. Dec Tibetans protest against the communist rule; Dalai Lama flees to India.	1959 "Three Hard Years" start, widespread famine created by the Great Leap Forward.		1959 April. Member of the editorial board of the poetry journal, *Epoch*. Sept. Admitted to History Department at Christian Tunghai University, Taichung.
	1960 Sino-Soviet split.	1960s Crackdowns on the magazines *Free China* and *Literary Star*.	1960 Publishes the first volume of poetry, *Shui zhi mei* [By the Waterside]. Transfers to the Department of Foreign Languages and Literature.

World	China	Taiwan	Yang Mu
1961 Berlin War erected.		1961 *Literary Star* publishes Li Ao's essay, "Lao Ren Yu Bang Zi," which introduces Cultural Polemics in the East-West Context.	1961 Chief editor of *Dongfeng*, a campus magazine.
	1962 Socialist Education Movement.	1962 Hu Shi dies.	1962 Sets up "The Cavemen Society" with his classmates.
			Studies Daoist philosophy, the classical prose of Han Yu and Liu Zongyuan, and *Shijing* [the Book of Songs] and *Chu ci* [Chu Elegies].
			1963 Jan. Publishes the second volume of poetry, *Huaji* [Flower Season].
			June. Graduates from Christian Tunghai University.
			October. Leaves for Quemoy and performs mandatory military service on the frontier island. Writes many lyrical essays, including a series entitled "Letters to Keats."

World	China	Taiwan	Yang Mu
	1964 "Learn from the People's Liberation Army" Movement.	1964 Li [Bamboo Hat] Poetry Society and *Li Poetry Magazine* are founded.	1964 July. Returns from Quemoy.
			Sept. Attends the Iowa Writers Workshop (directed by Paul Engle), University of Iowa.
	China and France establish diplomatic relations.	Relations with France severed.	Starts learning Old English with John C. McGalliad.
1965 US steps up military involvement in Vietnam.	1965 "A Critique of the New Historical Play *Hai Rui Dismissed from Office*" published.	1965 Cessation of US aid.	1965 Takes Comparative Literature as an elective; studies German.
			Member of the editorial broad of *Xiandai wenxue* (Modern Literature).
	1966-76 Emergence of model revolutionary plays during Great Proletarian Cultural Revolution.		1966 Feb. Receives MFA from the University of Iowa (thesis title: *The Lotus Superstition and Other Poems*).

World	China	Taiwan	Yang Mu
	1966 Great Proletarian Cultural Revolution begins. *Quotations from Chairman Mao* (The "Little Red Book") is widely read.	1966 Kaohsiung Export Processing Zone is inaugurated.	1966 August. Publishes *Ye Shan sanwenji* [First Essays of Ye Shan], and Chinese translation of Federico Garcia Lorca's *Romancero Gitano*. Sept. Marries Chen Shaocong; enters the doctoral programme in Comparative Literature at the University of California, Berkeley (academic advisor: Chen Shih-hsiang). Nov. Publishes third volume of poetry, *Dengchuan* [Boat Lantern].
			1967 Starts to learn Greek. Studies English Poetics with Josephine Miles, Early English Literature with Alain Renoir, and Medieval European Literature with Philip Damon. Publishes *"Shijing* guo feng de zhiwu he shi de biaoxian jiqiao" [A Study of the *Shijing* Vegetation and Its Poetic Function].

World	China	Taiwan	Yang Mu
1968 Anti-Vietnam War protests in US; student uprisings throughout Europe.	1968 Red Guard units fan out over China, aiming to destroy the feudal past and the bourgeois present; museums and libraries are pillaged; books and newspapers, notes and writings of intellectuals, art and religious statues are destroyed.	1968 Nine Years Free Education.	1968 Studies Japanese. Takes courses on Philology with Peter A. Boodberg, and Drama of Yuan and Ming dynasties with Cyril Birch. Witnesses the anti-war protests and student movements on Berkeley campus.
1969 *Apollo 11* makes first moon landing. Alexander Solzhenitsyn is expelled from Soviet Writers' Union.			1969 Publishes a volume of selected poems, *Fei du ji* (No Crossing, 74 poems written between 1956 and 1966). Passes the Qualifying Examinations for the Ph.D. in Comparative Literature candidacy.
1970 Nobel Prize in Literature: Alexandr Solzhenitsyn.		1970s Rise of Modernist Literature. Crackdown on the magazine *The Intellectuals*.	1970 Begins editing, with Lin Hengzhe, *Xinchao congshu*, published by Zhiwen Press. Becomes lecturer in Chinese and Comparative Literature at the University of Massachusetts, Amherst.

World	hina	Taiwan	Yang Mu
1971 Indo-Pakistan War, leads to the creation of Bangladesh.	1971 US Secretary of State Henry Kissinger secretly visits Beijing.	1971 People's Republic of China replaces Taiwan at United Nations (UN) and on the UN Security Council.	1971 Receives Ph.D. in Comparative Literature from the University of California, Berkeley (dissertation title: *Shih Ching: Formulaic Language and Mode of Creation*).
Jan. and April. Students in Taiwan, Hong Kong, and the US protest against the Japanese claim on the sovereignty of Diaoyutai Islands.		The first international comparative literature conference in the East takes place at Tamkang University.	March. Promoted to assistant professor. Publishes his fourth volume of poetry *Chuanshuo* [Legends], with an Afterword by Yip Wai-lim.
23 May. Prof. Chen Shih-hsiang (1912-71), Yang Mu's thesis supervisor, dies at Berkeley.			His poem, "Shier xingxiang lianxiqu" [Etudes: The Twelve Earthly Branches] receives the 1st Shi Zong Award.
			Dec. Moves to Seattle; becomes assistant professor in Chinese and Comparative Literature Department at the University of Washington, Seattle.

World	China	Taiwan	Yang Mu
	1972 US President Nixon visits China	1972 Modern Poetry Debate. Guan Jieming and Tang Wenbiao criticize new poetry, claiming that its language is too westernized, the use of symbols is not local and the themes are not related to social concerns. Yu Guangzhong and Yan Yuanshu rebut the charges.	1972 Adopts the pen-name Yang Mu when he publishes "Nianlun" [Tree Rings] in *Chun wenxue* No.62.
	US and China issue Shanghai Communiqué.		March. Chief editor for the special issue on "A Retrospect on Modern Chinese Poetry" in *Modern Literature* No. 46.
			Publishes (in English) "Sartorial Emblems and the Quest."
1973 US troops leave Vietnam.		1973 Yang Kuei renews attention in the literature of Taiwan under the Japanese occupation.	1973 Promoted to associate professor at the University of Washington, Seattle.
		Cessation of US military aid.	June. Travels to Europe.
		Lin Huaimin founds the Cloudgate Dancing Theatre.	Editor for *Micromegas: Taiwan Issue* [English translation of modern Chinese poems], published by the University of Massachuetts.

World	China	Taiwan	Yang Mu
1974 Alexander Solzhenitsyn is forced into exile after publishing the first volume of *The Gulag Archipelago*.	1974 Campaign to criticize Lin Biao and Confucius.		1974 March. Publishes a book on literary criticism, *Chuantongde yu xiandaide* [The Traditional and the Modern].
			June. Co-edits with Yu Guangzhong a special issue on poetry in *Zhongwai wenxue* (*Chung Wai Literary Monthly*).
			Visits the Confucius temple in south Taiwan.
			Sept. Promoted to associate professor in Chinese Literature and Comparative Literature.
			Nov. Publishes (in English, under the name C. H. Wang) *The Bell and the Drum: Shih Ching as Formulaic Poetry in an Oral Tradition*, published by University of California Press.
			Publishes (in English) "The Countenance of the Chou."

World	China	Taiwan	Yang Mu
			1975-76 Visiting Professor at the Department of Foreign Languages and Literatures, National Taiwan University, Taipei.
		1975 President Chiang Kai-shek dies; three television stations stop broadcasting colored TV programmes for three days.	1975 May. Publishes *Yang Mu zixuanji* (Selected Works of Yang Mu, 54 pieces of prose, with prefaces, chronology of events, and a list of publications).
			Sept. Publishes the fifth volume of poetry, *Ping zhong gao* [Manuscripts in a Bottle].
1975 Unification of Vietnam			Publishes (in English) "Towards Defining a Chinese Heroism."

World	China	Taiwan	Yang Mu
1976 The 40th anniversary of the death of Lorca.	1976 Jan. Zhou Enlai dies.		1976 Publishes a volume of lyrical essays, *Nianlun* [Tree Rings] in January, and "Xiandai de Zhongguoshi" [Modern Chinese Poetry] in the literary supplement of *United Daily* in February.
	April. Gang of Four suppress mourning for Zhou in Tiananmen Square.		June. Presents a talk on modern poetry in Hong Kong.
	Sept. Mao Zedong dies and Deng Xiaoping purged.		Sets up with Ye Burong, Hongfan shudian (a publishing house).
	Oct. Gang of Four arrested.		Serves on the editorial board of *Wenxue pinglun* [Literary Review] and *Hongfan wenxue congshu* (Hongfan literature series).
			Aug. Returns to teach in Seattle.
			Oct. Divorced.

World	China	Taiwan	Yang Mu
	1977 Deng Xiaoping is rehabilitated.	1977 Presbyterian Church in Taiwan declares a proclamation advocating the independence of Taiwan.	1977 Publishes a volume of miscellaneous essays, *Baikelai jingshen* (The Spirit of Berkeley); and reprints *First Essays of Ye Shan*, with a new preface.
		Aug 20. Yu Guangzhong publishes an article "Here Comes the Wolf," triggering the Native Soil Literature Debate.	Publishes (in English) "Chou Tso-jen's Hellenism."
			Publishes (in English) "From Chinese Modern Poetry to Modern Chinese Poetry."
			Translates (into Chinese) Ernest Robert Curtius, *Europaische Literatur und Lateinisches Mitelalter*, Chapter one.
1978 Edward Said, *Orientalism* is published.	1978 Four Modernizations Programme begins.	1978 Chiang Ching-kuo elected president.	1978 Publishes his sixth volume of poetry, *Beidou xing* [Song of the Big Dipper].
			Hosts a colloquium commemorating the May Fourth at the University of Washington.
	Scar Literature is started with the publication of Lu Xinhua's *Scar*.		Publishes *Yang Mu shiji I: 1956-1974* [Collected Poems of Yang Mu, Volume 1: 1956-1974].
			Serves as external examiner for the Graduate School of the Chinese University of Hong Kong.

World	China	Taiwan	Yang Mu
			1978-79 Visiting Professor at the Department of East Asian Studies, Princeton University.
			Publishes (in English) "The Bird as Messenger of Love in Allegorical Poetry."
		1979 Jan. Marries Xia Yingying.	
1979 Sino-Vietnamese War; "boat people" begin to flee to Hong Kong.	1979 Jan. 1. Establishment of diplomatic relations between PRC and the US	1979 US ends recognition of Taiwan but passes the Taiwan Relations Act.	Publishes verse drama *Wu Feng* in *United Daily* in February, and the play appears in book form in April.
	Dissidents put up wall posters calling for democracy, the "fifth modernization." This Democracy Wall movement is crushed by the government in the fall.	*Formosa* magazine first published.	Receives Zhongshan Literary Award for New Poetry.
		Dec. Formosa Incident in Kaohsiung on the International Human Rights Day.	
	An East-West comparative literature conference is held at the Chinese University of Hong Kong.		Publishes "Sanbainian jiaguo: Taiwan shi 1661-1925" [Taiwan Poetry: 1661-1925].
			Publishes a collection of literary criticisms, *Wenxue zhishi* [Literary Knowledge].

World	China	Taiwan	Yang Mu
1980-88 Iran-Iraq War	Early 1980s Scar Literature is succeeded by Reflection Literature.	1980s Growth of Nativist Literature and Military Compound Literature.	1980 Jan. *Wu Feng* receives *China Times*'s Special Literary Award for Narrative Poetry.
	The blossoming of Misty Poetry; the leading Misty poets include Bei Dao, Gu Cheng and Shu Ting.		March. First son Wang Changming, Bruce born.
1980 May. Kwangju Incident in South Korea: the armed Special Forces troops kill civilians and students in a demonstration.	1980 Sept. Premier Hua Guofeng is replaced by Zhao Ziyang.	1980 Feb 28. The mother and daughters of Lin Yixiong, the leader of the opposition party, are murdered.	Publishes "Beige wei Lin Yixiong zuo" [A Song of Sorrow for Lin Yixiong] in *Ba Fang* [Eight Directions] in Hong Kong
			Oct. Publishes the seventh and eighth volumes of poetry, *Jinji de youxi* (Forbidden Games) [Taboo Games] and *Haian qi die* [Seven Turns of the Coast].

World	China	Taiwan	Yang Mu
	1981-87 Campaign against bourgeois liberalization.		1981 Jan. Honorary Advisor to the Writers' Association of Singapore.
	1981 Gang of Four sentenced.		March. A trip to mainland China: visits Beijing, Xian, Chengdu, Chungxin, the Yangtze Gorges, Yichang, Wuhan, Shanghai, Hangzhou, and Zhaoxin.
	Communist Party formally denounces Cultural Revolution and reappraises Mao Zedong.		
	Hu Yaobang replaces Hua Guofeng as General Secretary of the Communist Party.		August. Edits two volumes of the *Anthology of Modern Chinese Prose Essays*
			Sept. Promoted to professor of Chinese and Comparative Literature at University of Washington, Seattle.

World	China	Taiwan	Yang Mu
1982 Falklands War	1982 Jan. 11. Deng Xiaoping puts forward the concept of "one country, two systems" for the first time.		1982 Hongfan reprints *Tree Rings*, with a new preface.
The border between Spain and Gibraltar is partially reopened.			Publishes a volume of lyrical essays, *Sousuo zhe* [The Quester].
Margaret Thatcher initiates talks on the future of Hong Kong.			Edits and publishes four volumes of Feng Zikai's *Selected Works*.
			Dec. Attends a seminar on Literary History organized by the University of Hong Kong.
			Publishes (in English) "The Weniad: A Chinese Epic in *Shih Ching*."
			1983-84 Visiting professor in the Department of Foreign Languages and Literatures at National Taiwan University, Taipei.
	1983 Campaign against "spiritual pollution" (i.e. against Western cultural influence).		1983 Co-translates *Wu Feng* with Cissie Kwok, published by Indiana University Press.
1983 Dec. The British government decides to return Hong Kong to China in 1997.	Sept. 20. Deng Xiaoping reaffirms China's position that it will recover the sovereignty of Hong Kong in 1997.		Editor of two volumes of Zhou Zuoren's *Selected Works* published in July.
	Mid-1980s Emergence of Root-searching Literature.		Publishes "Xiandaishi de Taiwan yuanliu" [The Taiwanese Origins of Modern Poetry].

World

1984 Dec. 20. Zhao Ziyang and Margaret Thatcher sign the Sino-British Joint Declaration in Beijing.

China

Taiwan

1984 President Chiang re-elected.

Chiang picks Lee Teng-hui, a Taiwanese agricultural economist, as his vice-president.

Spring. Debates over "Chinese consciousness" versus "Taiwanese consciousness."

Inauguration of *Unitas: A Literary Monthly*.

Yang Mu

1984 The first term, Adjunct professor in the Chinese Department at National Tsing Hua University, Taipei.

Jan. Publishes a collection of essays on literary criticism, *Wenxue de yuanliu* [Origins of Literature].

April. Starts writing "Interchanges," a weekly column on social issues for *United Daily*.

May. Attends the conference organized by the International PEN in Japan; visits Kyoto.

"Lu Ji *Wen Fu* jiaoshi" [A Comparative Interpretation of Lu Ji's *Essays on Literature*] appears in the *Bulletin for Literature, History and Philosophy* of National Taiwan University. The work is subsequently published in book form by Hongfan in 1985.

Edits and publishes Xu Deshan's *Selected Stories*.

Publishes "Xinshi de chuantong quxiang" [The Traditional Orientation of Modern Poetry].

World	China	Taiwan	Yang Mu
			Yang Mu
1985 The border between Gibraltar and Spain is fully opened. Joint talks on the future of Gibraltar are held between Spain and the UK.		1985 Libel of *Neo Formosa Weekly* (Fabulous Island); Chen Shuibian and the others involved jailed for a year.	1985 Edits and publishes Xu Deshan's *Selected Essays*.
			April. Attends a Conference on Hong Kong Literature in Hong Kong.
Feb. Lama Yeshe, who passed away in 1984, is reincarnated and born a Spanish boy, Osel Hita Torres, in Granada			July. Publishes a collection of editorials (written for *United Daily), Jiaoliudao* [Interchanges].
	1986 Mo Yan publishes *Red Sorghum*, which is later adapted into a film directed by Zhang Yimou in 1987.	1986 Political reform: Guomindang allows multi-party democracy.	1986 Jan. Attends the conference of the International PEN in New York.
		Sept. Establishment of Democratic Progressive Party (DPP), the first genuine opposition party.	April. Publishes the ninth volume of poetry, *You ren* [Someone].

World	China	Taiwan	Yang Mu
1987 Tibetan demonstrations for independence.	1987 Jan. Students demonstrations begin to grow.	1987 July 15. Martial law lifted by President Chiang, followed by a media boom and increasingly active cultural and commercial exchange across the Taiwan Straits.	1987 May Publishes *Shan feng hai yu* [Storms over Hills and Ocean: Memoirs I], which wins him *China Times* Literary Award for Prose Essays in November.
	Purge of leading intellectuals including Liu Binyan and others.		Publishes a collection of miscellaneous essays, *Fei guo huoshan* [Flying over the Volcano].
	Zhao Ziyang replaces Hu Yaobang as General Secretary of the Communist Party. Li Peng becomes Premier.	Nov. Government permits visits to mainland China for "humanitarian" purposes, followed by the blossoming of Family Visits Literature.	August, Attends a conference on Drama in Hong Kong, stays at the Guest House of the Chinese University of Hong Kong.
	Late 1980s Emergence of New Realist Fiction.		Edits Xu Zhimo's *Selected Poems*, published in November.
1988 Olympic Games in Seoul, Korea.	1988 Mainland Chinese are allowed to visit Taiwan.	1988 Restrictions on newspapers lifted.	1988 Publishes (in English, under the name C. H. Wang) *From Ritual to Allegory: Seven Essays in Early Chinese Poetry*.
	Inquiry into post-Mao modernism culminates in the debate over "pseudomodernism" versus "genuine modernism."	President Chiang dies; Vice President Lee Teng-hui steps in.	Summer. Makes a trip to New England and New York with his family.

World	China	Taiwan	Yang Mu
	1988 *Red Sorghum*, directed by Zhang Yi-mou, receives Golden Bear Award at the Berlin International Festival.	1988 Guomindang opens its 13th congress. It democratizes many of its rules and procedures and elects a majority of Taiwanese to its standing committee.	1988 Lectures on Classical Poetry at the University of Colorado; takes a trip to the mountains.
			Serves as Acting Chairman of the Department of Comparative Literature, at the University of Washington, Seattle.
1989 Fall of Berlin Wall.	1989 April. Hu Yaobang dies.	1989 *A City of Sadness*, directed by Hou Xiaoxian, receives Golden Lion Award in the Biennale Venice Film Festival.	1989 Publishes *Yishoushi de wancheng* [The Completion of a Poem], which is elected one of "The Ten Best Books of the Year" by *China Times*.
Feb. Marial Law in Tibet	A series of demonstrations near Tiananmen Square start in April; students and intellectuals protest against corruption and call for democratic reform.	Dec. The first democratic election held.	March. Publishes two volumes of *Xiandai Zhongguoshi xuan* [Anthology of Modern Chinese Poetry], co-edited with William Tay.
Islamic regime in Iran pronounces a death sentence on Salman Rushdie for his *Satanic Verses*.	May. Mikhail Gorbachev visits Beijing; Sino-Soviet relations "normalized."		
Dec. Dalai Lama awarded Nobel Prize for Peace.	May 21. One million people march in Hong Kong to protest the imposition of martial law in Beijing.		
	June 4. June Fourth Incident: PRC troops suppress the protests in Tiananmen Square and cause many deaths and severe injuries.		

World	China	Taiwan	Yang Mu
		Early 1990s Rise of urban culture contributes to the blossoming of urban literature.	
1990 Aug. Iraq attacked Kuwait.	1990 Asian Games in Beijing	1990 Guomindang formally ends state of war with PRC.	1990 Nov. Receives Wu Sanlian Award (Literature).
Oct. Unification of Germany		Taiwan authorities announce the termination of the "Period of Mobilization."	Publishes (in English) "The Double Plot of T'ao-hua shan."
			Dec. Edits the manuscripts of his uncollected poems; re-reads "The Story of the Five Concubines."
1991 Collapse of the Soviet Union.		1991 DPP drafts constitution for Taiwan independence opposed by ruling Guomindang and Beijing.	1991 Publishes *Fangxiang gui ling* [Direction Back to Zero: Memoirs II] in May and his tenth volume of poetry, *Wanzheng de yuyan* [A Complete Fable] in September.
Jan.-April. Gulf War			
Prof. Paul Engle (1908-91) dies in Iowa.			Sept 1. Goes to Hong Kong with his family. Appointed professor of literature at the Hong Kong Universiy of Science and Technology. Stays in Wanchai until they move to the university hostel at Clear Water Bay.

World	China	Taiwan	Yang Mu
			1991–94 Professor at the Hong Kong University of Science and Technology.
			1992 Publishes "Shi guanshe yu fanyi wenti" [Poetic Referentiality and the Problem of Translation].
	1992 Yu Hua publishes *To Live*, which is adapted to film by Zhang Yimou in 1994.		
		1992-93 Cross-Strait talks.	
	1993 Jiang Zemin becomes General Secretary of the Communist Party.	1993 Ex-Guomindang politicians form the "New Party."	1993 Publishes a collection of essays on aesthetics, *The Sceptic: Notes on Poetical Discrepancies*.
		All political prisoners are freed	Publishes English translations of poetry in *Forbidden Games and Video Poems: The Poetry of Yang Mu and Lo Ch'ing*, translated by Joseph R. Allen.
1993-2001 Bill Clinton president of the US.	Koo-Wang Talks (Koo Chen-fu and Wang Daohan) in Singapore.		Edits and annotates *Tang shi xuanji* [Anthology of Tang Poetry].

World	China	Taiwan	Yang Mu
1994-96 The first Chechen War.			1994 August. Visits the Wuling Farm.
			Dec. The contract with HKUST ends.
1994 Institution of South African democracy.			
1995 World Trade Organization (WTO) founded in Geneva.	1995 On the eve of the Chinese New Year, Jiang Zemin announces "8-point Proposal" for the peaceful reunification.	1995 February 28, Lee Teng-hui apologizes to the public for February 28th Incident.	1995 Publishes a collection of lyrical essays, *Xingtu* [Asterism] and *Yang Mu shiji II* [Collected Poems of Yang Mu, Volume 2: 1974-1985].
Sept. Eileen Chang (1920-95) dies in Los Angeles.		Lee Teng-hui announces his "Six Principles" in response to Jiang's "8-point Proposal." Lee makes an unofficial visit to the US, jeopardizing ties with Beijing.	August. Serves as adjudicator for the Literary Award (poetry) organized by the Hong Kong government.
			Oct. Visits the National Dong Hwa University at Hualian. Participates in the setting up of the Departments of Chinese and Foreign Languages, as well as the College of Humanities and Social Sciences.

World	China	Taiwan	Yang Mu
1997 Labour Party victory in the UK ends eighteen years of Conservative government.	1997 February. Deng Xiaoping dies at 92.	1995-96 Legislative elections. Guomindang majority reduced.	1996 March. Returns to Hualian to vote in the presidential election. This is the first vote he has ever cast for a civic post. Peng Mingmin is the candidate he votes for.
British handover of Hong Kong to China.	July 1. Celebrates the return of Hong Kong to China. Tung Chee-hwa is the Chief Executive of the Hong Kong Special Administrative Region.	1996 Crisis in Taiwan Straits as Beijing stages war games to coincide with Taiwan's first direct presidential election; Lee Teng-hui wins in this election.	April. Publishes a collection of essays, *Tingwu zhi ying* [A Hawk Perches at Noon].
Jiang Zemin visits the US.		National Dong Hwa University at Hualian officially opens, with three departments and four research institutes. The unique Research Institute of Ethnic Relations offers undergraduate courses suitable for aborigines in the College of Humanities and Social Sciences.	August. Dean of College of Humanities and Social Sciences, National Dong Hwa University, Hualian.
		1997 March Dalai Lama visits Taiwan.	1997 Edits Xu Zhimo's *Selected Prose.*
		Nov. DDP wins an overwhelming victory in regional election	Publishes *Selected Poems of W. B. Yeats*, translated into Chinese with an Introduction and Notes.
			Publishes the eleventh volume of poetry *Shiguang mingti* [Temporality Proposition].
			Publishes *Xi wo wang yi* [Then as I Set Off: Memoirs III].

World	China	Taiwan	Yang Mu
1998 Anglo-American bombing of Iraq. Northern Ireland Assembly established. Asian financial crisis slows growth in China, Hong Kong and Taiwan.	1998 During his visit to China Bill Clinton publicly reiterates that the US adheres to the "one China" policy, abides by the principles of the three China-US Joint Communiqués, and that the US Government does not support the positions of "Taiwan independence," "one China, one Taiwan," or "two Chinas," and Taiwan's membership in any international organizations of sovereign nations ("Three No" policy).	1998 Guomindang secures absolute majority in elections to Legislative Council.	1998 Publishes *No Trace of the Gardener: Poems of Yang Mu*, translated by Michelle Yeh and Lawrence R. Smith. May. Presents a paper exploring the use of allusion in ancient Chinese and Greek cultural discourses in a colloquium on the Comparative Study of Ancient Cultures at the University of Oregon, Eugene. May. Attends Bruce's graduation ceremony at Lakeside school in Seattle. Sept. Bruce enters Columbia University, New York. Dec. Publishes the first draft of Chinese translation of *The Tempest* by Shakespeare in *Ziyou shi bao* (Liberty Times).
1999 NATO's accidental bombing of Chinese embassy in Belgrade sparks crisis in Sino-US relations.	1999 Portugal hands back Macau. Chinese threats over reference to "separate states" status. China and the US agree on the terms of China's entry into WTO.	1999 Lee Teng-hui openly defines the Cross-Straits relations as "state to state" relations and declares his "two states theory," which attempts to separate Taiwan from mainland China. Earthquake in Taichong.	1999 Sept. Publishes the bilingual version of William Shakespeare's *The Tempest*. Publishes "Shi yu dikang" [Poetry of Resistance].

World	China	Taiwan	Yang Mu
2000 Nobel Prize in Literature: Gao Xingjian. The second Chechen War, Grozny seized by Russian troops.	2000 New strains in China-Taiwan relations.	2000 Taiwan Affairs Office and Information Office of the State Council release the White Paper titled "The One-China Principle and the Taiwan Issue."	2000 Feb. Visits Bruce in New York with Yingying.
Mar. Putin wins the Presidential election in Russia.	Feb. Beijing releases a White Paper on PRC's Taiwan policy, proposing a deadline for re-unification. War threats mount.	*Crouching Tiger, Hidden Dragon,* directed by Ang Lee, receives Best Foreign Language Film in Academy Award.	Mar. Publishes "Shiluo de zhihuan – wei Chechen er zuo" [The Lost Ring – for Chechnya] in *China Times.*
Oct. Committee on International Relations of the US House of Representatives passes the revised Taiwan Security Enhancement Act.		Mar. Chen Shuibian of DPP wins presidency; overturns Guomindang dominance. Lee Teng-hui resigns as chairman of Guomindang.	April. Visiting professor at the Centre for Oriental Cultural Studies, Charles University, Prague, the Czech Republic.
		Oct. Information Office of the State Council releases the White Paper titled "China's National Defence 2000."	Sept. Winner (Literature) of the Literature and Arts Award of the 4th National Culture and Arts Foundation.
			Yue Jie Dance Group performs Yang Mu's poem "She de lianxi san zhong" [Snake: Three Etudes] on stage in Taipei.

World

2001 G. W. Bush becomes president of the US; revival of National Missile Defence System.

September 11th Incident. A series of coordinated suicide attacks by al-Qaeda upon the US. Excluding the 19 hijackers, 2,974 people die in the attacks.

China

2001 Beijing is awarded the 2008 Olympic Games.

2002 Nov. The SARS epidemic appears to have started in Guangdong Province of China.

Taiwan

Yang Mu

2001 Feb. Yang Mu's mother dies.

Publishes a collection of critical essays, *Yinyu yu xianshi* [Metaphor and Reality] in March; and his twelfth volume of poetry, *She Shi* [Intervention] in June.

April. Attends "Chinese Creative Writing and the Prospect of Chinese Culture," a seminar organized by Chinese Civilization Centre, The City University of Hong Kong.

July 6. Completes his terms of Deanship, and moves out of the National Dong Hwa University.

2002 Jan. Director of the Institute of Chinese Literature and Philosophy, Academia Sinica, Nankang.

May Attends Bruce's Commencement at Columbia in New York.

Publishes *Shiqu de letu* [The Happy Land of Our Conceit], a collection of critical essays.

Publishes *Patt beim Go*, a collection of poems edited and translated into German by Susanne Hornfeck and Wang Jue.

Yang Mu	Taiwan	China	World
2003 Jan. Publishes *Qilai qian shu* [The Former Book of Mount Qilai].	2003 Aug 15. *INK: A Literary Monthly* founded	2003 Hu Jintao becomes General Secretary of the Communist Party.	2003 SARS outbreak. In February 2003, the disease spreads all over the world and on March 12, 2003 the World Health Organization issues a global alert. There are 8273 probable cases over the world and 775 deaths.
Chung Wai Literary Monthly publishes "Chorus: A Special Issue on Yang Mu."		1st July. Half a million demonstrate against HKSAR policy in Hong Kong.	
Aug. Adjudicator for the Biannual Literary Award of Hong Kong.			
Publishes (in English) "Alluding to the Text, or the Context."			
Oct. Yang Mu's father dies.			
2004 Dec. Completes his terms of Directorship at Academia Sinica.	2004 President Chen Shuibian re-elected.	2004 August. The XVIIth Congress of International Comparative Literature Association takes place in Hong Kong.	2004 Dec. Tsunami in Indonesia. An undersea earthquake occurred in the Indian Ocean triggering a series of devastating tsunamis along the coasts of the Indian Ocean. More than 225,000 people killed.
Publishes "Taiwanshi yuanliu zaitan" [The Origins of Taiwanese Poetry Revisited].			
Oct. Lectures "Chouxiang yu shuli" [Abstraction and Alienation] at Tokyo University, Japan.			
Publishes *Quelqu'un m'interroge à propos de la vérité et de la justice*, a collection of poems edited and translated into French by Angel Pino and Isabelle Rabut.			
Nov. A trip to France.			

World	China	Taiwan	Yang Mu
2005 July 7 and 21, Terrorist Attacks in London.	2005 Dong Chee-hwa steps down; Donald Tsang Yam-kuen becomes the Chief Executive of the Hong Kong Special Administrative Region.	2005 Lien Chen, Chairman of the Guomindang visits Beijing.	2005 July. Distinguished Senior Research Fellow. Academia Sinica.
		Ma Ying-jeou elected the Chairman of the Guomindang.	Publishes *Renwen zongji* [Literary Pattern: Tracks and Traces].
			Publishes *Lüeying jiliu* [Shadows in the Torrent].
		Brokeback Mountain, directed by Ang Lee, receives Golden Lion Award in the Biennale Venice Film Festival.	
		2006 Ma Ying-jeou steps down	2006 Jan. Completes his term of service at Academia Sinica and officially retired from government service in Taiwan.
			Mar. Publishes *Kakkouazami no uta: Youboku sishu*, a collection of poems edited and translated into Japanese by Ueda Tetsuji.
			Publishes the thirteenth volume of poetry *Jiekechong* (Diaepsis Patelliformi) [A Scale Insect].
			Oct. Pao's Distinguished Professorship at Hong Kong University of Science and Technology.

World	China	Taiwan	Yang Mu
2007 Global financial crisis caused by the US sub-prime problem surfaces		2007 *Lust, Caution*, directed by Ang Lee, receives Golden Lion Award in the Biennale Venice Film Festival.	2007 May Publishes *Yi shi* [Of Translation: Collected Essays].
			June Winner of the "International Prize for Literature Written in the Chinese Language," Malaysia.
			July Retires from the University of Washington.
			Publishes *Yingshi hanyi ji* [English Poetry in Chinese Translation].
			Publishes a Japanese version of *Qi lai qian shu* (Translator: Ueda Tetsuji).
			18 Nov. Four of his poems ("The Moment the Wind Blows," "Tonight, Glowed with Sunset," "River Lau,' and "Take You Home, Back to Hualian") are composed into songs by Lin Daosheng and performed at the Hualian International Music Festival 2007.

Select Bibliography

Abrams, M. H. *The Mirror and the Lamp: Romantic Theory and the Critical Tradition*. New York: Oxford University Press, 1953.

—. *Natural Supernaturalism: Tradition and Revolution in Romantic Literature*. New York: Norton Library, 1973.

Adams, Hazard. *Philosophy of the Literary Symbolic*. Tallahassee: University Presses of Florida, 1991, c. 1983.

—. *Critical Theory since Plato*. Rev. ed. Fort Worth: Harcourt Brace Jovanovich College Publishers, 1992.

Adorno, Theodor W. "Lyric Poetry and Society." *Telos* 20 (1974): 56-71.

Ahmad, Aijaz. "Jameson's Rhetoric of Otherness and the 'National Allegory'." *Social Text* 17 (1987): 3-25.

—. "The Politics of Literary Postcoloniality." *Race and Class* 36 (1995): 1-20.

Allen, Joseph R. *In the Voice of Others: Chinese Music Bureau Poetry.* Ann Abor: University of Michigan Press, 1992.

—. *Forbidden Games and Video Poems: The Poetry of Yang Mu and Lo Ching* Seattle: University of Washington Press, 1993.

Althusser, Louis. *Lenin and Philosophy and Other Essays*. Trans. Ben Brewster. London: NLB, 1971.

Anderson, Benedict. *Imagined Communities: Reflections on the Origin and Spread of Nationalism.* New York: Verso, 1991.

Appiah, Kwame Anthony. "Is the Post-in Postmodernism the Post-in Postcolonial?" *Critical Inquiry* 17 (Winter 1991): 336-357.

Appiah, Kwame Anthony and Henry Louis Gates, eds. *Identities*. Chicago: University of Chicago Press, 1995.

Apter, Emily. *The Translation Zone: A New Comparative Literature*. Princeton: Princeton University Press, 2006

Arac, Jonathan. *Huckleberry Finn as Idol and Target: The Functions of Criticism in Our Time*. Madison: University of Wisconsin Press, 1997.

Aristotle. *Aristotle's Theory of Poetry and Fine Art*. Trans. Samuel Henry Butcher. New York: Dover, 1951.

Aronowitz, Stanley. "Reflections on Identity." *October* (1992): 91-103.

Ashcroft, Bill, Gareth Griffiths, and Helen Tiffin, *The Empire Writes Back: Theory and Practice in Post-Colonial Literatures.* London: Routledge, 1989.

Bakhtin, Mikhail M. *The Dialogic Imagination: Four Essays.* Trans, Caryl Emerson and Michael Holquist. Austin: University of Texas Press, 1981.

—. *Speech Genre and Other Late Essays*. Trans. Vern W. McGee. eds. Caryl Emerson and Michael Holquist. Austin: University of Texas Press, 1986.

Barthes, Roland. *Image-Music-Text*. Trans. Stephen Heath. London: Fontana Press, 1977.

—. *Roland Barthes*. Trans. Richard Howard. London: Macmillan Press, 1977.

Bassnett, Susan. *Comparative Literature: A Critical Introduction*. Oxford: Blackwell, 1993.

Bassnett, Susan and Andre Lefevere, eds. *Translation, History and Culture*. London: Cassell, 1995.

Benjamin, Walter. *Illuminations*. Trans. Harry Zohn. London: Fontana Press, 1992.

Berger, John. *Ways of Seeing*. New York: BBC and Penguin Books, 1972.

Bernstein, Charles, ed. *The Politics of Poetic Form*. New York: Roof, 1990.

Bhabha, Homi. K. "Culture's In-Between." *Questions of Identity*. eds. Stuart Hall and Paul de Guy. London: SAGE, 1996. 53-60.

—. "The Third Space: Interview with Homi Bhabha." *Identity, Community, Culture, Difference*. ed. Jonathan Rutherford. London: Lawrence & Wishart, 1990. 207-221.

—, ed. *Nation and Narration*. London: Routledge, 1990.

—. "The World and the Home." *Social Text* 31/32 (1992): 141-153.

—. *The Location of Culture*. London: Routledge, 1994.

Birkerts, Sven. "'Poetry' and 'Politics'." *Margin* 4 (Autumn 1987): 55-62.

Blackham, H.J. *Six Existentialist Thinkers*. London: Routledge, 1994, c. 1961.

Bloom, Harold. *Yeats*. New York: Oxford University Press, 1970.

—. *The Anxiety of Influence*. New York: Oxford University Press, 1973.

—, *et al. Deconstruction and Criticism*. New York: Continuum, 1979.

—. "The Dialectics of Poetic Tradition." *Critical Theory since Plato*. ed. Hazard Adams. Rev. ed. Fort Worth: Harcourt Brace Jovanovich College Publishers, 1992. 1184-89.

Bowra, Maurice. *The Romantic Imagination*. Oxford: Oxford University Press, 1950.

Brooks, Cleanth. *The Well-wrought Urn: Studies in the Structure of Poetry*. Rev. ed. London: Dennis Dobson, 1968.

Browne, Nick, *et al.* eds. *New Chinese Cinemas: Forms, Identities, Politics*. Cambridge: Cambridge University Press, 1994.

Buber, Martin. *I and Thou*. Trans. Walter Kaufmann. New York: Touchstone, 1996.

Cai Yuanhuang. "Gaobai yu mianju – Zhongguo xiandaishi zhong de 'wo'" [Mask and Confession – "I" in Chinese modern poetry]. *Chung Wai Literary Monthly* 8.11 (April 1980): 106-121.

Cai Zongqi. *Configurations of Comparative Poetics: Three Perspectives on Western and Chinese Literary Criticism*. Honolulu: University of Hawai'i Press, 2001.

Calinescu, Martin. *Five Faces of Modernity: Modernism, Avant-Garde, Decadence, Kitsch, Postmodernism*. Durham: Duke University Press, 1987.

Chambers, Iain. *Border Dialogues: Journeys in Postmodernism*. London: Routledge, 1990.

Chambers, Iain and Lidia Curti, eds. *The Post-colonial Question: Common Skies, Divided Horizons*. London: Routledge, 1996.

Chang, Yvonne Sung-sheng. *Modernism and the Nativist Resistance: Contemporary Chinese Fiction from Taiwan*. Durham and London: Duke University Press, 1993.

—. "Beyond Cultural and National Identities: Current Re-evaluation of the *Kominka* Literature from Taiwan's Japanese Period." *Journal of Modern Literature in Chinese* 1.1 (July 1997): 75-107.

—. *Literary Culture in Taiwan: Martial Law to Market Law*. New York: Columbia University Press, 2004.

Chatterjee, Partha. *The Nation and Its Fragments: Colonial and Post-colonial Histories*. Princeton: Princeton University Press, 1993.

Chen Chung-min *et al*. eds. *Ethnicity in Taiwan Social, Historical, and Cultural Perspectives*. Taipei: Institute of Ethnology, Academia Sinica, 1994.

Chen Fangming. "Ping *Zhixu de chengzhang*" [A Review of *The Growth of Order*]. *Shuping shumu* [Reviews and Catalogues] 7 (September 1973): 6-18.

—. "Jiantao minguo liushisan nian de shiping" [An Assessment of the Poetry Criticisms of 1974]. *Chung Wai Literary Monthly* 3.2 (June 1974): 31-53.

—. "Liangan de duihua: fangwen Yang Mu xiansheng" [A Dialogue across the Sea: Interview with Yang Mu]. *Shi he xianshi* [Poetry and Reality] Taipei: Hongfan, 1977. 155-75.

Chen Lili. "Outer and Inner Forms of *Chu-kung-tiao*, with reference to *Pien-wen* and Vernacular Fiction." *Harvard Journal of Asiatic Studies* 32 (1972): 124-149.

Chen, Lucy J. "Literary Formosa." *Formosa Today*. ed. Mark Mancall. New York: Praeger, 1964. 137-141.

Chen Qianwu (Heng Fu). "*Taiwanshi de wailai yingxiang*" [The Foreign Influences on Taiwan Poetry] *Li* 146 (August 1988): 4-20.

Chen Shih-hsiang. "In Search of the Beginnings of Chinese Literary Criticism." *University of California Publications in Semitic and Oriental Philology*. XI (1951): 45-63.

—. "Metaphor and the Conscious in Chinese Poetry under Communism." *Chinese Communist Literature*. ed. Cyril Birch. New York: Frederick A. Praeger, 1963. 39-59.

—. "The *Shih-ching*: Its Generic Significance in Chinese Literary History and Poetics." *Bulletin of the Institute of History and Philology, Academia Sinica* XXXIX (1969): 371-413.

—. *Chen Shih-hsiang wencun* [Collected Essays of Chen Shih-hsiang]. eds. Ye Shan and Lin Hengzhe. Taipei: Zhiwen, 1972.

Cheung, Dominic. *The Isle Full of Noises: Modern Chinese Poetry from Taiwan*. New York: Columbia University Press, 1987.

Chi, Pang-yuan *et al.*, eds. "Poems and Essays." Vol. 1 of *An Anthology of Contemporary Chinese Literature – Taiwan: 1949-1974* Taipei: National Institute for Compilation and Translation, 1975.

Chi, Pang-yuan, and David Der-wei Wang, eds. *Chinese Literature in the Second Half of a Modern Century: a Critical Survey*. Bloomington and Indianapolis: Indiana University Press, 2000.

Chow, Rey. *Woman and Chinese Modernity: The Politics of Reading between East and West*. Minneapolis: University of Minnesota Press, 1991.

—. *Writing Diaspora: Tactics of Intervention in Contemporary Cultural Studies*. Bloomington and Indianapolis: Indiana University Press, 1993.

—. "The Old/New Question of Comparison in Literary Studies: A Post-European Perspective." *ELH* 71.2 (Summer 2004): 289-311.

Chow Tse-tsung, "The Early History of the Chinese Word *Shih* (Poetry)." *Wen-lin: Studies in the Chinese Humanities.* ed. Chow Tse-tsung. Madison: Wisconsin University Press, 1968.

—. "Shici de dangxiemei: lun zhongguo shige de shuqing zhuliu he ziran jingjie" [The Beauty of Immediacy in *Shi* and *Ci* – On the Lyric Tradition and Vision of Nature in Chinese Poetry]. *Gudian wenxue* [Classical Literature] 7.2. Taiwan: Xuesheng shuju, 1985. 683-727.

Chun, Allen. "From Nationalism to Nationalizing: Cultural Imagination and State Formation in Post-war Taiwan." *The Australian Journal of Chinese Affairs* 31 (January 1994): 49-69.

—. "An Oriental Orientalism: The Paradox of Tradition and Modernity in Nationalist Taiwan." *History and Anthropology* 9.1 (1995): 27-56.

Chung, Ling (Zhong Ling). *Xiandai zhongguo miusi: Taiwan nüshiren zuopin shilun* [The Modern Chinese Muses: Critical Essays on the Works of Taiwanese Poetesses]. Taipei: Lianjing, 1989.

Clifford, James. "Diaspora." *Cultural Anthropology* 9.3 (August 1994): 302-338.

—. "Notes on Theory and Travel." *Inscriptions* 5 (1989): 177-188.

—. "Travelling Cultures." *Cultural Studies*. eds. Lawrence Grossberg, Carl Nelson and Paula A. Treicher. New York: Routledge, 1992. 96-116.

Culler, A. Dwight "Monodrama and the Dramatic Monologue." *PLMA* xl (1975): 366-85.

Culler, Jonathan. *Structuralist Poetics: Structuralism, Linguistics and the Study of Literature*. London: Routledge & Kegan Paul, 1975.

—. *The Pursuit of Signs: Semiotics, Literature, Deconstruction.* Ithaca: Cornell University Press, 1982.

—. *On Deconstruction: Theory and Criticism after Structuralism.* Ithaca: Cornell University Press, 1982.

—. "Comparing Poetry," Presidential Address to the Conference of American Comparative Literature Association in 2001, *Comparative Literature* (Summer 2001): vii-xviii.

Damrosch, David. *What is World Literature?* Princeton: Princeton University Press, 2003.

Davidson, Michael. "Palimtexts: Postmodern Poetry and Material Text." *Postmodern Genres.* ed. Marjorie Perloff. Norman and London: University of Oklahoma Press, 1988.

Davis, A. R. "China's Entry into World Literature." *Journal of Oriental Society of Australia* 1 and 2 (December 1967): 43-50.

De Man, Paul. *Allegories of Reading: Figural Language in Rousseau, Nietzsche, Rilke and Proust.* New Haven: Yale Univeristy Press, 1979.

—. "Hypogram and Inscription: Michael Riffaterre's Poetics of Reading." *Diacritics* 11.4 (1981): 17-35.

—. *Blindness and Insight: Essays in the Rhetoric of Contemporary Criticism.* Minneapolis: University of Minnesota Press, 1983.

—. *Resistance to Theory.* Minneapolis: University of Minnesota Press, 1986.

—. *Romanticism and Contemporary Criticism.* eds. E. S. Burt *et al.* Baltimore: Johns Hopkins University Press, 1993.

De Sélincourt, E., ed. *The Poems of John Keats.* London: Methuen and Co., 1905.

Denton, Kirk A. *Modern Chinese Literary Thought: Writings on Literature, 1893-1945.* Stanford: Stanford University Press, 1996.

Derrida, Jacques. *Of Grammatology.* Trans. Gayatri Chakravorty Spivak. Baltimore: Johns Hopkins University Press, 1974.

—. *Writing and Difference.* Trans. Alan Bass. Chicago: University of Chicago Press, 1978.

—. "The Parergon." *October* 9 (Summer 1979): 3-40.

—. "Scribble (writing-power)." *Yale French Studies* 58 (1979): 117-147.

—. *A Derrida Reader: Between the Blinds.* ed. Peggy Kamuf. New York: Columbia University Press, 1991.

—. *Acts of Literature.* ed. Derek Attridge. New York: Routledge, 1992.

—. *Dissemination.* Trans. Barbara Johnson. Chicago: University of Chicago Press, 1981.

Dirlik, Arif. "Culturalism as Hegemonic Ideology and Liberating Practice." *Cultural Critique* 6 (Spring 1987): 13-50.

—. *The Post-colonial Aura: Third World Criticism in the Age of Global Capitalism.* Colorado: Westview Press, 1997.

—. "Place-based Imagination: Globalisms and the Politics of Place." In manuscript (March 1997): 1-50.

Dreyfus, Hubert L. and Paul Rabinow. *Michel Foucault: Beyond Structuralism and Hermeneutics.* Chicago: University of Chicago Press, 1982.

Duara, Prasenjit. *Rescuing History from the Nation: Questioning Narratives of Modern China.* Chicago: University of Chicago Press, 1995.

—. "De-constructing the Chinese Nation." *Chinese Nationalism.* ed. Jonathan Unger. Armonk, NY: M. E. Sharpe, 1996. 31-55.

Ďuršin, Dionýz. *Theory of Interliterary Process*. Bratislava: Veda, 1989.

Eagleton, Terry. *The Ideology of the Aesthetic*. Oxford: Blackwell, 1990.

—. *Ideology: an Introduction*. New York: Verso, 1991.

Easthope, Antony. *Poetry as Discourse*. London and New York: Metheun, 1983.

Eliot, T. S. *On Poetry and Poets*. New York: Noonday Press, 1961.

—. *Collected Poems 1901-1962*. London: Faber and Faber, 1962.

Eoyang, Eugene. *Two-Way Mirrors: Cross-cultural Studies in Glocalization*. Lanham: Lexington Books, 2007.

Fanon, Frantz. *The Wretched of the Earth*. Trans. Constance Farrington. New York: Grove Press, 1963.

Fishelov, David. *Metaphors of Genres: The Role of Analogies in Genre Theory*. University Park: Pennsylvania State University Press, 1993.

Fitter, Chris. *Poetry, Space, Landscape: Towards a New Theory*. Cambridge: Cambridge University Press, 1995.

Flaubert, Gustave. *Madame Bovary*. Trans. Alan Russell. Middlesex: Penguin, 1950.

Fokkema, Douwe and Elrud Ibsch. *Theories of Literature in the Twentieth Century: Structuralism, Marxism, Aesthetics of Reception, Semiotics*. New York: St. Martin's Press, 1995.

Foucault, Michel. *The Archaeology of Knowledge*. Trans. A. M. Sheridan Smith. London: Tavistock Publications, 1972.

—. *Power/Knowledge: Selected Interviews and Other Writings 1972-1977*. Trans. Colin Gorden *et al*. New York: Pantheon, 1977.

—. "The Order of Discourse." *Untying the Text: A Post-structuralist Reader*. ed. Robert Young. Boston: Routledge & Kegan Paul, 1981. 48-77.

—. *The Foucault Reader*. ed. Paul Rabinow. New York: Pantheon, 1984.

—. "Technologies of the Self." *Technologies of the Self*. eds. Luther H. Martin *et al*. Amherst: University Press of Massachusetts, 1988. 16-49.

—. *Essential Works of Foucault 1954-1984*. 2 volumes. ed. Paul Rabinow. Vol. 1. New York: New Press, 1997.

Frank, Joseph. *The Widening Gyre: Crisis and Mastery in Modern Literature*. Bloomington: Indiana University Press, 1963.

Freedman, Ralph. *Life of a Poet: Rainer Maria Rilke*. New York: Farrar, Straus and Giroux, 1996.

Freud, Sigmund. *The Future of an Illusion*. Trans. and ed. James Strachey. New York: Norton, 1989.

Frye, Northrop. *Anatomy of Criticism*. Princeton: Princeton University Press, 1957.

Gálik, Marián. "Interliterariness as a Concept in Comparative Literature." *Comparative Literature and Comparative Cultural Studies*. ed. Steven Tötösy de Zepetnek. West Lafayette, Indiana: Purdue University Press, 2003. 34-44.

Geertz, Clifford. *The Interpretation of Cultures.* New York: Basic Books, 1973.

Gittings, Robert, ed. *Letters of John Keats.* London: Oxford University Press, 1970.

Goethe, Johann Wolfgang von. *The Autobiography of Johann Wolfgang von Goethe.* Trans. John Oxenford. Chicago and London: University of Chicago Press, 1974.

—. *Goethe: Selected Verse.* Trans. David Luke. London: Penguin, 1986.

Goldblatt, Howard, ed. *Worlds Apart: Recent Chinese Writing and Its Audience.* Armonk, NY: M. E. Sharpe, 1990.

Goldman, Merle, ed. *Modern Chinese Literature in the May Fourth Era.* Cambridge, MA: Harvard University Press, 1977.

Gordon, Michael R. "Rights Group Says Russians Executed Grozny Civilians." *The New York Times* (6 February 2000).

Guillén, Claudio. "On the Literature of Exile and Counter-exile." *Books Abroad* L.2 (Spring 1976): 271-280.

Gurr, Andrew. *Writers in Exile: The Identity of Home in Modern Literature.* Sussex: Harvester Press, 1981.

Haft, Lloyd, ed. "The Poem." Vol. III of *A Selective Guide to Chinese Literature 1900-1949.* Leiden: E. J. Brill, 1989.

Hall, Stuart. "Cultural Identity and Diaspora." *Identity, Community, Culture, Difference.* ed. J. Rutherford. London: Lawrence & Wishart, 1990. 222-237.

Hartman, Geoffrey. *Saving the Text: Literature/ Derrida /Philosophy.* Baltimore and London: Johns Hopkins University Press, 1981.

Harvey, David. *The Condition of Postmodernity: An Enquiry into the Origins of Cultural Change.* Cambridge: Blackwell, 1997, c. 1990.

Heaney, Seamus. "Above the Brim." *Homage to Robert Frost.* Joseph Brodsky, Seamus Heaney and Dreck Walcott. New York: Farrar, Straus and Giroux, 1996. 57-88.

Heidegger, Martin. *Poetry, Language, Thought.* Trans. Albert Hofstadter. New York: Harper and Row, 1975.

Hightower, James R. "Han Yu as Humorist." *Harvard Journal of Asiatic Studies* 44.1 (1984): 5-27.

Hoagwood, Terence Allan. *Skepticism and Ideology.* Iowa City: University of Iowa Press, 1988.

Hokenson, Jan Walsh. "The Culture of the Context: Comparative Literature Past and Future." *Comparative Literature and Comparative Cultural Studies.* ed. Steven Tötösy de Zepetnek. West Lafayette, Indiana: Purdue University Press, 2003. 58-75.

Hošek, Chaviva and Patricia Parker, eds. *Lyric Poetry: Beyond New Criticism.* Ithaca: Cornell University Press, 1985.

Hsia Chi-an (Xia Jian). "Baihuawen yu xinshi" [The Vernacular and New Poetry]. *Xiandai Zhongguo wenxue pinglun xuanji* [Critical Essays on Modern Chinese Literature]. ed. Joseph S. M. Lau. Hong Kong: Union Press, 1970. 92-111.

Hsia Chi-ts'ing (Xia Zhiqing). *A History of Modern Chinese Fiction*. New Haven: Yale University Press, 1971.

—. *A History of Modern Chinese Fiction*. 3rd edition. With an introduction by David Der-wei Wang. Bloomington and Indianapolis: Indiana University Press, 1991.

Hsu Kang (Xu Gang). "Writing Taiwan: Strategies of Representation – An International Symposium on Chinese Literature from Taiwan." *Modern Chinese Literature* 10 (1998): 269-273.

Huang Churen, "Time as Running Water: From Temporal Indicators in Classical Poetry to Chinese Concept of Time" ["Shijian ru liushui: you gudianshige zhong de shijian yongyu tan dao zhongguo ren de shijian guan"]. *Chung Wai Literary Monthly* (April 1981): 70-88.

Hühn, Peter. "Watching the Speaker Speak: Self-Observation and Self-Intransparency in Lyric Poetry." *New Definitions of Lyric: Theory, Technology, and Culture*. ed. Mark Jeffreys. New York and London: Garland Publishing, 1998. 215-244.

Jakobson, Roman. "Closing Statement: Linguistics and Poetics." *Style in Language*. ed. Thomas A. Sebeok. New York: Wiley, 1960. 350-377.

—. "Shifters, Verbal Categories, and the Russian Verb." *Word and Language*, Vol. 2 of *Selected Writings*, 2nd ed. The Hague: Mouton, 1971. 130-147.

James, William. *Principles of Psychology*. Vol. 1. New York: Henry Holt & Co., 1890.

Jameson, Fredric. *The Political Unconscious: Narrative as a Socially Symbolic Act*. Ithaca: Cornell University Press, 1981.

—. "Third-World Literature in the Era of Multinational Capital." *Social Text* 15 (Fall 1986): 65-88.

—. *Postmodernism, or The Cultural Logic of Late Capitalism*. Durham: Duke University Press, 1991.

Jefferson, Ann and David Robey. *Modern Literary Theory: a Comparative Introduction*. London: Batsford, 1982.

Jeffreys, Mark. *New Definitions of Lyric: Theory, Technology, and Culture*. New York and London: Garland Publishing, 1998.

Johnson, Barbara. *The Critical Difference: Essays in the Contemporary Rhetoric of Reading*. Baltimore: Johns Hopkins University Press, 1980.

Joseph, Sister Miriam. *Shakespeare's Use of the Art of Language*. New York: Columbia University Press, 1947.

Kao, Yu-kung and Tsu-lin Mei. "Meaning, Metaphor, and Allusion in T'ang Poetry." *Harvard Journal of Asiatic Studies* 38.2 (1978): 281-356.

Kaplan, Caren. *Questions of Travel: Postmodern Discourses of Displacement*. Durham and London: Duke University Press, 1996.

Keynes, Geoffrey. *Blake: Complete Writings*. London: Oxford University Press, 1966.

Kinkley, Jeffrey C., ed. *After Mao: Chinese Literature and Society 1978-1981.* Cambridge, MA and London: The Council on East Asian Studies/ Harvard University Press, 1990.

Koelb, Clayton and Susan Noakes, eds. *The Comparative Perspective in Literature: Approaches to Theory and Practice.* Ithaca and London: Cornell University Press, 1988.

Kristeva, Julia. *Desire in Language: A Semiotic Approach to Literature and Art.* ed. Leon S. Roudiez. Trans. Thomas Gora, Alice Jardine, and Leon S. Roudiez. New York: Columbia University Press, 1980.

Lai Ruihe. "Shi Ye Shan de 'Gei Shijian'" [Deciphering Ye Shan's "To Time"]. *Dragons Poetry Quarterly* 9 (1973): 205-6.

Langbaum, Robert. *The Poetry of Experience: The Dramatic Monologue in Modern Literary Tradition.* Chicago and London: University of Chicago Press, 1985, c. 1957.

Langer, Susanne K. *Feeling and Form.* New York: Charles Scribner's Sons, 1953.

Larrain, Jorge. *Ideology and Cultural Identity: Modernity and the Third World Presence.* Cambridge: Polity Press, 1994.

Larson, Wendy and Anne Wedell-Wedellsborg, eds. *Inside Out: Modernism and Postmodernism in Chinese Literary Culture.* Aarhus, Denmark: Aarhus University Press, 1993.

Lau, D. C., ed. *A Concordance to the Huainanzi.* CUHK ICS The Ancient Text Concordance Series. Hong Kong: Commercial Press, 1992.

Lau, Joseph S. M., ed. *Xiandai Zhongguo wenxue pinglun xuanji* [Critical Essays on Modern Chinese Literature]. Hong Kong: Union Press, 1970.

Layoun, Mary N. "Fictional Formations and Deformations of National Culture." *South Atlantic Quarterly* (Winter 1988): 53-73.

Lee, Gregory. *Troubadours, Trumpeters and Troubled Makers.* London: Hurst & Co., 1996.

Lee, Ou-fan, Leo. *The Romantic Generation of Modern Chinese Writers.* Cambridge, MA: Harvard University Press, 1973.

—. "Modernism and Romanticism in Taiwan Literature." *Chinese Fiction from Taiwan.* ed. Jeannette L. Faurot. Bloomington: Indiana University Press, 1980. 6-30.

Legge, James. *The Chinese Classics.* 3 Vols. Taipei: SMC, 1991.

Li Zushen. "Zhongnian shiren de zhizhuo yu youhuan: ping Yang Mu de *Yishou shi de wancheng*" [The Obsession and Anxiety of a Middle-aged Poet: a Review of Yang Mu's *The Completion of a Poem*]. *Unitas* 5.7 (May 1989): 185-187.

Liao Binghui. "Zai Taiwan tan houxiandai yu houzhimin lunshu" [Discoursing Postmodernity and Post-coloniality in Taiwan]. *Houzhimin lilun yu wenhua rentong* [Postcolonial Criticism and Cultural Identity]. ed. Zhang Jingyuan. Taipei: Rye Field, 1995. 213-232.

—. "Taiwan and the Hyphenated Chinese Public Sphere." Paper presented at The Second International Symposium on Cultural Criticism. The Chinese University of Hong Kong, Hong Kong (4-6 January 1996): 1-33.

Liao Xuelan. *Taiwan shishi* [History of Taiwan Poetry]. Taipei: Wuling Publishing Company, 1989.

Lin, Julia. *Modern Chinese Poetry: An Introduction.* Seattle: University of Washington Press, 1972.

—. *Essays on Contemporary Chinese Poetry.* Athens: Ohio University Press, 1985.

Lin Shuangbu. *Taiwan xin Yuefu* [Taiwan New *Yuefu*]. Taipei: Grassroot, 1996.

Lin Shuen-fu. *The Transformation of the Chinese Lyrical Tradition: Chiang Kuei and Southern Sung Tsu Poetry.* Princeton: Princeton University Press, 1978.

Lin Weio. "Xin xi gujin yuanjin, wenyi yuyan jiangjie" [A Mind that Connects the Ancient and Modern, Far and Near; A Writing that Crosses Linguistic Barriers]. *United Daily* (9 March 2005).

Liu, James. *The Arts of Chinese Poetry.* Chicago: University of Chicago Press, 1962.

—. *Chinese Theories of Literature.* Chicago: University of Chicago Press, 1975.

—. "Towards a Synthesis of Chinese and Western Theories of Literature." *Journal of Chinese Philosophy* 4 (1977): 1-24.

Liu, Lydia. *Translingual Practice: Literature, National Culture, and Translated Modernity – China, 1900-1937.* Stanford: Stanford University Press, 1995.

Liu Xie. *The Literary Mind and the Carving of Dragons.* Trans. Vincent Yu-chung Shih. Hong Kong: Chinese University Press, 1983.

—. *Wenxin diaolong yizheng* [Exegeses on *The Literary Mind and the Carving of Dragon*] Vol. 1. ed. and annotated Chan Ying. Shanghai: Shanghai guji chubanshe, 1989.

Lorca, Federico Garcia. *Federico Garcia Lorca: Gypsy Ballads.* Trans. Havard, Robert G. Warmister, England: Aris and Philips, 1990.

Luo Qing. "Xifang wenxue yu zhongguo xinshi" [Western Literature and Chinese New Poetry]. *Chung Wai Literary Monthly* 9.12 (May 1981): 82-90.

Lupke, Christopher. "Modern Chinese Literature in the Postcolonial Diaspora." Ph.D. Diss. Cornell University. Ann Arbor: UMI, 1993.

Lyotard, Jean-Francois. *The Postmodern Condition: A Report on Knowledge.* Trans. Geoff Bennington and Brian Massumi. Minneapolis: University of Minnesota Press, 1984.

Macura, Vladimir. "Culture as Translation." *Translation, History and Culture*, eds. Susan Bassnett and Andre Lefevere. London: Cassell, 1995. 64-70.

Martin, Charles. "The Three Voices of Contemporary Poetry." *The New Criterion* (April 2004): 34-37.

Martin, Helmut. "The History of Taiwanese Literature: Towards Cultural-Political Identity – Views from Taiwan, China, Japan and the West." *Hanxue yanjiu* 14.1 (June 1996): 1-49.

McClintock, Anne. "The Angel of Progress: Pitfalls of the Term 'Post-Colonialism'." *Social Text* 31/32 (1992): 84-98.

McDougall, Bonnie S. *The Introduction of Western Theories into Modern China, 1919-1925*. Tokyo: Centre for East Asian Cultural Studies, 1971.

McDougall, Bonnie S. and Kam Louie. *The Literature of China in the Twentieth Century*. London: Hurst & Co.; Hong Kong: Hong Kong University Press, 1997.

McGann, Jerome J. *The Romantic Ideology*. Chicago: University of Chicago Press, 1983.

Metzger, Erika A., and Michael M. Metzger, eds. *A Companion to the Works of Rainer Maria Rilke*. New York: Camden House, 2001.

Miao, Samuel. *Creating Another Self: Voice in American Poetry*. Kirksville, Mussouri: Thomas Jefferson University Press, 1995.

Mill, John Stuart. *Essays on Poetry*. ed. F. Parvin Sharpless. Columbia: University of South Carolina Press, 1976.

Miller, J. Hillis. *Topographies*. Stanford: Stanford University Press, 1995.

Miner, Earl. *Comparative Poetics: An Intercultural Essay on Theories of Literature*. Princeton: Princeton University Press, 1990.

Miyoshi, Masao. "A Borderless World?" *Global/Local: Cultural Production and the Translational Imaginary*. eds. Rob Wilson and Wimal Dissanayake. Durham: Duke University Press, 1996. 78-106.

Murphy, Bruce. "The Exile of Literature: Poetry and the Politics of the Other(s)." *Critical Inquiry* 17:1 (Autumn 1990): 162-73.

Owen, Stephen. *Traditional Chinese Poetry and Poetics: Omen of the World*. Madison: University of Wisconsin Press, 1985.

—. "The Anxiety of Global Influence: What is World Poetry?" *The New Republic* (19 Nov. 1990): 28-32.

—. *Reading Chinese Literary Thought*. Cambridge, MA: Harvard University Press, 1992.

—. "Traditions and Talents." *The New Republic* (22 Feb. 1993): 38-41.

Palandri, Angela J. "Contemporary Chinese Poetry from Taiwan." *Tamkang Review* 1.2 (1970): 67-88.

Perkins, David. *A History of Modern Poetry: From the 1890s to the High Modernist Mode*. Cambridge, MA: Harvard University Press, 1976.

—. *A History of Modern Poetry: Modernism and After*. Cambridge, MA: Harvard University Press, 1987.

Perloff, Marjorie. *Poetic License: Essays on Modernist and Postmodernist Poetry*. Evanston: Northwestern University Press, 1990.

—, ed. *Post-modern Genres*. Norman and London: University of Oklahoma Press, 1988.

Pinsky, Robert. *The Situation of Poetry: Contemporary Poetry and Its Traditions*. Princeton: Princeton University Press, 1976.

Pound, Ezra. *ABC of Reading*. London: Faber & Faber, 1991, c.1951.

—. *Selected Letters 1907-1941 of Ezra Pound*. New York: New Directions, 1971.

—. *Literary Essays of Ezra Pound*. ed. T. S. Eliot. Westport: Greenwood Press, 1979.

Prasad, Madhava. "A Theory of Third World Literature." *Social Text* 31/32 (1992): 57-83.

Rader, Ralph Wilson. "The Dramatic Monologue and Related Lyric Forms." *Critical Inquiry* 3 (1976): 131-151.

Richter, David H. "Dialogism and Poetry." *Studies in the Literary Imagination* XXVIII. 1 (Spring 1990): 9-27.

Ricoeur, Paul. *A Ricoeur Reader: Reflection and Imagination*. ed. Mario J. Valdés. New York: Harvester Wheatsheaf, 1991.

Riffaterre, Michael. *Semiotics of Poetry*. Bloomington: Indiana University Press, 1984.

Rilke, Rainer Maria. *Letters to a Young Poet*. Trans. M. D. Herter Norton. Revised edition 1954. New York and London: Norton, paperback edition, 1993.

—. *Sonnets to Orpheus*. Trans. Edward Snow. New York: North Point Press, 2004.

Robbins, Bruce. "Comparative Cosmopolitanism." *Social Text* 31/32 (1992): 169-186.

Rubinstein, Murray A., ed. *The Other Taiwan: 1945 to the Present*. Armonk, NY: M. E. Sharpe, 1994.

Rutherford, Jonathan, ed. *Identity, Community, Culture, Difference*. London: Lawrence & Wishart, 1990.

Safran, William. "Diaspora in Modern Societies: Myths of Homeland and Return." *Diaspora* (Spring 1991): 83-99.

Said, Edward W.. *Orientalism*. London: Routledge and Kegan Paul, 1978.

—. *The World, the Text, and the Critic*. Cambridge, MA: Harvard University Press, 1983.

—. "Orientalism Reconsidered." *Cultural Critique* 1 (Fall 1985): 89-107.

—. "Intellectuals in the Post-Colonial World." *Salmagundi* 70-1 (Summer 1986): 54-55.

—. "Representing the Colonized: Anthropology's Interlocutor." *Critical Inquiry* 15 (Winter 1989): 205-225.

—. "Yeats and Decolonization." Terry Eagleton, Fredric Jameson and Edward Said. *Nationalism, Colonialism and Literature*. Minneapolis: University of Minnesota Press, 1990. 69-95.

—. *Culture and Imperialism*. London: Vintage, 1993.

—. *Reflections on Exile and Other Essays*. Cambridge, MA: Harvard University Press, 2000.

—. "Introduction to the Fiftieth-Anniversary Edition." Erich Auerback, *Mimesis: The Representation of Reality in Western Literature*. Fiftieth-Anniversary edition. Trans. Willard R. Trask. Princeton: Princeton University Press, 2003. ix-xxxii.

Salvesen, Christopher. *The Landscape of Memory: A Study of Wordsworth's Poetry*. London: Edward Arnole 1970, c. 1965.

Schank, Stefan. *Rainer Maria Rilke*. Munich: Deutscher Taschenbuch Verlag, 1998.

Schönhaar, Rainer. "Towards a Transcultural Concept of Comparative Literature in View of the Changes in Present-day China." *China's New Role in the International Community: Challenges and Expectations for the Twenty-First Century*. eds. Heinz-Dieter Assmann and Karin Moser v. Filseck. Frankfurt am Main: Peter Lang, 2005. 245-256.

Scott, James C. *Domination and the Art of Resistance: Hidden Transcripts*. New Haven: Yale University Press, 1990.

Sessions, Ina Beth. "The Dramatic Monologue." *Modern Language of America* LXII (1947): 503-516.

Shaw, Thomas A. "The Semiotic Mediation of Identity." *Ethnos* 22.1 (1994): 83-119.

Shih, Vincent Y. C. "A New Linguistic Form: Modern Chinese Poetry in Taiwan." *Tamkang Review* 1.2 (1970): 59-66.

Shils, Edward. "Ideology and Civility: On the Politics of Intellectuals." *The Swanee Review* 66 (1958): 450-480.

Shohat, Ella. "Notes on 'Post-colonial'." *Social Text* 31/32 (1992): 99-112.

Shozo, Fujii. *Taiwan Bungaku Kono Hyakunen*. Trans. Zhang Jilin. Taipei: iFront Publishing Company, 2004.

Smith, Barbara Herrnstein. *Poetic Closure: a Study of How Poems End*. Chicago: University of Chicago Press, 1968.

Sontag, Kate and David Graham, eds. *After Confession: Poetry as Autobiography*. Saint Paul, Minnesto: Graywolf Press, 2001.

Spender, Stephen. "Letter to a Young Writer." *Encounter* 3 (March 1954): 4-5.

—. *The Making of a Poem*. New York: Norton, 1962, c. 1955.

—. *The Imagination in the Modern World*. Washington D.C.: Library of Congress, 1962.

Spivak, Gayatri Chakravorty. "Can the Subaltern Speak?" *Marxism and the Interpretation of Culture*. eds. C. Nelson and L. Grossberg. Basingstoke: Macmillan Press, 1988.

Stewart, Frank, Arthur Sze, and Michelle Yeh, eds. *Mercury Rising: Featuring Contemporary Poetry from Taiwan*. Honolulu: University of Hawai'i Press, 2003.

Teeple, John B. *Timelines of World History.* 1st American ed. London; New York: DK, 2002.

Todorov, Tzvetan. *Mikhail Bakhtin: The Dialogic Principle.* Trans. Wlad Godzich. Minneapolis: University of Minnesota Press, 1984.

Tomlinson, John. *Cultural Imperialism: A Critical Introduction.* Baltimore: Johns Hopkins University Press, 1991.

Tu Wei-ming. "Cultural China: The Periphery as Centre." *Daedalus* 120:2 (1991): 1-32.

—. ed. *The Living Tree: The Changing Meaning of Being Chinese Today.* Stanford: Stanford University Press, 1994.

Waldron, Arthur. "The Great Wall Myth: Its Origin and Role in Modern China." *Yale Journal of Criticism* 2.1 (1989): 67-90.

Waley, Arther, trans. *The Book of Songs: The Ancient Chinese Classic of Poetry.* New York: Grove Weidenfeld, 1987.

Walzer, Michael. *Thick and Thin: Moral Argument at Home and Abroad.* Notre Dame: University of Notre Dame Press, 1994.

Wang, C. H. *The Bell and the Drum:* Shih Ching *as Formulaic Poetry in an Oral Tradition.* Berkeley, Los Angeles, London: University of California Press, 1974.

—. "Poetry Ablaze, and Ambiguous." *Caliban* 1 (1986): 50-55.

—. *From Ritual to Allegory: Seven Essays in Early Chinese Poetry.* Hong Kong: Chinese University Press, 1988.

Wang, Jing. "Taiwan Hsiang-t'u Literature: Two Directions in the Evolution of a Literary Movement." *Chinese Fiction from Taiwan.* ed. Jeannette L. Faurot. Bloomington: Indiana University Press, 1980.

Watson, Burton, trans. *Selected Poems of Su Tung-p'o.* Port Townsend: Copper Canyon Press, 1994.

Wellek, René. *Discriminations: Further Concepts of Criticism.* New Haven and London: Yale University Press, 1970.

—. *Concepts of Criticism.* New Haven: Yale University Press, 1963.

Wesling, Donald. *Bakhtin and the Social Moorings of Poetry.* Lewisburg: Bucknell University Press, 2003.

William, Patrick and Laura Chrisman, eds. *Colonial Discourse and Post-colonial Theory: A Reader.* New York: Columbia University Press, 1994.

Wimsatt, W. K. *The Verbal Icon: Studies in the Meaning of Poetry.* London: Methuen, 1954.

Wong Lai-ming, Lisa (Huang Liming). "Liangzhong jiedu 'Changan' de shiyan: chuantongde yu xiandaide" [Two Readings of 'Changan': the Traditional and the Modern]. *Fu Xi Poetry Journal* 3 (June 1997): 86-94.

—. *Framings of Cultural Identities: Modern Poetry in Post-colonial Taiwan with Yang Mu as a Case Study.* Ph.D. Diss. The Hong Kong University of Science and Technology. Ann Arbor: UMI, 1999.

—. "Landing on a Home: Negotiations of Cultural Identity in Modern Taiwan Poetry." *Lun Heng* (Hong Kong) 5.1 (June 2000): 1-47.

—. "Writing Allegory: Diasporic Consciousness as a Mode of Intervention in Yang Mu's Poetry of the 1970s." *Journal of Modern Literature in Chinese* 5.1 (July 2001): 1-28.

—. "Heyuan zhiyou? Yang Mu shi zhong de bentu yu shijie" [How Is It Far? The Local and the Global in Yang Mu's Poetry] "Chorus: Special Issue on Yang Mu." *Chung Wai Literary Monthly* 31 (January 2003): 133-160.

—. "A Thing of Beauty is a Joy Forever: Yang Mu's 'Letters to Keats'." *The Keats-Shelley Review* (UK) 18 (September, 2004): 188-205.

—. "(Un)tying a Firm Knot of Ideas: Reading Yang Mu's *The Skeptic*." *Connotations: A Journal for Critical Debate* 12. 2-3 (2002/2003): 292-306.

—. "Taiwan, China, and Yang Mu's Alternative to National Narratives." *CLCWeb: Comparative Literature and Culture* 8.1 (March 2006).

—. "Epiphany in Echoland: Cross-cultural Intertextuality in Yang Mu's Poetry and Poetics." *Canadian Review of Comparative Literature* 31.1 (March 2004): 27-38.

—. "The Making of a Poem: Rainer Maria Rilke, Stephen Spender and Yang Mu." *The Comparatist* 31 (2007): 130-147.

Wu Qiancheng. *Ganxing dingwei: wenxue de xiangxiang yu jieru* [Where Sensibility Dwells: Literary Imagination and Intervention]. Taipei: Yunchen wenhua, 1994.

—. *Hangxiang Aierlan: Yeci yu Saierte xiangxiang* [Sailing to Ireland: Essays on W. B. Yeats and the Celtic Renaissance]. Taipei: New Century Publishing Company, 1999.

Xiao Xiao. "Xiangchou yu xiangchou de jiaoti" [Shifting from Homesickness to Home]. *Xiandai shi zonghengguan* [Modern Poetry from Different Perspectives]. Taipei: Wenzhizhe, 1991. 31-41.

Xu Huizhi, "Shaonian zhi yan – Aichou zhi xin" [The Youthful Eyes – The Sorrowful Heart]. *United Daily* (2 March 1998).

Xu Wenwei. "Shenke yu duoqing de shuqing shengyin" [An Intense and Diverse Lyrical Voice]. *Zhongguo shibao* [China Times] (28 May 2006).

Yang Mu. *Shui zhi mei* [By the Waterside]. Taipei: Lanxing shishe, 1960.

—. *Huaji* [Flower Season]. Taipei: Lanxing shishe, 1963.

—. *Dengchuan* [Boat Lantern]. Taipei: Wenxing, 1966. [1966a]

—. *Ye Shan sanwen ji* [First Essays of Ye Shan]. Taipei: Wenxing, 1966. [1966b]

—. *The Lotus Superstition and Other Poems.* MFA Diss. University of Iowa, 1966. [1966c]

—. *Fei du ji* [No Crossing (74 poems 1956-66)]. Taipei: Xianrenzhang, 1969.

—. *Chuanshuo* [Legends]. Taipei: Zhiwen, 1971.

—. *Ping zhong gao* [Manuscripts in a Bottle]. Taipei: Zhiwen, 1975. [1975a]

—. *Yang Mu zixuanji* [Selected Works of Yang Mu]. Taipei: Liming wenhua, 1975. [1975b]

—. *Nianlun* [Tree Rings]. Taipei: Siji, 1976. [1976a]

—. "Yingguo shiren Shibande" [Spender, the English Poet]. *Epoch* 43 (March 1976): 4-8. [1976b]

—. *Bokelai jingshen* [The Spirit of Berkeley]. Taipei: Hongfan, 1977. [1977a]

—. *Ye Shan sanwen ji* [First Essays of Ye Shan]. Taipei: Hongfan, 1977. [1977b]

—. *Beidou xing* [Song of the Big Dipper]. Taipei: Hongfan, 1978. [1978a]

—. *Yang Mu shiji I (1956-1974)* [Collected Poems of Yang Mu, Volume 1: 1956-1974]. Taipei: Hongfan, 1978. [1978b]

—. *Wu Feng*. Taipei: Hongfan, 1979. [1979a]

—. *Chuantongde yu xiandaide* [The Traditional and the Modern]. Taipei: Hongfan, 1979. [1979b]

—. *Wenxue zhishi* [Literary Knowledge]. Taipei: Hongfan, 1979. [1979c]

—. *Jinji de youxi* [Taboo Games]. Taipei: Hongfan, 1980. [1980a]

—. *Haian qi die* [Seven Turns of the Coast]. Taipei: Hongfan, 1980. [1980b]

—. *Sousuo zhe* [The Quester]. Taipei: Hongfan, 1982.

—. "Wu Feng." Trans. Cissie Kwok and Yang Mu. *Twentieth Century Chinese Drama: An Anthology*. ed. Edward M. Gunn. Bloomington: Indiana University Press, 1983. 475-513.

—. *Wenxue de yuanliu* [Origins of Literature]. Taipei: Hongfan, 1984.

—. *Jiao liu dao* [Interchanges]. Taipei: Hongfan, 1985. [1985a]

—. *Lu Ji's* Wen Fu *Jiaoshi* [A Comparative Interpretation of Lu Ji's *Essays on Literature*]. Taipei: Hongfan, 1985. [1985b]

—. *You ren* [Someone]. Taipei: Hongfan, 1986.

—. *Fei guo huoshan* [Flying Over the Volcano]. Taipei: Hongfan, 1987. [1987a]

—. *Shan feng hai yu* [Storms over Hills and Ocean: Memoirs I]. Taipei: Hongfan, 1987. [1987b]

—. *Yishou shi de wancheng* [The Completion of a Poem]. Taipei: Hongfan, 1989.

—. *Wanzheng de yuyan* [A Complete Fable]. Taipei: Hongfan, 1991. [1991a]

—. *Fangxiang gui ling* [Direction Back to Zero: Memoirs II]. Taipei: Hongfan, 1991. [1991b]

—. "Selected Poems of Yang Mu." Trans. Lisa Lai-ming Wong. With an Introduction and an Appendix: "On Translating the Musicality in Yang Mu's Poetry." MA Diss. City Polytechnic of Hong Kong, Hong Kong, 1992.

—. *Yi shen* [The Skeptic: Notes on Poetical Discrepancies]. Taipei: Hongfan, 1993.

—. *Xingtu* [Asterism]. Taipei: Hongfan, 1995.

—. *Yang Mu shiji II (1974-1985)* [Collected Poems of Yang Mu, Volume 2: 1974-1985]. Taipei: Hongfan, 1995.

—. *Tingwu zhi ying* [A Hawk Perches at Noon]. Taipei: Hongfan, 1996.

—. *Shiguan mingti* [Temporality Proposition]. Taipei: Hongfan, 1997. [1997a]

—. *Xi wo wang yi* [Then as I Set off: Memoirs III]. Taipei: Hongfan, 1997. [1997b]

—. Trans. *Yeci shixuan* [Selected Poems of W. B. Yeats]. Taipei: Hongfan. 1997. [1997c]

—. *No Trace of the Gardener: Poems of Yang Mu*. Trans. Lawrence R. Smith and Michelle Yeh. New Haven: Yale University Press, 1998.

—. Trans. *Baofengyu* [The Tempest]. Taipei: Hongfan, 1999.

—. *Yinyu yu xianshi* [Metaphor and Reality]. Taipei: Hongfan, 2001.

—. *She shi* [Intervention]. Taipei: Hongfan, 2001.

—. *Shiqu de letu* [The Happy Land of Our Conceit]. Taipei: Hongfan, 2002.

—. *Yang Mu, Patt beim Go: Gedichte chinesisch-deutsch*. Trans. Susanne Hornfeck and Wang Jue. Munchen: Al Verlag, 2002.

—. *Qilai qian shu* [The Former Book of Mount Qilai]. Taipei: Hongfan, 2003.

—. "Mist and My Other Self," in "Great Masters' Love Poems in Manuscript." *United Daily* (22 July 2003).

—. "The Origins of Taiwanese Poetry Revisited." *United Daily* (27 November 2004).

—. "Abstract and Estranged: Where Time Would Surely Forget Us." *United Daily* (28-31 December 2004).

—. *Quelqu'un m'interroge à propos de la vérité et de la justice*. Trans. Angel Pino and Isabelle Rabut. Paris: You Feng, 2004.

—. *Renwen zongji* [Literary Pattern: Tracks and Traces]. Taipei: Hongfan, 2005.

—. *Lüeying jiliu* [Shadows in the Torrent]. Taipei: Hongfan, 2005.

—. *Kakkouazami no uta: Youboku shishu*. Trans. and ed. Tetsuji Ueda. Tokyo: Shichosha, 2006.

—. *Jiekechong* [A Scale Insect]. Taipei: Hongfan, 2006.

—. *Yi shi* [Of Translation: Collected Essays]. Hong Kong: Cosmos Books, 2007.

—. Trans. *Yingshi hanyi* [English Poetry in Chinese Translation]. Taipei: Hongfan, 2007.

Yang Mu and Yu Guangzhong, eds. "Special Issue on Poetry." *Chung Wai Literary Monthly* 3.1 (June 1974).

Yeats, W. B. *Essays and Introductions*. London and Basingstoke: Macmillan Press, 1985, c. 1961.

Yeh, Michelle (Xi Mi). *Modern Chinese Poetry: Theory and Practice since 1917*. New Haven: Yale University Press, 1991.

—. "Chayi de youlü: Yige huiying" [The Anxiety over Difference: A Rejoinder]. *Jintian* [Today] 1 (1991): 94-6.

—. "Du shi biji: Yang Mu" [Poetry Reading Notes: Yang Mu]. *Unitas* 192 (October 2000): 26-31.

Yeh, Michelle, and N. G. D. Malmgvist, eds. *Frontier Taiwan: An Anthology of Modern Chinese Poetry*. New York: Columbia University Press, 2001.

Yip Wai-lim. "Afterword." *Legends*. Yang Mu. Taipei: Zhiwen, 1971. 117-136.

—. *Zhixu de shengchang* [The Growth of Order]. Taipei: Zhiwen, 1971.

Young, Robert J. C.. *Untying the Text: A Post-structuralist Reader* Boston: Routledge & Kegan Paul, 1981.

—. *Colonial Desire: Hybridity in Theory, Culture and Race*. London: Routledge, 1995.

Yu, Pauline. "The Poetics of Discontinuity: East-West Correspondences in Lyric Poetry." *PMLA* 94.2 (March 1979): 261-74.

—. "Alienation Effects: Comparative Literature and the Chinese Tradition." *The Comparative Perspective on Literature: Approaches to Theory and Practice*. eds. Clayton Koelb and Susan Noakes. Ithaca: Cornell University Press, 1988. 162-175.

Yu Yingshi, *Lishi renwu yu wenhua weiji* [Historical Figures and Cultural Crisis]. Taipei: Dongdai, 1995.

Zeng Chenchen. "Sound of Water Mountains: Sea Imagery in Yang Mu's Poetry and Prose." In manuscript.

Zhang Longxi. *The Tao and the Logos: Literary Hermeneutics, East and West*. Durham: Duke University Press, 1992.

—. "Out of the Cultural Ghetto: Theory, Politics and the Study of Chinese Literature." *Modern China* 19.1 (January 1993): 71-101.

Zhang Mo. *Xiandaishi de touying* [Projections of Modern Poetry]. Taipei: Taiwan Commercial Press, 1967.

Zhang Mo *et al.*, eds. *Zhongguo dangdai shida shiren xuanji* [Selected Works of the Ten Major Contemporary Chinese Poets]. Taipei: Yuancheng wenhua tushu, 1977.

Zhao Tianyi, *Hunsheng hechang – Li shixuan: Taiwan jingshen de yinyu* [Mixed Choral Singing – Selections from *Li Poetry Magazine*: A Metaphor of Taiwan Spirit]. Kao-hsiung: Wenxue Taiwan zazhishe, 1992.

Zheng Jiongming, ed. *Taiwan jingshen de jueqi: "Li" shilun xuanji* [The Emergence of Taiwan Spirit: Selected Poetic Theories of *Li Poetry Magazine*]. Kao-hsiung: Wenxuejie zazhishe, 1989.

Žižek, Slavoj. *Enjoy Your Symptom! Jacques Lacan in Hollywood and Out*. New York: Routledge, 1992.

Index

New Comparative Poetics

This series publishes contributions which explore new territory in the ever-evolving field of comparative literature. Its monographs, written in English or in French, typically deal with the interaction between various authors, literary genres and societies or cultures, if necessary drawing on literary theory.

The term "comparative" is not restricted to the study of different national literatures. It also refers to comparative studies within a single linguistic culture, e.g. in a multicultural society or a postcolonial country. The series seeks to re-assess the complex relationship between margin and center, emphasizing, whenever possible, a non-Eurocentric perspective.

Series Editor : Marc MAUFORT
Université libre de Bruxelles (Belgique)

Series Titles

N° 15– Jean WEISGERBER, *Pierrot ou Bérénice ? Les Lettres européennes entre peuple et élites (XVIIe siècle)*, 2004.

No.14– Xavier GARNIER, *Le récit superficiel. L'art de la surface dans la narration littéraire moderne*, 2004.

N° 13– Dirk DE GEEST & Reine MEYLAERTS (eds.), avec la collaboration de – met medewerking van Gina BLANCKHAERT, *Littératures en Belgique. Diversités culturelles et dynamiques littéraires / Literaturen in België. Culturele diversiteit en literaire dynamiek*, 2004.

N° 12– Judith LABARTHE (dir.), *Formes modernes de la poésie épique. Nouvelles approches*, 2004.

No.11– Michel DELVILLE & Christine PAGNOULLE (eds.), *Sound as Sense. Contemporary US Poetry & / in Music*, 2003.

N° 10– Hoa Hoï VUONG, *Musiques de roman. Proust, Mann, Joyce*, 2003.

N° 9– Sineva Béné KATUNARIC, *André Malraux et Miroslav Krleža dans l'Europe littéraire de l'entre-deux-guerres* (provisional title), forthcoming.

No.8– Rebecca Hope FERGUSON, *Rewriting Black Identities. Transition and Exchange in the Novels of Toni Morrison*, 2007.

No.7– Marc MAUFORT & Franca BELLARSI (eds.), *Reconfigurations. Canadian Literatures and Postcolonial Identities / Littératures canadiennes et identités postcoloniales*, 2002 (2nd printing 2004).

No.6– Dirk VAN HULLE (ed.), *James Joyce: The Study of Languages*, 2002.

N° 5– Jean WEISGERBER, *La Muse des jardins. Jardins de l'Europe littéraire (1580-1700)*, 2002 (2nd printing 2003).

No.4– Marzena SOKOŁOWSKA-PARYŻ, *The Myth of War in British and Polish Poetry. 1939-1945*, 2002.

No.3– Eva DARIAS-BEAUTELL, *Graphies and Grafts. (Con)Texts and (Inter)Texts in the Fiction of Four Contemporary Canadian Women*, 2002.

No.2– Bart KEUNEN & Bart EECKHOUT (eds.), *Literature and Society. The Function of Literary Sociology in Comparative Literature*, 2001.

N° 1– Xavier GARNIER, *L'éclat de la figure. Étude sur l'antipersonnage de roman*, 2001 (2nd printing 2002).
